DOCTOR WHO

THE SEVENTIES

First published in 1994 by
Doctor Who Books
an imprint of Virgin Publishing Ltd
332 Ladbroke Grove
London W10 5AH

Copyright © David J. Howe, Mark Stammers & Stephen James Walker 1994
'Doctor Who' copyright
© British Broadcasting Corporation 1994

The moral rights of the authors has been asserted

Certain photographic illustrations
© BBC Photographs, Hulton Deutch, Syndication International,
Sue Willis, Bobi Bartlett, Barry Newbery, Mat Irvine, Allister Bowtell,
Bernard Lodge, Ian Scoones, National Readiological Protection Board, Chelton Oxon,
John Porter, Sandra Exelby, Graeme Wood, Jon Saville,
Kevin Davies, Ronald McDevitt, Sam Whalen.

This book is published by arrangement with BBC Books, a division of
BBC Enterprises Ltd. 'Doctor Who' is a registered trade mark of The
British Broadcasting Corporation

Cover and internal layout
designed by Mark Stammers Design, London

Printed and bound in Great Britain by
Butler & Tanner Ltd, Frome and London

David J. Howe
Mark Stammers
Stephen James Walker

PART ONE	Introduction	1
CHAPTER 1:	A New Beginning	3
CHAPTER 2:	Who Was Jon Pertwee	11
CHAPTER 3:	The Third Doctor: Man of Action	17
CHAPTER 4:	Season Seven: Exiled to Earth	21
CHAPTER 5:	Season Eight: A Masterful Season	31
CHAPTER 6:	Season Nine: Old Friends, Old Enemies	43
CHAPTER 7:	Season Ten: Ten Years in the TARDIS	53
CHAPTER 8:	Season Eleven: All Change	61
CHAPTER 9:	Who Was Tom Baker	69
CHAPTER 10:	The Fourth Doctor: Bohemian Eccentric	75
CHAPTER 11:	Season Twelve: Something Old, Something New	79
CHAPTER 12:	Season Thirteen: Worlds of Horror	89
CHAPTER 13:	Season Fourteen: Gothic Quality	99
CHAPTER 14:	Season Fifteen: Year of Transition	109
CHAPTER 15:	Season Sixteen: The Key to Time— A Universal Jigsaw	121
CHAPTER 16:	Season Seventeen: Crisis Point	133
PART TWO		
CHAPTER 17:	UNIT and the Companions	143
CHAPTER 18:	Doctor Who and the Daleks in Seven Keys to Doomsday	149
CHAPTER 19:	Exhibitions: On Display	153
CHAPTER 20:	Welcome to the Toyshop	155
CHAPTER 21:	Fandom Grows Up	173
CHAPTER 22:	End of an Era	175
	Indices	176

This one's for my parents, Ted and Sheila,
who didn't get a colour television until
part three of *The Sea Devils*!—DJH

For Fluff and Matthew Gregory
and baby Thomas — MS

For Michael, Jessica and Olivia Topley — SJW

Introduction

By the close of the sixties, *Doctor Who* had already been running for six seasons — a very creditable track record in comparison with most other series — and had become a well-established element of the BBC's family drama output. Few people in the UK could have been unaware of its existence, and many now followed a happy weekly ritual of gathering around the TV set at teatime on a Saturday evening to witness the latest exploits of the good Doctor and his companions in their battles against the evils of the Universe. World-wide, too, *Doctor Who* had won a huge following as the overseas sales arm of BBC Enterprises found eager buyers for the series in its Commonwealth and other markets.

The Doctor himself had appeared in two different incarnations — being portrayed first by William Hartnell as a kind-hearted but sometimes tetchy grandfather figure with flowing white hair and Edwardian clothes, and then by Patrick Troughton as an impish, dark-haired character, scruffily dressed in an old frock coat and baggy checked trousers — and had been joined by thirteen companions on his journeys through time and space. The stories had initially alternated between historical and science-based subjects, but had eventually come to focus almost entirely on the latter as successive production teams bowed to a perceived public preference for futuristic adventures featuring monstrous adversaries such as the Cybermen, the Ice Warriors, the Yeti and of course the dreaded Daleks — the creatures which had been credited with the series' early success and had since given rise to a veritable cornucopia of spin-off merchandise. The series had even spawned two cinema films, starring Peter Cushing as the Doctor, and a West End stage play entitled *The Curse of the Daleks*.

When its sixth season ended, however, *Doctor*

SEASONS

*When discussing **Doctor Who's** history, fans and media researchers generally divide it up into a number of separate seasons, each corresponding to a regular run of episodes in the original UK transmission sequence. The term 'season' is in fact an Americanism which gained currency in the UK only in the late seventies; before that, the word 'series' was generally used. For the sake of clarity, this book follows the standard convention.*

DOCTOR WHO?

*Throughout the sixties, the character of the Doctor was referred to as 'Doctor Who' each week in both the **Radio Times** and on the programme's closing credits. It wasn't until the eighties that the character's name was firmly established as being 'the Doctor', but during the seventies, there were two examples of the **Radio Times** listings crediting the character as such: **Image of the Fendahl** and **The Power of Kroll**. In this book we refer to the character as 'the Doctor' throughout as this has become the accepted practice.*

The first Doctor (William Hartnell). *Marco Polo.*

◀ **The second Doctor (Patrick Troughton) and his two companions, Zoe (Wendy Padbury) and Jamie (Frazer Hines).** *The Seeds of Death.*

PRODUCTION TEAMS

BBC production teams in the seventies generally consisted of a producer and a script editor, working full-time on a particular programme. The producer would have overall artistic and financial responsibility for the show, liaising with the various service departments and overseeing the work of individual directors and crews brought in to handle particular episodes or stories, while the relatively junior story editor would find and work with writers to provide the scripts. Around 1974, producers started to be assigned a production unit manager, who would look after the programme's finances on a day-to-day basis.

COMMISSIONING SCRIPTS

In a number of places in this book, reference is made to script editors commissioning scripts from writers. This is, in fact, a simplification of the BBC's procedures. Having asked a writer to write a storyline or a script, the story editor would in fact brief the Copyright Department formally to commission the work. Where commissioning dates are given in the text, these refer to the date when the story editor briefed the Copyright Department.

LOCATIONS

*During the seventies, location filming became far more prevalent than had been the case in the sixties, partly due to the introduction of lighter and more portable camera equipment, and partly due to there being less episodes per season, resulting in more time being available to make them. As a result there were often dozens of locations utilized when making a **Doctor Who** story and there is unfortunately insufficient room in a book of this scope to list them all. We have therefore only listed some of the more major locations to which the BBC has travelled while making the programme.*

The third Doctor with ▶ other early seventies regulars (Roger Delgado, Katy Manning and Nicholas Courtney).

The third Doctor (Jon Pertwee), a dashing man of action with a love for flamboyant clothes.

Who faced a period of uncertainty. Whereas previously it had been off the air for no more than eight weeks between seasons, this time there would be a longer break of over six months, during which the BBC would fill the Saturday teatime slot with a first batch of episodes from an imported American science fiction series called *Star Trek*. In addition, regular viewers knew that when the Doctor returned he would again be portrayed by a different actor and would be seen beginning a period of exile on 20th-century Earth as part of a sentence imposed on him by his own people, the Time Lords. Executives at the BBC, meanwhile, were becoming increasingly doubtful of the merits of continuing the series, in view of the steady decline in its average ratings and TV chart positions.

The fourth Doctor (Tom Baker), an eccentric bohemian character with a seemingly endless scarf.

The story of *Doctor Who*'s first six seasons is covered in *Doctor Who — The Sixties*. In this companion volume, we recount what happened during the years 1970 to 1979, when the Doctor appeared first as a dashing man of action with silver hair and a deeply-lined face, elegantly attired in frilly shirt and velvet jacket, and then as a wild-eyed bohemian with dark, curly hair and a toothy grin, sporting a battered felt hat and a long multi-coloured scarf.

We look at the changes in format and production style which saw the series reach new peaks of popularity and thus cement its status as a cherished national institution; detail the careers of the actors who portrayed the Doctor in his third and fourth incarnations; recall the friends who shared the Doctor's adventures and the enemies against whom they fought; examine the wealth of *Doctor Who*-related merchandise produced during this decade; describe the second West End stage production; and chronicle the continued growth of fan interest in the series.

Join us on another trip back in time, to re-live, remember and, above all, enjoy a little slice of TV history.

DJH, MS and SJW

February 1994

CHAPTER ONE

A New Beginning

T here had always been a certain ambivalence towards *Doctor Who* within the upper echelons of the BBC, where it was regarded by some as being rather 'low brow' and unsuitable for tea-time family viewing. This ambivalence grew even more pronounced after 1967 when Sydney Newman, the series' originator and strongest supporter, completed his five-year contract as Head of Drama and left to take up a new post with the Associated British Pictures Corporation. Terrance Dicks recalls that even as early as the spring of 1968, when he joined the series as assistant script editor, there were rumblings that it was perhaps no longer justifying its place in the schedules and should be allowed to come to a natural end as soon as its current star, Patrick Troughton, decided to leave:

'Almost the first thing I heard when I came to join as assistant script editor was that the BBC were actually thinking of taking the show off. I thought,

BESSIE

Peter Bryant realized that, as the stories of season seven would be set entirely on Earth, the TARDIS would become all but redundant. He therefore set about providing an alternative means of transport for the Doctor. This was to be a yellow Victorian-style roadster, with the distinctive number-plate WHO 1, which the Doctor nicknamed Bessie.

The car was bought by the BBC as one of a number of limited edition kits designed by Siva Engineering Sales of Weymouth, Dorset, and was custom-made for the series. The fibreglass shell was designed to fit directly on to an E93A Ford chassis of the type used from the late 1940s through to 1958 for the Ford Popular, Prefect and Anglia ranges. The basic kit cost £160 and comprised the fibreglass body, seats, bonnet with foam cushioning and brackets, mock artillery wheel trims, mudguards, radiator, running boards and fuel tank. On top of this Bessie had a number of optional extras, costing £182. These included bulb horns, luggage trunk, coach lamps, Cibie headlamps, hood and side curtains, battery box, seat covers, screen and body straps and carpets. With a chassis and engine taken from a Ford Popular, the total cost of the car was around £500.

Bessie could not be officially registered as WHO 1 as that number-plate was already owned by someone – Mr Aubrey Stevens, Clerk to the Magistrates for Alton, Alresford and Petersfield. This meant that on public roads it could be driven only with police permission or, in long shot, with its legal number-plate, MTR5.

The design of the car was copyrighted to the makers and, on 7 October 1969, Peter Bryant was sent a memo by BBC Enterprises' General Manager for Radio and TV Entertainment, pointing out that this was unfortunate as it would allow merchandising rights to be operated outside the BBC's jurisdiction. BBC Enterprises were concerned also to learn about the phasing out of the TARDIS police box, as it was licensed to several manufacturers for use on their products.

Jon Pertwee clowns around with some Yeti hands at his introductory photocall.

THE INTRODUCTION OF COLOUR

The establishment of a colour TV service in Britain had been under consideration since 1943, when it was discussed by the secret Hankey Committee set up by the Government to make recommendations for the 'reinstatement and development of the television service' after the Second World War. In the early fifties, a five-year plan for the BBC envisaged that colour transmissions could 'start in 1956/57, increase during 1957/58 and could be enlarged when the new studios at Television Centre, all of which will be equipped for colour, become available at the beginning of 1959'.

As things transpired experimental transmissions in the 625-line phase alternation line (PAL) colour system began from the BBC's original Alexandra Palace studios on 10 October 1955. At the turn of the decade, six of the new Television Centre studios were fitted with colour-compatible equipment, and, on 1 July 1967, BBC2 finally became Europe's first colour television network.

*Only a few 'launching' programmes were transmitted in colour to start with. These included the topical arts programme **Late-Night Line Up**, which in November 1967 ran a colour interview with visual effects designer Jack Kine about some of the effects for **Doctor Who's** fifth season. The commencement of the full colour service, comprising some 80 per cent of BBC2's output, was held back until 2 December 1967, and was confined initially to only four transmitter regions – London, the Midlands, the South and the North.*

There were strong economic pressures to move into colour. It would boost the sales of new TV sets and open up further markets for British programmes overseas – particularly in the USA, where there had been colour transmissions since the fifties, albeit in a different technical standard developed by the National Television System Committee (NTSC). On 16 May 1969, therefore, the Postmaster General gave the go-ahead for BBC1 and the rival ITV network to follow BBC2's lead, and both began a colour service on 15 November that year (restricted initially to the larger regions).

Jon Pertwee poses for an early photocall in his *Doctor Who* costume.

"That's a great start to my career; three months and that will be the end of it." For a while, they did actually consider ending it, because even then it had been going for a pretty long time in television terms. The viewing figures were okay but they weren't marvellous any more. So I was actually involved in looking around for something to replace the show.'

In the event, even though Troughton did indeed relinquish the role of the Doctor in 1969, a decision had already been taken to go ahead and make a further season of stories for transmission in 1970.

'We couldn't come up with anything which seemed as good,' says Dicks, who had by then become script editor proper, 'so eventually it was decided to recast — to get a new Doctor — and to start again.'

Peter Bryant, *Doctor Who*'s producer at the time, has a slightly different recollection of the situation:

'The BBC were always talking about killing the series off, for some extraordinary reason that I've never been able to understand, but I don't remember anything in particular being said about stopping it when Patrick Troughton left.

'I mean, there might have been talk of finding a new idea to replace it, but that frequently happened. One was always on the lookout for new

ideas. However, I don't recall being specifically briefed to look for a replacement — and I'm sure I would remember if I had been.'

Derrick Sherwin, Bryant's deputy producer at the end of the Troughton era, agrees:

'I certainly wasn't aware of any desire on the part of the BBC hierarchy to finish the series. There was always the possibility at the end of a season that it might not be renewed for another year, but that was the same for any show whatever it might have been.'

A number of new series ideas that Sherwin had himself been involved in developing at that time have sometimes been assumed to have been intended for the *Doctor Who* slot. Again, however, he denies this:

'One of the reasons Peter and I were so busy on *Doctor Who* at the end was that we were also working on two episodes of a potential new series called *S.P. Air*, which I wrote and revamped from an original idea called *Highway to Action* by Jon Rollason and Keith Williams. It was about a special body within the RAF which had political authority and investigated things "under the counter" rather than above board — a sort of troubleshooting team — and the RAF offered us some facilities for it. But those episodes were actually made and transmitted, and it wasn't intended for the same slot as *Doctor Who*. It was fairly hard-nosed, and was really for adults.'

Other ideas under discussion at one time or another included a series of Jules Verne-type stories and a remake of Nigel Kneale's *Quatermass* science-fiction serials of the fifties. However, Sherwin maintains that none of these was considered as a potential replacement for *Doctor Who*:

'You see, as a producer at the BBC, you had to decide what you wanted to do next and then promote it, to try to get it on the road. You were supposed to find your own ideas for new series. The Jules Verne proposal was certainly one that I came up with, but there were a number of others — probably 15 or 20 ideas — that I developed, which for one reason or another didn't get past the BBC executives.'

Although a new season of *Doctor Who* did eventually get the go-ahead, several developments combined to ensure that it would be in many respects very different from those which had preceded it. For one thing, it would have far fewer episodes.

Doctor Who's first five production blocks between September 1963 and July 1968 had consisted of an average of about 43 episodes each, but the sixth, lasting from September 1968 to June 1969, was given a reduced allocation of only 34 episodes. This was in line with the general trend towards slightly shorter seasons in TV drama series at that time, and also represented a more manageable workload for the production team and the regular cast — both Patrick Troughton and his predecessor, William Hartnell, had previously requested a reduction to around 26 episodes per year, feeling that the gruelling schedule was placing unreasonable demands upon them.

One consequence of this cutback in output was that, for the first time in the series' history, all the episodes in a production block were transmitted as part of the then current season, season six, with none being held over to launch the following year's run of transmissions. This in itself would have been sufficient to bring about a reduced episode count for the first season of the seventies but, as an added factor, the seventh production block would consist of even fewer episodes. The regular cast's contracts specified a minimum of 21 episodes to be made between 13 September 1969 and 26 May 1970, and the number eventually allocated was 25. Season seven would consequently be only 25 episodes long, and this would set a rough precedent for every other season of the decade.

Another major innovation for season seven was the fact that it would be made and transmitted in colour.

Important though the advent of colour was, its immediate impact on *Doctor Who* should not be overestimated. The BBC had long been anticipating the introduction of colour, and all the necessary equipment had been in place for years. In addition, while it certainly allowed for the development of new and more sophisticated electronic effects techniques, its implications for the series' design aspects were less far-reaching than might perhaps be thought. BBC designers had routinely worked in colour even in the days of black and white TV, finding that this generally made for more convincing and atmospheric pictures and assisted actors in giving believable performances. Aside from the need to avoid obvious pitfalls, such as putting an extra in a brightly coloured costume which might distract the viewer's attention from the principal cast, the main problems encountered with the new technology were the higher image definition, which meant that scenery, costumes and make-up all had to be more finely detailed — and therefore more costly — than before, and the lack of sophistication of the early colour cameras, which meant that only a limited range of tones could be used together in any one shot.

If the start of colour transmissions had relatively little impact on *Doctor Who*'s production process, it had even less on its viewers. In 1970, colour TV sets were still very much a luxury item, found in only a small minority of British homes. Even by 1972, only about 17 per cent of the nation's population were able to receive colour transmissions. For many, the early seventies would be just as much a black-and-white era as the sixties had been.

Of far greater significance to *Doctor Who*'s regu-

Pertwee at a *Radio Times* photocall midway through the making of his first season.

COLOUR REGIONS

*Those BBC regions capable of receiving colour transmissions at the time **Spearhead From Space** was broadcast in January 1970 were as follows:*

TRANSMITTER	SERVING
Crystal Palace	Area around London
Winter Hill	South Lancashire
Sutton Coldfield	Area around Birmingham
Emley Moor	South Yorkshire
Black Hill	Central Scotland
Rowbridge	Central Southern England
Dover	East Kent and parts of East Sussex

PRODUCTION BASE

*By 1970, the **Doctor Who** production office was firmly established in Room 505 of Union House, a BBC-owned building overlooking Shepherd's Bush Green in London. (It had moved there early in 1964, having previously been in Room 512 of the adjoining Threshold House.) The making of the series continued to be based around the BBC's various premises and facilities in this west London area, and with one exception – season fifteen's **Horror of Fang Rock** – all the seventies stories had their studio recordings done at Television Centre. This large, torus-shaped complex of administrative offices and production studios (one of them, TC1, the largest in Europe) had been built in White City in the early sixties and was fully equipped for colour recording. Filmed inserts continued to be shot at the BBC's Television Film Studios in Ealing, while model work and other visual effects sequences were filmed in a variety of locations, including Television Centre's so-called Puppet Theatre – a small studio sometimes used for puppet productions – and outside facilities such as Bray Studios. Rehearsals during seasons seven and eight took place in a number of different outside rehearsal rooms, but from season nine onwards were usually conducted at the BBC's newly-built Rehearsal Block in North Acton.*

BARRY LETTS
PRODUCER

*Barry Letts started his career as an actor. He began in repertory in York whilst also working for a local radio station in Leeds. After a chance meeting with BBC producer/director Rex Tucker, Letts started working with him first on radio and then on television. His first television appearance was with Patrick Troughton in a 1950 production of **Gunpowder Guy**, about Guy Fawkes. Eventually Letts decided he wanted to go into directing and attended the BBC's director's course in 1967. He worked on episodes of **Z Cars** and **The Newcomers** before directing the six-part **Doctor Who** story **The Enemy of the World** in 1967. Following this he became producer of **Doctor Who** in 1969. After he left **Doctor Who** in 1974 he found himself marking time by working as a sort of assistant to Head of Drama Ronnie Marsh until he decided to return to directing and approached various producers for work. It was because of this that he came to direct **The Android Invasion** for **Doctor Who** in 1975. Straight after that came a production of **The Prince and the Pauper** for John McCrae. However, McCrae was promoted to Head of Drama for a New Zealand TV station, and so Letts was asked to take over as producer of the classic serials on BBC1. In the late seventies and early eighties Letts returned to **Doctor Who** for a time as executive producer. He continued to work as a director, particularly on the classic serials which were at that time being produced by Terrance Dicks. In 1993, Letts wrote a new radio production of **Doctor Who** called **The Paradise of Death**.*

The second Doctor (Patrick Troughton) bids farewell to his companions Zoe (Wendy Padbury) and Jamie (Frazer Hines) at the conclusion of *The War Games*.

lar audience were the major changes that the production team had decided to make to the series' format. As Derrick Sherwin recalls, he and Peter Bryant agreed that a radical rethink was called for:

'The series had become very fanciful and gone heavily into monsters from outer space, which I found very tedious and unbelievable. The only

The third Doctor in ▶ costume.

reason everyone watched was to see what the latest monster was like — whether it had got fur on or a silver head or one eye at the back of its ear, or whatever. The series wasn't going anywhere, the viewing figures were dropping, so I sat down with Peter Bryant to work out what we could do about this. I said the only thing I could think of was to look back, see what had been successful in the past and try to learn from that.

'I went to the BBC's archives and managed to dig out some episodes of the very first *Quatermass* serial. (The writer, Nigel Kneale, was my neighbour at the time!) We screened them, and the production was so appalling that we found them hysterically funny. We rolled about laughing! But what the producers had been trying to do — and what ultimately they achieved in *Quatermass and the Pit* — was to get some reality into it. So I said that this was the solution; that what we had got to do with *Doctor Who* was to forget wobbly jellies in outer space and create some reason for bringing the stories down to Earth.

'We couldn't do this with just the Doctor and his two companions, we had to have some other means, so I came up with the idea of UNIT, the United Nations Intelligence Taskforce. I sat down and wrote a couple of pages about this special Taskforce, specifically with members from all nations, which had been set up to investigate funny things happening in space or the possibility of UFOs or whatever. It was basically an army in-

Captain Turner (Robert Sidaway) and Jamie in a UNIT helicopter in a scene from *The Invasion*, the story that introduced the concept of UNIT to *Doctor Who*.

TERRANCE DICKS
SCRIPT EDITOR/ WRITER
Born in East Ham, London, in 1935, Terrance Dicks was educated at the local grammar school and went on to read English at Downing College, Cambridge. After two years' national service in the army, he got a job as an advertising copywriter. This lasted for five years, during which time he started writing radio scripts as a sideline. Eventually he switched to full-time freelance writing, first on plays and comedy series for radio and then in television on programmes like **The Avengers** *and* **Crossroads**. *Following some five years as script editor on* **Doctor Who**, *ending in 1974, he returned to a freelance writing career. Later he produced some of the BBC's classic serials. Aside from his contributions to the* **Doctor Who** *TV series, he has also written two spin-off plays –* **Doctor Who and the Daleks in Seven Keys to Doomsday** *in 1974 and* **Doctor Who – The Ultimate Adventure** *in 1989 – and well over fifty novelizations. Today he is one of the UK's most prolific authors of children's fiction.*

telligence unit — with special powers and, on some occasions, special weapons — which had access to scientists and laboratories and all the kinds of things that Doctor Who might need. It gave us an identifiable group within which to work on special occasions and of course a reason for bringing the Doctor in. It was constructed fairly methodically and thoughtfully in the first instance, to serve a very specific purpose for at least a year's run.'

UNIT made its debut in the Patrick Troughton adventure *The Invasion*, the first story in the series' sixth production block; and, as Sherwin explains, this was always intended as just the first step in a process of moving towards a more permanent Earth-bound setting — something which would have happened even if Troughton had not decided to leave:

'The idea was always to bring it down to Earth gently and then to stay there for a long period of time. Quite apart from dramatic considerations, another factor was that budgets were being cut and we were being asked to do more. Don't forget that we were going from black and white into colour, which was an expensive exercise, and we had to have a run of productions that we could afford. We couldn't keep on creating spaceships and monster suits all over the place and going out to the back end of nowhere to film alien planets — it just wasn't on, with the financial restrictions which existed.'

The fact that the groundwork for the series' seventh production block was being laid right at the beginning of the sixth lends weight to the assertion by Peter Bryant and Derrick Sherwin that there was, at that point, no real danger of the series being cancelled. Indeed, actor Nicholas Courtney, who played UNIT's commanding officer Brigadier Lethbridge-Stewart, recalls that it was during the making of *The Invasion*, in the autumn of 1968, that he was first asked if he would be willing to reprise the role throughout the whole of the 1970 season — an invitation he readily accepted.

Having decided that *Doctor Who* should be brought down to Earth, to get away from the more fantasy-based storylines which Derrick Sherwin characterized as 'funny planets and weird frogs and people with trees growing out of their ears', the production team were then faced with the task of explaining in plot terms the sudden curtailment of the Doctor's journeys through space and time, and also the latest transformation of his appearance. The concluding story of season six was originally to have been written by Sherwin himself, but nothing came of this idea. It was left instead to script editor Terrance Dicks and his regular co-writer Malcolm Hulke to supply the answers in their scripts for *The War Games*, the epic ten-part replacement story which marked the end of Patrick Troughton's tenure as the Doctor. In doing so, they also devised some of the secrets of the Doctor's past, which had been

▲ The second Doctor (Patrick Troughton) is exiled to Earth by the Time Lords. *The War Games.*

DERRICK SHERWIN
PRODUCER

Derrick Sherwin worked initially as a junior set designer and scenic artist in the theatre. This led to a number of other jobs including scene shifter, stage manager and lighting designer. Finally, interrupted only by a two-year spell in the Royal Air Force, he became an actor – a profession he was to pursue for many years in theatre, films and television. Eventually, while continuing to act, he also began to work as a freelance writer, mostly on TV plays and series such as Z Cars and Crossroads. Late in 1967, he was interviewed by BBC Head of Serials Shaun Sutton and offered the job of assistant story editor on Doctor Who. After Doctor Who, he worked on Paul Temple from 1970 until 1971 before leaving to found an independent production company called SkiBoy to make the series SkiBoy in 1974. In the early eighties he ran the very first computer animation company, Electronic Arts, before returning to independent TV production. He has also continued to work as a freelance writer, working both in England and America.

Jon Pertwee pictured ▲ at his London home on 3 February 1956 wearing one of a collection of garments which he designed and, with the help of an established tailoring organization, had made for a show to be held ten days later at the Men's Trade Fair in the Royal Albert Hall.

Jon Pertwee with co-stars Helen Chasen (left) and Judy Cornwall in a 1961 publicity shot for The Navy Lark.

shrouded in mystery during the series' first six years.

As *The War Games* moves towards its conclusion, the Doctor is taken prisoner by his own people, the previously-unnamed Time Lords, and placed on trial for interfering in the affairs of other races. Found guilty, he is sentenced to a period of exile on 20th-century Earth and told that he must again take on a new appearance. A number of suggested faces are displayed on a large screen, but none meets with his approval. Suddenly, to his indignation, he is himself up on the screen, and his image begins to break up, multiply and revolve as the Time Lords trigger his second regeneration. The final image is of the protesting figure of the Doctor, his face in shadow, slowly spinning off into blackness.

Thus it was that the Doctor was banished to begin his next incarnation stranded on Earth, where it would be a logical development for him to hook up with UNIT for a further succession of adventures.

The most daunting challenge was finding an actor to star as the new Doctor himself. The principal responsibility for this fell to Peter Bryant, in consultation with Derrick Sherwin.

'I went through *Spotlight*, the casting directory,' says Bryant, 'and thought and thought and thought

about it. My first choice was Ron Moody, who had played Fagin in the musical *Oliver!* I felt he would bring something special to the role. When I approached him, though, he turned it down.

'The other person I had in mind was Jon Pertwee. Again, that was on the basis that he was somebody who had the personality to bring something to this difficult, nebulous part, which on paper means nothing.'

'I was in a radio programme called *The Navy Lark*,' Pertwee later recalled, 'and one day one of the other actors, Tenniel Evans, said, "Why don't you put yourself up to play Doctor Who. I understand that Patrick Troughton is leaving." I said "Why the hell would they want me? I'm a sort of eccentric character actor." He replied, "I think you would make a very good Doctor Who." So I rang my agent and told him, and there was a terrible pause. I said, "All right, forget it, I suppose it wasn't a very good idea." He answered, "No, no. It comes as a bit of a shock, that's all. I'll ring them up."

'He phoned the BBC, told them he had heard that Patrick Troughton was leaving and that he wanted to suggest one of his clients to take over. The producer said, "Who's that?" When my agent told him, there was a long pause. My agent said, "Sorry, we'll forget all about it!" The producer then said, "May I read you our short list?" So he read the list, and my name was second — and none of us had any idea! That was how I got the job.

'I went to see Shaun Sutton, who was Head of Drama at the BBC and a very old friend — we'd started in the business together. I said, "How do you want this played?" and Shaun replied, "Well — as you." I said, "What is me? I don't know what I am!" You see, I had always "hidden under a green umbrella" — meaning one has always played character parts. I had never played "me". He told me, "We know what you are, that's why you've been cast, and if you play it as you, it will come out all right." So Doctor Who was me!'

Peter Bryant's expectation was that Pertwee would give the Doctor a lighter, more whimsical quality:

'I hadn't met Jon Pertwee before I cast him, but I knew a lot about his work and thought he would bring some comedy into the programme. It had been getting a bit heavy towards the end of Patrick Troughton's stint and I felt it badly needed lightening. He was such a multi-talented man, Jon. He could sing, he could play the guitar, he could do funny voices and he looked very good. All these things I thought he would contribute to *Doctor Who*. He had great authority, too, when he wanted to use it. He'd been in the business a long time; he knew his way around.'

In the event, although a few touches of whimsical humour would be apparent in his earliest episodes, Pertwee ultimately played the Doctor in a predominantly straight, serious vein, and his interpretation of the role was not at all as Bryant had envisaged.

The series' new star signed his contract for season seven on 21 May 1969 and was presented to the press at a special photocall held at the BBC Pictorial Publicity premises in Cavendish Place, just across the road from Broadcasting House in London's West End, on Tuesday 17 June, four days after the recording of Patrick Troughton's final episode and four days before its transmission.

An early priority after Jon Pertwee's selection for the role was to design the new Doctor's costume.

'I originally wanted something in grey, frightfully elegant and beautifully tailored,' says Pertwee, 'but the BBC weren't keen on that idea. Then one day I was asked to do a photographic session, and they told me to wear what I liked for it. I went home and found my grandfather's old smoking jacket and his Inverness cape, in a very tatty condition. I put these on with a frilly shirt from a

Jon Pertwee in characteristic pose as the third Doctor.

fashion house called Mr Fish and a pair of dark trousers with buckles. I came out in this outfit more for a giggle than anything else, but the BBC thought it was fabulous. They wondered how they could explain it in terms of the story and if the Doctor could go on wearing things like this. "Sure," I said, "I'll wear different coloured velvets and he'll be an eccentric, very natty dresser, an elegant dilettante. I can play it like a Regency buck." They liked that idea, and it gave me a hook to hang my character on.'

Season seven costume designer Christine Rawlins, however, recalls that there was a little more to it than this:

'Around that time, there was a BBC series called *Adam Adamant Lives!*. Adam Adamant was a Victorian adventurer who came back to life in present day London. He dressed in period costume, complete with cloak, and I remember thinking that something rather "romantic" like this would make a good contrast to the previous Doctor. That Jon Pertwee was thinking along the same lines was an agreeable coincidence, though whatever Jon had wanted I'm sure the producer would have endorsed.'

The costume was made by distinguished tailor Arthur Davey and the final details worked out in two fittings, which took place on 27 August and 4 September 1969.

▲ **A series of action poses taken at a *Radio Times* photo session.**

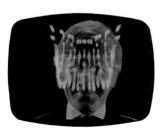

The new opening title ▲ sequence.

PETER BRYANT
PRODUCER

*Peter Bryant started out as an actor and, in the fifties, was one of the stars of the BBC soap opera **The Grove Family**. Later he took a temporary job as an announcer for BBC Radio, and this led to a permanent appointment. He also began to write radio scripts as a sideline. On the strength of this, and because he had a good theatrical background, he was transferred to the Radio Drama Department, where he worked as a script editor. Eventually he became head of the whole Drama Script Unit, as well as producing and directing. After about seven years he decided he would like to cross over to TV. He approached Head of Serials Shaun Sutton and was given an initial six-month attachment, assigned to work alongside departing story editor Gerry Davis on **Doctor Who**. He went on to become both script editor and producer of the series. After leaving the BBC in the early seventies he was involved in independent productions ranging from theatrical shows to TV commercials. He now works primarily as a literary agent.*

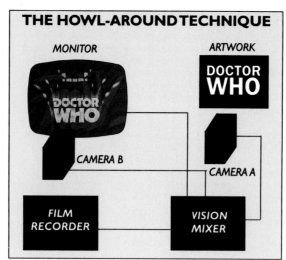

THE HOWL-AROUND TECHNIQUE

'Jon was extremely positive and professional,' notes Rawlins, 'and cared very much about the "look" of the whole production.'

Not only had Patrick Troughton decided to leave the series at the end of season six, but so too had his co-stars, Frazer Hines and Wendy Padbury. Their departure — explained by the simple expedient of having the Time Lords return the Doctor's companions Jamie and Zoe to their respective points of origin — meant that a completely new team of regulars had to be assembled for season seven.

The production team had already gained Nicholas Courtney's provisional agreement to return in the role of Brigadier Lethbridge-Stewart, and the actor signed his contract on 27 May 1969. The third and final member of the regular cast to be chosen was Caroline John, a young classical actress who successfully auditioned for the role of the Doctor's new assistant, scientist Liz Shaw, after sending in to the production office a glamorous modelling shot of herself, which she hoped would help to change her image.

The first studio work to be done for the season was the filming of a new title sequence. Like the two sixties sequences, this was the responsibility of BBC graphic designer Bernard Lodge and made use of an effect known as howl-around, which entails pointing a TV camera at a screen displaying the camera's own output and then filming the resultant feedback patterns. As with the Patrick Troughton sequence, the effect was realised in the studio by electronic effects specialist Ben Palmer, the designer whose pioneering work with howl-around had first inspired Lodge to use it for *Doctor Who* back in 1963.

'When we were asked to do the first colour title sequence in 1969,' recalls Lodge, 'I had expected colour television would give us even more won-

derful abstract shapes than we had achieved in black and white, but in fact the results were very disappointing. In the light of that, the obvious thing to do was to shoot some more black and white patterns and then try to colour the images. This time I introduced some concentric diamonds into the feedback patterns, and I was a bit more careful about the photography of Jon Pertwee's face than I had been about that of Patrick Troughton's. I deliberately arranged the photograph with a symmetrical back-light hitting the left and right sides, leaving a kind of shadow right down the middle of the face.

'We put the colour in using a very primitive form of optical printer. Between the camera and the projector were coloured gels arranged in the patterns we wanted — a bull's-eye shape, for example. Because the camera was focused on the projector, the colour gel plane was soft, giving a blurred edge to the colours.'

Lodge experimented with a number of different photographs of Jon Pertwee when compiling the sequence, including a three-quarter length shot of the actor with his arms held out to either side, palms forward, in a gesture of salutation. Eventually, however, he settled on a simple portrait shot.

For the first time, Lodge was also asked to create a closing title sequence for the series — during the sixties, the closing titles had generally been rolled over a plain black background. He designed this in the same style as the new opening titles, again using the familiar howl-around effect.

To go with the new titles, the BBC Radiophonic Workshop provided a slightly revamped arrangement of Ron Grainer's theme music. This was essentially the same as that used for the latter Patrick Troughton serials but had some additional sound effects overlaid and, rather than simply being faded down at the end, was given a more positive conclusion.

The start of the new season was heralded by a full-page colour photograph of Jon Pertwee's Doctor on the front cover of the BBC's listings magazine, *Radio Times*, dated 1 January 1970. This was one of a number of shots taken by a *Radio Times* photographer, Ray Rathborne, specifically for that purpose, mid-way through the making of the season. Unusually, however, no major article appeared inside the magazine to back up the cover photograph.

The new Doctor's debut episode, *Spearhead from Space* part one, was eventually transmitted at 5:15:53 on the evening of Saturday 3 January 1970. A new era had begun.

CHAPTER TWO

Who Was Jon Pertwee

J on Pertwee was born on 7 July 1919 in the Chelsea area of London. His parents Roland and Avice had conceived him on Armistice Day — 11 November 1918 — when having a child had been the furthest thing from their minds. They had in fact been living apart and had bumped into each other quite by chance during the celebrations at London's Piccadilly Circus. The resultant son was named John (after the apostle and disciple) Devon (after the county) Roland (after his father) Pertwee (an Anglicized version of the true family name, Perthuis de Leillevaux) — although he later changed the spelling of John to Jon.

Jon was the second son of Roland and Avice, his brother Michael being three years his senior. Shortly after Jon's birth, his mother divorced Roland and married his best friend, a Frenchman named Louis de la Garde. Jon and Michael remained with their father and went to live in Caterham-on-the-Hill in Surrey.

The Pertwee family had a long connection with showbusiness and the performing arts. Roland was a noted actor and playwright and a great friend of Gerald du Maurier; his great aunt was the opera singer Eva Moore whose daughter, Jill Esmond, used to bring her then husband, Laurence Olivier, to tea with the Pertwees while Jon was in his teens.

Jon joined Aldro, a boarding school in Eastbourne, at the age of seven and a half, but was later expelled for swinging from chain to chain in the toilets. Before starting at his next school he met A.A. Milne, a friend of his father's, and also Milne's son, Christopher Robin. Jon still recalls being introduced to Christopher's toys, Piglet, Owl, Kanga, and, of course, Pooh Bear.

Jon next attended Wellington House preparatory in Westgate-On-Sea in Kent, and while there he developed an almost overwhelming desire to become an actor. The school's head, the Reverend Percy Underhill, and his wife, encouraged him in this direction, allowing him to write, produce, direct, act in, do the make-up and play the music for numerous evenings' entertainment for his fellow pupils and teachers.

After Wellington House, Jon moved to the public school of Sherborne in Dorset, from where he was subsequently 'superannuated' — expelled — for threatening one of the prefects. He next moved to

◀ A 1951 publicity photo.

NAMES

Over the years, Jon Pertwee has seen his name misspelt or mispronounced innumerable times. Here are some of his favourites:

Tom Peetweet; Jon Peterwee; Jon Peartree; Mr Twee; Saniel Pertwee; Mr Pardney; Mr Bert Wee; John Peewee; Newton Pertwee; Mr Pickwick; Miss Jane Partwee; Master J Peewit; Mr Pertweek; Joan Pestwick; J Pertineee; John Between; Mr and Mrs Jon Perkee; J Parpertwuwe; Jan Putrid

THE SPARE PART PEOPLE

*During his time as the Doctor, Jon Pertwee wrote with his friend, actor Reed de Rouen, a script for a seven-part **Doctor Who** story which has been referred to variously as **The Labyrinth, The Brain Drain** and **The Spare Part People.** This was rejected by the production team as being unsuitable, partly because its setting in a labyrinth of ice tunnels would have made it too expensive to realize.*

THE FILMS OF JON PERTWEE

Dinner At The Ritz (1936); A Yank At Oxford (1938); The Four Just Men (US title: The Secret Four) (1939); There Ain't No Justice! (1939); Young Man's Fancy (1939); Penny And The Pownall Case (1948); Trouble In The Air (1948); A Piece Of Cake (1948); William Comes To Town (aka William At The Circus) (1948); Murder At The Windmill (US title: Murder At The Burlesque) (1949); Helter Skelter (1949); Stop Press Girl (1949); Dear Mr Prohack (1949); Miss Pilgrim's Progress (1950); The Body Said No! (1950); Mr Drake's Duck (1951); Will Any Gentleman ...? (1953)*; The Gay Dog (1954); Knock On Wood (1954)* (uncredited, doubling for Danny Kaye); A Yank In Ermine (1955)*; It's A Wonderful World (1956); The Ugly Duckling (1959); Just Joe (1960); Not A Hope In Hell (1960); Nearly A Nasty Accident (1961); Ladies Who Do (1963); Carry On Cleo (1964)*; I've Gotta Horse (aka Wonderful Day) (1965); You Must Be Joking! (1965); How To Undress In Public Without Undue Embarrassment (1965); Carry On Cowboy (1965)*; Carry On Screaming (1966)*; A Funny Thing Happened On The Way To The Forum (1966)*; Up In The Air (1969)*; Under The Table You Must Go (1969)*; The House That Dripped Blood (1970)*; There's A Girl In My Soup (1970)*; Four Against The Desert (1974)*; One Of Our Dinosaurs Is Missing (1976)*; Adventures Of A Private Eye (1977)*; Wombling Free (1978)**; No 1 Of The Secret Service (1978)*; The Water Babies (1979)**; The Boys In Blue (1983)*; Have You Ever Heard Of The Milky Way (1985)*; Carry On Columbus (1992)*

Dates are release dates, not production dates
* = colour film
** = colour film, voice only

With co-star Dani Sheridan in the 1965 film *How to Undress in Public without Undue Embarrassment*.

Frensham Heights, starting there at the age of 16.

It was at Frensham Heights that Jon had his first taste of 'real' theatre as the school staged productions of *Twelfth Night* and *Lady Precious Stream*. Jon played parts in both, and was even mentioned in local newspaper reports as having given 'an outstanding performance'.

After leaving school, Pertwee auditioned for the Central School of Dramatic Arts. Despite the fact that his uncle was a teacher there and a friend of the principal, he failed the audition dismally. The principal informed him in no uncertain manner that he had a malformation of the mouth and as a result was cursed with a very sibilant 'S'. Undaunted, he promptly auditioned for, and was accepted by, the Royal Academy of Dramatic Arts (RADA), joining in 1936.

His stay at RADA was curtailed, however, as he was 'asked to leave' for refusing to play the part of a 'Greek Wind' in the chorus of Euripides's *Iphigenia*. Thanks to his friendship with the sons of Hugh McKay and Eleanor Elder, he was subsequently able to secure a place in their Arts League of Service Travelling Theatre. This travelling group had started up in 1919 and Pertwee's arrival coincided with their last tour before being forced out of business. He was billed as a 'juvenile character actor'.

Following the demise of the Arts League of Service, Pertwee was determined to join another good repertory company. In 1937, after many weeks seeking employment, he managed to secure an engagement with J. Baxter-Somerville's Repertory Players at the Springfield Theatre in Jersey, where he worked with Val Blanchard, better known in later life as MacDonald Hobley. This association lasted only a short time, Pertwee being dismissed from the company for a couple of pranks. It was while in Jersey that he decided to alter the spelling of his first name from John to Jon after seeing it misprinted that way on a billing.

Several small stage roles followed while Pertwee attempted to gain a permanent position with a company. In April 1938 he joined the Rex Lesley-Smith Repertory Players at the West Pier in Brighton. There he appeared in *Love from a Stranger* and *Candida*, amongst other productions.

Following this, Pertwee worked for a company at the Festival Theatre in Cambridge before putting repertory work behind him and returning in late 1938 to London to try to make his name in the West End. During 1938 and 1939 he obtained small parts in *Judgement Day*, a comedy concerning Van der Lubbe, a pawn in the Berlin Reichstag fire trial, *To Kill a Cat* (written by his father) at the Aldwych Theatre and *Goodbye Mr Chips* at the Q Theatre. He also made his debut on radio,

As the soothsayer with Charles Hawtrey in *Carry On Cleo* (1964).

SELECTED TV APPEARANCES

*Six-Five Special (BBC);
Dangerous Cargo (ITV 1957);
Can Do (ATV 1958); Sunday
Night At The London
Palladium (BBC 1958); The
Amazing Adventures Of
Commander Highprice (BBC
'50s); Evans Above (BBC '50s);
Round The Bend (1956);
Glencannon (Gross-Krasne
1959); Ivanhoe (Sydney Box
1959); The Dickie Henderson
Show (Associated Rediffusion
1963); Five O'Clock Club (ITV
1965); Jon Pertwee Show (BBC
1966); The Good Old Days
(BBC 1966); Jackanory (BBC
1966/67/69); The Rolf Harris
Show (BBC 1969); Call My
Bluff (BBC 1969); Going For A
Song (BBC 1971); Doctor Who
(BBC 1970–1974); Pebble Mill
At One (BBC 1973/74); Blue
Peter (BBC 1974); Whodunnit?
(Thames 1974–78); The Goodies
(BBC 1975); Worzel Gummidge
(Southern 1979–81); Worzel
Gummidge Down Under
(1986–87); Give Us A Clue (ITV
1985); The Little Green Man
(Central 1985)*; The Curious
Case Of Santa Claus (C4 TV
film 1987); Three Of A Kind;
Superted*; The Little Green
Man (1988)*; Virtual Murder:
A Torch For Silverado (BBC
1992); That's Entertainment
(ITV 1994); Noel's House Party
(BBC 1994); Young Indiana
Jones (1994).*

*=Voice only

SELECTED RADIO APPEARANCES

*Marmaduke Brown ('30s);
Young Widow Jones ('30s);
Stella Dallas ('30s);
Mediterranean Merry-Go-
Round (BBC 1946); Captain
Kettle (BBC 1947); Up The Pole
(BBC 1947–52); Listen My
Children (BBC 1948); The
Waterlogged Spa (BBC 1948);
Puffney Post Office (BBC
1950); Pertwee's Progress (BBC
1955); The Navy Lark (BBC
1959–77); London Lights (BBC
1962); The TV Lark (BBC 1963);
Superman (BBC c.1991);
Doctor Who: The Paradise Of
Death (BBC 1993).*

narrating *Lillibulero* with Leo Genn and Ralph Truman in Northern Ireland.

Also in the cast of *To Kill a Cat* was an actor called John Salew, who played several characters in popular radio soap operas of the day such as *Marmaduke Brown*, *Young Widow Jones* and *Stella Dallas*. At Salew's suggestion, Pertwee auditioned for work in these shows. The producer, American Jack Hayes-Hunter, was so impressed with the young actor that he decided to hire him — to play the parts previously held by Salew!

Salew never spoke to him again, but Pertwee had managed to break into commercial radio and he stayed there for the next two years. To supplement his income, he also worked as an extra at Denham Film Studios, appearing in numerous productions including *Dinner at the Ritz* (1936), *A Yank at Oxford* (1938), *Young Man's Fancy* (1939) and *The Four Just Men* (1939), many of them written by his father. It was in *The Four Just Men* that he spoke his first lines on film.

During this period, Pertwee was living with a half-Dutch, half-Singhalese woman called Carlotta Joachim Sid'Kithan, and this relationship helped settle him into a happy domestic life. His career and home life were both put on hold, however, when the Second World War broke out and he joined the Navy, becoming Ordinary Seaman Pertwee P/JX178358. He was stationed initially at Portsmouth Naval Barracks, then moved to *HMS St Vincent* in Portsmouth Harbour as a wireless operator and from there to *HMS Collingwood*, a nearby stone-frigate, as a trainee telegraphist.

On 29 November 1940, Pertwee was drafted onto *HMS Hood*, one of the biggest battle cruisers in the world, and stationed at Scapa Flow in the Orkney Islands for almost six months, during which time his girlfriend Carlotta left him and returned to Ceylon. He was then transferred to the ship *Dunluce Castle* to train as an Officer Cadet. Shortly afterwards, on 24 May 1941, *HMS Hood* had its fateful battle with the *Bismark* in which it was hit and sunk in less than 90 seconds. Of the 1,415 men on board — many of whom had been Pertwee's friends and colleagues — only three survived.

Following an incendiary bomb attack on the barracks at Portsmouth, Pertwee suffered a severe blow to the head which slightly displaced the retina in his right eye. As a result, he was dropped from the Officer Cadet course and became Sub-Lieutenant Pertwee, RNVR Special Branch, posted to *HMS Valkyrie* in the Isle of Man as a Divisional Officer.

Whenever possible during the war, Pertwee continued his theatrical work with appearances in shows and galas for fellow servicemen. On the Isle of Man, he formed a small company of local amateurs and servicemen and staged events at the Gaiety theatre. The first production of the Service

With Harry H. Corbett ▶
in *Carry On Screaming*
(1966).

SELECTED THEATRE APPEARANCES

To Kill a Cat; See You Inside; Touch It Light (1957–58); A Funny Thing Happened on the Way to the Forum (1963); There's a Girl in my Soup (1966); Who Needs Marriage?; Oh Clarence; The Bedwinner (1974); Irene (1977); SuperTed (1985); Worzel Gummidge; Doctor Who – The Ultimate Adventure (1989); Dick Whittington (1989); Aladdin (1990/1 and 1991/2); Scrooge – The Musical (1992/3 and 1993/4).

**With second wife ▲
Ingeborg.**

**At home with Ingeborg ▲
and his children Sean
(aged 8) and Dariel (11) in
April 1973.**

Players, as they came to be known, was *Night Must Fall* by Emlyn Williams in April 1942, and this was followed by a presentation of *George and Margaret*. When he wasn't performing with the Players, Pertwee was working with a Concert Party company, which he had also formed, to entertain the crew of *HMS Valkyrie* and the Manx locals.

From the Isle of Man, Pertwee was next posted to the Security Staff of Naval Intelligence in Great Smith Street, Westminster, where he found himself working alongside James Callaghan, later to become Prime Minister. Following the winding down of this section of Naval Intelligence, he was then appointed to the Naval Broadcasting Section where he, together with the actor Lieutenant Commander Kim Peacock RNVR, was to produce and record programmes for the 'pleasure and edification' of the armed services.

In 1946, Pertwee joined the cast of *HMS Waterlogged*, the Naval edition of Eric Barker's forces radio show *Mediterranean Merry-Go-Round*, after having been sent to investigate the production for 'irregularities'. It was in this series that he was first able to indulge his flair for accents, playing Commander Highprice and the schizophrenic efficiency expert Robin Fly. The fictional *HMS Waterlogged*, stationed at Sinking-in-the-Ooze, subsequently became the subject of a spin-off show entitled *The Waterlogged Spa*, which began on 17 September 1948. Pertwee remained in the cast, creating characters like Svenson the Norwegian seaman ('Er-yaydon yowdon yaydon, neggerdicrop dibombit'), the Bugler from Plymouth Barracks, the stuttering Mr Cook and, perhaps most famous of all, the Postman ('What does it matter what you do as long as you tear 'em up?'). He also starred as the latter character in *Puffney Post Office*, a spin-off from *The Waterlogged Spa*, which began on 21 April 1950.

Towards the end of the forties, following his departure from the Navy, Pertwee joined a vaudeville troupe, June and Wallace, and played a

character called Mister Burp in a revue entitled *Up the Pole*. This later transferred to radio, four seasons being produced between 1947 and 1952. Like many other radio stars, he was also in demand for music hall appearances and films, and was contracted to the Associated British Pictures Corporation (ABPC) to appear in their productions.

Pertwee received star billing in films for the first time in 1953 in *Will Any Gentleman . . . ?* (which also featured William Hartnell). He stood in for American comedian Danny Kaye, to whom he bore more than a passing resemblance, for London scenes of *Knock on Wood* and played a conductor in *It's a Wonderful World*.

Television was a relatively new medium when Pertwee was asked if he would front some 'TV spectaculars'. Following a successful run of these he appeared with David Jacobs in a production called *The Amazing Adventures of Commander Highprice*, recreating his character from *Mediterranean Merry-Go-Round*, and with Norman Evans in *Evans Above*. Eventually he was offered his own series and, although he suggested a sitcom format, was asked to make it a sketch show. Pertwee did a series of six programmes but felt that his talents were in acting and entertaining rather than as a comedian.

In 1959, the Head of Programmes for BBC Radio, Michael Standing, invited him to front a new series, and asked if he could come up with a suitable idea. The result was *The Navy Lark*, which was based very much upon Pertwee's wartime experiences. *The Navy Lark* was a great success and ran for almost 20 years. It starred Pertwee, Leslie Phillips and Dennis Price, and the main supporting cast were Ronnie Barker, Michael Bates, Richard Caldicot, Heather Chasen, Judy Cornwall, Tenniel Evans and, replacing Dennis Price from the second season onwards, Stephen Murray. June Whitfield and Norma Ronald appeared as guests in a few seventies episodes. Pertwee's characters were the conniving CPO Jon Pertwee, the incomprehensible Commander Wetherby, the schizophrenic Vice-Admiral Burwasher and — in the seventies — the evil oriental genius the Master. The series temporarily ended in 1962 and was reformatted for 1963 as *The TV Lark*, with the same characters running a TV station. This was badly-received, however, and after only ten episodes the characters rejoined the Navy!

Pertwee had married actress Jean Marsh in 1955 after meeting her while filming *Will Any Gentleman . . . ?*, but their relationship was to be short-lived. He met his second wife-to-be, Ingeborg Rhosea, while on a skiing holiday in Kitzbühel in February 1958. He had broken his leg at the time

With Kenneth Williams in *Carry On Cowboy* (1965).

CO-OP CAKES
The character of the Doctor was often used to promote other products and projects, but none so tangential as when Jon Pertwee lent his name to a book of baking recipes released by the Co-Op in 1973. The book contains recipes contributed by entrants to a national newspaper's competition and has nothing to do with **Doctor Who** *whatsoever, however the back cover is given over to an artwork illustration of Pertwee apparently saying: 'Men go shooting off to outer space but it's really their inner space that matters most. I'm sure I'm not the only one who likes to be adventurous at meal times. When the meal I'm eating is home cooked, but doesn't cost the earth, then I know I'm getting the best of all worlds.'*

ALIEN APPEARANCE
Among the many promotional appearances given by Jon Pertwee, was one in March 1974 when Pertwee, together with his new 'flying car' attended an event at the Co-Op Superstore in Glenfield, Leicester.

and was effectively out of action when he met the German woman, who was also a stranger in a strange place. Pertwee was divorced from Marsh in 1960 and married Rhosea on 13 August the same year at Bourne End in Buckinghamshire. He has two children from his second marriage — a daughter, Dariel, and a son, Sean.

During the sixties, Pertwee concentrated on film acting and appeared in several productions of note, including three of the popular *Carry On* films produced by Peter Rogers. He was a soothsayer in *Carry On Cleo*, a Scottish scientist in *Carry On Screaming* and a blind and deaf sheriff in *Carry On Cowboy*.

In 1969, he played an actor who was transformed into a vampire in Hammer Films' production *The House that Dripped Blood*. By the time the film was released in 1970, he was already starring as the Doctor in the seventh season of *Doctor Who*.

Ever the man of action, Pertwee insisted on doing some of his own stunts on *Doctor Who* — although he had a regular stunt man and double, Terry Walsh, to take care of the really dangerous stuff. While filming a particularly vigorous scene he aggravated a spinal injury originally sustained during the Second World War and, as every movement was agony, had to have his back strapped up. Eventually he opted for surgery to try to resolve the problem, having some of the nerves in his spinal column cut, but this proved unsuccessful. Thereafter he used infra-red lamps and pain killers to try to overcome the agonizing back ache,

which was so bad at times that he was forced to perform certain episodes of *The Navy Lark* tied down to a chair to prevent unnecessary movement.

Shortly after leaving *Doctor Who* in 1974, Pertwee returned to the small screen hosting a quiz show called *Whodunnit?* for Thames TV. This involved a group of actors acting out a crime — with clue-dropping everywhere — while a panel of celebrities, including resident panellists Patrick Mower and Anouska Hemple (later replaced by Liza Goddard), attempted to guess 'whodunnit'. The show had already been running for one season with Edward Woodward as host, and Pertwee was asked to take over after making an appearance as a guest panellist.

In the late seventies, Pertwee managed the enviable feat of bringing to the screen a series, *Worzel Gummidge*, in which he was to enchant a whole new generation of children. This came about after Willis Hall and Keith Waterhouse, the eventual

◀ **As the host of *Whodunnit?* with regular celebrity guests Liza Goddard and Patrick Mower.**

Jon Pertwee ▲ and friend.

Jon Pertwee at home ▲ with his first wife Jean Marsh, in 1956.

ROAD SAFETY

In the mid-seventies, Jon Pertwee lent his name to a series of road safety television advertisements with the catchphrase SPLINK. The fact that this never really caught on is perhaps due to the rather obscure origin of the acronym: find a safe place to cross and stop; stand on the pavement near the kerb; look all round for traffic and listen; if traffic is coming, let it pass; when there is no traffic near, walk straight across the road; keep looking and listening for traffic while you cross.

writers of the series, asked if he would play Gummidge as a version of his famous Postman character in a proposed film they had written from Barbara Euphan-Todd's books. After about five years of trying to interest companies in the film, Pertwee finally had some success with Southern Television and so asked Hall and Waterhouse to prepare a pilot script. The resulting series proved phenomenally popular, as Pertwee had always believed it would be, running for several seasons and spawning a number of one-off specials. When Southern lost its franchise and its successor, TVS, declined to take up the series, Pertwee managed to secure a co-production deal for further episodes to be made in New Zealand.

Following the completion of *Worzel Gummidge Down Under*, Pertwee appeared in stage productions of the children's cartoon series *SuperTed* (he had earlier provided the voice of Spotty Man for the TV series), of *Worzel Gummidge* and of *Scrooge — The Musical*, as well as in several Christmas pantomimes. On film he provided a number of the voices for a cartoon adaptation of Charles Kingsley's *The Water Babies* and had a cameo role in *Carry On Columbus*, the 1992 revival of the *Carry On* films. On television he was in the BBC series *Virtual Murder*, playing an ageing Spanish arsonist in an episode called *A Torch for Silverado*.

In addition to his TV, radio and stage appearances, Pertwee has over the years lent his talents to many sound recordings, notably records of songs from *Worzel Gummidge* and a series of story-telling and song records for children. He also recorded 'Who is the Doctor?', a version of the *Doctor Who* theme, in 1972.

In the early eighties he again turned his hand to writing, producing the first volume of his memoirs under the title *Moon Boots and Dinner Suits*. This was published in hardback by Elm Tree Books in 1984.

Pertwee has returned several times to *Doctor Who* since the end of his regular stint as the Doctor. He appeared in the 20th anniversary story *The Five Doctors* in 1983 and starred in the stage play *Doctor Who — The Ultimate Adventure* in 1989. He presented two of BBC Video's special *Doctor Who* releases — one looking at the era of the second Doctor, *The Troughton Years*, and a similar tape looking at his own era, *The Pertwee Years*, which were recorded together in the spring of 1991. He narrated one of the BBC Audio Collection's *The Missing Stories* cassettes, *The Tomb of the Cybermen*, recorded in 1991 and released in 1993. Also in 1993, he reprised his role as the Doctor for two different projects. The first was a five-part serial called *The Paradise of Death* which was broadcast

Jon Pertwee as Worzel Gummidge, a role he made his own.

on BBC Radio 5 and simultaneously released on audio cassette in the BBC Radio Collection. The second was a two-part skit entitled *Dimensions in Time*, put together for that year's *Children in Need* charity appeal, which was intended to be viewed through special 3-D glasses.

Other *Doctor Who*-related projects included two video releases from Reeltime Pictures. The first, *Myth Makers 15: Jon Pertwee — The Third Doctor* (1989), was a straightforward interview tape while the second, *Return to Devils End* (1993), saw the actor reunited with some of his co-stars for a return visit to the principal location of the season nine story *The Dæmons*. In addition, Pertwee has attended innumerable *Doctor Who* conventions and conferences all over the world, including the very first convention in 1977.

Despite continued problems with his back, and latterly with his legs, Pertwee has always enjoyed taking part in challenging sports like scuba diving, speedboat racing and biking. He has spent much of his leisure time at a holiday home in Ibiza and is always in demand to appear in cabaret and to provide after-dinner speaking services. Throughout much of his career, spanning over five decades on stage, radio, film, television — and even a time spent working with Billy Smart's Circus — he has been a staunch supporter of and fund raiser for the Grand Order of Water Rats, a charity which cares for elderly and retired members of the acting profession. Membership of the Water Rats is by invitation only, and he is proud to be associated with the organization. Above all else, Jon Pertwee has always had a deep respect for others in his profession, and has remained a showman to the core.

CHAPTER THREE

The Third Doctor: Man of Action

During *Doctor Who*'s first six seasons, very little had been disclosed about the Doctor's background. It was only in *The War Games*, the last story of his second incarnation, that viewers had finally seen his home planet and learned of his origins as a Time Lord. Placed on trial by three members of this incredibly powerful race and accused of interference in the affairs of other planets, he was ultimately sentenced to a period of exile on 20th-century Earth and also to a further transformation of his appearance.

When the third Doctor arrives on Earth at the beginning of his debut story, *Spearhead from Space*, he immediately collapses due to the after-effects of his regeneration and is taken to the nearby Ashbridge Cottage Hospital. There, previously unknown facts are revealed about his physiology. For a start, he is found by the medical staff to have two hearts, blood completely unlike any known human type and a pulse of only ten beats per minute. Then, on being wounded in the head after a failed kidnap attempt, he enters a self-induced recuperative coma during which his brain activity falls close to zero — a remarkable ability which is to save his life in a number of later adventures, such as *The Dæmons, Planet of the Daleks* and *The Monster of Peladon*.

Recovering, the new Doctor soon demonstrates that he has retained the magpie instincts of his predecessors. Sneaking out of his hospital room, he comes across a doctors' changing area from which he helps himself to a frilly shirt and cravat, a smart jacket and trousers and, left there by a visiting bigwig, a red-lined cloak and a fedora hat. This establishes his personal style for the remainder of his third incarnation as being that of a dapper gentleman favouring velvet smoking jackets, crisp shirts with ruffled fronts and cuffs and sharply-creased black trousers — in short, as his first incarnation later observes in *The Three Doctors*, a dandy.

▲ The third Doctor in action.

◀ The third Doctor in his vintage roadster Bessie. *Doctor Who and the Silurians.*

In contemplative mood. ▲
Death to the Daleks.

A behind the scenes ▲
shot from *Terror of the
Autons.* The Doctor is
warned about the Master's
arrival on Earth by a fellow
Time Lord (David Garth).
Note the blue CSO screen
behind the actors.

The Brigadier (Nicholas ▲
Courtney) and Liz Shaw
(Caroline John), two UNIT
members who became the
Doctor's allies during his
exile on Earth.

The Doctor races into action as the Brigadier (Nicholas Courtney) watches. *Doctor Who and the Silurians.*

Not content with stealing some of the bigwig's clothes, the Doctor also makes off with his elegant red vintage roadster; and, although he is later persuaded to return it, he subsequently obtains a similar, bright yellow model of his own, which he nicknames Bessie. This is symptomatic of a penchant for exotic forms of transport, which he indulges with vehicles such as a three-wheeled trike (*Day of the Daleks*), a jet ski (*The Sea Devils*), a one-man hovercraft (*Planet of the Spiders*), an autogiro (*Planet of the Spiders*) and a spacecraft-styled flying car of his own design (*Invasion of the Dinosaurs* and *Planet of the Spiders*).

Needing a base of operations during his exile, the Doctor enters into an uneasy alliance with his old acquaintance Brigadier Lethbridge-Stewart of the United Nations Intelligence Taskforce. Thereafter he is often to be found in the UNIT laboratory, proving to be an inveterate tinkerer with a passion for gadgetry of all kinds. His favourite tool is the sonic screwdriver, a remarkable piece of engineering used only sparingly by his second incarnation but now pressed into service to perform a wide variety of different functions: acting as an electronic key (*Inferno*); detonating land mines (*The Sea Devils*); detecting traces of antimatter (*The Three Doctors*); setting off marsh gas explosions (*Carnival of Monsters*); indicating a safe path across an electrified floor (*Death to the Daleks*); and even, with the addition of a small spinning mirror, hypnotizing Aggedor, the sacred beast

of Peladon (*The Curse of Peladon*).

The Doctor's first priority after his arrival on Earth is to repair the TARDIS console. Deeply resentful of the Time Lords' sentence of exile, he makes a number of unsuccessful attempts to overcome their deactivation of his ship and their blocking of his memory of time travel law and the relevant dematerialization codes. At one point during *The Claws of Axos*, his UNIT colleagues suspect that he may even have betrayed them to the parasitic Axons in order to regain the ability to travel in time and space — although, as it turns out, this is simply a ruse of his to lure the aliens into a trap.

It is perhaps due in part to his frustration at his inability to escape from Earth that this Doctor initially exhibits a certain degree of high-handedness or even arrogance towards the humans around him. He gives particularly short shrift to self-important bureaucrats such as the civil servant Chinn in *The Claws of Axos*:

DOCTOR: My dear Mr Chinn, if I could leave I would, if only to get away from people like you, and your petty obsessions! England for the English — good heavens man!

CHINN: I have a duty to my country.

DOCTOR: Not to the world?

The Doctor and Jo (Katy Manning) flee from the Ogrons. *Day of the Daleks.*

▲ The Doctor prepares for his forthcoming battle with *The Sea Devils.*

▲ The Doctor relaxes after his first battle with the Master. *Terror of the Autons.*

▲ The Doctor and his friends Professor Clifford Jones (Stewart Bevan) and Jo Grant (Katy Manning) fight environmental pollution in *The Green Death.*

Other pompous establishment figures who feel the sharp edge of his tongue include ill-tempered scientist Professor Stahlman in *Inferno* and civil servants Brownrose in *Terror of the Autons* and Walker in *The Sea Devils.* The Doctor is however ready to revise his attitude if his preconceptions prove unfounded, as is demonstrated by this exchange from *Invasion of the Dinosaurs*:

BRIGADIER: Doctor, this is the Rt. Hon. Charles Grover, Minister with Special Powers.

(THE DOCTOR, ENGROSSED IN HIS WORK, DOES NOT REPLY.)

GROVER: I do apologize for the interruption, Doctor. I realize how busy you are.

DOCTOR: I'm glad somebody does!

GROVER: I understand you may be able to help us find a solution to this crisis.

DOCTOR: Yes, I sincerely hope so.

(SUDDENLY HE LOOKS UP.)

Aren't you the chap who started the Save Planet Earth Society?

GROVER: I had something to do with it.

DOCTOR: You also wrote that book, *Last Chance for Man*, didn't you?

GROVER: Yes, that's right.

DOCTOR: Oh, my dear Grover, I'm delighted to meet you. This planet needs people like you.

As his exile continues, the Doctor does in fact mellow quite considerably, becoming more accepting of his enforced sojourn on Earth and of his position as UNIT's scientific adviser. This is well illustrated by his developing friendship with the Brigadier. At first, their relationship is an almost purely professional one, based on mutual need and convenience. The Doctor needs the Brigadier to provide him with accommodation, laboratory facilities and an official identity, while the Brigadier needs the Doctor to help him combat the many alien menaces with which he is faced. The Time Lord certainly makes little secret of his distaste for the Brigadier's military approach to problems, protesting at the end of *Inferno* that he has had all he can stand of 'this pompous, self-opinionated idiot'. Gradually, however, a firm friendship develops between the two men, to the extent that by *Planet of the Spiders*, the final adventure of his third incarnation, the Doctor is even addressing the Brigadier by his first name, Alistair, and taking him out to the theatre — albeit in the line of research.

The third Doctor as he ▲ appeared in his debut season.

On the planet Exxilon ▲ with MSC officer Peter Hamilton (Julian Fox). *Death to the Daleks.*

The Doctor takes to a hovercraft in a thrilling chase sequence in the penultimate episode of *Planet of the Spiders*.

By the time his sentence of exile is finally lifted by the Time Lords at the end of *The Three Doctors*, the Doctor has lost the burning desire he once felt to get away from Earth. In fact, although he does make a few 'proving flights' in the TARDIS, he subsequently returns of his own volition to continue his work at UNIT. When, at the end of *Planet of the Spiders*, his ship materializes in its accustomed place in the corner of the UNIT laboratory, he comments that it has brought him 'home'.

Part of his motivation for maintaining his association with UNIT is clearly the great affection he feels towards his second assistant Jo Grant, a scatter-brained blonde who quickly endeared herself to him despite his initial instinct to send her packing. When Jo eventually decides to give up her adventures with him in order to marry Nobel prize-winning ecologist Professor Clifford Jones, he appears deeply upset, slipping quietly away from the celebratory party and driving off alone into the sunset — a sentimental and melancholy side of his nature that viewers had rarely witnessed before.

Perhaps the most notable aspect of this Doctor's character, though, is his propensity for throwing himself headlong into perilous situations. He is frequently seen speeding to a trouble spot in Bessie or one of his other outlandish vehicles, or else running into danger, cloak flying in the breeze, and tackling his enemies physically using Venusian aikido — his own brand of the martial arts. Whereas the first Doctor showed only a limited inclination towards violent confrontation, and the second none at all, the third seems positively to relish it. Amongst his many daring exploits, he undergoes a trial-by-combat against King Peladon's champion (*The Curse of Peladon*), engages the Master in an impressive display of swordsmanship (*The Sea Devils*), undertakes a hazardous spacewalk (*Frontier in Space*) and takes part in some thrilling high-speed chases (in stories such as *Invasion of the Dinosaurs* and *Planet of the Spiders*).

It is incidents such as these which serve to establish the enduring image of the third Doctor as that of a dashing yet fiercely moral adventurer, an elegant caped crusader taking the Earth under his wing and doing battle with hordes of monstrous alien invaders. Truly a man of action.

CHAPTER FOUR

Season Seven: Exiled to Earth

Viewers' first taste of the new, action-orientated *Doctor Who* was provided by *Spearhead from Space*. This four-part story sees the Doctor exiled to 20th-century Earth where, having recovered from the after-effects of his latest regeneration, he reluctantly agrees to help his old acquaintance Brigadier Lethbridge-Stewart of UNIT to investigate a mysterious meteorite shower. The meteorites turn out to be hollow globes containing the Nestene consciousness, a disembodied alien intelligence with an affinity for plastic. A Nestene agent, Channing, has already infiltrated a nearby plastics factory and is using the energy from the globes to animate Autons — mannequin-like figures and realistic replicas of senior establishment figures — with the aim of taking over and colonizing the Earth.

Aided by a newly-recruited UNIT scientist, Dr Elizabeth Shaw, the Doctor manages to thwart this scheme with the use of an electro-convulsion transmitter which repels the Nestene consciousness into space and thereby neutralizes the monstrous tentacled form that it was creating for itself in a tank within the factory. Channing, himself revealed to be no more than a sophisticated Auton, is likewise deactivated.

Following this incident, the Doctor agrees to join forces with UNIT in return for access to equipment and facilities with which he can attempt to overcome the Time Lords' grounding of the TARDIS and thereby regain his freedom to travel through time and space.

Although he was involved in setting up the production of *Spearhead from Space* and even attended some of the initial location filming which took place in mid-September 1969, Peter Bryant was by this point taking a back seat on *Doctor Who*, having been given a new assignment to troubleshoot an ailing BBC series entitled *Paul Temple*. Derrick Sherwin therefore took the producer's credit on this story, as he had on the last story of season six. His task was by no means a straightforward one, however, as a number of unexpected complications arose. For one thing, he found himself having to make an unscheduled cameo appearance, playing the part of a commissionaire at UNIT's underground car park.

'The actor we'd originally cast couldn't act,' laughs Sherwin, who had himself worked as an actor in the fifties and sixties, 'so I said, "Get that uniform off — I'll do it myself!" It was a stupid little

SEASON SEVEN

CODE	TITLE
AAA	SPEARHEAD FROM SPACE
BBB	DOCTOR WHO AND THE SILURIANS
CCC	THE AMBASSADORS OF DEATH
DDD	INFERNO

RATINGS

Figures in millions

15			
14			
13			
12			
11			
10			
9			
8			
7			
6			
5	AAA	BBB	CCC	DDD

Story code

Channing (Hugh Burden) ▲
in *Spearhead from Space*.

Liz Shaw (Caroline John). ▲
***Doctor Who and the Silurians*.**

The Doctor and Liz. ▲
***Doctor Who and the Silurians*.**

CSO

*The first use of colour separation
overlay (CSO) in* **Doctor Who**
was in part four of **Doctor Who
and the Silurians.**
*Chronologically in terms of the
recording, a scene where Major
Baker is kidnapped in the caves
was the first use – one of the
background cave walls has been
created via CSO. Later in the
recording order, the Doctor and Liz
descend into the caves under
Wenley Moor and discover a giant
Tyrannosaurus Rex. This creature
was in fact a man-sized costume,
superimposed into the caves using
CSO. The effect was also utilized to
place an image of Major Baker
onto the Silurians' monitor screen.*

part which had only a couple of lines, but the guy couldn't get it right, so I threw him off the set.'

Of far greater seriousness was a problem which arose after the completion of the initial location filming, and which almost resulted in the production being cancelled altogether:

'There was a BBC strike at the time and the studio cameramen were working to rule,' recalls Sherwin. 'I had written a *Thirty Minute Theatre*, an all studio production, and it was suddenly switched in the schedules to be recorded that week as it needed relatively little direction and the cameras couldn't go far wrong. On *Doctor Who*, though, it threw us out of kilter as it meant we couldn't go into the studio. This was Jon Pertwee's first story, remember, and of course he was in a dead sweat! I said, "Don't worry, don't worry, I can mount the whole thing on film, given a fortnight or three weeks run up." So I discovered some BBC training premises out in the country, a lovely old building, where we could find every location we needed. I took everyone down there and we shot the whole story on 16mm film!'

This additional shooting was carried out in two main blocks, the first from 8 to 23 October 1969 and the second from 29 October to 5 November 1969. A further day's work was then required on 22 November 1969 — by which time production of the following serial was already well advanced — apparently to remount the climactic scenes of the Nestene creature bursting from its tank, which had proved unsuccessful on the first attempt.

In the end, as Sherwin notes, Jon Pertwee turned out to be quite happy about this unexpected change of plan, which made *Spearhead from Space* the only *Doctor Who* story ever to have been shot entirely on film as opposed to videotape:

'He was terribly nervous about doing the series — he had never done drama before — and I told him that if anything went wrong we could simply stop and do another take. The fact that he could treat it like a film reassured him, and then he got used to it. It finally gave him the confidence, because he found the character.'

Director Derek Martinus also felt that the change of plan brought fringe benefits:

'We looked around for locations and luckily found a wonderful place down in Evesham, and it all worked a treat.

'I enjoyed it because we were able to improvise a lot, based on the facilities we found at the location. One example is a sequence where the

Doctor is seen taking a shower, which wasn't in the script: it wasn't until we saw the location with its antique shower unit that we could spot the potential.

'Jon was great. He was full of energy, and a great improviser. He was fairly confident about his ability to play the part, but I don't think he knew the Doctor as a character at all. He was playing it very much by ear, experimenting a lot — especially with comedy. I had to tone down some of his wilder excesses, and in fact the onus was very much between me and Jon because the show was actually changing producers at the time and Derrick wasn't around an awful lot. It was a tremendously exciting — and tiring — time for us all.'

The change of producers to which Martinus refers was occasioned by a request from Peter Bryant for Derrick Sherwin to be allowed to move off *Doctor Who* and join him on *Paul Temple*.

Having been turned down by a number of other candidates, including director Douglas Camfield, the opportunity to take over from Sherwin was eventually accepted by Barry Letts, a popular actor who had recently moved into directing, one of his earliest jobs in that capacity having been the season five *Doctor Who* story *The Enemy of the World*.

Letts officially began his first job as a producer on 20 October 1969, joining script editor Terrance Dicks and assistant script editor Trevor Ray on the series' production team. Bryant and Sherwin had brought Ray in during the making of season six as a potential successor to Terrance Dicks, feeling that he might fit in better with their more informal style of working. Letts, however, immediately hit it off with Dicks and found that they had very similar ideas about how the series should be made. Ray therefore became effectively redundant and, shortly after Letts's arrival, he too moved off *Doctor Who* and on to *Paul Temple*. He was briefly replaced by Robin Squires — a young former pop singer who had written a novel about the music business and gained an attachment to the production team — but he too moved on and the post of assistant script editor was then abolished.

The arrival of a new producer had relatively little impact on the style and content of season seven as most of the scripts had already been chosen by this point. It had been decided at an early stage that the season should be subdivided into only four stories — one four-parter and three seven-parters — on the basis that this would allow for each to be allocated a reasonably high proportion of the budget, ensuring improved production values. It had also been decided that the general tone

Mullins (Talfryn Thomas), the Brigadier (Nicholas Courtney), Channing (Hugh Burden) and Liz Shaw (Caroline John) in Ashbridge Cottage Hospital. *Spearhead from Space.*

DAVID WHITAKER
WRITER

*Born in Knebworth in 1928, David Whitaker started his career in the theatre, writing, acting and directing for a wide range of companies, including the York Repertory Group. There, one of his plays, **A Choice of Partners**, was seen by a member of the BBC Script Department and he was commissioned to adapt it for television. On the strength of this, in 1957, Donald Wilson invited him to join the Department's staff. For the next few years, Whitaker's work covered plays, situation comedies, light entertainment features and spectaculars, musical biographies – the most notable being **Hello Ragtime** – and series such as **Compact** and **Garry Halliday**. After leaving the **Doctor Who** production team he maintained a successful writing career – including a period of work in Australia – until his death on 4 February 1980.*

of the series should become rather more adult than in the past, in line with Derrick Sherwin's preferences and with the pressing need to widen the series' viewing audience.

In consultation with Bryant and Sherwin, Terrance Dicks had invited Robert Holmes to write *Spearhead from Space*, originally called *Facsimile*, on the strength of a storyline commissioned around April 1969. Holmes had recently been responsible for two season-six stories, *The Krotons* and *The Space Pirates*, which had been generally well received. A number of elements in *Spearhead from Space* were in fact based on incidents in the 1965 AA/Merton Park science-fiction film *Invasion*, for which Holmes had also provided the storyline.

On 25 June 1969, the production team had also commissioned *Doctor Who*'s original story editor, David Whitaker, to develop one of the season's seven-part stories from an outline he had sent in unsolicited for a second Doctor adventure reported to have been called *The Invaders from Mars*. This outline, which had been accepted on 1 May 1969, concerned the arrival on Earth of a group of alien ambassadors whose presence proves lethal to human beings, leading to the mistaken assumption that they are hostile invaders.

Another of the seven-parters had been developed from a storyline entitled *The Monsters* com-missioned on 18 August 1969 from Malcolm Hulke, whose previous credits on the series had been as co-writer of *The Faceless Ones* with David Ellis and of *The War Games* with Terrance Dicks. Hulke's initial reaction on learning of the idea of the Doctor's exile to Earth had been one of disappointment, as he feared that this would limit the series to just two types of story: 'alien invasion' and 'mad scientist'. In the event, however, he neatly side-stepped this potential pitfall by developing a scenario suggested by Dicks in which the Doctor was faced with a very different type of challenge. Transmitted as the second story of the season under its final title *Doctor Who and the Silurians*, this was a thought-provoking tale which presented no stereotype 'villains' and no easy answers.

Summoned by the Brigadier to an underground research centre at Wenley Moor, the Doctor and Liz Shaw learn from its highly-strung director, Dr Lawrence, that work on a new type of nuclear reactor is being hampered by inexplicable power losses and by an unusually high incidence of stress-related illness amongst the staff. The Doctor becomes convinced that the root of these problems lies in a nearby cave system. Investigating, he discovers that the caves are in fact the base of a group of highly intelligent reptiles, termed Silurians, whose civilization flourished on Earth before the rise of man. The creatures went into hibernation millions of years ago but have now been revived

MALCOLM HULKE
WRITER

*Malcolm Hulke did not begin writing professionally until he was in his thirties, and much of his work was in advancing the cause of television writing, through his talks and lectures and in particular his book **Writing For Television in the '70s**. Other books included **Cassell's Parliamentary Directory** and **The Encyclopedia of Alternative Medicine and Self Help**. In the sixties he wrote for television series like **Danger Man**, **Gideon's Way**, **The Protectors** and **The Avengers** for which he contributed four episodes with Terrance Dicks, and five episodes writing on his own. In the early sixties he, together with Eric Paice, wrote the children's serials **Target Luna** (1960), **Pathfinders in Space** (1960), **Pathfinders to Mars** (1961) and **Pathfinders to Venus** (1961). He was also script editor of **Crossroads** for many years, and novelized several plots from that series. His last **Doctor Who** script was **Invasion of the Dinosaurs** and he also completed several **Doctor Who** novelizations in the Target book range, the last of which, **The War Games**, was completed just before his death on 6 July 1979.*

by the power from the research centre.

The Doctor strives for peace between reptiles and humans, arguing that the Earth is big enough for both races to share. He manages to gain the trust of the old Silurian leader, but then a rebellious and intolerant young Silurian seizes power and releases a deadly virus which threatens to wipe out mankind. When the Time Lord finds an antidote, the Silurians immediately retaliate by taking over the research centre and preparing to destroy the Van Allen Belt, a natural barrier which shields the Earth from solar radiation harmful to humans but beneficial to reptiles. The creatures are tricked into returning to their caves when the Doctor overloads the reactor, threatening to cause a nuclear explosion. The Time Lord intends to reopen negotiations between the two species but, to his disgust, the Brigadier has the Silurian base blown up.

Much of the pre-production work on *Doctor Who and the Silurians* had been done by Peter Bryant and Derrick Sherwin, the former of whom was even credited as producer on some of its rehearsal scripts, and Barry Letts had been in charge for only three weeks by the time its location filming began on 13 November 1969.

'The BBC doesn't teach you how to be a drama producer,' Letts later reflected. 'She just picks you up by the scruff of the neck and drops you in it, if you take my meaning. You'll have been a director, an actor, a writer or a script editor perhaps and so you'll have learned a bit of doggy-paddle. If you swim hard enough you stand a chance of surfacing after a while.'

The first full studio session for the story, and indeed for the season as a whole, took place in TC3 — Television Centre Studio 3 — on Monday 8 December 1969. All went smoothly on that occasion, when the principal recording for episode one was carried out, but the same could not be said of the following week's session in TC1. At this point in *Doctor Who*'s history, increasing use was being made of out-of-story-sequence recording, and Monday 15 December had been designated for completion of all the cave sequences required for the entire story, to be edited in at the appropriate points during post-production. A specialist fibreglass firm in Wembley had been contracted to build the cave set but had failed to follow designer Barry Newbery's instructions, and the results proved near-calamitous. Newbery explains what happened:

'I went along after they had been working on it for a while — this would have been about four weeks before it was needed — and discovered that they hadn't made a framework for it at all. They

had spread fibreglass rovings over sacking, in various odd shapes, and it was all floppy. I told the BBC's Scenic Services people that I thought this wouldn't work, but they said, "Oh, it'll be all right, you don't have to worry about it." I then explained the situation to Barry Letts, who had just become producer of *Doctor Who*, and said, "Cancel it, it won't work, they don't know what they're doing." However, he didn't — and couldn't really — go against Scenic Services' advice.

'Anyway, I kept going back at regular intervals, and I could see that it still wasn't working, but no one took notice of my warnings. Eventually it came to the day of recording, and I rang Barry Letts from the studio at seven o'clock in the morning and told him "You haven't got a set!" It was just lying there flat on the floor, and no one knew how to make it stand up! That was the only time I ever had a sleepless night working on *Doctor Who*. Usually I knew what I was doing, but on this occasion I had no control over events. Why the contractors didn't follow my drawings, I'll never know.

'Fortunately, I'd had a number of black gauzes artist-painted with rock wall effects, and some rock pieces made out of a PVC material in the BBC workshops. In the studio they looked fine, so the director did all he could with the parts of the set that remained, and it actually worked quite well. However, we still had to have an extra, unscheduled studio day later on to make up for what had been lost. By that time, I'd had a chance to put together some sort of a replacement set: a ramped area covered with a material called expanded clay, which looks like shingle and sand.'

This extra, unscheduled studio session took place on Sunday 21 December 1969, the day before the principal recording for episodes two and three was carried out.

'Later,' says Newbery, 'there was a sort of inquest about the fibreglass set, and people were pointing the finger at me because it hadn't worked. I had to remind them that I'd been saying it wouldn't work ever since the first week!'

Partly because of these problems, *Doctor Who and the Silurians* proved to be something of a landmark story, as it ultimately led to the phasing out of the one-episode-per-week recording routine that *Doctor Who* had followed up to that point.

'Barry Letts asked me how we could get around the problem of sets being damaged,' explains Newbery. 'Every time they were taken in and out of the studio there was a tremendous amount of wear and tear on them, due mainly to the amount of handling involved but also to the scene shifters

A Silurian, revived from its long hibernation.
Doctor Who and the Silurians.

The Silurians' pet Tyrannosaurus Rex. *Doctor Who and the Silurians*.

being a bit blasé about scenery. I said to him, "If you have a set in straight from the workshop, you should use it just once in the studio and get everything you need for all the episodes of the story. Then any damage that's done when it's taken away won't matter, because you'll never see it again. And if you do your studio work in blocks of two days, to allow for more of this out-of-sequence recording, I think you'll find that you get a better-looking product."

'So, on my advice really, that's what Barry decided to do, and it was introduced later that season. It was a technique which was already commonly used on other BBC shows, but *Doctor Who* had almost always been done one day a week — it was traditional — and everybody had taken it for granted that that was how it should be.'

Letts also remembers this important development:

'Every time we came to plan a show there was an argument. Scenery said our requirements were too demanding, we said no they weren't. So I called a big meeting, as big as possible. I got all the scenic servicing people, the studio management, my head of department, the top studio planners, everyone together at the Centre for a discussion.

'I said it seemed to me that what was needed was early information — to decide on the sets required for each show and get them sorted out in rough much earlier than we had been doing, then get in touch with the scenic people concerned and discuss it with them. I said it also seemed to

me that the big snag was the fact that we did one episode per week. It didn't give anybody time to plan anything, and it also meant that each week we were having to put up and take down all these heavy sets, which was a great pity. So, speaking as an ex-actor, I thought it would be advantageous if we could do two a fortnight instead of one a week. If we planned our scenery such that the two episodes would use more or less the same sets, that would make it possible.'

Unexpectedly, *Doctor Who and the Silurians* was not the only input that writer Malcolm Hulke was called upon to make to the season. His second contribution came about due to problems which had arisen on David Whitaker's story, now retitled *The Carriers of Death*. The production team had been unhappy with the three episodes so far completed by Whitaker, and Trevor Ray, then still working as the series' assistant script editor, had been assigned to rewrite the first of them, earning a staff contribution fee of £150. This new draft had been sent to Whitaker by Sherwin under cover of a letter dated 11 August 1969:

Herewith our attempt at doing the first episode along the lines we feel the series should run. As you will see when you read the script, we are approaching the series from a much more realistic point of view; in other words the style is somewhat more sophisticated than we have previously used in other serials. This is why we found your episodes as written didn't quite work for us and felt that the best way to indicate the 'style' was to write the first episode.

TITLE TATTLE

*During season seven, some variations were made to the standard **Doctor Who** title sequence.*

*At the start of each episode of **Spearhead from Space**, the camera zooms in on the story title so that it appears to rush towards the viewer. The closing sequences of these episodes are also noteworthy. For the first, a coloured filter gives the picture a yellow/green tint, while for all four episodes the music accompanying the credits fades down part way through – at a different point each time – and another part of the theme simultaneously fades up, the net result being a rather disjointed-sounding edit.*

*The second story's title is shown on screen as **Doctor Who and the Silurians** – the only time that a TV story title has included the words 'Doctor Who and...' although the closing credits for **The Gunfighters: The OK Corral** in 1966 stated that the next story would be 'Doctor Who and the Savages'.*

*For the third story, the opening sequence is split into two sections. It runs as usual up to the point when the **Doctor Who** logo fades away, then a short teaser is shown, then the sequence starts up again. The title of the story appears as **The Ambassadors** first, then the words **Of Death** zoom into view below.*

*For **Inferno**, the opening sequence fades out after the **Doctor Who** logo, and the title, author and episode number are then slowly brought into focus over stock footage sequences of volcanic eruptions.*

▲ Dr Quinn (Fulton Mackay). *Doctor Who and the Silurians*.

LOCATIONS

Spearhead from Space
BBC Training Centre,
Wood Norton;
Guinness Factory, Acton

Doctor Who and the Silurians
Milford Chest Hospital,
Milford, Surrey;
Godalming, Surrey;
Transmitter station,
Hog's Back, Surrey

The Ambassadors of Death
Wycombe RDC Sewage
Purification Works, Little
Marlow, Bucks;
North Thames Gas
Works, Southall;
Spade Oak Quarries,
Nr Little Marlow, Bucks;
Marlow Wier, Mill
Road, Marlow

Inferno
Berry Wiggins & Co,
Kingsnorth-on-the-
Medway, Kent

**Designer Barry ▼
Newbery's concept
painting for the cave sets
in Doctor Who and the
Silurians.**

Do read it and come in and see us on Wednesday with your reactions. This isn't by any means the final first episode, but we hope this will give you some idea of what we are after.

We are, at the moment, attempting to do breakdowns of Episodes Two and Three, so that you can see how we would like to follow up. If these are completed in time we'll shoot them off to you by taxi.

See you Wednesday.

Despite these efforts, Whitaker's subsequent redrafts still failed to meet with the production team's approval. Terrance Dicks explains how Malcolm Hulke then became involved:

'It was one of those cases where a story just goes wrong, through no inherent fault of the writer. David Whitaker did about three or four rewrites in all, and it still wasn't working. Every time a new draft was done to change one thing, it would end up throwing something else out. When that happens, you eventually arrive at a point where the writer has got so wrapped up in the story that he can't give you anything new.

'It was at about this time that David announced that he was moving to Australia to do some work there. So what I did was arrange to have David paid off in full, which I insisted upon for all the work he'd done on the scripts, and then handed the drafts to Mac Hulke to rewrite with a fresh eye.'

Ray's first episode was retained virtually intact, but around November 1969 Hulke extensively revised Whitaker's second and third episodes and wrote the remainder from scratch, using the original ideas as a guideline. It was however agreed at the request of Whitaker's agent that he should still receive sole writer's credit on the transmitted story, which was retitled *The Ambassadors of Death*.

This adventure sees the Doctor taking part in a UNIT investigation into the mysterious events surrounding the Mars Probe 7 expedition. British Space Control has had no contact with the Probe's three astronauts since it started back from Mars seven months ago, and the Recovery 7 rescue mission has now run into similar difficulties. Although this second ship does eventually get back to Earth, the astronauts are kidnapped shortly after landing. Liz Shaw then notices that the ship's Geiger counter is at maximum, indicating that it must have been exposed to a lethal level of radiation. It soon becomes clear, however, that the ship's occupants are not the human astronauts after all, but a trio of radiation-dependent alien ambassadors who have swapped places with them.

The Doctor undertakes a solo flight in Recovery 7 to dock with the Mars Probe 7 vessel still orbiting in space. There he is intercepted by a huge alien spaceship and taken on board, where he finds the real astronauts unharmed but hypnotized to believe that they are being held in quarantine after the completion of their mission. The aliens' Captain threatens to destroy the Earth unless their three ambassadors are soon released.

Returning to Earth, the Time Lord discovers that the kidnapping of the ambassadors is all part of a complex scheme devised by ex-astronaut General Carrington to discredit the aliens and thereby convince the world's authorities to wage war against them. Carrington's xenophobia stems from the fact that the aliens accidentally killed one of his crew members on the earlier Mars Probe 6 expedition. With the help of UNIT, the Doctor is able to thwart his plans and arrange for the safe exchange of the ambassadors for the astronauts.

After *The Ambassadors of Death* had been transmitted, Terrance Dicks wrote to David Whitaker on 6 July 1970 to acknowledge the importance of his original ideas in securing the story's success:

Now that the tumult and shouting has died, just thought I would drop a line to say that Ambassadors of Death was one of our most popular serials last year. Viewing figures reached nine million at one point and part of the first episode was shown to an international drama conference, to great acclaim!

I'm quite convinced that the success of the show was very much due to the strength of your original story-line and hope you weren't too unhappy with the final result.

The Brigadier (Nicholas Courtney), Liz Shaw (Caroline John) and the Doctor (Jon Pertwee) direct the alien ambassadors in a move to recapture British Space Control. *The Ambassadors of Death*.

The director of *The Ambassadors of Death* was Michael Ferguson who, having also worked on *Doctor Who* during the sixties, was very conscious of the changes the series had undergone:

'I think one of the most important milestones for *Doctor Who* was the move into colour. Colour technology enabled all kinds of effects to be done which had been impossible before. I was very lucky to be around at that time. Barry Letts and I did a lot of work together to explore the possibilities of colour separation overlay (CSO).'

Letts explains the principle of this electronic effect, known outside the BBC as Chromakey:

'Basically, CSO is used to combine two pictures to achieve a third. For example, one camera shoots a picture of an actor against a plain-coloured background — usually blue, though green, red or yellow are sometimes used. Wherever the camera "sees" blue, the CSO apparatus will replace it with the output of another camera, which becomes the background in the final picture. As a result the actor can be put into any setting you like, even a model.'

As Ferguson recalls, everyone was keen to take full advantage of the new technology:

'I had a lot of discussions with the script editor, Terrance Dicks, about how we might develop ideas and realize a story slightly more visually than had

been done in the past, when the tradition had been for the director to turn the script into pictures quite literally.

'Much of the work I did on *The Ambassadors of Death* arose out of the opportunities opened up both by the advent of colour and by the new approach being taken to the production, such as the willingness to use stunt men and devise sequences based around what they felt they could offer.'

The stunts on *The Ambassadors of Death* were arranged and performed, as on many late-sixties and early-seventies stories, by an organization called HAVOC, run by leading stunt man Derek Ware. Some impressive action sequences were achieved with their assistance, although at the end of the day Barry Letts had cause to wish that they had been rather *less* spectacular:

'I think if *The Ambassadors of Death* taught me one thing it was the importance of keeping a close eye on the budget. Directors are a very enthusiastic breed who, quite naturally, always want the very best for their story. The problem lies in so far as what they push for invariably comes down to a question of more money. This is where the producer comes in, as arbiter of the whole season, to decide how money is to be apportioned throughout all the serials.

'The main example I can quote for *The Ambassa-*

MUSIC

Story	Composer
Spearhead from Space	Dudley Simpson
Doctor Who and the Silurians	Carey Blyton
The Ambassadors of Death	Dudley Simpson
Inferno	No specially composed music

*Season seven was the last time that the incidental music for **Doctor Who** was recorded prior to the studio recording. From season eight onwards, the music would be composed after recording from a video playback.*

*In realizing the score to **Doctor Who and the Silurians**, composer Carey Blyton conducted the following musicians: Paul Harvey (clarinet, bass clarinet, contra-bass clarinet), Michael Oxenham (clarinet, sopranino, descant recorder), Neill Sanders (horn), Vivian Joseph (cello), Gordon Kember (piano) and Stephen Whittaker (percussion).*

*In addition to Dudley Simpson's score, **Spearhead from Space** features Fleetwood Mac's 'Oh Well – Part One' by Peter Green as the background to a montage of shots of the plastics factory producing dolls. **Inferno** was the last **Doctor Who** story to have no specially composed incidental music. Instead it featured a number of stock tracks: Delia Derbyshire's 'The Delian Mode' and 'Blue Veils and Golden Sands'; 'Homeric Theme', 'Battle Theme', 'Souls in Space' and 'Attack of the Alien Minds' by St. George; 'Mysterious Sounds' by the Telecast Orchestra, conducted by Elliott Mayes; 'Build up to...' by Vorhaus; 'Electric Links' by Eric Peters; and 'Cosmic Sounds No. 5' and 'Crazy Sounds No. 4', composer unknown.*

▲ The alien Captain (Peter Noel Cook). *The Ambassadors of Death*.

'Creating the alien within the space suit meant building up the actor's face with very fine latex rubber, with blue make-up foundation underneath, to make the face appear irradiated when the special electronic colour overlay process was used,' Marion explained. 'On some parts of his face we used tissue and wet latex. Only the human eyes remained recognizable.'
Marion Richards, make-up designer for **The Ambassadors of Death,** *interviewed in the Radio Times dated 7 May 1970*

NOTES

Shared Set

The rocket capsule set used for **The Ambassadors of Death** *was also seen in the episode* **Re-Entry Forbidden** *of the BBC science-fiction series* **Doomwatch,** *which was recorded two days prior to its use in* **Doctor Who.** *It had been decided at the suggestion of their respective designers, David Myerscough-Jones and Ian Watson, that as both series required a set of this type they should build just one and split the costs between them.*

Primords

The hideous creatures into which people were transformed in **Inferno** *were never named in the dialogue of the transmitted episodes, but were identified in the closing credits as Primords.*

Cut Scene

The fifth episode of **Inferno** *was originally to have featured a scene where a radio announcer gave details of emergency measures being taken after the penetration of the Earth's crust in the alternative universe. This was edited out before transmission, however, as producer Barry Letts felt it was too obvious that the announcer was played by Jon Pertwee using one of his many disguised voices. The scene was however retained in copies of the episode sold overseas.*

Stock Footage

Inferno made use of a number of pieces of footage from Contemporary Films for the scenes of volcanic eruptions.

A behind the scenes shot of the alien Captain (Peter Noel Cook). *The Ambassadors of Death.*

The aliens' spaceship. *The Ambassadors of Death.*

dors of Death is the scene where the villains attempt to hijack the three astronauts on their return to Earth. I can't remember the script exactly, but I think all this scene involved originally was one Land Rover and a few heavies with guns. Michael Ferguson was, and is, a very good director with a terrific eye for film, and all during my first month or so as producer he was continually seeking me out with ideas he'd had for making this scene more visually exciting. Of course, being fairly green, and with a lot of my own director's instincts still prevailing, I was saying, "Yes, yes, yes" to all this. By the end of the day, we'd got something like a five-minute sequence involving helicopters, motor bikes, smoke bombs, explosions — the whole works. On film it looked tremendous, but you should have been there the day the bill arrived!

'As a production office we didn't actually write out any cheques ourselves. Nevertheless, every programme had to work within the budget it was given, with heavy penalties imposed if the limit was ever exceeded. So with *The Ambassadors of Death*, the biggest problem I had to face was looking around for cuts we could make in the show to pay for this enormously expensive bit of filming.'

By the time Letts took over as producer, only the last of the season's three seven-part stories remained to be chosen. The early favourite for

this slot was a submission by Brian Wright entitled *The Mists of Madness*, the initial outline for which had been commissioned by Peter Bryant and Terrance Dicks on 17 February 1969. This eventually proved unsuitable, however, so Letts and Dicks then turned their attention to two other possibilities: Don Houghton's *Operation: Mole-Bore* and Charlotte and Dennis Plimmer's *The Shadow People*, the storylines for which were commissioned on 16 November and 27 November 1969 respectively. After reading Houghton's four-page outline, delivered on 4 December, the production team felt sufficiently confident that on 9 January 1970 they commissioned him to write a full set of scripts under the revised title *The Mo-Hole Project*; and it was with this story that they eventually decided to proceed.

Retitled *Project Inferno* and then finally, around the end of May 1970, *Inferno*, Houghton's story centred around an experimental drilling project designed to penetrate the Earth's crust and release a previously untapped source of energy. UNIT's involvement begins when they are called in to provide security cover for the project, which is under the control of Professor Stahlman, the scientist after whom the new discovery — Stahlman's gas — has been named. Dismissing the concerns of Executive Director Sir Keith Gold (renamed from the story outline's Sir Keith Mulvaney), Stahlman is exceeding all safety margins in order to expedite the work. Soon, however, the drill head starts to leak an oily green liquid which, on contact with the skin, transforms people into vicious primeval creatures with a craving for heat.

The Doctor is accidentally transported by the partially repaired TARDIS control console into a parallel universe where England is ruled by a military dictatorship. The drilling project is at a more advanced stage here and, thwarted by his friends' ruthless *alter egos*, the Time Lord is unable to prevent the penetration of the Earth's crust, which causes a succession of violent eruptions and ultimately the planet's destruction.

Escaping back to his own universe, where the drilling is still in progress, the Doctor tries to warn of the impending disaster. At first he is disbelieved, but his words are borne out when the power-crazed Stahlman is himself transformed into one of the hideous primordial creatures. The Doctor, aided by oilman Greg Sutton, kills Stahlman with ice-cold blasts from fire extinguishers and, with only moments to spare, is finally able to shut down the drilling.

As Barry Letts and Terrance Dicks recall, it was they who suggested *Inferno*'s 'parallel Earth' subplot as a way of helping to sustain the story over its seven-episode length. If so, however, this must have been at a very early stage of their discussions with Don Houghton, as the idea was included in the writer's storyline dated November 1969. The only change of substance made at the scripting stage was the introduction of the story's hideous primordial monsters, which had not been part of Houghton's original idea. Although unnamed in the dialogue, these creatures were termed Primords in the closing credits of the transmitted episodes.

In a letter of 29 June 1970, responding to a viewer's enquiries, Houghton described some of the research which had gone into his storyline:

The story behind Inferno was almost as dramatic as that which appeared on the TV screen. After I had conceived the idea I began to research the whole project. I had read, some years ago, of a plan to drill down through the Mohorovic Discontinuity. It was to be the Americans' contribution to the Geophysical Year. They chose a spot, evidently, somewhere in the Pacific. There was a lot of publicity about it — and then, suddenly, silence. When I started making enquiries about it last year the authorities became very cagey about the entire business. The whole thing seemed to be shrouded in a thick veil of secrecy. The American Embassy told me that all information about the project was 'Classified' — and no data whatsoever could be released. The US Information Service told me that the project was progressing satisfactorily — but then two days later telephoned me urgently to say that

Professor Stahlman (Olaf Pooley), Sir Keith Gold (Christopher Benjamin) and Greg Sutton (Derek Newark) in the project control room. *Inferno.*

the Mo-Hole had been abandoned — but gave no reason. The British Science Museum told me that they were certain that the Americans were still drilling — but that they had received no data or infor-

▲ **The Primord Stahlmann (Olaf Pooley).** *Inferno.*

▲ **Stahlmann and the Brigade Leader (Nicholas Courtney).** *Inferno.*

DON HOUGHTON
WRITER

Don Houghton was born in 1930 in Paris and started writing for radio in 1951. In 1958 he moved to television and film. In the seventies he was one of Hammer Films' primary writers with credits including **Dracula AD 1972** (1972), **The Satanic Rites of Dracula** (1974), **The Legend of the Seven Golden Vampires** (1974) and **Shatter** (1976). On television he wrote for **Emergency Ward 10** in the sixties, **Crossroads** (for which programme he was also script editor for a time), contributed two stories for **Ace of Wands** (1970/71), six episodes of **New Scotland Yard** (1972/73), two episodes of **The Professionals** (1978), the fifth **Sapphire & Steel** story (1981) and one episode of **C.A.T.S. Eyes** (1985). He created and wrote for the Scottish soap opera **Take The High Road** and in 1984 was the executive story editor on **Hammer House of Mystery and Suspense**. He has written at least two novels, **Column of Thieves** and **Blood Brigade**. He was married to actress Pik Sen Lim who appeared as Captain Chin Lee in the second of Houghton's two Doctor Who stories, **The Mind of Evil**. He died in July 1991.

A rehearsal shot of Jon Pertwee (out of costume), John Levene and Nicholas Courtney (minus moustache) on the set of the Brigadier's commandeered office in the project complex. *Inferno.*

TREVOR RAY
ASSISTANT SCRIPT EDITOR

Following Trevor Ray's brief stint on Doctor Who he moved across to join outgoing Doctor Who producers Peter Bryant and Derrick Sherwin on Paul Temple in 1970. In 1976 he wrote the seven-part children's drama series Children of the Stones, transmitted by HTV in early 1977. In 1977 he worked on the six-part series Raven with Jeremy Burnham. He is seen playing the British Rail ticket collector who collapses from the Silurian virus in part six of Doctor Who and the Silurians.

ROBERT HOLMES
WRITER/SCRIPT EDITOR

Robert Colin Holmes was the youngest ever commissioned officer in the Queen's Own Cameron Highlanders, serving in Burma. After demob he joined the police and passed out top of his year at Hendon Police College. He eventually moved to court work, and left the force to become a court reporter and journalist. His work as a sports reporter took him to the Midlands, where he became the final editor of John Bull Magazine, at the same time submitting material to Granada TV for Knight Errant. Other early TV work included Emergency Ward 10, Ghost Squad, Public Eye, Undermind (his first science fiction) and Intrigue. His first work for Doctor Who was a commission to write The Space Trap, later retitled The Krotons. Subsequently he went on to become one of the series' most popular writers, responsible for more than a dozen televised stories. He also had a successful period as Doctor Who's script editor between 1974 and 1977. He scripted much TV drama during the seventies and eighties, including a Wednesday Play (The Brilliant New Testament) and episodes of Doomwatch, Dr. Finlay's Casebook, Dead of Night, The Regiment, Warship, Spy Trap, Dixon of Dock Green, and he adapted the BBC's 1981 science-fiction thriller serial The Nightmare Man from David Wiltshire's novel. He was working on further Doctor Who episodes when he died, after a short illness, on 24 May 1986.

Section Leader Shaw (Caroline John). *Inferno.*

mation from the Mo-Hole for nearly three years. So what has really happened to the bore? Have they discovered something awful down there? Are they frightened of releasing some terrifying force? And what is the mystery? Perhaps my story was not so fantastic after all. Anyway, without specific information I had to invent the Primords — and the catastrophe. One wonders what the outcome might have been if my good friend, Jon Pertwee, had not been on hand to safeguard us!

It was on *Inferno* that Barry Letts's plan of moving to a two-episodes-per-fortnight recording schedule finally came to fruition. The production went far from smoothly, however, as after the completion of the location filming in April 1970 the story's director, Douglas Camfield, became seriously ill — the result of an adverse reaction to some new medication he was taking for a long-standing heart condition. As Camfield noted in a later interview, it was Barry Letts himself who provided the solution to this problem:

'It might have been possible, even at that late stage, to bring in another director who wasn't already tied up with *Doctor Who*, but this would have meant starting all over again as few directors would be content with someone else's leftovers. Consequently Barry stepped in and took over, much to everyone's relief and admiration. There was still a lot of work to do on it, but he approached the task with the same professionalism he has always shown. More than that, although he finally did about 80 per cent of the work, he gave me all the credit. The show went out under my name.'

All in all, season seven had been something of

a baptism of fire for Letts. It could however be considered a successful start to his tenure as producer, being well received by critics and public alike. Although the average ratings and weekly chart positions fell slightly during the course of its run, from 8.2 million viewers per episode and 62nd place respectively for *Spearhead from Space* to 5.6 million viewers per episode and 69th place respectively for *Inferno*, these figures still compared very favourably with those for season six. Even more encouragingly, the average audience appreciation index actually climbed slightly from around 55 per cent for *Spearhead from Space* to 60 per cent for *The Ambassadors of Death* and *Inferno* — better than had been achieved by any second Doctor episode. While still falling some considerable way short of the peak levels of popularity the series had reached during its second season back in the mid-sixties, this seemed to confirm that the change of style initiated by Peter Bryant and Derrick Sherwin had paid off.

'I think I'm right in saying that it was a good six weeks into the season before we got the go-ahead to prepare for the next one,' says Letts. 'Terrance Dicks and I were badgering the powers that be to give us the go-ahead, because we couldn't get ourselves sorted out in terms of getting scripts written in time to record them. We managed it but, for a while, everyone was waiting to see how the new Doctor, and the new look of the show, was taken to by the audience, and what the viewing figures were, before they committed themselves.

'It was also said to me, as the new producer, that it would be a good idea if I could look around and see if I could find some idea for something to take *Doctor Who*'s place in the Saturday slot, if it were scrapped. I did have one idea, but that never came to anything.'

The idea that Letts devised was entitled *Snowy Black* and concerned the exploits of an innocent Australian cowboy trying to come to terms with city life in London — a forerunner of sorts to the *Crocodile Dundee* films of the late eighties. Letts had even got to the point of lining up an actor, Mark Edwards, to take the title role in the series but, before the first scripts were commissioned, *Doctor Who* was finally given a reprieve and *Snowy Black* was no longer needed.

Following the success of season seven, the last episode of which was recorded on 29 May 1970 and transmitted less than a month later on 20 June 1970, *Doctor Who* had a firm foundation on which to build for the rest of the decade. Flexibility had always been the key to the series' fortunes, however, and further important changes lay in store in season eight.

CHAPTER FIVE

Season Eight: A Masterful Season

Barry Letts had never been altogether happy with the new-style *Doctor Who* he had inherited from Peter Bryant and Derrick Sherwin. He considered it a mistake for the series to be set entirely on Earth and disliked the concentration on seven-part stories, feeling that the drama rarely sustained itself over such an epic length. For season eight, he was able to bring his own creative influence fully to bear.

'*Doctor Who* was a cheap show,' recalls Letts. 'They'd been scrabbling around for years trying to make something out of nothing. Once I found out how much money I had actually got to work with, I analysed what had happened in the past and realized that there were certain items, such as visual effects and costumes, on which we almost always overspent. I therefore went to the powers that be and pointed out that if that money was going to be spent anyway, we might as well have it up front. They saw the logic of that and agreed.

'We had worked out some provisional budgets for season eight and then, when it became obvious that *Doctor Who* was going to be a success, I started adding in other things, such as an extra bit of filming here and there. In this way I gradually increased the amount of money that was available. We ended up with much more money for the second season than we had had for the first, and that enabled us to break it up more sensibly with regard to the length of the individual stories.'

Terrance Dicks remembers that the BBC's Head of Serials was also very much in favour of this change:

'Ronnie Marsh was a big supporter of *Doctor Who*. He liked the idea of the "first night" — the excitement generated by the start of a new story — and asked for as many as possible in a season. So in the second Pertwee season we introduced a greater number of stories.'

Letts and Dicks had quickly developed a very good working relationship, spending many hours discussing all aspects of the series' production. They were keen to achieve, amongst other things, a varied mix of stories within each season. While opting to retain the basic exile scenario, with the Doctor acting as UNIT's scientific advisor, they therefore determined that during season eight there should be at least one adventure in which the TARDIS ventured back into outer space. They also felt that the series should become rather lighter in tone than had been the case in the recent past,

SEASON EIGHT	
CODE	TITLE
EEE	TERROR OF THE AUTONS
FFF	THE MIND OF EVIL
GGG	THE CLAWS OF AXOS
HHH	COLONY IN SPACE
JJJ	THE DÆMONS

RATINGS

Figures in millions

```
15
14
13
12
11
10
 9
 8
 7
 6
 5
    EEE FFF GGG HHH JJJ
    Story code
```

◀ **The Master (Roger Delgado) and Jo Grant (Katy Manning) join the regular team. *Terror of the Autons*.**

The Master (Roger ▲ Delgado) at Rossini's circus. *Terror of the Autons.*

THE ORIGINAL AUTONS

A number of plot elements in **Terror of the Autons** *were suggested by script editor Terrance Dicks when commenting on writer Robert Holmes's original scene breakdown for the story. These included: the circus boss and his band of thugs; the radio telescope; the idea of Jo being hypnotized by the Master while checking out the plastics factory; the activation of the killer daffodils by a radio signal, rather than by rainfall as Holmes had intended; and the appearance of a Nestene energy creature at the climax of the final episode. Dicks later amended Holmes's draft scripts to include some additional introductory material for Jo and to remove all but one of the troll dolls which were originally to have played as large a part in the Master's plans as the killer daffodils. In addition, he substituted a sequence involving an air strike for one depicting an artillery attack as some hoped-for co-operation from the Army had failed to materialize and the production team wanted to keep the use of stock footage to a minimum. Head of Serials Ronnie Marsh later requested that the story's final line of dialogue be changed – the Doctor was originally to have said that his battle with the Master would continue: 'Until I destroy him. Or until he destroys me.' Marsh objected to this as he considered it too stark and explicit.*

It appears the Master is ▶ defeated as the Autons lie deactivated around him. *Terror of the Autons.*

Jo visits Devil's End. *The Dæmons.*

with a greater focus on characterization.

One element of season seven with which Letts and Dicks had been particularly dissatisfied was the character of Liz Shaw. They felt that the independent, self-confident scientist had little need to rely on the Doctor for explanations and so failed to fulfil the basic dramatic functions of aiding plot exposition and acting as a point of audience identification. Their decision to drop a companion between seasons was the first time that a companion had left the series without a specially written farewell scene. Caroline John was upset at this decision, but, as she was pregnant at the time — a fact that was unknown to Letts or Dicks — realized that her time on the show would have been limited anyway.

'Barry clearly wanted to take things in his own direction,' recalls the actress. 'On top of this, I had never established the best kind of rapport with Jon Pertwee, who I think basically saw the show in a very traditional light and didn't want a companion who in any way matched up to him in terms of intelligence. Coupled with this, I had married and decided that I wanted to start a family, so that was obviously a priority in personal terms. That was that; I left after we finished *Inferno* and I never got to say a proper goodbye to the Doctor or the Brigadier!'

To replace Liz, the production team came up with a character called Josephine Grant — or Jo for short. An impetuous young woman, assigned to UNIT as a result of some string-pulling by an influential relative, Jo would frequently run into danger and require rescuing by the Doctor, who could take her under his wing in a way that would have seemed condescending with her predecessor. Jo also provided the writers with an easy-to-use cipher for any plot information that they needed to convey to viewers. The original outline for her character was as follows:

The Doctor destroys a bomb planted by the Master while Mike Yates (Richard Franklin) and Jo Grant look on. *Terror of the Autons.*

Glamorous young female intelligence agent newly attached to UNIT. Keen, professional, lots of charm. Works with the Doctor. Needs to be involved in the story in an active way, not just as a screaming heroine or passing the Doctor's test tubes. Not a scientist, though with enough basic background to know what's going on.

A large number of highly attractive actresses were auditioned for the role, including Anouska Hemple and Shakira Baksh, and Letts and Dicks eventually chose the bubbly, somewhat scatter-brained and very short-sighted Katy Manning, whom they had almost missed seeing altogether as she had got lost and gone to the wrong room.

The production team also decided at this point to enlarge the UNIT team by giving the Brigadier a new second-in-command more suited to his status than the relatively lowly Sergeant Benton. This was Captain Yates, who was also envisaged as a possible love interest for Jo — although, in the event, little came of this in the transmitted stories. His original character outline was as follows:

The Brigadier's no. 2. A tough cheerful young soldier, very competent but a shade too easy-going and casual for the Brigadier's liking. Makes fun of Jo, in an affectionate way.

Two main candidates for this role emerged at audition. The first, Ian Marter, had to withdraw when he realized that Yates was to be a regular, explaining that he was already committed to other work. The second, Richard Franklin, was then offered the part, and readily accepted.

Another, even more significant innovation for season eight was the introduction of a new villain, the Master, who was ultimately to prove almost as popular as the Doctor himself. A renegade Time Lord dedicated to evil, the Master was created by Barry Letts and Terrance Dicks as an arch-enemy or Moriarty figure for the Doctor, who they felt bore a number of similarities to Sherlock Holmes. He was described in the following character outline:

A lapsed Time Lord of equal, perhaps even senior, rank to the Doctor. Now on the run from the Time Lords.

Sinister, polished, charming. A manipulator of others for evil ends, with a vested interest in chaos and misrule, which he turns to his own profit.

He will co-operate with any evil force but will readily double-cross his evil allies if things get sticky. Completely selfish and ruthless.

Tends to use a variety of roles and aliases, often based on his title. Masters, Masterson, Le Maître, Il Maestro. Always chooses a distinguished and affluent role for himself. Uses a naturally dominant personality amounting almost to hypnosis, to bring others under his sway. (But they can sometimes break loose.)

LOCATIONS

Terror of the Autons
  Black Park Cottage, Fulmer, Bucks;
  Hodgmore Wood, Bucks;
  Robert Brothers Circus, Edmonton

The Mind of Evil
  Dover Castle, Kent

The Claws of Axos
  Dungeness Power Station, Kent;
  Dungeness Beach, Kent

Colony in Space
  'The Old Baal Pit' China Clay Quarry, Plymouth, Devon

The Dæmons
  Aldbourne, Wiltshire

Am I mistaken or do I detect a note of tiredness in BBC1's 'Dr. Who' saga?

My suspicions were alerted early in the present adventure when one of the mysterious Lords of Time suddenly materialized wearing a bowler and carrying an umbrella!

And this in a Saturday serial which has always taken itself seriously and shown a pride in its inventiveness.

Those faceless plastic dummies may have had a nightmare quality when they first appeared, but creating monsters is like telling jokes – old ones (unless they are in the Dracula class) really won't do.

Matthew Coady writing in the Daily Mirror

Stuntman Terry Walsh ▲ has make-up applied during location filming of scenes as an Auton policeman. *Terror of the Autons.*

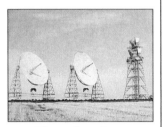

The radio telescope ▲ at the Ministry of Technology, Beacon Hill research establishment. *Terror of the Autons.*

STOCK FOOTAGE

*In part four of **Terror of the Autons**, shots of a fighter plane came from the RAF.*

*To achieve the effect of flames seen by the Doctor as he is attacked by the Keller Machine in part one of **The Mind of Evil**, footage was obtained from the Movietone Library.*

*A brief shot of a toad in the church graveyard in the opening moments of **The Dæmons** came from BBC stock; in part three, a shot of a fighter plane came from the RAF; and, also in part three, a shot of a helicopter exploding came from Movietone.*

The Doctor holds the mask with which the Master deceived UNIT and made good his escape at the conclusion of *Terror of the Autons*.

A long-standing and implacable enemy of the Doctor, he is the force of evil bound to oppose the Doctor's force of good.

Important note:

The Master has a chameleon-like ability to adapt to any society in which he finds himself. He will therefore be completely natural and convincing in his various human roles. He must not be written as a moustache twirling villain of melodrama, or given melodramatic dialogue; if anything his evil quality should be underplayed, though never forgotten.

In this instance, only one actor was ever considered for the role.

'I'd worked with Roger Delgado quite a lot when I was an actor myself,' explains Letts, 'having first met him in the York Repertory Company. When Terrance and I decided that the Doctor needed a "Moriarty", I at once said, "And I know exactly the actor to play him." The part was almost devised with Roger in mind.

'He was always precisely right, always finding that nice balance between smoothness and villainy, which was the hallmark of the Master.'

So pleased were the production team with their conception of the Master that they decided to have him included in every story of season eight. Where writers had already started work on ideas or scripts, they were briefed to amend them in order to incorporate the new character. One planned six-parter entitled *The Cerebroids*, the storyline for which had been commissioned from writer Brian Wright on 24 June 1970, ultimately proved unsuitable — for reasons unknown — and was written off.

The opening story of the season was a Robert

Holmes four-parter entitled *Terror of the Autons*, the first episode of which was transmitted on 2 January 1971 and saw the series being featured for the second year in succession on the front cover of *Radio Times*.

Shortly after arriving on Earth in his TARDIS, which materializes disguised as a horsebox at a circus, the Master steals from a museum the last Nestene energy unit surviving intact from their attempted invasion in season seven's *Spearhead from Space*. Investigating, the Doctor is tipped off about the Master's involvement by a Time Lord emissary.

The Master meanwhile uses his hypnotic abilities to take control of a small plastics firm, where he organizes the production of deadly Auton dolls, chairs and daffodils. Humanoid Auton dummies distribute the daffodils — designed to spray a suffocating plastic film over the victim's mouth and nose — by giving them away to members of the public in a fake promotional campaign. The Master plans to activate the flowers with a signal from a radio telescope, which he will then use to bring the main Nestene Consciousness to Earth.

The Doctor manages to persuade the Master that the Nestenes will have no further use for him once they arrive. The two Time Lords then work together to send the Consciousness back into space. Once the danger is past, the Master escapes to fight another day.

The plot of *Terror of the Autons* — the storyline and scripts for which were commissioned on 28 April and 2 June 1970 respectively under the working title *The Spray of Death* — bore a number of similarities to that of the first Auton story, *Spearhead from Space*. Both featured plastics factories with financial problems, and the Master's involvement in the former mirrored Channing's in the latter. In terms of production style, however, the two were quite different. Whereas *Spearhead from Space* had a cold, realistic, almost documentary feel — an effect somewhat heightened by the fact that it was shot entirely on film — *Terror of the Autons* had a larger-than-life quality and brought a newfound family atmosphere to the UNIT set-up, reflecting the changes instituted by Barry Letts. Even so, the story attracted criticism from some quarters over its use of everyday objects as deadly weapons and its depiction of two policemen as masked Auton killers. As a result of this, the production team decided that in future the series' horror content should be strictly limited to a fantasy context and not linked with things likely to be found in the viewer's own home.

The season's second story, Don Houghton's *The

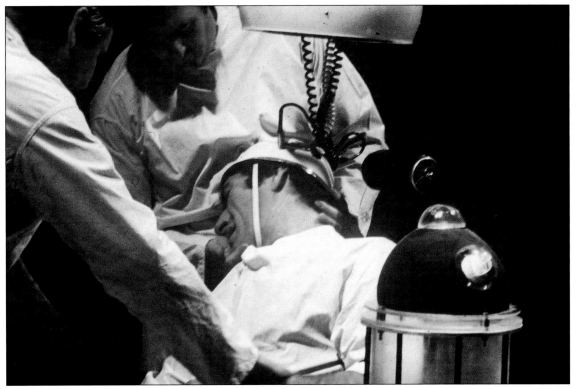

Barnham (Neil McCarthy) undergoes the Keller process. The Keller Machine stands on the right. *The Mind of Evil.*

▲ Jo ministers to the unconscious Doctor in the cell where they are being held hostage in Stangmoor Prison. *The Mind of Evil.*

▲ The banned Thunderbolt missile hijacked by the Master and the Stangmoor prisoners. *The Mind of Evil.*

Mind of Evil, sees the Doctor and Jo visiting Stangmoor Prison to witness a demonstration of the Keller Machine — a device claimed to be capable of extracting the negative emotions from hardened criminals. The Doctor's scepticism seems to be borne out when a prisoner called Barnham collapses whilst undergoing the treatment. The Brigadier, meanwhile, is in charge of security at a World Peace Conference, where tension mounts as documents go missing and the Chinese delegate dies in mysterious circumstances. To complicate matters further, Captain Yates is away on another mission, transporting a banned Thunderbolt missile across country to be destroyed.

The Doctor joins the Brigadier at the conference and together they foil an attempt by the Chinese delegate's aide, Captain Chin Lee, to kill the American delegate. It transpires that Lee is under the hypnotic control of the Master — otherwise known as Professor Emil Keller.

The Master uses the evil impulses stored within the Keller Machine — in truth the container for an alien mind parasite — to cause a riot at Stangmoor. He then enlists the convicts' aid to hijack the Thunderbolt missile. His plan is to use the weapon to blow up the peace conference and thereby start World War Three. Shielded by Barnham, who is now immune to the effects of the parasite, the Doctor transports the Keller Machine to the nearby airfield where the missile is being held. Using it to keep the Master occupied, he reconnects the mis-

sile's auto-destruct circuit and gets clear just before the Brigadier triggers it. The parasite is presumed destroyed in the resulting explosion, but the Master manages to escape in a van, running Barnham down in the process.

The Mind of Evil (working titles: *The Pandora Machine, Man Hours* and *The Pandora Box*) was commissioned on 3 July 1970 on the strength of a story treatment commissioned on 29 June 1970. Don Houghton created the part of Captain Chin Lee especially for his actress wife Pik-Sen Lim, who had thought up a number of the plot ideas, and this casting suggestion was gratefully accepted by director Timothy Coombe when put to him by Barry Letts. Letts had chosen Coombe for this story because of the quality of his work on *Doctor Who*

▲ The Axons in humanoid form (Patricia Gordino and Bernard Holley). *The Claws of Axos.*

◄ Mailer (William Marlowe) (out of shot on left) and his fellow prisoners hold the Doctor and Jo at gunpoint in the Governor's office at Stangmoor Prison. *The Mind of Evil.*

A behind the scenes ▶ shot of the filming of the Chinese dragon conjured up telepathically by Captain Chin Lee to attack Senator Alcott, the American delegate at the peace conference. Producer Barry Letts and director Tim Coombe were disappointed with the final result, terming it 'Puff the Magic Dragon', and consequently used only brief shots of it. *The Mind of Evil*

ROGER DELGADO
THE MASTER

Roger Caesar Marius Bernard de Delgado Torres Castillo Roberto was born on 1 March 1918 in London. After leaving school he started working in a bank but resigned after 18 months and joined the Nelson Repertory Company in Leicester in 1938. When he was called up for National Service, Delgado was turned down by the British Army and Airforce because of his French mother and Spanish father, but he eventually joined the Royal Leicester Regiment and served in Europe, Burma and India. Following the end of the war, Delgado joined the York repertory company and in 1950 he started work with the BBC Drama Repertory. He worked in radio for the next 20 years and also enjoyed much success in the theatre, with productions like Man About the House, Guinea Pig *and* The Diplomatic Baggage. *On the big screen, Delgado appeared first in* The Captain's Glory, *and other roles followed, including* The Power and the Glory, The Battle of the River Plate *(aka* Pursuit of the Graf Spee *1957),* Terror of the Tongs *(1961),* First Man into Space *(1959) and* The Mummy's Shroud *(1967). On television he appeared in* Quatermass II, Danger Man, The Saint, The Power Game, Crossfire *and* Randall and Hopkirk (Deceased) *amongst others, as well as playing the villain Mendoza in the 1961 series* Sir Francis Drake. *It was while working on the subsequently cancelled film* Bell of Tibet *in 1973 that Delgado was killed when a chauffeur-driven car ran off the road outside Neveshir in central Turkey on 18 June. His last TV work was for an episode of* The Zoo Gang.

An Axon in its non-humanoid form. *The Claws of Axos.*

and the Silurians and also his ability to handle action-based crowd scenes like those of the prison riot. To add to the authenticity of the scenes involving the Thunderbolt missile, Letts arranged to borrow a genuine ground-to-air guided missile from the Royal Air Force, who proved most amenable — particularly after he let slip how much help the series had received from the Army in making the season-six story *The Invasion*.

Due mainly to the high cost of mounting a battle scene between UNIT troops and escaped convicts on location at Dover Castle, *The Mind of Evil* went well over budget. Further filming costs were incurred in reshooting some sequences for which the original negative had been damaged and in scheduling an extra day's work to remedy a shortage of close-ups in the battle scene footage. In the latter case, the expense was kept to a minimum by having members of the production crew, including Coombe himself, appearing in place of actors.

The season's third story, *The Claws of Axos*, came about as a result of a curious twist of fate. Writers Bob Baker and Dave Martin had sent in to the BBC a comedy script about life in the Army but, by some quirk of the internal mail system, this had ended up on Terrance Dicks's desk.

'I read it with some bafflement,' recalls Dicks, 'as it had nothing whatsoever do with *Doctor Who*! It was however very funny and well written, so I got in touch with Bob and Dave — known collectively as

the Bristol Boys, because that was where they lived — and after some discussion they wrote us a storyline.'

This storyline, commissioned towards the end of 1969 under the title *The Gift*, proved to be unworkable in its original form.

'What came back,' explains Barry Letts, 'was something at least twice as thick as a complete script — and with very full pages! We started reading it, and it had some lovely ideas. It began with a spaceship, shaped like a skull, landing in Hyde Park. Now, this caused us some concern, as there was no way we could ever have achieved it on screen. Then, as we continued reading, we found that there was one good idea after another, but none of them seemed to tie together. There was an enormous quantity of very good ideas, but the story had no structure to it — and it would have filled about 26 episodes!'

'We started with the idea of a brain,' recalls Bob Baker, 'the brain being able to project itself into the various forms that it wanted to make. Therefore there were ganglia and nerve endings which could produce the shape of a human being and fool the Earthmen into thinking that that was what they were actually like. There was also — as was the case with all our stories — a kind of other level, which was that of trade or capitalism, and the idea of Axonite as a substance capable of beguiling the Earthmen into thinking, "Ah, here's the chance for a great trade," and that by allowing the aliens in they could make some money out of them.'

A heavily revised storyline entitled *The Friendly Invasion* was commissioned in April 1970, and scripts for the four-part story were eventually commissioned on 11 September (episode one), 18 October (episode two) and 29 October 1970 (episodes three and four). The working title for the first episode was *The Axons*, but after this had been delivered the production team asked the writers to rename the story *The Vampire from Space*, Terrance Dicks noting in a letter of comment dated 9 October 1970 that this had the 'right melodramatic *Doctor Who* ring'. The final change of title to *The Claws of Axos* was made at a very late stage, Barry Letts having decided that the 'vampire' reference had unduly horrific connotations, and the story's title sequence had to be hastily re-recorded as a result.

The Claws of Axos opens with an alien spaceship approaching Earth and being detected on monitoring equipment at UNIT HQ, where the Brigadier is entertaining two visitors — Chinn, a pompous civil servant making a security inspection, and Bill Filer, an American agent sent to discuss the threat of the Master. Despite an attempt by Chinn to have it destroyed with missiles, the ship lands on Earth close to the Nuton power station in England. Filer, ignoring Chinn's warning not to get involved, goes to investigate. A tendril emerges from the ship and drags him inside, where he is held captive.

When the UNIT team arrive on the scene they are joined by Hardiman and Winser, two scientists from the Nuton complex, and pick up a radio message in which the ship's occupants plead for help. The Doctor, Hardiman, Winser, Chinn and the Brigadier all enter the ship and are met by a group of gold-skinned humanoids calling themselves Axons. The Axons claim that their ship, Axos, is damaged and that they need time in which to repair it. In return, they offer Axonite, a substance which can cause animals to grow to enormous sizes and thus end food shortages. The Doctor is suspicious, but Chinn eagerly obtains a sample for analysis.

The Doctor subsequently discovers that Axos, the Axons and Axonite are all part of a single parasitic entity brought to Earth by the Master so that it can feed on the planet's energy. The Axons send a duplicate of Filer to kidnap the Doctor, but the real Filer escapes and raises the alarm. The Axons then attack in another form — blobby, many-tentacled monsters — and take the Doctor and Jo prisoner. Axos, by threatening Jo, persuades the Doctor to reveal the secret of time travel. It intends to obtain the necessary power from the Nuton reactor, but the Master, having been captured by UNIT, is forced to help thwart this attempt.

The Doctor and Jo escape from Axos and return to Nuton. As the Axons attack in force, the Doctor pilots his TARDIS, with the Master on board, into the centre of Axos. He offers to link the two ships together to make one giant time machine, on condition that Axos in return helps

BOB BAKER
WRITER

Bob Baker was born in Bristol, the son of a signwriter, and made cartoon and live action films in his youth before going to art college to study painting and animation. When he left college he did some cartoon work for the BBC. He also renovated old houses, edited a pop magazine, did design work for other publications and was also a semi-professional musician, playing saxophone in a jazz-rock group. In 1967 he met up with Dave Martin, and in 1969 the two decided to start writing together. They completed about ten plays before one was finally accepted by HTV called **Whistle For It.** *Following this they collaborated for many years on series like* **SkiBoy** *(1974),* **Sky** *(1975),* **King of the Castle** *(1977) and worked on numerous stories for* **Doctor Who** *starting with* **The Claws of Axos** *in 1971. Baker became script editor for the detective series* **Shoestring** *in 1979, which was set in his home town of Bristol, and has continued to work in television, including devising* **Into the Labyrinth** *in 1981 and writing an episode for* **Smuggler** *(1981), and for the theatre. More recent work includes script editing* **Call Me Mister** *(1986) for the BBC and numerous scripts for European television.*

DAVE MARTIN
WRITER

David Martin was born in Hansworth, Birmingham and was heavily influenced by books at a young age. This interest led him to write and he has published several thrillers. To supplement his income he has worked at various times in hospitals, building pylons, houses, theatre and advertising, as well as numerous jobs in industry. His writing career didn't take off until he was over 30 and in 1969 he joined forces with Bob Baker. They contributed scripts to **Z Cars,** *one episode of* **Arthur of the Britons** *(1972), six episodes of* **Hunter's Walk** *(1974–1976) and* **Target** *(1978) as well as* **Doctor Who.** *One of their main contributions to the programme was the creation of K-9, the Doctor's robotic companion, suggested by Martin after his own dog was killed by a car. Martin later wrote four books aimed at very young children about the adventures of the mechanical hound. He has continued writing novels, as well as material for stage and television, including an episode for* **Into the Labyrinth** *in 1981.*

The Master, impersonating the Adjudicator, hears evidence from IMC's Captain Dent (Morris Perry) while his officer Morgan (Tony Caunter) looks on from the side table. *Colony in Space.*

Two Primitives ▲ in a colonist's dome. *Colony in Space.*

THIS IS YOUR LIFE

During the location filming for **Colony in Space**, *Jon Pertwee was 'surprised' by Eamon Andrews and his big red book for an episode in the popular ITV biography series* **This Is Your Life**. *Eventually transmitted on 14 April 1971, the half hour long programme covered Pertwee's career to date, featuring guest appearances from: Katy Manning, Ingeborg Pertwee (Jon's wife), Michael Pertwee (Jon's brother), Macdonald Hobley, Dr Michael Colbourne (Jon's step-brother), Bob Tilburn and Ted Briggs (survivors of the attack on* **HMS Hood**), *David Jacobs, Eric Barker, Bill Maynard, Dariel and Sean Pertwee (Jon's daughter and son), 'Elymir' (forger of 'Matisse' painting Pertwee nearly bought) and Ted Falcon-Barker (saved Pertwee's life in 1958).*

Jon Pertwee is surprised ▲ by a disguised Eamon Andrews for the *This Is Your Life* programme in 1971.

Jo enters the TARDIS for the first time. *Colony in Space.*

him to take revenge on the Time Lords for exiling him to Earth. This is merely a trick, however, and Axos is locked in a time loop from which it can never escape. The Doctor returns to Earth in the TARDIS, where he reluctantly admits to the Brigadier that the Master may also have escaped.

The director assigned to *The Claws of Axos* was Michael Ferguson, who recalls making extensive use of CSO and other video effects:

'Yes, I remember getting very greedy about effects around that time and coming up with all sorts of things that we could try. In a way, that arose out of the experiments Barry Letts and I had done with CSO, exploring its possibilities.

'I must have made myself very unpopular during editing when I discovered the video disc machine. This was a fairly crude device which could record pictures and play them back at different speeds. It was used mainly for action replays on sports programmes; the rest of the time it just sat there in the editing suite. Anyhow, I happened to find out that this machine was enormously sensitive — the engineers were always having to tweak it because the little pick-up heads which read the information from the concentric grooves on the disc would get out of sync and produce jagged,

distorted pictures. This seemed to me to be rather a nice effect, so every now and again I would go across to the machine and give it a little kick! I ran quite a lot of material through the system so that I could get these strange, jagged images. I used it on both *The Ambassadors of Death* and *The Claws of Axos*.

'The thing I remember most about *The Claws of Axos*, though, is the terrible weather we had on the four-day location shoot, which was done at Dungeness in January. The first day there was thick fog, so all the production value which had made me choose the location in the first place was completely obscured. The next day I think it snowed. The third day, as far as I can remember, there was brilliant sunshine. Then, on the last day, it rained! Fortunately, as this was *Doctor Who*, it didn't really matter — we simply blamed it on the visitors from outer space! I think you'll find there's a line in one of the early scenes where somebody says, "Doctor, they're reporting freak weather conditions in the area," or something to that effect. That's part of the joy of the programme: it's fantasy, and all things are possible.'

Malcolm Hulke's *Colony in Space* — the fourth story of the season, commissioned on 3 July 1970 under the working title *Colony*—saw *Doctor Who's* regular Saturday evening transmission time moved to 6.10 pm — an hour later than in the recent past. This change in timeslot was made in recognition of the increasingly large adult audience the series was winning; as a reaction to the criticisms levelled against the horror content of *Terror of the Autons*; and also to avoid clashing with the ITV science fiction series *U.F.O.*, which was now being shown in most ITV regions at 5.15 pm on Saturdays. Coinciding with the change, *Radio Times* ran a *Doctor Who* feature consisting of a three-page comic strip adaptation by Frank Bellamy of the opening scenes of *Colony in Space* and an article by Russell Miller drawing attention to the fact that, for the first time since Jon Pertwee took over as the Doctor, the TARDIS would be journeying to an alien world.

This journey is initiated by the Time Lords who, on discovering that the Master has stolen their secret file on the Doomsday Weapon, decide to send the Doctor to retrieve it for them. The Doctor and Jo — the latter seeing inside the TARDIS for the first time — arrive in the year 2472 on the desolate world of Uxarieus, where they meet a small group of colonists beset by crop failures and attacks from giant lizards. The Doctor investigates and discovers that a spaceship belonging to IMC — the Interplanetary Mining Corporation — has landed nearby. The ship's Captain Dent claims that IMC are the rightful occupants of the planet, which is to be

The Doctor is threatened by an IMC mining robot (John Scott Martin) fitted with false claws as Morgan (Tony Caunter) operates the control device. *Colony in Space.*

▲ **The Guardian (voiced by Norman Atkyns).** *Colony in Space.*

MUSIC

Dudley Simpson made extensive use of the BBC's Radiophonic Workshop to realize his season eight scores, working in close collaboration with Brian Hodgson, the man responsible for the series' special sound effects.

As well as the specially composed scores, several pieces of stock music were used during the season:

***Terror of the Autons** part two featured circus music from the record 'Spotlight Sequins No. 1' by Keith Papworth.*

***The Mind of Evil** part three featured material from a track called 'The Devil's Triangle' from King Crimson's LP 'In the Wake of Poseidon'. This is played on the radio in the car transporting the Master.*

***Colony in Space** part two was originally planned to feature thirteen seconds from a record called 'Tank' by Emerson, Lake and Palmer, but this idea was abandoned; part six does however feature 58 seconds of a track called 'Build up to...' by Vorhaus for the scenes of the destruction of the Doomsday Weapon.*

***The Dæmons** part two includes an excerpt from the fourth movement of the Orchestre Nationale Redefusion Française's 'Symphony Fantastique: March to the Scaffold', used for the TV coverage of the rugby highlights enjoyed by Benton and Yates.*

mined for valuable minerals needed on Earth. The colonists, however, dispute this.

It transpires that IMC have faked the lizard attacks with a robot in the hope of scaring the colonists away. Jo and a colonist named Winton sneak aboard their ship to try to find evidence against them, but are captured and held hostage. Winton subsequently escapes, while Jo is seized by the planet's native Primitives and taken into their underground city. The Doctor follows and discovers that the Primitives and their High Priests worship a large machine tended by a creature called the Guardian. Sensing that the Doctor is a good man, the Guardian frees both him and Jo.

An Adjudicator summoned from Earth to decide the fate of the planet turns out to be the Master. He forces the Doctor to take him to the underground city, where they learn that the machine worshipped by the Primitives is in fact the Doomsday Weapon, capable of destroying entire planets. Its radiation emissions have brought about the decline of the Guardian's race and are also responsible for the colonists' crop failures. The Doctor persuades the Guardian to destroy the Weapon rather than let it fall into the Master's hands. The two Time Lords get clear just in time as the machine explodes, and the Master then escapes in his TARDIS. The colonists, meanwhile,

attack the IMC men and force them to surrender. Their mission concluded, the Doctor and Jo return to Earth, arriving only a few seconds after they left.

Even though *Doctor Who* had now been moved to a later timeslot, BBC executives remained sensitive to potential criticisms about its suitability for family viewing. This led Ronnie Marsh to overrule one of director Michael Briant's casting decisions on *Colony in Space*. Briant had decided that

◄ **One of the alien High Priests.** *Colony in Space.*

NOTES

Auton Catering

By a curious coincidence, the location catering for **Terror of the Autons** *was handled by a company called Thermo Plastics Ltd!*

The Axons

The costumes for the Axon monsters were constructed by a freelance contractor, Jules Baker. Barry Letts was displeased with the result, however, and thereafter relied mainly on the BBC's own Visual Effects Department and Costume Department to meet requirements of this sort.

IMC Robot

The robot with which IMC terrorized the colonists in **Colony in Space** *was a prop built by a firm of freelance contractors, Magna Models, for £450. A further cost of £60.70 was incurred when the prop was damaged due to being left out overnight in the rain during location filming at St Austell, Cornwall.*

IMC Transport

The IMC buggies seen in **Colony in Space** *were lightweight Haflinger cross-country vehicles supplied by Steyr-Daimler-Pach (Great Britain) Ltd. They were returned in a damaged state following filming, costing the BBC an extra £74.40.*

The Cloven Hoof

The real name of the Cloven Hoof pub used by the Doctor and his friends as their base in **Devil's End** *was the Blue Boar. The Cloven Hoof sign which was hung outside during the filming of* **The Dæmons** *was later presented to the landlord and could be seen for many years afterwards on display in the bar. When the pub changed hands in the late eighties, however, the new landlord sold the sign (below) to a group of* **Doctor Who** *fans.*

Bok (Stanley Mason) and Azal (Stephen Thorne) in the cavern below the church. The Dæmons.

the story's principal villain, a particularly nasty and sadistic IMC officer named Morgan, would have more substance if played by a woman rather than a man. Consequently he had cast actress Susan Jameson in the role. Marsh, however, insisted that the character be changed back to a man, as Barry Letts explains:

'Ronnie Marsh was effectively the executive producer of *Doctor Who*, and he told me that we weren't to use a woman. He said, "I'm not going to have, at this time on a Saturday evening, a woman striding about with a whip and kinky boots on, being sadistic! No, no, no!" '

Marsh's decision did not go down well with Briant. 'I felt it was sexist, unenlightened, somewhat arrogant and really rather boring and stupid,' he states. 'I argued against it. I argued like mad, even from the financial point of view. The lady had already been cast and so had to be paid all the money she would have got for doing the job for six episodes!'

These arguments were to no avail, however, and the part of Morgan eventually went to actor Tony Caunter, who had been due to play another, more minor role in the story.

Colony in Space was followed by a five-parter entitled *The Dæmons*, which arose indirectly out of the introduction of Jo Grant. The production team had needed an audition piece when casting the

character, and for this purpose Barry Letts had written two short scenes, both featuring Captain Yates. The longer of the two involved Yates rescuing Jo from a church. 'After he's found her,' Letts recalls, 'he throws a book onto a strangely carved stone, and the book is immediately torn to shreds by a force he describes as being like an elemental piranha fish, waiting to tear her apart just as effectively. And at the very end Jo turns round and sees the Devil . . . It was quite an exciting little scene, in so far as Jo had to be terrified and brave and to do a jolly good scream at the end, which is what *Doctor Who* girls have to be good at doing.'

Letts had long been interested in tales of black magic, having been particularly thrilled as a boy by Dennis Wheatley's *The Devil Rides Out*, and was very pleased with the way this audition piece had worked. He subsequently commented to Terrance Dicks that it was a pity they could not have a black magic story in the series itself, to which Dicks replied, 'Why not?' Letts therefore decided to expand his short audition piece into a full story:

'I wanted to write *The Dæmons* as a proving vehicle for myself. As the producer (and a fairly new one at that), I'd been busy telling writers how I felt *Doctor Who* should be done, but for a long time I'd thought, "It's all very well telling other people how it should be done, maybe I ought to have a go myself. . ." '

Letts did not however want to write the story entirely on his own, so to help him he contacted a local friend by the name of Robert Sloman. Sloman had never written for television before but was an established playwright, with West End credits to his name. The two men found that they could work very well together, brainstorming ideas between them and then tying them down into a sound dramatic format, and they quickly came up with the basic plot of *The Dæmons*, the scripts for which were commissioned on 6 January 1971 under the working title *The Demons*. In order to circumvent possible Writers' Guild objections to a producer writing for his own show, they adopted the pseudonym Guy Leopold, made up from their respective middle names.

The story centres around the English village of Devil's End, where the local white witch, Miss Hawthorne, is protesting against a nearby archaeological dig which she believes will lead to disaster. In charge of the dig is Professor Horner, who maintains that the site, known as the Devil's Hump (amended from Devil's Dyke in the writers' original scripts), is nothing more sinister than the burial mound of a Bronze Age chieftain and that his plan to open it at midnight on 30 April — the ancient occult festival of Beltane — is merely a publicity stunt. Watching TV coverage of the event at UNIT HQ, the Doctor realizes that Miss Hawthorne is right and rushes off with Jo to try to put a stop to the dig.

Also present in Devil's End is the Master, posing as the new vicar, Mr Magister. As midnight approaches, he presides over a black magic ceremony in a cavern beneath the church and calls on a creature called Azal to arise. The Doctor and Jo reach the Devil's Hump just too late to prevent Horner from opening it. An ice-cold wind bursts forth, killing Horner and leaving the Doctor frozen solid. The Doctor is taken to the local pub, the Cloven Hoof, where Jo phones UNIT for help. Benton and Yates arrive in the UNIT helicopter but, before the Brigadier and his troops can join them, a heat barrier appears and cuts the village off from the outside world.

Recovering, the Doctor deduces that Azal is the last of an alien race known as the Dæmons, who have the ability to change their size by absorbing or releasing energy and have aided mankind's development throughout history. Azal will appear three times, and on the last occasion will decide whether to transfer his huge powers to another or to destroy the planet as a failed experiment. The Master hopes to be the recipient of Azal's powers, but instead they are offered to the Doctor. When the Doctor declines, arguing that the human race should be allowed to develop at its own pace, Azal decides to kill him. Jo then offers herself in the Doctor's place and, unable to comprehend this act of self-sacrifice, the Dæmon is destroyed as his attack rebounds on him. The Master is finally captured by UNIT and taken away to await trial for his crimes against humanity.

The *Quatermass* influence which had been such an important factor in the conception of the Doctor's exile to Earth can still be detected in *The Dæmons*, several aspects of which are reminiscent of *Quatermass and the Pit*. In that 1958/59 serial, an archaeological dig uncovers a long-buried alien spaceship, emanations from which have given the local area a reputation for hauntings and apparitions. Professor Quatermass later discovers that the ship contains creatures who have guided Mankind's development for their own ends and whose gargoyle-like features have entered into folklore as the images of goblins and demons. As the story reaches its climax, a TV news team is caught up in an eruption of psychic energy from the excavation site and the alien menace manifests itself as a huge creature towering over the area — a menace which is ultimately defeated only through an act of supreme self-sacrifice by one of Quatermass's associates. All these plot elements are closely mirrored in *The Dæmons*.

The Master (Roger Delgado). *The Dæmons.*

Another influence was the work of Erich von Daniken, a researcher who gained some notoriety in the seventies for claiming to have discovered archaeological evidence of alien visitations throughout Earth's history. Particularly suggestive

▲ **Katy Manning relaxes on location in Aldbourne for** *The Dæmons.*

▲ **Jon Pertwee and Stephen Thorne pose for a publicity shot during studio recording for** *The Dæmons.*

▲ **John Levene poses on location for** *The Dæmons.*

◀ **Bok (Stanley Mason).** *The Dæmons.*

The Master is captured ▲ by UNIT troops after an unsuccessful attempt to escape in Bessie at the end of *The Dæmons*.

ROBERT SLOMAN
WRITER

Robert Sloman was born in Oldham, the son of a famous rugby league player, and brought up in Plymouth. After service in the RAF, he graduated from university and became an actor. The experience taught him enough to construct plays and write dialogue and he eventually left acting to take up writing. He met his wife, Mary, in repertory and they have two children. At the time he was commissioned by Barry Letts to co-write **The Dæmons** *for* **Doctor Who**, *Sloman was an established playwright who had enjoyed success in London's West End with shows like* **The Tinker** *starring Edward Judd, and he had also written productions for the provinces and Europe, as well as scripts for radio, film and television. He worked for the* **Sunday Times** *during the day. Sloman contributed four scripts for* **Doctor Who**, *all co-written with Barry Letts:* **The Dæmons, The Time Monster, The Green Death** *and* **Planet of the Spiders**. *He still writes occasionally but spends much of his time switching between Devon and Spain, and pursuing hobbies which include flying, gliding, sailing and watching television.*

A behind the scenes shot of the filming of a UNIT Land Rover breaking through the heat barrier surrounding Devil's End. The Dæmons.

of this source is the revelation that the Devil's Hump, which appears to be the burial mound of a Bronze Age chieftain, is in fact the resting place of Azal's spaceship. As Robert Sloman concedes, 'I suppose von Daniken's *Chariots of the Gods*, which proved that there were spacemen on Earth before we arrived, may well have had something to do with *The Dæmons*.'

The initial filming for *The Dæmons* took place over the period 19—30 April 1971 in the picturesque village of Aldbourne in Wiltshire, seven miles north west of Hungerford. Location work at this point in the series' history usually followed the standard technique of shooting with a single film camera, each scene being repeated several times from a variety of different angles so that a selection of the resulting footage could later be edited together for use in the finished programme. On *The Dæmons*, however, there was so much film work to be done that, as an experiment, three film cameras were taken to the location and used in a multi-camera set-up, similar to the way electronic cameras were used in a TV studio, thus cutting down considerably the number of takes which had to be done and saving a great deal of time. The cameras were 'crystal locked' together so that all three could be started and stopped simultaneously by remote control.

Even using this technique, it still proved very difficult to complete all the filming in time, owing to extreme weather conditions. Mid-way through the shoot, a freak snow fall caused the loss of a morning's work, and the snow had to be washed away to allow filming to proceed in the afternoon.

The Dæmons brought to an end a season which had seen the series' ratings rise from 7.3 million viewers at the start of *Terror of the Autons* to 8.3 million by the final episode of *The Dæmons*, hitting an impressive high of 9.5 million for episode three of *Colony in Space*. The regular cast of Pertwee, Manning, Delgado, Courtney, Levene and Franklin had soon formed a very effective team, and their *esprit de corps* was evident in the transmitted episodes.

This season had in many respects laid down a template for the remainder of Jon Pertwee's time as the Doctor. Under the guidance of Barry Letts and Terrance Dicks, *Doctor Who* had discarded the gritty realism of the previous year and been steered back more towards a family audience. While UNIT continued to represent an important element of the format, characterization and humour had been given precedence over military hardware and action set-pieces; and while in season seven the Doctor's relationship with the Brigadier had been one of uneasy mutual convenience, during season eight it had become one of obvious friendship. The Doctor himself had also mellowed, losing the harder edges of his rather arrogant season-seven persona and becoming a debonair and reassuring uncle figure, albeit still a man of action. All these developments would be maintained in later seasons as, following the successful experiment of *Colony in Space*, the emphasis started to shift slowly back towards stories set in outer space.

CHAPTER SIX

Season Nine: Old Friends, Old Enemies

Season nine saw *Doctor Who* enjoying a period of stability. It had the same main cast and production team as season eight and was made in much the same style, continuing the mixture of stories set on near-contemporary Earth, where the Doctor operated as UNIT's scientific adviser, and occasional forays to other worlds, where he acted as an agent of the Time Lords. There were however a number of differences between this season and its immediate predecessor. Perhaps most noticeable was the fact that the Master appeared in only two of the five stories.

'Looking back,' says Barry Letts, 'I must admit that we overdid the Master in his first year. He was the main villain in every single story, and after a while the audience twigged this and started looking for him. So in later seasons we restricted him to one or two appearances.'

This decision was well received by Jon Pertwee, who was reportedly displeased that the Master was coming almost to equal the Doctor in terms of his popularity with the viewing audience.

The less frequent use of the Master also left the way clear for stories devoted to other adversaries; and, for the first time since Pertwee's arrival as the Doctor, a decision was taken to bring back some of the traditional monsters for which *Doctor Who* had become famous during the sixties. The first episode of the new season, recorded with the second over 4 and 5 October 1971 and transmitted on 1 January 1972, was publicized with a Frank Bellamy-painted *Radio Times* front cover, the headline of which really said it all: 'The Daleks are back!'

The production team, conscious that viewers were clamouring in ever increasing numbers for the return of the Daleks, had been considering this move for some time. In early 1971 they had approached Terry Nation to see if he would be willing to write a new story for his creations. Nation had some four years earlier withdrawn his permission for their use in *Doctor Who* as he was attempting to launch them in their own series.

SEASON NINE

CODE	TITLE
KKK	DAY OF THE DALEKS
MMM	THE CURSE OF PELADON
LLL	THE SEA DEVILS
NNN	THE MUTANTS
OOO	THE TIME MONSTER

RATINGS

Figures in millions

Story code

◀ **The third Doctor encounters his old adversaries, the Daleks.** *Day of the Daleks.*

The crew on location for ▲ *Day of the Daleks*, filming the scene where the Daleks and their force of Ogrons emerge into the 20th-century time zone from a disused railway tunnel.

The Controller (Aubrey Woods), a collaborator with the Daleks, attempts to justify his actions to a captive Jo and the Doctor. *Day of the Daleks*.

That attempt had long since come to nothing, however, so he was now happy for them to return to their original home. Although too busy to write a story himself, being fully occupied on the ITC film series *The Persuaders*, he indicated that he would have no objection to the Daleks being included in another writer's story for the 1972 season. This was confirmed in a letter which his representatives, ALS Management, sent to Terrance Dicks on 22 April 1971.

After briefly considering a Robert Sloman submission entitled *The Daleks in London*, Letts and Dicks abandoned the idea of commissioning a completely new story and decided instead to have the Daleks incorporated into an existing set of scripts written by Louis Marks, who had previously contributed *Planet of Giants* to season two.

Marks's story — the scene breakdown for which had been commissioned on 22 January 1971 on the basis of a second draft storyline accepted on 27 October 1970 — was originally called *The Ghost Hunters* and then retitled *Years of Doom* at the scripting stage. It told of a group of guerillas from a nightmarish future Earth travelling back in time to the 20th century in a bid to prevent the nuclear war which led to their situation, only to discover that by interfering in the course of history they themselves had actually *caused* the war. Although intrigued by this time paradox idea, Letts and Dicks felt that an extra element was needed, particularly if the story was to be used to launch the new season, and that the Daleks would provide this element. Marks was therefore asked to revise his scripts accordingly, and was paid an additional fee for doing so.

Under terms agreed on 15 June 1971, Nation would receive £25 per episode for the use of the Daleks in Marks's story and would also be credited as their originator in the closing titles. Dicks sent him copies of the scripts on 13 July 1971, and he replied a week later to confirm that he was content

with them. Describing the story as 'a very good and exciting batch of episodes', he went on to write:

I have a few suggestions for what (I think) will improve some of the Daleks' dialogue and I'll let you have my notes quite soon. But you're the script editor and you can decide whether you think they're improvements or not.

Look forward to talking to you about the second coming of the Daleks before very long.

The transmitted story — retitled *Day of the Daleks* at the production team's request — opens with Sir Reginald Styles, organizer of a World Peace Conference, narrowly surviving an assassination attempt by a combat-uniformed guerilla who suddenly vanishes like a ghost. UNIT troops discover another of the guerillas lying unconscious in the grounds of Styles's house. Unknown to them, he has been set upon by huge, ape-like creatures called Ogrons. The Doctor deduces that the guerilla comes from about 200 years in the future and that a device found with him is a time machine — a deduction confirmed when he operates the device and the man fades back to his own time, much to the amazement of those in the ambulance taking him to hospital.

While Styles is away, the Doctor and Jo keep watch at his house. The guerillas attack again, but the Time Lord is able to convince them that he is not the man they want. One of their party, Shura, is later injured in an encounter with an Ogron. Jo, meanwhile, accidentally activates one of the guerillas' time machines and is transported into the 22nd century. When the guerillas return there, the Doctor goes with them. To his horror, he learns that the Earth of this period is a slave world ruled by the Daleks with the help of Ogron guards and human collaborators.

Jo and the Doctor are both taken prisoner at the Dalek base, but the guerillas rescue them and try to enlist the Doctor's help. They explain that they are attempting to kill Styles because in the 20th century he caused an explosion at the World Peace Conference, starting a series of wars which left humanity vulnerable to Dalek conquest — a history that they wish to change. Sceptical of this theory, the Doctor realizes that the explosion was actually caused by Shura in a misguided attempt to fulfil his mission. Hurrying back to the 20th century with Jo, he has Styles's house evacuated just in time. Daleks and Ogrons arrive in pursuit, but are destroyed when Shura detonates his bomb.

Louis Marks was not the only sixties *Doctor Who* writer with a story under consideration at around the time season nine was in its early planning stages.

Anat (Anna Barry) and her force of guerrillas escort Jo and the Doctor across the barren terrain of 22nd-century Earth. *Day of the Daleks.*

▲ The Doctor and Jo are recaptured by the Ogrons after a desperate attempt to escape on a trike. *Day of the Daleks.*

Bill Strutton — writer of season two's *The Web Planet* — had a storyline entitled *The Mega* commissioned on 19 October 1970 and Ian Stuart Black — who had scripted *The Savages* and *The War Machines* for season three and *The Macra Terror* for season four — had one entitled *The Space War* commissioned on 28 October 1970. Strutton's story progressed a little further than Black's, a full script for the first of its four episodes being commissioned on 28 October 1970, but in the end neither proved suitable. More fortunate was Brian Hayles — previously responsible for season three's *The Celestial Toymaker*, season four's *The Smugglers*, season five's *The Ice Warriors* and season six's *The Seeds of Death* — who was commissioned on 14 May 1971 to write a full set of scripts for a four-part story, reportedly under the working title *The Curse*. This was based on an untitled outline that Hayles had agreed in discussion with the production team after they had turned down two of his own ideas, entitled *The Brain-Dead* and *The Shape of Terror*.

The Curse of Peladon, as it was eventually renamed, was transmitted as the second story of season nine, although it had originally been intended as the third. This late change in running order was designed to achieve a better balance between Earth-based and alien settings and constituted the first instance in the series' history of complete stories being shown in a different order from that in which they were made.

Like *Day of the Daleks*, *The Curse of Peladon* featured the reappearance of one of the Doctor's popular adversaries — in this case, the Ice Warriors. As Brian Hayles noted, this renewed focus on established monsters was a conscious policy on the part of the production team:

'They weren't my original intention. My original intention was to give a new kind of villain that role. But the BBC felt that they were a popular monster and they asked me to bring them back.

'I liked the Ice Warriors, but I don't think I would have wanted to have brought them into every adventure I wrote.

'I wanted to develop them because I felt that, as had been done with the Cybermen, I could dip into their lifestyle every couple of thousand years or so, and it would be nice to see how they had developed. At the same time they could continue only if they were popular.'

On this occasion, Hayles introduced a novel twist by portraying the Ice Warriors as reformed characters:

'Here was a question that, having done them twice as the dirty villains, I wanted to play a trick; to turn the thing upside down. Very often when you find monsters like the Ice Warriors or the Daleks or the Cybermen, you know that they're going to be villainous. We started off the serial and as soon as they appeared everybody would

DALEK COMPETITION

*The **Radio Times** for 1–7 January 1972 not only featured **Doctor Who** on its front cover but also included a competition to win one of two 'Mark 7 Daleks' – battery-operated models with a control panel mounted on a rod at the back. The aim of the competition was to write in no more than 400 words the conclusion to a new Dalek story for which the opening by Terry Nation was printed in the magazine. Each entrant was also required to provide a minimum of three drawings or paintings to illustrate aspects of the story, which was set on the nightmarish planet Destron and involved a battle between Daleks and humans to capture a fantastic arsenal of weapons created by a now-extinct indigenous species.*

Filming the Sea Devils ▲ on location at Portsmouth. *The Sea Devils*.

Ian Scoones' design ▲ sketch for the Federation ambassador Arcturus. *The Curse of Peladon*.

Colonel Trenchard ▲ (Hugh Morton) and the Master use a signalling device to summon the Sea Devils. *The Sea Devils*.

Jo, masquerading as a princess from Earth, meets Alpha Centauri (Stuart Fell) and Izlyr, the Ice Lord (Alan Bennion). *The Curse of Peladon*.

say "Aha, they're into something dirty." But then we turned them around and they became, in a sense, the co-heroes of the plot, with a certain nobility of purpose. If you followed their psychology, though, they were still basically the same people. It simply happened that, for once, their motivation was similar to the Doctor's — although even he suspected them during the evolvement of the plot. He accepted their help very reluctantly, because he knew they would turn nasty at the drop of a scale or something.'

The Curse of Peladon sees the Doctor and Jo making a test flight in the TARDIS and unexpectedly arriving on the storm-swept planet Peladon. Seeking shelter, they find themselves in the citadel of King Peladon, where the Doctor is mistaken for a human dignitary summoned to act as Chairman of a Committee of Assessment considering the planet's application to join the Galactic Federation. The other Committee members — Alpha Centauri, Arcturus and, from Mars, the Ice Lord

Izlyr and his Warrior subordinate Ssorg — have already arrived, but their deliberations have been interrupted by the mysterious death of one of the King's closest advisors, Chancellor Torbis.

High Priest Hepesh, who opposes the planet's union with the Federation, attributes Torbis's death to the ancient Curse of Aggedor, the sacred beast of Peladon. When further incidents occur, the Doctor concludes that a saboteur is at work. At first he suspects the Ice Warriors, but the guilty parties are eventually revealed to be Hepesh and Arcturus, who have allied themselves in an attempt to prevent Peladon from joining the Federation. Arcturus has managed to convince Hepesh that the Federation would only exploit the planet for its mineral riches, whereas this is in fact his own race's intention.

Arcturus is destroyed with a blast from Ssorg's sonic gun, but Hepesh escapes into the secret network of tunnels beneath the citadel, where he foments rebellion amongst the guards. The rebels storm the citadel and take the King prisoner. Hepesh then orders Aggedor — a real beast he has been using for his own ends — to kill the Doctor. The Doctor, however, has tamed Aggedor, and it is Hepesh who dies, putting an end to the rebellion. The Doctor and Jo leave as the true delegate from Earth arrives.

The Curse of Peladon was the first Jon Pertwee story to feature no location-filmed material. This made it a relatively inexpensive production and also helped to enhance the claustrophobic 'ghost story' atmosphere of the script.

The script itself was one of an increasing number

King Peladon (David Troughton) tries to persuade Jo to intercede on his behalf with the Federation committee. *The Curse of Peladon*.

The Federation delegates Arcturus (operated by Murphy Grumbar, voiced by Terry Bale) and Izlyr (Alan Bennion). *The Curse of Peladon*.

to make an oblique allegorical comment on contemporary social issues, the debates concerning Peladon's accession to the Galactic Federation mirroring those concerning the United Kingdom's entry into the European Community. This was a trend promoted by both Barry Letts and Terrance Dicks, who were keen that the series should work on more than one level and be thought-provoking as well as entertaining.

Malcolm Hulke's six-parter *The Sea Devils*, made immediately before *The Curse of Peladon* but transmitted immediately after it, was the third story in succession to feature the return of some old adversaries — this time, adversaries who had made their debut earlier in the third Doctor's own era, rather than in the sixties.

The story begins with the Doctor and Jo visiting the Master, who — following his capture by UNIT at the end of season eight's *The Dæmons* — is now the sole occupant of a high-security prison situated on an island off the south coast of England. The prison Governor, Colonel Trenchard, mentions that ships have been mysteriously disappearing out at sea, and the Doctor decides to investigate. At a nearby naval base, he meets the commanding officer, Captain Hart, and discovers that the sinkings have centred around an abandoned sea fort. He and Jo then hire a boat and go out to the fort, where they are attacked by a humanoid reptile — termed a 'Sea Devil' by one of the men on the fort — which the Time Lord identifies as an amphibious breed of the prehistoric creatures that he encountered in a Derbyshire cave system shortly after his exile to Earth (as seen in season seven's *Doctor Who and the Silurians*).

It transpires that the Master, aided by a misguided Trenchard, is stealing electrical equipment from the naval base in order to build a machine that will revive the Sea Devils from hibernation and thus enable them to reclaim the planet they believe is rightfully theirs. After a reconnaissance submarine disappears, the Doctor takes a diving bell down to the Sea Devils' underwater base to try to encourage peace. His efforts are frustrated by a depth charge attack ordered by a pompous politician, Walker, but in the confusion he manages to free the captured submarine crew and escape with them back to the surface.

The Doctor tries to persuade Walker to allow him another attempt at negotiating peace, but in the meantime the Sea Devils capture the naval base. The Master has the Doctor taken back to the Sea Devils' control centre and forces him to help finish the machine which will revive the creatures' colonies all over the world. The Doctor sabotages the machine and the two Time Lords escape together just before the base is destroyed in a huge explosion. The Master then flees in a stolen hovercraft.

Commissioned on 29 March 1971 under the

▲ **Three frames taken from visual effects designer Ian Scoones's extensive storyboards for the model filming of *The Curse of Peladon*.**

BRIAN HAYLES
WRITER
*Born on 7 March 1930 in Portsmouth, Brian Hayles set out to be a sculptor and taught art in Canada. Returning to England, he continued to teach, while writing in his spare time. He eventually turned to writing full time. His work included shows as diverse as radio's **The Archers** and television's **United!**, **Legend of Death** (1965), **Public Eye** (1968), **Out of the Unknown** (1969–1971), **Doomwatch** (1970–1972) and **The Regiment**. His last TV work was **The Moon Stallion** in 1978 which he also novelized. His film work included the 1978 adventure movie **Warlords of Atlantis** which was followed by **Arabian Adventure** (1979). It was while working on the latter that he died on 30 October 1978.*

The Doctor in danger as he attempts to escape from the Sea Devils. *The Sea Devils.*

The Doctor and ▲
Sondergaard (John Hollis)
ponder the factors which
have led to the evolution
of *The Mutants*.

LOUIS MARKS
WRITER

*Having gained a philosophy
doctorate from Oxford University,
Louis Marks made the perhaps
surprising career move of becoming
a TV scriptwriter. He broke into the
business in 1959, and the following
year contributed three scripts to the
last season of Sapphire Films'* **The
Adventures of Robin Hood**. *This
led on to a longer stint as script
editor and writer on the Associated
Rediffusion crime drama* **No
Hiding Place**. *In 1970, he joined
the BBC as a script editor, and
amongst the many memorable
programmes he was responsible for
commissioning were Nigel Kneale's
cult classic* **The Stone Tape** *in
1972 and in the same year a series
of six supernatural dramas entitled*
Dead of Night, *all produced by
Innes Lloyd. More recently, Marks
has produced drama for the BBC,
his credits including* **The Lost
Boys, The Crucible, A Month in
the Country, Precious Bane** *and the BBC's classic serial for
1994,* **Middlemarch**.

POWER CUTS

*Many viewers found themselves
unable to watch episodes of* **The
Curse of Peladon** *and* **The Sea
Devils** *due to power cuts arising
from industrial action taken by the
National Union of Mineworkers
which left power stations short of
coal. The sporadic regional
blackouts lasted for 20 days, finally
ending on 2 March 1972.*

Ky (Garrick Hagon) and ▶
the Doctor in the caves on
Solos. *The Mutants.*

**The Doctor encounters the Mutants in the caves
on the surface of the planet Solos. *The Mutants.***

working title *The Sea Silurians, The Sea Devils* presented a marked contrast to the studio-bound *The
Curse of Peladon*. It was granted a ten-day location shoot around the Portsmouth area and included some memorable scenes on the No Man's
Land sea fort, built in 1860 as part of Prime Minister Lord Palmerston's plan to reinforce the coastal
defences against possible attack by the French.
The production also benefited from a great deal
of co-operation by the Royal Navy, who readily
agreed to Barry Letts's request for assistance.

'The big thing we got from the Navy,' recalls
director Michael Briant, 'was *HMS Reclaim*, the
diving vessel. It was based at Portsmouth at this
time, so there was no question of going anywhere
but Portsmouth to film. We then had to find all
our other locations within that vicinity.'

The Navy allowed Briant's team to film at the
HMS Fraser naval base near Southsea and, with
the agreement of visual effects designer Peter Day,

created all the explosions and smoke effects required on location. They also provided a large
amount of stock footage — including sequences of
submarines diving and surfacing and ships on
manoeuvres — and waived their normal royalty
payment for this as they considered that the publicity derived from the programme would be sufficient recompense.

The action-packed nature of the story gave rise
to plenty of work for Derek Ware's HAVOC stunt
team. Ware put his own expert swordsmanship to
use in arranging a protracted sword fight between
the Doctor and the Master, and no fewer than six
stuntmen were required to achieve the climactic
sequence of the Sea Devils storming the naval
base. This, however, was the last time that HAVOC
would work on *Doctor Who*: one member of the
team, Terry Walsh, had left to form his own group,
PROFILE, and subsequently took over as the series' regular stunt arranger.

The next transmitted story, a six-parter entitled
The Mutants (working titles: *Independence* and *The
Emergents*), was the second to be accepted from
writers Bob Baker and Dave Martin, who had continued to bombard the production office with ideas
following their success the previous season with *The
Claws of Axos*. The first three episodes were commissioned individually between May and August
1971, and the remainder together in September 1971.

In this story, the Time Lords again operate the
TARDIS by remote control, and the Doctor and Jo
find themselves undertaking a mission to deliver
a sealed message pod to an unknown party aboard
a Skybase orbiting the planet Solos in the 30th
century. Solos is due to gain independence from
Earth's dwindling empire, but its sadistic Marshal
is determined to prevent this as it would mean
the end of his comfortable life of authority. He
arranges the murder of the Earth Administrator
and, with his chief scientist Jaeger, plans to transform Solos's atmosphere into one more suited to
humans. Ky, a Solonian rebel, is falsely accused
of the murder and flees to the planet's surface,
taking Jo with him. The Doctor follows and is reunited with them in an old thæsium mine.

Ky turns out to be the intended recipient of the
Time Lords' message pod, which opens automati-
cally when given to him. Inside are a number of
stone tablets carved with ancient inscriptions, but
their meaning is a mystery. The Doctor's party then
meet up with Sondergaard, a human scientist who
has been leading a hermit-like existence in the mine
workings while searching for a cure for the mutat-
ing disease which threatens the Solonians. Together,
the Doctor and Sondergaard decipher the inscriptions, deducing that the mutations — colloquially

termed Mutts — are actually part of a natural life-cycle, in which thæsium radiation plays a vital role.

The Doctor retrieves a crystal from a cave where the radiation is concentrated, and returns to the Skybase in order to analyse it. On his arrival, however, he is recaptured by the Marshal. With his friends held hostage, he is forced to perfect the machine with which Jaeger plans to transform Solos. Sondergaard, meanwhile, gives Ky the crystal, which turns him first into a mutant and then into an ethereal super-being — the ultimate stage of the Solonians' life-cycle. Jaeger is killed when the Doctor sabotages his machine, and the Marshal is vaporized by Ky. Leaving Ky and Sondergaard to supervise the transformation of the other Solonians, the Doctor and Jo depart in the TARDIS.

The idea of a creature gradually metamorphosing into a beautiful super-being was suggested to Bob Baker and Dave Martin by Barry Letts, drawing on a storyline entitled *The Mutant* which he himself had unsuccessfully submitted to *Doctor Who's* then script editor Gerry Davis around 1966. Further suggestions were then made by Terrance Dicks after the writers had completed a draft script for their first episode and a detailed outline for each of the other five. In a letter dated 3 August 1971 he told them:

Well, you've done it again haven't you?

The script of Episode One followed by the outline of Ep. 2 lulled me into a false sense of security. Reality began to slip away somewhere around Episode Three, and by the end of Episode Six I was suffering from a full case of script editor's angst, a condition producing low moans and a tendency to claw the temples, curable only by large doses of Macon at the Lime Grove Bar!

In plainer terms I still like Episode One, feel the outline of Episode Two works reasonably well, and that the story careers steadily off the rails thereafter. However, don't be too discouraged. I think the basic elements are all there and only need rationalising and simplifying.

I suggest the following course of action. I will now commission Episode Two, subject to the enclosed notes and would like you to deliver this within the next couple of weeks. In the meantime, I will be working ahead with Barry on Episodes Three to Six, and we'll go ahead and commission further scripts when we have a mutually agreed storyline.

Amongst the changes requested by Dicks and Letts were the removal of two subplots, one involving cloning and the other an influx of refugees from Earth; the introduction of the radio-

One of the Solonian Mutants; discovered to be part of a natural evolutionary cycle leading ultimately to a race of ethereal super-beings. The costume is one of many impressive designs for the series by James Acheson. *The Mutants*.

active cave idea; and the ending of the story with the Marshal receiving his come-uppance from a transformed Ky.

The draft scripts for all six episodes were completed by 25 October 1971 and the final edited versions by early February 1972. Dicks then wrote again to Baker and Martin on 5 February, sending them their copies of the finished scripts:

TRAILERS

*The **Radio Times** cover and accompanying feature were not the only pre-publicity that **Day of the Daleks** received. Over the Christmas period leading up to the start of the new season, viewers of BBC1 were given frequent opportunities to see two specially-shot trailers showing Daleks gliding around familiar London landmarks. Although bearing no relation to the actual plot of **Day of the Daleks**, these were highly reminiscent of the clips used back in 1964 to promote **The Dalek Invasion of Earth** – appropriately enough, given that both stories depicted a 22nd-century Earth under Dalek rule. The fact that this was the Daleks' second invasion in the same time period was something to which **Day of the Daleks** itself alluded, although another continuity reference, telling of the defeat of the humanized Dalek faction at the end of the civil war seen in the creatures' last story, season four's **The Evil of the Daleks**, was cut at the video editing stage for timing reasons.*

STOCK FOOTAGE

***Day of the Daleks** parts two and three each feature nine seconds of BBC stock footage of stars, for the effect of travelling through the time vortex.*

***The Sea Devils** part one features a clip from the Oliver Postgate children's series **Clangers**, which the Master watches on a screen in his cell. Part three features some footage from an Admiralty film called **Where No Breezes Blow**, as does part five along with extracts from **The Navy is a Ship** and **Defence in Depth**.*

***The Time Monster** part one features footage from Contemporary Films showing scenes of volcanic eruptions – as seen previously in season five's **The Enemy of the World** and season seven's **Inferno**. Part three features material from Visnews of a V1 doodlebug rocket.*

◄ **Ky in his fully evolved state as a Solonian super-being. *The Mutants*.**

EXPERIMENTAL SESSIONS

Three experimental studio sessions took place during production of season nine. The first, for **Day of the Daleks**, *was on 7 September 1971 in TC4. Its main purpose was to try out some CSO effects using yellow as the keying colour, to see if this would give a better result than the blue normally used – a suggestion made by director Paul Bernard. The opportunity was also taken to rehearse a number of other effects. Stuntman Rick Lester, who played one of the Ogrons in the story, stood in for Jon Pertwee during this session, while an unknown actress stood in for Katy Manning. A second, gallery-only session was held on 20 March 1972 to experiment with some CSO effects for* **The Mutants**. *Lastly, a session took place on 27 March in TC4A to complete the CSO tests for* **The Mutants** *and to try out a number of effects for* **The Time Monster**, *including the ageing make-up required to be worn by actor Ian Collier in the role of lab assistant Stuart Hyde and the 'suit of lights' to be donned by stuntman Marc Boyle as the monstrous Kronos.*

WRONG NAME

When Malcolm Hulke wrote **Doctor Who and the Silurians**, *he had the reptile creatures identified as 'Silurians' because they had supposedly originated in the Silurian era of Earth's past. By the time* **The Sea Devils** *came to be written, the production team had realized that the creatures could not in fact have come from that period as reptiles had not developed then. A line was therefore written into* **The Sea Devils** *in which the Doctor corrects this previous assumption, explaining that the creatures should really be referred to as 'Eocenes'.*

The Doctor and Jo in the TARDIS control room in *The Time Monster*. This was the first appearance of a new TARDIS interior set designed by Tim Gleeson. The set received only a luke warm reaction from the production team. It subsequently warped in storage and was never used again.

Stuart Hyde (Ian Collier) and Dr Ruth Ingram (Wanda Moore) with Sergeant Benton (John Levene) in Cambridge. *The Time Monster*.

Here at long last are your scripts.

Changes have been fairly minimal and mostly for production or policy reasons. E.G. The changing of 'Munt' to 'Mutt', since it was felt at a higher level that lines like 'Munt mad he is' were open to misinterpretations! Similarly, I've moderated the violence of the Marshal's language here and there, but this has been mostly a matter of changing words rather than lines.

We've had to cut down film sequences, and simplify studio action a little, but again this has been purely for practical reasons.

I've also added a few lines of explanation here and there for the sake of viewers whose minds don't move as fast as yours do.

Ignore the description of 'Super Ky' as a globe. After much agonised discussions with the Special Effects department, he has now reverted to something very much like your original description.

In fact, as always with your work, any changes I've made have been in the causes of possibility, clarity and occasionally, decency! I don't think I've once changed a line because I didn't like it, and there are few other writers to whom I could say this.

Very much in keeping with the production team's own concerns were the story's central themes of the evils of pollution and colonialism.

'It was supposed to be a satire on the British Empire,' recalls director Christopher Barry, 'but we played it down because I don't think that *Doctor Who* is really the place for such obvious political comment.'

Although disappointed by this slight change of emphasis, the writers were generally happy with the transmitted version. 'It had a good story over the six parts,' says Baker, 'and contained, I feel, some fairly strong comments about Empire and the Vietnam war.'

Having first worked on *Doctor Who* back in 1963 — coincidentally on a story also entitled *The Mutants* — Barry was very conscious of the changes the series had undergone over the years, particularly in areas such as location filming, video editing and electronic effects, all of which were far more sophisticated in the mid-seventies than had been the case a decade earlier.

'*The Mutants* was interesting,' he notes of the third Doctor story, 'because of the amount of modelwork in it. I've always liked using lots of effects. I remember having a model of the cavern in which the Doctor finds the crystal. It would have needed a very expensive lighting rig to light this huge cavern on location, so instead we built a fibreglass model, which was translucent, and lit it from behind. The actors were put in using CSO.

'The visual effects designers were always trying to extend the medium and, if they convinced me they could do it, I'd say, "Great, let's have it, and we'll try to get the budget for it." That was always difficult, because producers would give money for visual effects without ever knowing how much they were going to cost in the end, so they needed an elastic purse. I don't recall whether or not *The Mutants* went over budget, but I should think it did. Some of the effects were very good, particularly by the standards of those days.'

The next story, *The Time Monster*, was another six-parter, bringing the total number of episodes in season nine to 26 — one more than in seasons seven and eight. This marginal increase in allocation would be maintained for the remainder of

The humanoid face of Kronos (Ingrid Bower). *The Time Monster.*

**Queen Galleia (Ingrid Pitt), wife of King Dalios –
the elderly ruler of Atlantis.** *The Time Monster.*

▲ **The Master attempts to seduce Galleia.** *The Time Monster.*

the Pertwee era, allowing the production team to adopt a regular pattern of two four-part stories and three six-part stories per season.

Like the previous season's closing story *The Dæmons*, *The Time Monster* was written as a collaboration between Barry Letts and Robert Sloman. Letts's responsibilities as producer again prevented him from admitting authorship, so on this occasion Sloman took the on-screen credit.

The story itself had much in common with *The Dæmons*, in that it blended science fiction with mythology and placed an unusually high degree of emphasis on developing the series' regular characters — the UNIT team and their arch-enemy the Master.

The Master's latest scheme sees him taking on the guise of an eminent research scientist, Professor Thascales, in order to make use of the facilities of the Newton Institute in Cambridge. There he has constructed a device known as TOMTIT — transmission of matter through interstitial time — with which he intends to gain control of Kronos, a powerful creature from outside the boundaries of time. When the creature is summoned, it proves to be uncontrollable, and the Master flees. The Doctor, having detected the time disturbance and traced it to its source, is able to shut TOMTIT down.

Although his laboratory is placed out of bounds,

the Master manages to sneak back and reactivate TOMTIT. He uses it first to ensnare Krasis, High Priest of the fabled city of Atlantis, and then to attack the UNIT forces by way of a series of timeslips, culminating in the appearance of a V1 flying bomb from the Second World War.

The Master takes Krasis back to ancient Atlantis in his TARDIS in the hope of gaining access to the city's temple and stealing the sacred Crystal of Kronos, with which he believes he can finally dominate the creature. The Doctor follows in his own TARDIS, taking Jo with him. He is unable to prevent his enemy from seducing Queen Galleia and staging a coup, but Galleia turns against the Master when she learns that he has caused the death of her elderly husband, King Dalios. The Master then unleashes the full fury of Kronos, leading to Atlantis's destruction.

The two Time Lords escape in their respective TARDISes and confront each other in the time vortex. The Doctor threatens to trigger a time ram — a devastating collision between the two ships — in order to thwart the Master's schemes, but cannot bring himself to do it. Jo, held hostage by the Master, has no such qualms, and operates the controls herself. Instead of being destroyed, the two TARDISes reappear in a strange void presided over by Kronos — who now appears in the form of a beautiful female face. The time ram has released Kronos from the Master's influence and, in

LOCATIONS

Day of the Daleks
Harvey House, Green Dragon Lane, Brentford, Middx;
Bull's Bridge, Hayes, Middx

The Curse of Peladon
No location work

The Sea Devils
HMS Reclaim;
Norris Castle, Cowes, Isle of Wight;
No Man's Land Sea Fort, Solent

The Mutants
Chiselhurst Caves, Kent;
Finsbury Caves, Stonehouse Farm, Kent

The Time Monster
Heckfield Heath, Nr Reading, Berks;
Old Church Farm, Hartley Wintney, Hants

MUSIC

Story	Composer
Day of the Daleks	Dudley Simpson
The Curse of Peladon	Dudley Simpson
The Sea Devils	Malcolm Clarke
The Mutants	Tristram Cary
The Time Monster	Dudley Simpson

*Malcolm Clarke replaced John Baker who dropped out of doing the music for **The Sea Devils** at a late stage.*

THE BRAIN-DEAD

*The Brain-Dead was one of two unsuccessful storylines that Brian Hayles submitted to the **Doctor Who** production office shortly before he wrote **The Curse of Peladon**. An Earth-based story, it pitted the UNIT team against the Ice Warriors, whose plan – involving the use of a network of comsats (communications satellites) – was described as follows:*

'Their new weapon is the 'Z' beam, which can in effect reduce most substances to subzero temperatures, and when used full force, can effect absolute zero – fatal to human beings, with their high proportion of H_2O. However, the beam is capable of pinpoint accuracy, and when aimed at the brain, freezes it, producing a zombie – easily and instantly imprinted to serve the Ice Warrior cause.

'The 'Z' beam is used first of all via the comsat, to take over the receiving station, with its vital 'dish'. The imprinted engineers will then, under instruction, construct a giant version of the 'Z' beam transmitter. This involves taking over a neighbouring frozen food factory, an ideal cover under which to operate until the next major step in the plan. The freeze centre transmitter is then connected to the radio dish, now rigged to transmit. The 'Z' beam is then bounced off the immediate comsat to each of the comsat chain, and from them to all normal receiving stations throughout Earth. In an instant, the majority of Earth's industrial, political and military organizations will be under Ice Warrior control. With major resistance wiped out, the ensuing invasion will be easy. After that, with more 'Z' beams operating, the planet can be reconditioned to the Martian climate needed by the invaders.'

The Brigadier at first suspects that the problems at the comsat station are the work of an environmental pressure group, the Isolationists, but the Doctor manages to convince him of the truth. They then fight together against the Ice Warriors, led by Commander Kulvis, and their zombies – the eponymous Brain-Dead. The Doctor finally discovers how to turn the Ice Warriors' own weapon against them:

'Freezing metals to absolute zero renders them super-conductive, with a nil resistance to voltage. Just as the critical build-up is reached for the 'Z' beam to operate globally, Dr. Who effects an electrical power connection with the transmitter resulting in the spectacular destruction of the Ice Warriors and their slaves ... the Brain-Dead.'

Kronos the Time Monster (Marc Boyle). *The Time Monster*.

gratitude, she agrees to return the Doctor and Jo to Earth in their TARDIS. She plans to subject the Master to perpetual torment, but the Doctor pleads on his behalf and he too is allowed to go free.

The Time Monster's time travel elements recalled some of the historical flavour which had been an important aspect of *Doctor Who*'s format during its earliest years but which had been phased out in the latter part of the sixties. They also enabled Robert Sloman to develop an idea he had conceived while out walking his dog one day near his home in London:

'Through some curious meteorological phenomena I saw a plane flying through low cloud layers. It sounded very much like a V1 which I had heard when I was in the Air Force during the war, and from this came the idea of a timeslip.'

Another aspect of *The Time Monster* with which Barry Letts was particularly pleased was the light it threw on the Doctor's own character:

'Terrance Dicks and I are great talkers and great listeners, and throughout our years together we were constantly striving to find a "rationale" for *Doctor Who*; an "ethic" if you prefer. I was very clear in my mind about what the Doctor would do and what he wouldn't do. He was a flawed knight in shining armour, but flawed only in so far as he was "human". In other words, he was a knight who had left part of his armour at home and had

knocked up the rest out of old tin cans.

'In *The Time Monster*, the Doctor talks about his old teacher on the hillside who inspires him with his greed, a greed to experience all the wonders of these new worlds he goes to. There's nothing wrong with experiencing such wonders as an end, but what is wrong, and what is thus wrong in the Doctor's character, is the craving for it. *The Time Monster* paints him as an only semi-enlightened being — someone who sees more clearly into reality than we do, who sees more clearly into his own motivations than we see into ours, because he is further along the path, so to speak, but who is by no means fully enlightened. Unlike the old hermit, he is no Parsifal, no Buddha. On the contrary, the very fact that he stole the TARDIS in the first place, to escape and to satisfy his craving, is the key to the flaw that makes him fallible.'

When the final episode of *The Time Monster* was transmitted on 24 June 1972, recording of the story having been completed on 24 May, it brought to an end a season which had seen *Doctor Who* continuing to build on its recent success. The average ratings and weekly chart positions both showed a marked overall improvement for the third year in succession — peaking at eleven million viewers and 20th position respectively for the second episode of *The Curse of Peladon* — and the series' future had rarely looked more secure. The policies pursued by Barry Letts and Terrance Dicks were paying handsome dividends.

CHAPTER SEVEN

Season Ten:
Ten Years in the
TARDIS

We always used to try to think of a gimmick to launch each of our seasons,' says Terrance Dicks.

Previous gimmicks had been the introduction of the Master and the return of the Daleks. For the opening story of season ten, which also celebrated *Doctor Who*'s tenth anniversary on air, it was an adventure in which the third Doctor would join forces with his two predecessors to fight a phenomenally powerful adversary.

'I don't think you could ever say one person thought up the idea of *The Three Doctors*,' continues Dicks, 'because it was probably the most obvious storyline to do once we knew we wanted to do an anniversary show. Indeed it would be fair to say that hardly a week went by without at least one letter coming into the office suggesting just such a meeting of all the Doctors. So the difficult task was not so much bringing Jon Pertwee together with Bill Hartnell and Pat Troughton, it was what sort of story one would write from there onwards.'

Bob Baker and Dave Martin were the writers assigned this task, and they submitted a suggested outline early in 1972, while their season nine story *The Mutants* was still in production. Dicks replied in a letter dated 8 March 1972:

First the good news. The 'Three-Doctor' idea is definitely on. William Hartnell and Patrick Troughton have given provisional agreement.

But I'm afraid we're not happy about the approach you suggest in your story idea, interesting and imaginative though it is. Bitter experience has taught us that stories set in dreamland, fairyland, limbo or any other metaphysical setting simply don't grab our audience, because the 'It's only a sort of dream' makes them lose interest. Everything must be physically real, a real planet with real dangers and monsters. I think we should have a meeting on your next visit and thrash things out. My own thinking on the story, as far as it goes, is as follows.

◀ **The second and third Doctors join forces in The Three Doctors.**

SEASON TEN

CODE	TITLE
RRR	THE THREE DOCTORS
PPP	CARNIVAL OF MONSTERS
QQQ	FRONTIER IN SPACE
SSS	PLANET OF THE DALEKS
TTT	THE GREEN DEATH

RATINGS

Figures in millions

15	
14	
13	
12	
11	
10	
9	
8	
7	
6	
5	

RRR PPP QQQ SSS TTT
Story code

A photocall for *The* ▲ *Three Doctors* is held in the garden of William Hartnell's house as Hartnell's ill-health makes it difficult for him to travel.

WHEEZING AND GROANING

In 1973, the sound effect of the TARDIS materializing and dematerializing, was finally classified by the BBC as music, and composer Brian Hodgson of the BBC's Radiophonic Workshop was officially credited for his contribution to the series on the internal BBC documentation. Hodgson had first worked out what effect he wanted to achieve and then created the base sound by rubbing a key along the strings inside a standard household upright piano.

BESSIE GETS A REFIT

The Doctor's vintage roadster, Bessie, had broken down several times during the making of season ten, so Barry Letts had it sent to a company called Glentura Plastics for a refit. The car was given a new chassis, a new gearbox and a larger capacity engine, which in turn necessitated the use of some new body parts, including in particular a more rounded saddle bonnet. Fully resprayed, the car was back at the BBC in time for location filming on **The Green Death.**

The Time Lord President (Roy Purcell) discusses with the first Doctor the progress of the fight against Omega. *The Three Doctors.*

Omega (Stephen Thorne) contemplates the reflection of his own mask. *The Three Doctors.*

A rehearsal shot on the UNIT lab set with the actors playing Gel Guards – Omega's blob-like servants – wearing only the lower parts of their costumes. *The Three Doctors.*

The Time Lords come up against some almighty peril involving an opponent of almost equal powers to their own, perhaps a set of anti Time Lords, Lords of Evil, like your Death figure. So great is the danger that the Time Lords feel that even the Doctor will be unable to cope. They therefore bend the rules of time and allow the Doctor to meet and ally with his other selves, thus tripling his powers.

I think the Doctors would at first be in opposi-

tion to each other, or at least unwilling allies, finally combining to solve the problem. As for the setting, I quite like the idea of a 'death world' not in the spiritual sense but in that of Harry Harrison's novel — a planet where every life form animal, vegetable and mineral is savagely hostile.

These are a few early thoughts. Would you like to start thinking round them and perhaps jot a few preliminary ideas down by or before our next meeting. If you could arrive a bit earlier we could fit in a script conference on 27th or 28th March, your last two recording days. I enclose a copy of the Dr. Who book which will not only save you 25 pence but provide useful information on the Doctor's past.

Working from Dicks's suggestions, Baker and Martin came up with a revised storyline under the working title *The Black Hole*, which drew inspiration from sources as diverse as Greek mythology and L. Frank Baum's *The Wonderful Wizard of Oz*. The central premise was that the three Doctors would be brought together by the Time Lords to do battle with Ohm, a legendary figure from their race's own history, who now inhabited a world of antimatter in the heart of a black hole. This was approved by the production team, although Barry Letts requested that the villain's name be amended to Omega as he felt that Ohm was too jokey (OHM being WHO turned upside-down and reversed). The story was subsequently retitled *The Three Doctors* to achieve maximum publicity for the unique teaming of Pertwee, Troughton and Hartnell.

Letts had by this time discovered that Troughton was committed to other work until November 1972 — some three months after the season would normally have gone into production — so, for the second year running, the stories would have to be made out of transmission sequence. *The Three Doctors* was in fact the third story to go before the cameras, leaving only a relatively short gap between the start of its studio recording on 27 November and the transmission of its first episode on 30 December.

Another problem, which became apparent only just before the story's location filming was carried out over 6—10 November, was that Hartnell was too ill to play a full part in the proceedings. He had for some years been suffering from a circulatory complaint called arteriosclerosis, and this had now become so bad that he was unable to remember dialogue or even to stand unsupported for any length of time.

'It was obvious that he would never be able to play the extensive part which had been written

Pletrac (Peter Halliday), Vorg (Leslie Dwyer) and Shirna (Cheryl Hall) gather around the Inter Minorians' eradicator weapon and the molten remains of the wrecked Miniscope. *Carnival of Monsters.*

▲ **The Time Lord President considers the danger posed by Omega.** *The Three Doctors.*

▲ **The Gel Guards beseige the TARDIS in the UNIT lab.** *The Three Doctors.*

for him,' recalls Terrance Dicks, 'so I hurriedly had to rewrite the script — in particular the final episode, where he was due to appear with Pat and Jon in a dramatic showdown with Omega. Instead I confined Bill to a few scenes where he would appear on the screen of the TARDIS scanner to deliver advice to his other truculent selves.'

In the event, Hartnell's scenes were all pre-filmed on 6 November 1972 at the BBC's Television Film Studios in Ealing, the actor reading his lines from large cue cards held just out of camera shot. The photograph of the three Doctors taken for the *Radio Times* front cover, which was again used to publicize the start of the new season, was reportedly set up in Hartnell's own garage during a brief press call.

The Three Doctors opens with a cosmic ray research device picking up a blob of animated energy which dematerializes everything it touches. The creature expands and besieges the Doctor, Jo and Sergeant Benton in the TARDIS at UNIT HQ. The Doctor is forced to call on the Time Lords for help, but they are experiencing problems of their own: a black hole is rapidly draining off their energy. The only help they can give is to send the Doctor's earlier selves to join him.

The first Doctor, caught in a time eddy and able only to advise, deduces that the energy creature is a time bridge. The third Doctor and Jo then emerge from the TARDIS and 'cross' the bridge, being borne along a light stream to a strange world of antimat-

ter beyond the black hole. On Earth, the gel-like creature continues to wreak havoc, and the second Doctor is forced to take refuge in the TARDIS along with the Brigadier and Sergeant Benton. After consulting with his previous incarnation, he switches off the ship's force field, and the whole UNIT building is then transported through the black hole.

The instigator of these events is Omega, a legendary figure from Time Lord history whose solar engineering first provided the power for time travel. He has been trapped in the black hole ever since and now wants the Doctor to swap places with him, but the corrosive properties of the light stream have already taken their toll: his physical form has been destroyed, and only his will remains. Omega flies into a rage and threatens to destroy the Universe, but is tricked into touching the second Doctor's recorder — the only thing not converted to antimatter when the TARDIS passed through the black hole — and is consumed in the resulting supernova. Having bid farewell to his predecessors, who fade away to their rightful times and places, the third Doctor discovers that the Time Lords have now lifted his exile, restoring his freedom to travel in time and space.

Barry Letts decided that as an added boost to *Doctor Who* for its anniversary year he would commission a complete revamp of the famous theme music. The new arrangement was created on the Radiophonic Workshop's Delaware synthesizer by Paddy Kingsland with assistance from Brian

LOCATIONS

The Three Doctors
YMCA/Ministry of Defence Hotel, Hayling Rd; Springwell Reservoir, Rickmansworth; Summerfield Bungalow, Springwell Lane, Rickmansworth

Carnival of Monsters
Tillingham Marshes, Howe Farm; RIA Robert Dundas, Naval Dockyard, Chatham

Frontier in Space
Fullers Earth Works, Reigate, Surrey; Royal Festival Hall, South Bank, London

Planet of the Daleks
Beachfields Quarry, La Porte Industries Ltd, Cormonger Lane, Redhill, Surrey

The Green Death
Deri, Mid Glamorgan 'Scotch' factory, Merthyr Tydfill, Mid Glamorgan

BRIAN HODGSON
SPECIAL SOUNDS

Brian Hodgson joined the BBC Radiophonic Workshop in 1962 and almost the first sounds he was required to produce were the TARDIS's distinctive dematerialization noise and an alien voice for a new race of creatures called Daleks. Hodgson provided all of the special sounds for the series up until 1972 when he left the BBC to set up his own company. He returned to the Workshop and became its organizer in 1977, a position which he still holds.

MUSIC

All the incidental music for this season was composed by Dudley Simpson.

*The music used for the party to celebrate Jo and Cliff's engagement at the end of **The Green Death** was a track entitled 'It'll Never Be Me' from an LP called 'Even More Electric Banana' by the curiously named Electric Banana.*

A Drashig, one of the ▲ ferocious marsh creatures which breaks out of the Miniscope. *Carnival of Monsters.*

Pletrac (Peter Halliday). ▲ *Carnival of Monsters.*

Pletrac and Vorg relax after their narrow escape from the Drashigs at the conclusion of *Carnival of Monsters.*

Hodgson, who had been responsible for the series' sound effects ever since it had begun but was just on the point of handing over the reins to his colleague Dick Mills. Kingsland's version, which was more high-pitched and up-tempo than the original and had a 'twangy' quality to it, was well-received by Letts — but disliked intensely by everyone else who heard it. With just days to go before transmission, Letts was finally persuaded to revert to the old arrangement, even though this meant re-editing all the title sequences for the season's first three stories, onto which the new version had already been dubbed. The abandoned theme was however heard on ABC TV in Australia on the second episode of the season's second story, *Carnival of Monsters*, as BBC Enterprises inadvertently supplied the earlier edit (which also contained a few extra scenes).

Carnival of Monsters sees the TARDIS arriving on what appears to be a cargo ship, the SS *Bernice*, crossing the Indian Ocean in 1926. This, as the Doctor and Jo soon discover, is an illusion: the ship is in reality one of a number of exhibits trapped inside a Miniscope — a banned peepshow of miniaturized life-forms — on the planet Inter Minor. The travellers try to escape by entering another section of the Scope, but find themselves confronted by ferocious carnivores called Drashigs.

The Doctor eventually breaks out of the Scope and returns to full size. He learns that the device is owned by a pair of Lurman entertainers, Vorg and Shirna, who have brought it to Inter Minor in the hope of making a quick profit from the planet's hitherto reclusive natives. This hope has so far proved false, as the bureaucratic Inter Minorians are dissatisfied with the pair's credentials.

The Doctor's efforts to rescue Jo from the Scope, which is on the point of breaking down, are hampered by the schemes of two Inter Minorians, Kalik and Orum, who plan to dupe their superior, Pletrac, and overthrow the planet's president, Zarb, by al-

lowing the Drashigs to escape. Vorg destroys the Drashigs with an eradicator weapon and the Doctor, by linking the Scope to the TARDIS, finally manages to return all the exhibits to their points of origin. Jo materializes beside the wrecked Scope, and she and the Doctor then depart in the TARDIS.

Carnival of Monsters was developed by writer Robert Holmes from a storyline entitled *The Labyrinth*, which had been commissioned as early as 6 May 1971. The target completion date for the scripts was 1 June 1971, but Holmes eventually delivered the first episode on 1 September and the other three on 24 December. Under a new working title, *Peepshow*, this was the first story to be recorded for season ten. Owing partly to uncertainty surrounding the timing of Patrick Troughton's availability for *The Three Doctors*, it was in fact brought forward to be made immediately after *The Time Monster* as the final story of the ninth production block, which therefore consisted of 30 episodes in total. Its location work was carried out in early June 1972 and its first studio session took place on 19th and 20th of that month. Recording was then completed on 3—4 July, following which the regular cast and crew had a short break until location filming began on the next story, a six-parter called *Frontier in Space*, in mid-September.

Only one story seriously considered for inclusion in season ten subsequently failed to reach the screen. This was Godfrey Harrison's *Multiface*, a four-parter for which the storyline was commissioned on 5 August 1971. Harrison, the writer of the popular radio sitcom *A Life of Bliss*, was an old friend of Barry Letts, who was keen for him to work on the series, but his highly detailed storyline was eventually rejected on 29 February 1972 on the grounds that it was more science fantasy than science fiction. Terrance Dicks had by this time come to rely, in effect, on a regular team of writers, having been influenced in this regard by something Malcolm Hulke had told him about the approach taken by one of his sixties predecessors, Gerry Davis:

'Mac Hulke said "Gerry used to get a writer in, and he used to say, 'You and I are going to do a *Doctor Who* together. There is your name on the schedule. No matter how much work we have to put in, no matter how many rewrites we have to do, no matter how long it takes, you are going to write a *Doctor Who*.' If you say that to a writer, he doesn't mind how much he does for you, because he knows that at the end of the day there is going to be a show." That was very much what we tried to promote; this feeling that it was a collaboration.'

Frontier in Space was Malcolm Hulke's own

A reheasal shot taken on the studio set of the Draconian throne room. Katy Manning and Jon Pertwee, out of full costume, prepare for the scene where they are introduced to the Draconian Emperor (John Woodnutt). *Frontier in Space.*

contribution to the tenth anniversary season; and from the outset it was planned to link directly into the following story, another six-parter commissioned from Terry Nation on 11 May 1972 under the working title *Destination: Daleks*, to make up a celebratory twelve-part epic reminiscent of season three's *The Daleks' Master Plan*.

The story begins with the Doctor materializing the TARDIS in the hold of an Earth spaceship of the year 2540 in order to avoid colliding with it in hyperspace. Almost immediately the ship is attacked. The crew perceive the Doctor, Jo and the attackers as Draconians, members of an alien race whose empire rivals Earth's for control of the galaxy. The Doctor and Jo, however, see that the attackers are really Ogrons. The Ogrons stun everyone aboard and steal the cargo — including the TARDIS. A rescue ship takes the Doctor and Jo to Earth, where they are brought before the President and accused of spying for the Draconians. The Doctor is eventually sent to a penal colony on the Moon, while Jo is transferred into the custody of a Commissioner from Sirius 4 — in truth the Master. The Master subsequently rescues the Doctor from the Moon and locks him and his companion up aboard a stolen police spaceship. Once in flight, the ship is intercepted and captured by the Draconians.

Taken to the Draconians' home world, Draconia, the Doctor is able to convince the Emperor of the Master's scheme to provoke a war between the two empires by using the Ogrons and a hypnotic device which makes those affected see whatever they most fear. Jo is recaptured by the Master and taken to the Ogrons' bleak home planet, where he is also holding the Doctor's TARDIS. The Doctor follows, along with General Williams — an

The Master gloats over the captive Jo Grant aboard the police space ship he has commandeered in his guise as a Commissioner from Sirius 4. *Frontier in Space.*

▲ The Draconians. The masks were designed by director Paul Bernard and created by visual effects sculptor John Friedlander. *Frontier in Space.*

NOTES
Time Scan Images
The short sequence of the first Doctor seen on the Time Lords' scanner in the first episode of **The Three Doctors** was shot in the garden of William Hartnell's own cottage in Grove Hill, Sussex. The sequence of the second Doctor was filmed at Harefield Lime Works near Rickmansworth – the same location used for the scenes set on Omega's planet.

Title Sequence Variations
The closing credits for episodes two, five and six of **The Green Death** presented a departure from the norm, as Bernard Lodge's standard title sequence film was run upside-down and backwards.

Maggot Moments
Some of the giant maggots used in **The Green Death** were constructed from stuffed condoms. Fox skulls were used to provide the hissing mouths and teeth of the more elaborate props used in close up.

▼ Two Ogrons. *Frontier in Space.*

The Doctor with fellow ▲ prisoner Professor Dale (Harold Goldblatt) under guard in the prison on the Moon. *Frontier in Space.*

The Daleks arrive on ▲ the Ogrons' home planet. *Frontier in Space.*

Visual effects designer ▲ Ian Scoones makes final adjustments to the Ogron spaceship model before filming of the scene where it docks with the Master's police ship. *Frontier in Space.*

The police ship on the ▲ surface of the Moon. *Frontier in Space.*

A Dalek uncovers an attempt by the Doctor and Thal leader Tarron (Bernard Horsfall) to enter their base disguised under Spiridon cloaks. *Planet of the Daleks.*

emissary from the President of Earth, who has also been convinced of the truth — and a Draconian Prince. There the Time Lord learns that the instigators of the Master's plot are the Daleks, who want a war to break out so that they can invade in the aftermath.

The Doctor and his party are placed in the Master's custody as the Daleks leave to prepare their forces, but they manage to escape with the aid of his hypnotic device, which Jo has purloined. Williams and the Draconian Prince depart to warn their respective peoples of the Daleks' intentions. The Doctor, though, is injured in the confusion. Jo helps him into the TARDIS, where he sends a telepathic message to the Time Lords. . .

Jon Pertwee has often declared the Draconians to he his own personal favourites of all the creatures encountered during his tenure as the Doctor, citing in particular the wide range of facial movement afforded the actors by the use of halfmasks. These masks were designed by the story's director, Paul Bernard, and made out of latex by sculptor John Friedlander, who endeavoured to give each of them a slightly different appearance. The masks for the three principal Draconians were made from casts of the actors' own faces, but for the extras the plaster former was built up over an existing head cast of comedian Dave Allen. Finishing touches, such as colouring and facial hair, were added by make-up designer Sandra Shepherd and her assistants.

Frontier in Space was the final production to feature Roger Delgado as the Master. Some seven months later, on 18 June 1973, a hired car in which the actor was being driven to a film location in Neveshir, Turkey, ran off the road and plunged into a ravine, killing him outright. He had in fact already decided to leave *Doctor Who*, having found that his semi-regular status since season eight made it difficult for him to obtain other work, but his tragic death robbed viewers of the chance to see a final dramatic showdown between the Doctor and the Master.

'We were planning a story,' says Barry Letts, 'where the Master would be destroyed in an enormous cosmic explosion, and it would always be left ambiguous as to whether it was an accident, whether it was a consequence of his malevolence, or whether in the end he couldn't bring himself to destroy the Doctor and allowed himself to be sacrificed instead. It never got any further than that, and then poor Roger was killed. It would have been quite a story, I think.'

In an unintentionally prophetic letter to the *Doctor Who* Fan Club a few weeks before his death, Delgado had written: 'Although the Master will soon no longer be with you, he will remember with affection the time he spent chilling your spines.'

The Master's exit from the series was even more abrupt than it should have been, owing to problems encountered in the making of the climactic final scenes of *Frontier in Space.* Malcolm Hulke's intention had been that the Master's hypnotic device should cause the Ogrons to see images of the fearsome predator that they worshipped as a god. Paul Bernard, however, was dissatisfied with the costume designed for the creature and elected to omit it from these scenes, adapting them accordingly. The Master consequently vanished from the action quite suddenly. In the event, Barry Letts and Terrance Dicks disliked the new ending, feeling that it lacked impact. They therefore asked director David Maloney to record a new scene for the end of *Frontier in Space* during his own studio sessions for the following story, now retitled *Planet of the Daleks.* The editing in of this new scene, set in the TARDIS interior, was carried out on 6 February 1973, at the end of the second studio session for *Planet of the Daleks* (*The Three Doctors* having been made in between the two six-part stories).

The TARDIS's point of arrival in *Planet of the Daleks* is a hostile jungle on the planet Spiridon. Jo sets out alone to find help for the Doctor, who has fallen into a coma as a result of the wound he sustained at the end of *Frontier in Space.* She meets a party of Thals and is left in hiding aboard their crashed spaceship while they go to the Doctor's aid. The Time Lord, now recovered, learns of their mission to destroy a party of Daleks sent here to learn the native Spiridons' secret of invisibility.

The Doctor and one of the Thals are captured by the Daleks and taken to their base. Another Thal spaceship then crash-lands in the jungle, and

Dave (Talfryn Thomas), one of the Welsh miners, attempts to halt a sabotaged lift cage while the Brigadier and the Doctor look anxiously on. *The Green Death.*

▲ The Doctor and Tarron try to work out a means of escape from the lower levels of the Dalek city on Spiridon. *Planet of the Daleks.*

▲ The Thals: Rebec (Jane How), Codal (Tim Preece) and Latep (Alan Tucker) on the surface of Spiridon. *Planet of the Daleks.*

the survivors bring news that somewhere on Spiridon there is an army of ten thousand Daleks! Jo, meanwhile, meets a friendly Spiridon named Wester, who cures a deadly fungus disease she has contracted.

It transpires that the Daleks' army is frozen in suspended animation in a cavern below their base. The Doctor, with the help of the Thals, explodes a bomb in the cavern wall and thereby causes an ice volcano to erupt, entombing the army in a torrent of liquid ice. The newly-arrived Dalek Supreme and his aides are left stranded on Spiridon as the Thals steal their ship and the Doctor and Jo depart in the TARDIS.

Planet of the Daleks was notable for being the first TV production since 1964's *The Dalek Invasion of Earth* to feature some brand new Dalek casings. There were four in all, made by the BBC's Visual Effects Department. Although very faithful to the original shape, they were somewhat crude in construction, so the three surviving sixties Daleks were again pressed into service for all the main shots and sequences.

In addition to these seven standard Daleks, painted gun-metal grey, an eighth appeared in the form of the Dalek Supreme. This was not a BBC-owned prop but one of those constructed for the Aaru cinema films of the sixties. It had been in Terry Nation's possession for some years, and he agreed to loan it out for use in *Planet of the Daleks.* The Visual Effects Department carried out extensive repair work on it and made a number of modi-

fications, giving it a black-and-yellow colour scheme similar to that of the Dalek Supreme of sixties stories such as *The Daleks' Master Plan.* The new eyepiece was a domestic torch, rigged to flash on and off in synchronization with the dome lights, while the dome lights themselves were equally makeshift in construction, consisting of bulbs inside inverted glass jam jars!

The sequences of the huge Dalek army were achieved through the use of modelwork featuring commercially available Louis Marx toy Daleks, painted grey.

For the third year running, the season's final story was written as a collaboration between Robert Sloman and Barry Letts, and again it was Sloman who took the on-screen credit. Entitled *The Green Death*, this was another example of a story reflecting a contemporary social issue of concern to the production team.

'Several of the stories were inspired by interests of mine,' confirms Letts. '*The Green Death* came about after Terrance Dicks and I had read a series of pieces in an environmental magazine, *The Ecologist*, about the pollution of the Earth by man. The articles were very disturbing and made me wish I could do something positive about it.

'Terrance and I were talking about this and he said, "One of the things we could do is produce a *Doctor Who* story about pollution and get people thinking about it." So that was exactly what we did.'

DICK MILLS
SPECIAL SOUNDS

*Dick Mills started his career in 1958, working as a recording engineer for the BBC. At about the same time, the BBC established a Radiophonic Workshop in Maida Vale and Mills applied to work there full time. Among the first productions he assisted with were the BBC's productions of **Quatermass and the Pit** for television and **Song of a Quiet Street** for radio. When **Doctor Who** started in 1963, the Workshop was called upon to produce special sounds and also the distinctive theme music which was written by Ron Grainer and realized by Delia Derbyshire with assistance from Mills. Mills took over the creation of the special sounds for **Doctor Who** from Brian Hodgson in 1973 and continued to work on the series until 1989. In addition to his work on just about every television and radio production in that period which required special sounds of one form or another, Mills also harboured a love for tropical fish, writing numerous books on the subject and attending shows around the country. Dick Mills retired from the BBC in 1993.*

STOCK FOOTAGE

The National Coal Board provided footage used in part two of **The Green Death**, *showing the wheels at the pit head turning as the lifts are lowered into the mine.*

Jo and Professor Jones ▲
(Stewart Bevan). *The*
Green Death.

The giant maggots. ▲
The Green Death.

Stevens (Jerome Willis), ▲
the Director of Global
Chemicals, in his office.
The Green Death.

Another element that Sloman and Letts had to build into the story was the departure of the Doctor's assistant Jo Grant, actress Katy Manning having decided it was time to move on to other work.

The setting for *The Green Death* is the village of Llanfairfach in Wales, where a company called Global Chemicals has just gained a Government grant to build a full-scale refinery. The project is fiercely opposed by local ecologist Professor Cliff Jones, whose Wholeweal community has been dubbed the Nuthutch by the villagers. A strange death in some disused coal mines brings UNIT to the scene. The Doctor and Jo discover that the mine workings are seething with giant maggots and green slime — both fatal to touch — which have been produced by chemical waste pumped from the Global plant.

Stevens, the Director of Global, deliberately obstructs UNIT's investigation. It transpires that he and members of his staff have been taken over by BOSS — Biomorphic Organizational Systems Supervisor — a powerful computer with a will of its own. BOSS plans to seize power by linking itself to every other major computer in the world, but the Doctor uses a blue crystal — a souvenir from a brief visit made to the planet Metebelis 3 — to break its hold over Stevens, who then programs it to self-destruct. The maggots, on the point of pupating into giant insects, are destroyed with a type of fungus which a lucky accident at the Nuthutch has shown to be fatal to them.

Jo falls in love with Professor Jones and decides to leave UNIT in order to accompany him on an expedition up the Amazon — and also to marry him. The Doctor gives her the blue crystal as a wedding present.

'In *The Green Death*,' says Barry Letts, 'we had no intention of attacking high technology or big business in themselves, but rather the attitude that the maximization of profit is the *only* good; that economic growth must be maintained *at all costs*; that people don't matter a damn. A total greed is built into the system, as its sole motivation, quite independent of those who are running it. The computer, the BOSS, symbolized the whole dehumanizing result of such an attitude. He wanted it all for himself; he wanted the entire world. The machine would have taken over completely. Human beings would have been slaves.

'Alternative technology, on the other hand, is to be used in the service of humanity, in the search for a more human way of living. This quest has been a central concern of mine for many years — which is why *The Green Death* was a quite deliberate piece of propaganda.

'We quite expected that we would get into trouble; that we would have people accusing us of being anti-establishment, left wing and subversive. But in the event we didn't hear a peep from anybody, presumably because we were at the same time telling an intriguing and exciting story. Terrance and I always tried to make each *Doctor Who* story work on several different levels at once, from a children's show at the bottom to a play of ideas at the top, with a strong drama about real people somewhere in between.

'The subtext which was present in most, if not all, the stories of this period was that the ideal way of living is to be free. Now, by "free" I don't mean a kind of beat hippy existence, wandering through the world (or the Universe) with no cares or responsibilities, giving way to every impulse. Most of us are so conditioned by our personal histories — our upbringing, our emotional hang-ups, our cherished beliefs — that we have very little real freedom of choice. If we can learn to recognize these constraints as they come up in our lives, we have a chance of walking away from them — just as the Doctor did when he first ran away from the rigid world of the Time Lords. Then we can be free to choose for ourselves how to live — and maybe catch a glimpse of the real world behind the appearances. I suppose I'm talking about Zen, really. Or is it just a matter of finding out how to grow up?'

Location filming for *The Green Death* took place in Deri, South Wales. The schedule ultimately proved rather too ambitious, however, and director Michael Briant was unable to complete all the material he had originally planned. Consequently a number of sequences in the later episodes of the story had to be achieved by intercutting location footage with studio scenes shot on a CSO landscape.

The last of the three studio sessions for *The Green Death* took place on 29—30 April 1973 in studio TC3, and the story's final episode was transmitted less than a month later on 23 June 1973. Thus ended season ten, during which *Doctor Who* had again achieved a notable increase in average ratings, peaking at 11.9 million viewers for the final episode of *The Three Doctors*. The series' performance on the weekly TV chart had also shown a further overall improvement, the opening episode of *Planet of the Daleks* reaching as high as ninth position — the first time *Doctor Who* had been in the top ten programmes since episode six of *The Chase* hit number seven in 1965. Much of this continued success was attributable to close and highly effective teamwork, both in front of and behind the cameras. The death of Roger Delgado and the departure of Katy Manning had however created gaps in the team, and further changes lay just around the corner. . .

CHAPTER EIGHT

Season Eleven: All Change

When *Doctor Who* returned on 15 December 1973 with the first of a four-part story entitled *The Time Warrior* — the start of the new season having for the fifth year in succession been heralded by a *Radio Times* front cover — the most immediately noticeable change was that it bore a completely new title sequence, incorporating a distinctive diamond-shaped logo. This had been commissioned by Barry Letts from top BBC graphic designer Bernard Lodge, who had been responsible for all the previous sequences.

Letts wanted something different from the howl-around effect which had been used in the past, and Lodge decided to experiment with a technique called slit-scan which had been developed by director Stanley Kubrick and effects expert Douglas Trumbull for the film *2001: A Space Odyssey* in 1968. The slit-scan technique is a painstaking one in which a sequence is built up a frame at a time. It involves positioning a camera on a motorized track and, with the shutter locked on a single frame of film, moving it towards a slot behind which a pattern of colours is being passed. The next frame is created by repeating the procedure, with the pattern of colours starting from a slightly different position.

'I realized that the key factor was follow-focus,' recalls Lodge. 'All rostrum cameras have follow-focus, so that one can zoom down onto a picture and have the focus remain sharp as it is adjusted relative to the distance from the image. So the next thing I needed was a motor to pass something behind the slot. By luck, one of the companies we used outside the BBC had a motorized bench which moved from side to side as the camera moved up and down. All I had to do was to set up a fixed slot over the mobile bench.

'I decided to use a small circle instead of a linear slot — as long as the camera lens could get inside it, I knew that this would produce a tunnel effect rather than a wall of light and would require only one pass of the camera for each frame. I'd never seen a tunnel created in this manner, and felt it was something new. So we ended up with a tunnel effect but were left with a black circle in the middle. To cover this up, we superimposed an optical glow, as if there was light at the end of the tunnel.

◄ **Elisabeth Sladen makes her debut as journalist Sarah Jane Smith in *The Time Warrior*.**

SEASON ELEVEN	
CODE	TITLE
UUU	THE TIME WARRIOR
WWW	INVASION OF THE DINOSAURS
XXX	DEATH TO THE DALEKS
YYY	THE MONSTER OF PELADON
ZZZ	PLANET OF THE SPIDERS

RATINGS

Figures in millions

(Bar chart with vertical axis labelled 5 to 15; horizontal axis labelled UUU WWW XXX YYY ZZZ)

Story code

Irongron (David Daker). ▲
The Time Warrior.

Linx, the Sontaran ▲
warrior (Kevin Lindsay).
The Time Warrior.

TV's Dr. Who, actor Jon Pertwee is to quit the series after five years.

The 53-year-old actor has told the BBC he wants to return to the stage. He will make his last appearance as the eccentric Doctor in June.

"He will star in three more stories after the present one, including one about the Daleks," said producer Mr. Barry Letts today.
Aldo Nicolotti writing in an unknown newspaper, February 1974

A rehearsal shot taken ▶
on location at Peckforton
Castle for *The Time Warrior*.
John J. Carney, playing
Bloodaxe, wields an axe
above Jeremy Bulloch,
playing Hal the Archer,
while David Daker and
other members of the cast
and crew look on.

'The other thing that occurred to me was that if a linear slot made a wall and a circular slot made a tunnel, then a slot in the shape of the Doctor should produce a Doctor-shaped tunnel. So we took a photograph of the Doctor and traced round it to make a slot — it was a bit crude, but it worked.

'The image moving behind the circular slot was created using plastic shopping bags! I wanted something fairly science-fictiony and saw in photographic books some lovely stress-pattern photos taken using polarized filters. So I got strips of plastic bags and stretched them to create stress. The strips were then laid out between pieces of glass to keep them together and passed behind the slot. When filmed between polarizing filters, the plastic appeared multicoloured.

'To create the pattern behind the Doctor-shaped slot I used a prop built by the Visual Effects Department. I asked them for a piece of texture, then photographed that with a raking light and used the resulting transparency to create the tunnel wall.

'Another problem with the sequence was getting the Doctor's face to fade in. I remember asking the cameraman to fade it in while we were creating the tunnel, but he pointed out that it isn't possible to fade when the camera is locked on one frame. I thought about this and remembered someone who had produced fades by using polarized filters to block out the light. I therefore had a motor arrangement made where one filter was fixed and the other rotated through 90 degrees to fade the image. This was timed to move at the same speed as the camera and the image behind the slot, to give the right effect.

'It took us about three months to complete the sequence,' notes Lodge. 'A 30-second sequence with 25 frames per second adds up to a lot of frames (750 to be exact) and every one had to be created by this laborious process. It was horrible. I remember one day we were over the moon because we had managed to get four seconds of continuous film completed!'

Another important change coinciding with the first episode of *The Time Warrior* was the introduction of a new regular character, Sarah Jane Smith, to accompany the Doctor on his adventures. A different companion had originally been envisaged to fulfil this role but, as rehearsals began with the actress concerned, it became clear that a rethink was called for. The production team then devised Sarah who, as a freelance journalist, would have a plausible reason to get involved in dramatic situations and would also be capable and independent — attributes that Barry Letts was particularly keen to see maintained as he felt that the portrayal of earlier companions had left the series open to criticisms of sexism.

Auditions were held for the part of Sarah and the best candidate proved to be Elisabeth Sladen, who had been recommended to the production team by new Head of Serials Bill Slater on the strength of a performance she had given in *Z Cars* when he was its producer. Sladen was introduced to Jon Pertwee and immediately found favour with him, although she herself was initially unaware

Kevin Lindsay minus Sontaran mask. *The Time Warrior.*

Captain Yates, Sergeant Benton, a UNIT radio operator, the Doctor, Sarah and the Brigadier discuss the dinosaur invasion in the school building that UNIT have commandeered as their emergency HQ.

▲ Sarah meets Edward of Wessex (Alan Rowe) and his wife Lady Eleanor (June Brown) in their castle. The Time Warrior.

that the part was to be a regular one.

At the start of the story, Sarah is impersonating her aunt, virologist Lavinia Smith, in order to gain access to a research centre where top scientists are being held in protective custody while UNIT investigates the mysterious disappearance of a number of their colleagues. Sarah hopes to gain a 'scoop', but the Doctor immediately sees through her deception.

The missing scientists have in fact been kidnapped by a Sontaran warrior, Linx, and taken back in time to medieval England, where they are working under hypnosis to repair his crashed spaceship. The Doctor follows in the TARDIS, unaware that Sarah has stowed away on board. The bewildered Sarah initially believes that the Doctor is behind the kidnappings, but later realizes her mistake.

Since his arrival on Earth, Linx has been given shelter by a robber baron called Irongron. In return, he has provided Irongron with weapons from the future to use in attacks on neighbouring castles. The Doctor helps Sir Edward of Wessex to repel one such attack, then conspires with Sarah to drug the food in Irongron's kitchens so that the anachronistic weapons can be removed while the men are unconscious. He also enlists the help of one of the kidnapped scientists, Rubeish, to send the others back to the 20th century using Linx's primitive time travel equipment.

Linx tries to kill the Doctor, but Rubeish hits

him on the vulnerable probic vent at the back of his neck and renders him unconscious. Irongron, shaking off the effects of the drugged food, finds his weapons gone and believes that Linx has betrayed him. He goes to confront the Sontaran, but the now-recovered Linx shoots him down. As Linx gets ready to leave in his repaired ship, Hal — one of Sir Edward's archers — fires an arrow into his probic vent, killing him. The Doctor, Sarah and Hal escape just in time as the ship explodes, completely destroying the castle.

The Time Warrior started life as a storyline entitled *The Time Fugitive* commissioned from writer Robert Holmes at the end of February 1973. This was after another Holmes storyline entitled *The Automata*, commissioned on 16 January and delivered on 26 January, had been rejected as unsuitable. The setting of a story in medieval England was part of the production team's conscious policy of bringing back to *Doctor Who* some of its earlier historical aspect — albeit in stories with a sound science-fiction basis. Holmes was sceptical of this approach, as he later admitted:

'I resisted the suggestion vigorously, although I needed the money. Memory reminded me that *Doctor Who* was always least successful when venturing into history. Finally we compromised. I would send the Doctor into the past as long as he didn't meet any historical figures.'

Holmes wrote out his basic storyline and sent it to Dicks in the humorous form of a military

NOTES
Clairvoyant Clips
In the opening episode of Planet of the Spiders, the Doctor tests the abilities of the clairvoyant Professor Clegg by asking him to visualize some of the sonic screwdriver's past history. Clips from Carnival of Monsters and The Green Death were originally to have been shown as part of this sequence, but in the event only the former was used.

Pebble Mill At One
Patrick Troughton appeared on BBC1's lunchtime magazine programme Pebble Mill at One on 21 December 1973 to publicize the new season of Doctor Who. Also appearing were visual effects designer Bernard Wilkie, fan Matthew Jones – who had been pictured with Jon Pertwee on the Radio Times front cover two weeks earlier – and eight assorted monsters from the series.

SONTARAN DESIGN

*Of all the **Doctor Who** monsters introduced during the seventies, the Sontarans were the only ones to approach the popularity of their famous sixties counterparts such as the Daleks, the Cybermen and the Ice Warriors. As with those earlier creations, part of their success was due to their distinctive appearance, which in this instance was the responsibility of make-up designer Sandra Exelby and costume designer James Acheson.*

'The Visual Effects people had designed the costume and the facial features of the Sontaran up to a point,' recalls Exelby, 'but they couldn't do the whole thing as they needed time to design the spaceship. At our first planning meeting we all sat down and the director, Alan Bromly, tried to explain the kind of thing he wanted. I can't remember if it was I or James Acheson who suggested that he should look half man, half frog and have no neck. We thought the lack of a neck would enhance the impression of him being frog-like.'

'The head had been modelled by the effects sculptor John Friedlander,' confirms Acheson, 'We just had this very silly idea that he should have a helmet and that, when he took the helmet off, the head should be almost the same shape.'

'The actual making of the mask was the responsibility of Visual Effects,' explains Exelby, 'as at that time the Make-up Department didn't have any facilities for making prosthetics. They took a cast of the actor Kevin Lindsay's face and I went to help them do this. They then constructed the mask from latex and fibreglass (without the resin – just the glass matting used to build up the shape). The top lip actually went inside Kevin's own lip as a flap. The bottom lip was attached under his lip, so there was some movement there, and then I just painted his lip in the same sort of browny-green colour as the mask. I also had to attach the mask round his eyes, adding make-up there to blend it in.'

Sarah meets Mark (Terence Wilton), Ruth (Carmen Silvera) and Adam (Brian Badcoe) on board the fake space ship. *Invasion of the Dinosaurs.*

The London Underground comes under attack by one of the dinosaurs brought through time by Professor Whitaker. *Invasion of the Dinosaurs.*

communiqué between two Sontarans named Hol Mes and Terran Cedicks. The message ended with the recommendation that Jingo Linx be posthumously awarded the Galactic Hero's Cross, Second Class. The production team promptly commissioned a full set of scripts, and Holmes completed these under the revised working title *The Time Survivor* over the period 12 March to 2 April 1973.

The Time Warrior was made immediately after season ten's closing story, *The Green Death*. Its studio recording took place over 28—29 May and 11—12 June 1973 and brought to a close the series' tenth production block. Barry Letts had, uniquely during his tenure as producer, refrained from directing any of the stories of this block himself. This was so that he would have more time to devote to another science-fiction series that he and Terrance Dicks had been asked to devise and make for the BBC. Entitled *Moonbase 3*, it consisted of six 50-minute episodes, went into studio between June and August 1973 and was transmitted on BBC1 on consecutive Sunday evenings from 9 September 1973.

The first story of *Doctor Who*'s eleventh production block, which began location filming in late September 1973 (after a single morning's shoot had been carried out on 2 September), was a six-parter by Malcolm Hulke. Initially called *Timescoop*, it was later retitled *Invasion of the Dinosaurs* — although this was shortened to *Invasion* for the first episode in order to avoid giving away one of the major plot elements. Letts had decided to go ahead with a story featuring dinosaurs after being approached by a freelance effects designer, Clifford Cully of the Pinewood-based Westbury Design and Optical Ltd, who assured him that he could produce highly realistic models of such creatures. He later regretted his decision, as the models turned out to be unconvincing rod and cable controlled puppets with a very limited range of movement. They were filmed in some instances against two-dimensional sets made from photographic blow-ups and in others against yellow backdrops to allow for them to be inserted into live-actions shots using CSO.

Invasion of the Dinosaurs was also notable for introducing the Doctor's new car, referred to generally — though never in the transmitted episodes — as the Whomobile.

The story sees the Doctor and Sarah returning to 20th-century London, where they find the streets deserted, cars upturned and phones dead. Investigating, they are attacked by a creature which the Doctor identifies as a prehistoric pterodactyl. They escape the monster only to be arrested by the army and charged with looting. Their photos are sent with those of other suspected criminals to UNIT's emergency HQ, set up in an abandoned school, where Sergeant Benton recognizes them. After a close encounter with a Tyrannosaurus Rex, they are rescued by the Brigadier, who explains that London has been evacuated due to the sudden appearance of the dinosaurs.

The monsters are being brought through time by two scientists, Whitaker and his henchman Butler, as part of a conspiracy to clear London of people. The Doctor decides to capture a dinosaur and monitor it in order to learn the location of the time scoop, but his work is sabotaged first by Captain Yates and then by the regular Army's commanding officer General Finch, both of whom are involved in the conspiracy. Sarah visits Sir Charles Grover, the Government Minister in charge during the emergency, but discovers that he too is involved. Captured and hypnotized, she revives to find herself on board a spaceship with a group of people who believe that they have been in flight for three months and are *en route* to colonize another world. She soon realizes that the ship is just a mock-up and those on board have been duped. Grover then admits to her that the conspirators intend to use a time machine to return London to a 'Golden Age' before the Earth became polluted, so that they and the would-be colonists can start civilization afresh on a sounder basis.

Although framed as a traitor by General Finch, the Doctor persuades the Brigadier to assist him in mounting a raid on the underground headquarters of Operation Golden Age. Grover makes a last-ditch attempt to operate the time machine, but the Doctor has already changed the settings and he succeeds only in sending himself and Whitaker back to the era of the dinosaurs. The Brigadier arranges for the misguided Yates to be given a chance to resign quietly from UNIT after a period of sick leave.

It was on 8 February 1974, between transmission of episodes four and five of *Invasion of the Dinosaurs*, that the production team held a press conference to announce that Jon Pertwee would be leaving *Doctor Who* at the end of the season. Pertwee has since stated that he was given no choice but to leave when Head of Drama Shaun Sutton reacted unfavourably to a request he had made for an increase in his fee; others, however, recall that he was keen to move on, fearing that if he continued to turn down offers of alternative work they might soon dry up. In the press, he was quoted as saying that he wanted a break and that a major factor in his departure was the sadness he felt over the death of Roger Delgado and the gradual break-up of his team on the series.

This break-up was confirmed when Barry Letts and Terrance Dicks decided that they would also leave at the end of the current run of productions. They had first considered relinquishing their respective posts some two years earlier but had been persuaded by departmental superiors to prolong their highly successful stint on the series — prompting Dicks to quip that '*Doctor Who* is the only prison where time gets *added on* for good behaviour'.

Although Dicks was, as he recalls, less anxious to move on than either Pertwee or Letts, his was the first successor to be chosen. Writer Robert Holmes had approached the production team to put himself forward as a possible candidate for the script editor vacancy, and was delighted to discover that his name was already under consideration. He started to trail Dicks during the final stages of work on *Invasion of the Dinosaurs* and is credited on some BBC documentation as joint script editor of the season's third story — a Terry Nation four-parter with the working title *The Exxilons*, which had been commissioned on 2 July 1973 on the strength of a storyline commissioned on 23 March 1973. Holmes's dislike of the story's central monsters is reputed to have led him to suggest the final title change to *Death to the Daleks*, which summed up his feelings towards the Doc-

The Doctor and MSC officer Galloway (Duncan Lamont) form an uneasy alliance with the Daleks on the planet Exxilon. *Death to the Daleks*.

tor's greatest enemies.

Death to the Daleks begins with the TARDIS suffering a power loss and arriving on the planet Exxilon, where all electrical energy is being drained off by an unknown force. The Doctor and Sarah set out to explore and become separated after encountering the savage Exxilons. The Doctor meets up with an Earth expedition who tell him that a space plague is sweeping the galaxy and that the antidote, parrinium, can be found only on Exxilon. Their ship has also been disabled by the energy drain, so they are unable to leave with the much-needed mineral. Sarah, meanwhile, has come upon a magnificent white edifice with a flashing beacon on top. Before she can explore further, she is captured by a group of Exxilons and taken away to be sacrificed for

The savage Exxilons on the barren surface of their planet. *Death to the Daleks*.

▲ **Bellal (Arnold Yarrow), one of the more civilized faction of Exxilons who join forces with the Doctor and Sarah. *Death to the Daleks*.**

THE WHOMOBILE

The Whomobile was a custom-built vehicle specially commissioned by Jon Pertwee from designer Peter Farries, Chairman of the Nottingham Drag and Custom Club. Its registration number was WVO 2M and it was more properly called the Alien.

The main body of the vehicle was fourteen foot long by seven foot wide, with fins extending five foot from the ground, and consisted of a fibreglass shell constructed in only two sections – something other specialist designers had considered impossible and which took three months and six hundredweight of plaster to complete. This shell was then mounted on a four-inch box section chassis, shaped like an anchor and incorporating a sheet steel floorpan for added strength, and fitted with an aluminium 975cc Imp Sports Unit engine specially prepared by Chrysler UK. The car had three wheels – two for transmission and one for steering – which were concealed behind an eight-inch deep rubber skirt to give the illusion that it was in fact a hovercraft. Although capable of speeds in excess of 100 miles per hour, it was officially classified as an invalid tricycle!

Barry Letts was persuaded to feature the Whomobile in the series and it was quickly written into scenes in part four which had originally described the Doctor riding around on a motorbike. The car still lacked a proper roof and windscreens when filming took place in late September 1973, so Farries added a makeshift motorboat windscreen as a temporary measure to ensure it was legally roadworthy. By the time it made its second and last appearance in the series in *Planet of the Spiders* it had been fully completed.

Sarah in the Temple of ▲
Aggedor. *The Monster of
Peladon.*

Sskel (Sonny Caldinez) ▲
and Azaxyr (Alan Bennion).
The Monster of Peladon.

**A rehearsal shot of ▶
Frank Gatliff (playing
Ortron) with two partially
costumed Ice Warriors
and Alpha Centauri. *The
Monster of Peladon.***

LOCATIONS

The Time Warrior
*Peckforton Castle,
Tarporley, Cheshire*

Invasion of the Dinosaurs
*Numerous locations in
Central London*

Death to the Daleks
*ARC Quarry, Binnegar
Heath, Dorset*

The Monster of Peladon
No location work

Planet of the Spiders
*Mortimer Station,
Strathfield Mortimer,
Berks;
Tidmarsh Manor,
Tidmarsh, Berks;
Membury Airfield, Wilts*

defiling their city.

The Doctor and the humans see another spaceship land and are horrified when Daleks emerge. Luckily, the creatures' weapons have been rendered inactive by the energy drain. The two parties enter into an uneasy alliance but are subsequently set upon and taken prisoner by the Exxilons. They arrive at the cave in time for the Doctor to interrupt Sarah's execution, but he is then placed under sentence of death himself. The two travellers escape into some tunnels as the cave is attacked by a second force of Daleks who have previously remained concealed aboard their ship and have now armed themselves with mechanical guns.

In the tunnels, the Doctor and Sarah are befriended by Bellal, one of a group of civilized Exxilons. He tells them that the magnificent city above was created by his own race but then brought about their downfall. The Doctor, realizing that it is the city's beacon which is causing the energy drain, resolves to put it out of action. With Daleks in close pursuit, he and Bellal enter the city and, by passing a series of potentially deadly tests, manage to reach its centre. There the Time Lord uses his sonic screwdriver to give the controlling computer a brainstorm.

The Daleks' intention is to take all the parrinium and detonate a plague bomb on Exxilon so as to prevent others from approaching. As their ship takes off, however, it is destroyed in an explosion triggered by one of the human party who has stolen on board. Sarah then reveals that she and another of the humans had already smuggled off all the parrinium and transferred it to the Earth ship. The story ends with the Exxilons' city dissolving, causing the Doctor to muse that the universe now has only 799 wonders . . .

Death to the Daleks was directed by Michael Briant, who had been an assistant floor manager on the very first Dalek story back in 1963 and a production assistant on the epic *The Daleks' Master Plan* in 1965/66. Briant felt that the Daleks had

over the years been allowed to lose some of their original impact, and he wanted to reverse this trend. He gave instructions for their casings to be refurbished and repainted to resemble the colour scheme of their early black and white appearances and also asked designer Colin Green to reproduce the look of the original Dalek control rooms in his sets for their spaceship.

A perennial problem for directors of Dalek serials had been to find a way of getting the Dalek casings to move over rough terrain. On this occasion, when location filming took place between 13 and 19 November 1973 at the ARC Ltd sand and gravel pits at Gallows Hill in Dorset, Briant came up with two solutions: first, for simple scenes, he used the tried and tested method of laying down strips of sand-coloured hardboard for the Daleks to move across; secondly, for more complicated shots, he turned to the innovative technique of laying down linked sections of camera dolly track and mounting each Dalek on a dolly base such that it could be pulled along on a wire or surreptitiously pushed by one of the actors.

The season's penultimate story, *The Monster of Peladon*, forms — as its title suggests — a sequel to season nine's *The Curse of Peladon*. It sees the Doctor returning to Peladon to find that some 50 years have passed since his last visit and that the planet is now ruled by Queen Thalira — daughter of the late King Peladon — with advice from the intolerant Chancellor Ortron. The Doctor and Sarah are arrested by Ortron for trespassing on sacred ground but their names are quickly cleared by Alpha Centauri, who is now acting as the Galactic Federation's ambassador to Peladon.

A ghost-like image of the sacred beast Aggedor has been responsible for some deaths in the planet's trisilicate mines, heightening unrest amongst the miners. The Doctor investigates and discovers that the apparitions are really the result of the combined use of a matter projector and a directional heat ray by a human engineer, Eckersley. Eckersley is in league with a group of renegade Ice Warriors, led by Commander Azaxyr, in a plot to seize the trisilicate deposits for Galaxy 5, a power bloc at war with the Federation. Emerging from hiding, Azaxyr mounts an attack on the throne room and kills Ortron.

The Doctor turns the Aggedor hologram on the Ice Warriors, who are then dispatched by the miners. Eckersley flees, taking the Queen as a hostage, but the Doctor uses the real Aggedor creature to track him down. Eckersley is killed, but Aggedor also dies in the skirmish. With its plans thwarted, Galaxy 5 surrenders to the Federation. The Doctor is invited by Thalira to take over as her Chancellor but he declines, suggesting that the miners' leader Gebek would make a more suitable candidate.

The Monster of Peladon was very similar in style to *The Curse of Peladon* — the only other third Doctor story to feature no location-filmed sequences — and was made by many of the same team, including director Lennie Mayne and set designer Gloria Clayton. Actors Alan Bennion and Sonny Caldinez returned as usual to play the Ice Warrior commander and his deputy, and all the stock Ice Warrior costumes were dusted off and reused, with just a few replacement parts being made from scratch.

'*The Curse of Peladon* was so popular that the BBC asked me to do a follow-up,' recalled writer Brian Hayles. 'It wasn't conceived as a saga, although it had the potential to develop that way as the planet had itself a history behind it, in my mind at least. I suppose, having written *The Curse of Peladon*, I thought it would be nice to repeat the formula, but didn't expect to be asked. But the BBC did ask me, so it was they who evolved the saga rather than me.'

Also in common with *The Curse of Peladon*, and with many other stories of this period, *The Monster of Peladon* reflected some contemporary issues of interest to the production team.

'We weren't making a direct comment on the real-life miners' strike,' says Terrance Dicks, 'but obviously that kind of issue was in the air, and one can't just do a kind of old imperial story where the Galactic Federation comes to Peladon and brings the simple natives the benefits of civilization, like *Sanders of the River*. We are all well aware now that what happens when an advanced race meets a primitive race is not always to the benefit of the primitives. So one has got the conflict between the different factions. Obviously the miners would resist the new technology as it wouldn't be what they were used to and they would be frightened by it, and it might put some of them out of work . . . Obviously the ruling establishment would try to latch onto the technology and see what benefits were going to come from civilization . . .

'I would say it is a kind of general liberal consensus that in any strike there are rights and wrongs on both sides. In *The Monster of Peladon*, the Chancellor wants to preserve the old ways and the leader of the miners wants to look after his people. The tragedy is that both sides think that they are totally right and that the others are totally wrong. The Doctor is very much someone who can step back and look at both arguments. The Doctor always plays that role.'

Sarah is given shelter from the Spiders by Neska (Jenny Laird), Sabor (Geoffrey Morris) and Arak (Gareth Hunt). *Planet of the Spiders*.

Jon Pertwee's swan-song as the Doctor was a six-part story, *Planet of the Spiders*, written by Barry Letts in collaboration with Robert Sloman — although Sloman again took the on-screen credit.

The story begins with Sarah being tipped off by Mike Yates about the activities of a group of people at a rural meditation centre where he has been staying since the events of *Invasion of the Dinosaurs*. Unknown to the abbot K'anpo Rimpoche and his deputy Cho-je, these people are misusing the meditation rituals in order to make contact with powerful alien forces — forces which eventually manifest themselves in the form of a giant spider. The spider is in fact an emissary from the ruling council on the planet Metebelis 3, sent to recover the blue crystal which the Doctor found there and gave to Jo Grant in the season ten story *The Green Death*. It is the influence of such crystals which has caused the spiders to grow in size and enabled them to dominate the human colonists in whose ship they were inadvertently transported to the planet.

The Doctor and Sarah journey to Metebelis 3 and assist the humans in an attempt to overthrow the spiders. They then escape back to Earth in the TARDIS. The Doctor recognizes K'anpo as his former Time Lord guru and, at his prompting, realizes that he himself must put matters to rights by going to face his fear. Returning to Metebelis 3, he learns that the humans' revolt has ultimately met with failure. He demands an audience with the Great One — a huge mutated spider which the others revere — and offers her the crystal, which has earlier been returned to him by Jo. The Great One uses it to complete a huge crystal lattice which she believes will increase her mental powers to infinity. Instead, the rising power kills her. The other spiders also die as their mountain is destroyed in the resulting explosion.

K'anpo has meanwhile been killed while

▲ The Doctor with his Time Lord mentor K'anpo (George Cormack). *Planet of the Spiders*.

▲ Queen Thalira (Nina Thomas). *The Monster of Peladon*.

MUSIC

*Apart from **Death to the Daleks**, all the incidental music for this season was supplied by Dudley Simpson.*

*As one of the main themes of **Death to the Daleks** was the absence of electrical power, director Michael E. Briant decided against using synthesized incidental music, opting instead for a score composed by Carey Blyton and performed by the London Saxophone Quartet.*

***Planet of the Spiders** also featured some stock music. 'Music From The Himalayas: The Living Tradition' by Lama Chhopa was used for the meditation chanting, and for the sequences in the theatre, tracks from 'Selection' by P. Gerard were used.*

The Spider council ▲ members die following the destruction of the Great One in the final episode of *Planet of the Spiders.*

The surface of Metebelis 3. ▲ *Planet of the Spiders.*

PRODUCTION UNIT MANAGER

*The post of production unit manager was created by the BBC around the end of 1974, and the first to be appointed to **Doctor Who** was George Gallaccio.*

'The idea,' says Gallaccio, 'was to lighten the load of the production assistants by shifting over some of the organizational and costing aspects of their job to this new position. There were only five of us to begin with. I remember our first meeting together when we just sat down in a room and tried to work out what a production unit manager was going to do. Nobody told us how to do it. We had to work it out from scratch.'

Their main function, as things transpired, was to oversee the budgeting and expenditure of the series to which they were assigned, liaising closely with the producer.

*Gallaccio's stint as PUM lasted from season eleven's **The Monster of Peladon** until season thirteen's **The Seeds of Doom**. He was succeeded first by Christopher D'Oyly John, who handled just one season, and then by John Nathan-Turner, who took over for the remainder of the decade.*

The Great One in her cavern on Metebelis 3. *Planet of the Spiders.*

protecting Yates from an attack by the spider-controlled residents of the meditation centre, only to be reborn in the form of Cho-je — his own future self. When the Doctor is brought back to UNIT HQ by the TARDIS, having been fatally injured by the radiation in the Great One's cave, K'anpo appears and helps him to regenerate. Sarah and the Brigadier watch in amazement as their friend enters into his fourth incarnation . . .

Planet of the Spiders was consciously conceived as a Buddhist parable which addressed the Doctor's thirst for knowledge — a subject upon which Barry Letts and Robert Sloman had first touched in *The Time Monster.* 'There is nothing wrong with the acquisition of knowledge in itself,' notes Letts, who not only co-wrote the story but also directed it. 'Indeed it is the goal of any being who travels along a path of meditation towards Enlightenment. What is wrong is having a greed for that knowledge, as greed presupposes a preoccupation with the self, the ego. We know that in the beginning the Doctor stole a TARDIS to satisfy his greed for knowledge, and in *The Green Death* he steals one of the blue crystals for precisely the same reason.

'The spiders represent the aspects of the ego — the false self with which we identify, including all the greed and the avarice, which causes us suffering in Buddhist terms. The individual spiders latch onto people like that, exteriorizing the ego. Then, at the end of the story, the Doctor goes right inside the blue mountain. That symbolizes him going right inside himself, even though he knows it will destroy him; just as somebody going right to the end of Zen is willing to allow himself to be destroyed, the false ego being destroyed to find the real Self. He knows he will be destroyed, but knows also that he will be regenerated.

'What he is going to find is the Great One — the core of egoism, the central motivator of our lives which wants to be in control of the world. The way it wants to do this is to increase the power of the thinking mind, as opposed to the experiencing mind. In other words, the mind is trying to become the Buddha, is trying to become the Uncreated, the Unborn, the Whole, which is impossible. If anyone tries it, ultimately they're going to destroy themselves. So the Doctor goes in, confronts this, and sees that it is an impossibility. In fact he warns the Great One in scientific terms that it is impossible. The old man is destroyed and the new man is regenerated. Yes, it was all a quite deliberate parallel.'

For the benefit of the cast and crew, Letts even prepared a glossary of Buddhist terms extracted from a book called *The Message of the Tibetans.*

The story required considerable ingenuity on the part of the Visual Effects Department in order to realize the giant spiders. Various versions were made, including static props, wire operated puppets and a motor driven model — affectionately nicknamed Boris — which could scuttle across the floor under its own power. At Letts's suggestion, a more traditional string-suspended puppet was also created for certain shots. The Great One had to be redesigned and a new model made when Letts rejected the first attempt as being too horrific.

CSO was used extensively for scenes set on Metebelis 3, and also for a sequence of the Whomobile flying through the air. Letts, however, found some of the shots of the Metebelis landscape and the spider city very unconvincing and decided to drop them. Mainly because of this, episode four under-ran and scenes originally planned for the start of episode five had to be moved forward to compensate. This created a knock-on problem which Letts eventually solved by having episode six begin with a very lengthy reprise from the end of episode five, with additional material intercut.

Planet of the Spiders brought season eleven to a close, its last episode being transmitted on 8 June 1974. It was also the last story on which Terrance Dicks was credited as script editor, his hand-over to Robert Holmes having now been completed. Barry Letts, however, would remain to oversee recording of the final story of the series' eleventh production block, which would be held over to form the opening story of season twelve on transmission. That story, written by Dicks as his first job on returning to freelance work, would usher in a whole new era for *Doctor Who* and introduce a fourth Doctor in the person of a relatively unknown actor called Tom Baker.

CHAPTER NINE

Who Was Tom Baker

T homas Stewart Baker was born on 20 January 1934 and brought up in the Scotland Road area of Liverpool. His mother was a devout Roman Catholic and his father a Jew who had worked in a biscuit factory before joining the Navy.

'I was always looking for a way out,' reflects Baker, 'but how was I to manage it? I was from a poor background: from a house with no books and parents with no experience of how to form one's life. Here was a young man desperate to make his mark, fantasizing and dreaming. Not clever at school. Rather overgrown and therefore odd to look at. "Good heavens! Is he only eleven? But he's six foot one!" people said. In addition, I was skinny and had a curved back because I could hardly ever stand up straight.'

When a monk came to his school, St Swithens, to talk about monasticism, this fired his interest. Consequently, after leaving school at the age of 15 and working briefly as a waiter in Liverpool's Adelphi Hotel, he went to Jersey to join an order called the Brothers of Ploermel. Later he moved to Shropshire in England for his novitiate.

Baker followed the monastic life for six years before deciding at the age of 21 that it was not for him. He then found himself called up for National Service. He joined the Army's medical corps, and it was in this that he was able to rediscover his love of the performing arts.

'I had acted at school and had been offered a job at the Abbey Theatre in Dublin when I was 15, but my mother wouldn't let me go. But now I decided, "This is what I want to do." I've had some terrible moments of depression and sometimes I've felt really isolated and lost, but I've never wavered from that feeling.'

Upon leaving the Army, Baker obtained a drama scholarship from Liverpool. Before pursuing this, however, he joined the Merchant Navy and sailed on the Queen Mary for seven months. He eventually enrolled at the Rose Bruford Drama School in south-east London and his first professional job was reading poetry in a Soho coffee bar called the Partisan. Towards the end of the fifties he began to work with repertory companies around

◀ Tom Baker in uncharacteristically dapper attire.

THE FILMS OF TOM BAKER

The Winter's Tale (1966) (released 1968); ***Nicholas and Alexandra*** (1971); ***The Canterbury Tales*** (Italian title: ***I Racconti Di Canterbury***) (1971); ***Dear Parents*** (Italian title: ***Cari Genitori***) (1973); ***Vault of Horror*** (1973); ***The Golden Voyage Of Sinbad*** (1973); ***Luther*** (1973) (released 1976); ***The Mutations*** (1973); ***Frankenstein: The True Story*** (TV movie) (1973); ***The Zany Adventures Of Robin Hood*** (TV movie) (1984).

All films in colour.

Tom Baker at his first ▶ photocall after being announced as the fourth Doctor poses with Elisabeth Sladen and, in a Cyberman costume, Pat Gorman.

SELECTED TV APPEARANCES

Dixon Of Dock Green: The Attack (BBC 1968); *Market In Honey Lane: The Matchmakers* (ATV 1968); *George And The Dragon* (ATV 1968); *Dixon Of Dock Green: Number 13* (BBC 1968); *Softly, Softly: Task Force: Like Any Other Friday* (BBC 1970); *The Millionairess* (BBC 1973); *Arthur Of The Britons: Go Warily* (HTV 1973); *The Author Of Beltraffio* (BBC 1974); *Doctor Who* (BBC 1974–1981); *Read All About It* (BBC 1976); *Nationwide* (BBC 1976/1978/ 1980); *The Lively Arts: Whose Doctor Who* (BBC 1977); *The Multicoloured Swap Shop* (BBC, 1978); *Pebble Mill At One* (BBC 1979); *The Curse Of King Tut's Tomb* (HTV/Columbia TV film 1980); *The Book Tower* (Yorkshire 1977–1980); *The Hound Of The Baskervilles* (BBC 1982); *Jemima Shore Investigates: Doctor Zeigler's Casebook* (Thames 1983); *Remington Steele: Hounded Steele* (1984); *Under The Same Sky* (Thames 1984); *Jackanory* (BBC 1985); *Blackadder II: Potato* (BBC 1986); *The Life And Loves Of A She-Devil* (BBC 1986); *The Kenny Everett Show* (BBC 1986); *Boom!* (Channel 4 1989); *Hyperland* (BBC 1990); *The Chronicles Of Narnia: The Silver Chair* (BBC 1990); *Selling Hitler* (Euston Films 1991); *The Law Lord* (BBC 1991); *Medics* (Granada 1991–); *Cluedo* (ITV 1992); *Doctor Who: Dimensions In Time* (BBC 1993).

Tom Baker as the artist ▶ Moore in the film *Vault of Horror* (1974). This still was used by the film's designer as the basis of a 'self portrait' of the artist required to be seen during the action.

Britain, taking roles in numerous different productions.

It wasn't until the late sixties, at the age of 34, that his first big break came whilst appearing in a revue called *Late Night Lowther* — Lowther being the name of the pub in York where it was staged. Baker was

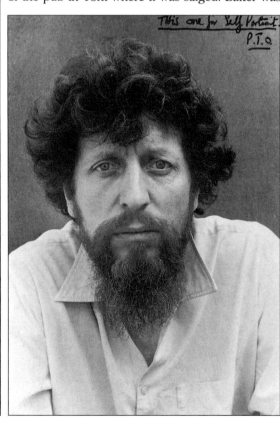

playing a dog called Clint in a sketch alongside Laurie Taylor impersonating the game show host Hughie Green, and was spotted by a talent scout from the National Theatre. He was subsequently interviewed by Lord Olivier and offered a job with the company, playing a horse called Rozinante in *The Trials of Sancho Panza* in 1968.

Lord Olivier liked Baker, and in 1970 got him an audition for the role of Rasputin in the film *Nicholas and Alexandra*.

'The film was made in Spain,' recalls Baker, 'at a time when I was in two plays at the National and rehearsing a third. I was shuttled back and forth to Spain to film my bits. I was whisked about in limousines and first-class plane seats. It was heady stuff. I was asked, "How does a working-class boy like you adjust to an air-conditioned Cadillac?" I replied, "Terribly easily." '

His performance having been very well-received, the actor subsequently went on a publicity tour of the USA to promote the film.

Baker had already appeared in one film prior to his role in *Nicholas and Alexandra*. This was *The Winter's Tale*, a record of an Edinburgh Festival stage production of the William Shakespeare play. Although made in 1966, the film was eventually released in 1968, in which year Baker also made his television debut with an appearance in an episode of *Dixon of Dock Green* called *The Attack*. Shortly after this he had a role in the series *Market in Honey Lane*, in an episode called *The Matchmakers* — reportedly one of the first major TV exposures of cockney rhyming slang. This was followed by parts in *George and the Dragon*, another episode of *Dixon of Dock Green* and *Softly, Softly: Task Force*.

'Concomitant with being an actor,' notes Baker, 'is that dreadful, exhausting state of being self-aware all the time, because you're marketing your appearance, you're marketing what you sound like. You're worried about whether you're ugly or going bald or getting fat. You're worried about dental bills or worried that no one wants you. In other words you are ill. To want to be an actor, especially these days, is to be ill. It's a kind of illness — this terrible pernicious itch to want what threatens you most, which is insecurity. Performers, like other people, are mesmerized by what threatens them most. They have to learn to love it and live with it and create out of it.

'Performers create out of anxiety, they don't create out of jolliness or a happy song. They have to exorcize the most terrible memories of the last effort, to forget past failures and hope all the time

As Prince Koura in the film *The Golden Voyage of Sinbad* (1973).

that they're going to please someone. Actors are just professional pleasers, like waiters!'

The early seventies were busy years for Baker as, on top of his occasional TV appearances, he gained work in several more films. These included Pasolini's *The Canterbury Tales* (1971), the Italian/French production *Dear Parents* (1973), the horror anthology *Vault of Horror* (1973) in which he played an artist called Moore in the 'Drawn and Quartered' segment, and the fantasy film *The Golden Voyage of Sinbad* (1973) portraying the evil Prince Koura.

His work for the National Theatre continued, too, and saw him taking roles in *The Merchant of Venice* (playing the Prince of Morocco in a production directed by Jonathan Miller), *The Idiot*, *The National Health* and *A Woman Killed with Kindness* during his two-and-a-half year stint with the company. Later he played leading parts at the Bristol Old Vic, received excellent reviews for his performance in *The Novelist* at the Hampstead Theatre Club and, in 1973, won the title role in *Macbeth* at the Shaw Theatre.

Also in 1973, Baker was cast as Pope Leo X in the film *Luther*, but his part was cut from some versions of the finished release. More successful was a horror film called *The Mutations* in which he co-starred with Donald Pleasance, playing a carnival freak called Lynch. The make-up for this

▲ The actor at an autograph signing at Windsor. One of many he took part in during his time as the Doctor.

DOCTOR WHO IS ON THE MOVE AGAIN

Talking to Tom Baker is an extraordinary experience. The eyes mesmerize and the voice enchants. Not only is he interesting, but he sounds so interested that he makes an exceptional listener too.

Sometimes his talk is so honest it has the shock of the confessional: 'I had a very religious mother, and I went to mass 21 times a week when I was a boy.' Attending constant funerals as an altar boy, he discovered a 'capacity to grieve. Of course, one never had breakfast, because one wasn't allowed to eat before communion, and I was standing by the graveside and it was so cold I began to weep as the old lady was lowered. We used to get a three-penny bit afterwards, but a man came over, squeezed my arm, and gave me a two-shilling piece, which confounded me. And it suddenly clanged in my little head – already rapacity was rearing at the age of eight – that he thought I was crying for his mother.'

In wartime Liverpool he was desolate because his house was left intact: 'All the children whose houses had been bombed were getting games from America with 'Greetings!' from the President. I prayed that my mother would be murdered on her way back from the pub where she worked. They'd have noticed me then. Odd, really, considering how much I loved her.'

Returning home many years later he found his parents dying in separate rooms, not having spoken for seven years. Knowing how hard his mother worked as a char to send him a few pounds when he was a student, he leaned over her guiltily to ask if there was anything she wanted: 'Yes,' she whispered, 'to outlive that old goat in the next room.' But she did not. 'When my brother told him the news, my father wept for all those wasted years, all that silence; wept and wept ... I felt sorry for him.'

From an article by Daniel Farson in Telegraph **Sunday Magazine in 1980.**

As the evil Prince Koura in the epic *The Golden Voyage of Sinbad* (1973) – a performance which convinced *Doctor Who* producer Barry Letts that Baker was the ideal choice for the role of the fourth Doctor.

took an hour to put on each day and by a strange coincidence the costume included a long scarf and a floppy hat, both of which were to become trademarks of the fourth Doctor — a part that the actor was offered very shortly afterwards.

Despite a number of recent roles — including that of a sea captain in a TV movie entitled *Frankenstein: The True Story* — Baker was down on his luck at the point when he was chosen to succeed Jon Pertwee as the Doctor. Three films in which he had landed major roles — *Isabella of Spain* with Glenda Jackson, *Three Men Went to War* with Ian McKellen and Anthony Quinn and *Jackson's War* with Richard Harris — had all been cancelled within six weeks of each other due to lack of funding, and for the past two months he had been working on a building site as a hod-carrier and tea-maker.

'I was desperately out of work and was terribly depressed by this. Suddenly, along came the possibility of playing Doctor Who. It was just a relief to play a major part!

'I was working very hard on a building site in Ebury Street, next door but one to where Mozart wrote his first symphony, when I got the job. The builders were actually very good to me and I have a happy memory of that, but of course I didn't want to be on a building site, because I hadn't much skill. I wanted to be an actor.

'When I got the part I had this feeling of just huge relief, and also one of great pride. I didn't tell my workmates I'd got the job. I had the day off and went to the BBC and then it was in the first edition of the *Evening Standard.* I knew they all took that paper — and bang, all was revealed! So there they were, looking over the tops of their papers at me. It was a great moment of pleasure. They were very proud of me — and I was very proud of them.'

Shortly after he was cast in *Doctor Who*, Baker also won the role of Mark Ambient in a BBC adaptation of *The Author of Beltraffio*, and this was to be just the first of a number of additional projects that he would undertake during his record seven-year stint as the Doctor.

In 1976, he appeared in a season of plays at the Library Theatre in Scarborough. His roles included Richard the Diplomat in Noel Coward's *Hay Fever*, Black Will in *Arden of Faversham*, an old man in David Bradley's *Boat in the Backyard* and Alphonse Silkenhand in Carl Stenheim's *The Strongbox.* The same year, he also lent his vocal talents to two LP records released by Decca on the Argo label. The first was a new *Doctor Who* adventure called *Doctor Who and the Pescatons*, while the second was an adaptation of Jules Verne's *Journey to the Centre of the Earth*. Decca were particularly pleased with the success of the *Doctor Who* release and wanted to do a follow-up, but Baker was less enthusiastic and the idea was eventually dropped. The actor had given all his earnings from the first record to a charity for spastic children.

1976 also saw Baker writing three showbusiness-type review columns for *The Times* (3 April, 5 June and 2 October editions), recording a radio drama by George Mikes called *Mortal Passion* and appearing as a guest reviewer on Melvyn Bragg's book programme *Read All About It*.

Spin-offs from the *Doctor Who* series included the aforementioned *Pescatons* record and, the year before, a nine-month stint writing a column in the weekly *Reveille* newspaper. In 1977, Baker, together with co-star Ian Marter and friend and producer James Hill, put together a script for a proposed *Doctor Who* film called *Doctor Who meets Scratchman*. The suggestion was that Vincent Price might play the Scratchman, or Devil, of the title, and that Twiggy might appear alongside Marter as companions to Baker's Doctor. Lanzarote was mooted as a possible location for the filming. Later, the title was changed to *Doctor Who and the Big Game* and the proposed location switched to Australia. Despite a great deal of work being put into it, lack of adequate finance meant that the project never got past the script stage.

From 1977 until 1980, Baker was the regular host of *The Book Tower*, a children's book review series for Yorkshire Television which he very much enjoyed making as he was a great lover of literature. In 1979, he also appeared as Hassan in the HTV/Columbia TV movie *The Curse of King Tut's Tomb*, although many of his scenes were lost in editing.

'It was in the works for months before,' he says of his departure from the programme in 1981. 'I struggled with all the arguments for and against staying, but seven years is a long time. I'd given the show all I felt I could give it, but I loved it so much that in other ways I didn't want ever to go.'

Not long after he had left *Doctor Who*, Baker was back on the nation's TV screens as Sherlock Holmes in a 1982 BBC production of Sir Arthur Conan-Doyle's *The Hound of the Baskervilles*. During the mid-eighties, though, typecasting from his success as the Doctor restricted his TV work to occasional appearances in shows as diverse as Thames TV's *Jemima Shaw Investigates* and the BBC's *Jackanory*, for which he read *The Iron Man*.

Tom Baker and Lalla Ward outside the registry office where they married on 13 December 1980. The marriage proved to be short-lived.

Blackadder II: Potato saw him playing an insane sea captain, and he appeared in *The Life and Loves of a She-Devil* as Father Ferguson, a cleric who is seduced by the She-Devil. He even made a guest appearance on *The Kenny Everett Show*.

In 1983, when the BBC decided to make a special *Doctor Who* story to celebrate the series' twentieth anniversary, Baker declined to take part.

'That was a decision I had to think long and hard about. The original plan was to have me with Lis Sladen and have us all come together at the end. I finally decided I wouldn't do it because I simply couldn't face the prospect of going back. It was too close to my leaving really, and I was very impatient. I didn't want to be seen with either new Doctors or old Doctors. In my own mind, I was the most recent. It was simply that I felt there was a danger that it could be very competitive. I felt it would just be a novelty scheme and I wasn't interested in novelty at the time. I was looking for good drama.'

In the end, Baker's appearance in *The Five Doctors* was restricted to a few clips from the story *Shada*, which had been left part-completed in 1979 due to a strike at the BBC.

Baker had found success playing the Doctor, and he carried this with him onto the stage, giving a series of critically acclaimed performances in *The Doctor's Dilemma* (1984), *She Stoops to Conquer* (1984) and *An Inspector Calls* (1987). He

▲ With co-star Sheila Allen in a publicity shot for a 1973 production of *Macbeth*.

▲ A 1990s publicity shot of Tom Baker.

▲ With Mary Tamm as Romana and K-9 in season sixteen of *Doctor Who*. Baker is wearing a plaster on his upper lip as he has been bitten by a dog.

With his trademark ▲ hat and scarf at another personal appearance during his time as the Doctor.

A publicity shot for the ▲ film *Nicholas and Alexandra* (1971), in which he played the monk Rasputin.

Tom Baker signs an autograph for one of the winners of a 'Design a Monster' competition.

also appeared in *Treasure Island* (1981), *Educating Rita* (1982), *Hedda Gabler* (1982) and, playing both Sherlock Holmes and Moriarty, *The Mask of Moriarty* (1985).

By the close of the eighties, Baker had begun to shake off his typecasting and gain regular TV work once more. In 1990 he played Puddleglum the Marsh Wiggle in an adaptation of C.S. Lewis's *The Silver Chair* — one of the BBC's *The Chronicles of Narnia* series. This was followed by parts in Euston Films' *Selling Hitler* and the BBC's *The Law Lord* and a regular role as Professor Hoyt in the Granada series *Medics*. In 1992 he appeared as Professor Plum in the ITV quiz programme *Cluedo*, which was similar in concept to the *Whodunnit?* show hosted by Jon Pertwee in the seventies.

Throughout the eighties and early nineties, Baker frequently provided voice-overs for commercials and corporate video projects. He also worked on a number of radio productions, including BBC Radio 4's *The Adventures of Lionel Nimrod* (1992), *The Genie and the Playwright* (1993) and *Lionel Nimrod's Inexplicable World* (1993).

The actor also appeared in two *Doctor Who*-related videos from Reeltime Pictures. The first was *Myth Makers 17: Tom Baker — The Fourth Doctor,* a 1989 interview tape in which he talked about his time as the Doctor. The second, a 1991 release called *Who on Earth is Tom Baker?*, was a far more personal look at his life, taking the format of Tom Baker talking to Tom Baker about Tom Baker. Other *Doctor Who*-related projects included narrating three of the BBC Audio Collection's Missing Stories cassettes, *The Evil of the Daleks* (1992), *The Power of the Daleks* (1993) and *Fury from the Deep* (1993), and presenting two 1992 BBC Video releases, one a compilation of the incomplete footage from *Shada* and the other a selection of clips from all the stories of his era under the title *The Tom Baker Years*. Finally, in 1993, Baker made a return appearance as the Doctor in *Dimensions in Time*, the two-part *Doctor Who*

skit produced for the Children in Need charity appeal.

During his long career, Baker has managed for the most part to keep his private life out of the public eye. On 26 April 1961 he married Anna Wheatcroft — the daughter of Alfred Wheatcroft, brother of the famous rose-grower Harry Wheatcroft — whom he had known since they were fellow students at drama school. They had two sons — Daniel born in 1961 and Piers in 1966 — but were divorced in 1966. In the late seventies, while working on *Doctor Who*, he had a relationship with a BBC designer, but the Corporation encouraged them to keep this quiet. More publicly chronicled was his marriage on 13 December 1980 to Lalla Ward, following her appearance in *Doctor Who* as Romana.

'We were incredibly aware of each other from the very first moment when Lalla joined the show,' Baker admits. 'She was in one story with me, then I went away during a break in the series. We came back to work together again and it happened. We fell in love. I realized after she left the programme I couldn't envisage living without her.'

The marriage lasted about 16 months and ended in separation and a second divorce. More recently Baker has married again, to television director and former actress Sue Jerrard.

'I wouldn't say I'm close to my children. I wouldn't say I'm close to anyone, except my wife. I don't have much capacity for friendship because of my self-centredness. I'm not generous enough to give to individuals. These things are heightened in actors when you are thinking about yourself all the time and worrying about where the next round of applause is coming from.

'I've lost my religion and sometimes I think I've lost everything in life because I'm a great betrayer. The title of my autobiography is going to be *All Friends Betrayed.* That's made me more anxious to hold onto my dear wife. I used to be very fragmented, and I do need to be adored. I feel this overriding security in her affection; she reassures me constantly. Now that I've located admiration, I'm hanging onto it for grim death.'

In many respects Tom Baker is the most enigmatic of all the actors to have played the Doctor. He can be both outgoing and intensely private. He has a wicked sense of humour which can both disarm and disorientate those who encounter it, leaving them unsure what to make of him.

One thing that is certain is that Tom Baker's contribution to *Doctor Who* was one of the greatest boosts the series ever received.

CHAPTER TEN

The Fourth Doctor: Bohemian Eccentric

Many of the fourth Doctor's characteristic traits are established during the course of his debut adventure, *Robot*, in which he quickly demonstrates that his style and demeanour are to be markedly different from those of his predecessor.

Whereas the third Doctor was the epitome of seventies elegance in his velvet smoking jackets, bow ties and frilly shirts, the fourth takes on the look of a slightly down-at-heel bohemian eccentric with a baggy jacket, broad-brimmed hat and long, trailing scarf. And whereas the popular image of the former was that of a dashing man of action, often using Venusian aikido — his own brand of unarmed combat — to tackle his enemies physically, the latter is introduced as someone whose preferred approach to problems is contemplation rather than action. On the rare occasions in *Robot* when he does become involved in violent confrontation, he seems to come out the winner almost without trying to, his opponents falling over him or tripping over his scarf.

In contrast to his predecessor's upright bearing is the new Doctor's tendency to sprawl or perch in unconventional positions. At one point, he even lies down for a short nap on his laboratory workbench at UNIT HQ. Like his second incarnation, he often appears oblivious to what is going on around him, or else preoccupied with child-like pursuits such as building a tower out of pieces of bric-a-brac, but this is merely a facade to disguise the fact that he is actually deep in concentration.

In common with all his previous incarnations, the fourth Doctor has a great regard for the

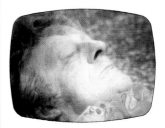
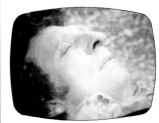

▲ **The Doctor's regeneration was achieved by recording Jon Pertwee first, then the videotape was rewound and Tom Baker changed places with Pertwee so that the images of their faces could be mixed seamlessly together. This was done on 2 April 1974.** *Planet of the Spiders.*

◄ **The fourth Doctor in his original costume as seen in season twelve.**

The Doctor in Highland ▲ garb in the season thirteen story *Terror of the Zygons.*

The fourth Doctor in ▲ cheerful mood. *Genesis of the Daleks.*

Tom Baker, Ian Marter ▶ (a fellow newcomer cast as companion Harry Sullivan) and Elisabeth Sladen pose for a publicity shot in Bessie.

The Brigadier and Sarah with the newly regenerated Doctor in the UNIT laboratory. *Robot.*

human race, as is highlighted in remarks he makes during his second adventure, *The Ark in Space,* on discovering a group of people in suspended

animation aboard an orbiting space-station after the apparent destruction of all life on Earth:

'Homo sapiens — what an inventive, invincible species. It's only a few million years since they crawled up out of the mud and learned to walk, puny defenceless bipeds. They've survived flood, famine and plague. They've survived cosmic wars and holocausts. And now here they are, out among the stars, waiting to begin a new life, ready to outsit eternity. They're indomitable . . . indomitable.'

This Doctor's attachment to Earth is, on the other hand, by no means as strong as his predecessor's. His first instinct on recovering from his regeneration at UNIT HQ is to make for the TARDIS and resume his journeys through time and space, and only some quick talking by journalist Sarah Jane Smith succeeds in detaining him long enough to arouse his interest in the latest crisis being faced by Brigadier Lethbridge-Stewart. As soon as the crisis is over, he is anxious to be on his way again:

DOCTOR: How about a little trip in the TARDIS? I'm just off.

SARAH: You can't just go!

DOCTOR: Why not? It's a free cosmos.

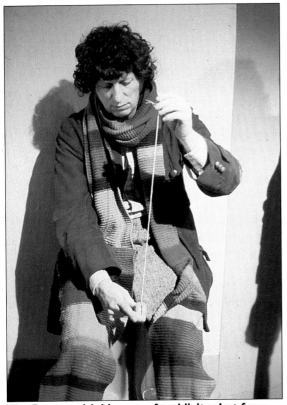

The Doctor with his yo-yo. A publicity shot from *Genesis of the Daleks*.

The Doctor visits Victorian London and adopts a suitable period attire. *The Talons of Weng-Chiang*.

▲ The Doctor searches for the third segment of the Key to Time in season sixteen's *The Stones of Blood*.

▲ A behind the scenes shot taken during the making of the season thirteen story *Terror of the Zygons*.

SARAH: The Brigadier . . .

DOCTOR: The Brigadier wants me to address the Cabinet, have lunch at Downing Street, dinner at the Palace and write 17 reports in triplicate. Well I won't do it! I won't, I won't, I won't!

Clearly this Doctor will never be content to remain at UNIT as their resident scientific adviser, and indeed he becomes increasingly reluctant to return there after each new journey in the TARDIS. When, in *Pyramids of Mars*, Sarah chides him on his pensive mood, reasoning that he should be happy to be going back to Earth, he tells her:

'The Earth isn't my home, Sarah. I'm a Time Lord . . . You don't understand the implications. I'm not a human being. I walk in eternity . . . It means I've lived for something like 750 years.'

Later in the same story, his alien nature is graphically illustrated by the cool detachment he shows on learning of the death of Edwardian scientist Laurence Scarman at the hands of his deceased brother, Professor Marcus Scarman, whose corpse has been possessed by the evil Sutekh:

SARAH: Sometimes you don't seem —

DOCTOR: Human . . . ?

SARAH: A man has just been murdered!

DOCTOR: Four men, Sarah. Five, if you include Professor Scarman himself. And they may be the first of millions unless Sutekh is stopped. 'Know thine enemy.' Admirable advice.

The Doctor has always been unpredictable, however, and his character changes and develops as his fourth incarnation progresses. While his thoughtful side remains apparent — one particularly notable example of this being an incident in *Genesis of the Daleks* in which he questions his right to destroy the Dalek race at birth — he gradually reverts towards the more physical approach to problems which he took during his third incarnation. In *The Seeds of Doom* he is seen to assault several of his adversaries, breaking a chair over the head of one of them, and even to wield a revolver; in *The Masque of Mandragora* he at one point lashes out with his feet to try to avoid capture and also takes part in a sword fight, as he does again in *The Androids of Tara*; and *The Deadly Assassin* and *The Talons of Weng-Chiang* provide further examples of him engaging his enemies in violent combat.

When he does employ such forceful tactics, however, it is almost always because he or one of his friends is under threat or in imminent danger.

Tom Baker with Dalek ▲ creator Terry Nation in a publicity shot intended for inclusion in the *Radio Times* with an article publicising *Genesis of the Daleks*. In the event, the article appeared only in some regional editions of the magazine.

The fourth Doctor in ▲ (from the top) *The Talons of Weng-Chiang, Image of the Fendahl* and, with Lady Adrasta (Myra Frances), *The Creature from the Pit.*

The Doctor with his ▶ faithful TARDIS. *The Stones of Blood.*

For the most part he shows a clear disposition towards reaching peaceful solutions; and he is unquestionably committed to preserving life wherever possible. He forbids his companion Leela from using poisonous janus thorns on her enemies, and chastises her for her tendency to rely on her hunting knife to get her out of difficult situations. He also shows a similar disapproval of violent behaviour by others — for example, private eye Duggan's propensity for throwing punches in *City of Death* (although ironically it is with one such punch that Duggan saves the day at the end of the adventure).

Although still essentially a hero, the fourth Doctor is a complex and fallible one. He can be irascible and moody, and his motives are sometimes obscure. The most striking example of this is to be found in *The Invasion of Time*, when he appears to aid the Vardans in an invasion of his home planet Gallifrey, acting in a brusque, overbearing and sometimes even irrational manner in order to conceal from the telepathic aliens his true motive of luring them into a trap.

This tendency towards deception and his wealth of knowledge and past experience are balanced, however, by a quality of naive innocence which makes him unwilling to think ill of any person or creature until presented with hard — and often painful — evidence of their villainy. Often he will

walk nonchalantly into a situation, introducing himself with a broad grin, only to find himself attacked or taken prisoner.

Perhaps the most significant shift in the Doctor's character during his fourth incarnation is his growing inclination to resort to tomfoolery to confuse and outmanoeuvre his enemies, accompanied by his adoption of a generally more outrageous and amusing disposition. His brooding, contemplative moods come to be offset by bursts of manic activity and he starts to assail his opponents with flippant retorts and cheeky wise-cracks.

These traits are brought to the fore when he is joined on his travels by a female Time Lord named Romana — and especially so after she regenerates into her more compatible second incarnation. There is an obvious rapport between the two, and their conversation is generally witty and sophisticated. There is at times even a hint of playful surrealism about their badinage, such as in the following instance as they prepare to descend from the top of the Eiffel Tower in *City of Death*:

ROMANA: Shall we take the lift, or fly?

DOCTOR: Let's not be ostentatious.

ROMANA: All right, let's fly then.

DOCTOR: That would be silly. We'll take the lift.

This seemingly humorous exchange is given added significance by a later incident in which the pair, having returned to the top of the Eiffel Tower, are then seen back on the ground again only moments later, so that it appears the only way they could have got down so quickly is indeed to have flown!

It is only in his last few adventures that the Doctor loses some of his usual carefree good humour and assumes a more serious, brooding demeanour; a relatively short-lived state of foreboding which portends his eventual regeneration.

All the aforementioned qualities and attributes combine to give the fourth Doctor a uniquely zany, off-the-wall personality. He is also a highly recognizable figure with his imposing stature, his outlandish attire, his dark curly hair, his broad toothy grin and his rich booming voice. For many viewers, this image of the Doctor — an extraordinary, wild-eyed man with an incredibly long scarf, attempting tricks with a yo-yo or gleefully proffering a bag of jelly babies — remains the most instantly memorable, eclipsing those of his predecessors and successors and arguably making him the most popular Time Lord of them all.

CHAPTER ELEVEN

Season Twelve: Something Old, Something New

It was Barry Letts who had the principal responsibility for choosing an actor to succeed Jon Pertwee in the role of the Doctor. One name he considered was that of 39-year-old comedian and former pop singer Jim Dale, well known for his appearances in the *Carry On* films. On the whole, though, he favoured casting someone rather older. Amongst those he considered possible were: Richard Hearne, whom he quickly discounted as the actor was set on the idea of play-

ing the part in the style of the popular Mister Pastry character he had created in the forties; Michael Bentine, who was quite keen to take the role but was ruled out on the grounds that he would be unhappy working on a series without being able to contribute to the scripting; and Graham Crowden, who was also quite enthusiastic but ultimately decided that he would not want to make such a long-term commitment to one project. A hot favourite eventually emerged in the person of Fulton Mackay, who had previously appeared as Dr Quinn in the

SEASONTWELVE	
CODE	TITLE
4A	ROBOT
4C	THE ARK IN SPACE
4B	THE SONTARAN EXPERIMENT
4E	GENESIS OF THE DALEKS
4D	REVENGE OF THE CYBERMEN

RATINGS

Figures in millions

Story code	Figure
4A	10
4C	11
4B	10.5
4E	9.5
4D	9

◀ **The Brigadier, Harry and the Doctor. Robot.**

THE SLIT SCAN PROCESS

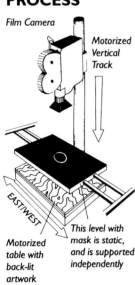

Film Camera

Motorized Vertical Track

EAST/WEST

Motorized table with back-lit artwork

This level with mask is static, and is supported independently

The camera tracks with the shutter locked on one frame of film. As the camera tracks either towards or away from the slot, the back-lit artwork travels laterally so that the colour or pattern passes behind the slot.

The next frame is exposed using the same procedure except that the artwork table starts its move in a slightly different position.

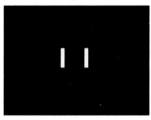

MASK

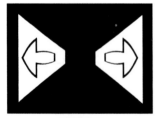

EFFECT

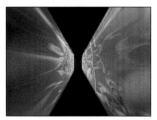

FINISHED IMAGE

season seven story *Doctor Who and the Silurians*, but still Letts remained undecided.

Many ideas were considered for the image of the new Doctor, including having him look like Albert Einstein and play a violin in the manner of Sherlock Holmes to emphasize his eccentricity.

'All of us who were involved in the casting,' says Letts, 'wanted a Doctor who would be radically different from Jon Pertwee's style of portrayal. It was no good just turning out a carbon copy as that would have given the audience the impression that the new Doctor was a watered down version of the previous one, and that would have been unfair to Jon's successor.'

While Letts was still searching for someone to fill the role, time was marching on and writers had to be briefed to start work on scripts for the fourth Doctor's initial run of stories. In view of the possibility that the part would eventually go to an actor of advanced years who would be unable to cope with strenuous physical action, the production team decided to introduce a new young male companion to undertake any 'rough stuff' which might be called for. So was born the character of UNIT's Surgeon-Lieutenant Harry Sullivan (apparently originally to have been called Harry Sweetman), who would be summoned to treat the Doctor in the aftermath of his regeneration. For this part Letts chose actor Ian Marter, whom he had cast as another naval character, First Officer John Andrews, in *Carnival of Monsters* and had earlier seen at audition for the role of Captain Mike Yates.

With time running short to decide on a new Doctor, Letts received inspiration from another source:

'Eventually it was my head of department, Bill Slater, who suggested Tom Baker. He'd directed him in a television version of Shaw's *The Millionairess*.

'Bill introduced me to him in the BBC Club at the Television Centre the following lunchtime and I felt at once that I'd found what I was looking for: a larger-than-life, eccentric, likeable character who commanded attention. But could he act? I knew he'd been at the National, and in the film of *Nicholas and Alexandra* playing Rasputin, but I'd never actually seen him.

'Tom solved the problem. Playing at Victoria was his latest film, *The Golden Voyage of Sinbad*. I went back to the office and said to Terrance, "Come on, we're going to the pictures."

'I was so impressed by what I saw that I rang Tom straight away and offered him the part.'

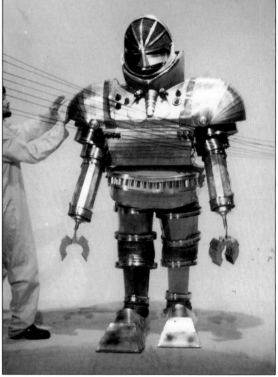

Costume designer James Acheson sets up a shot of the Robot (Michael Kilgarriff) bringing down some power cables against a yellow CSO backdrop. *Robot.*

As Baker recalls, it was his friendship with Slater's wife, Mary Webster, which led to his name initially being put forward to Letts, after he had written to the BBC seeking work.

With Baker cast as the Doctor, the next step was to decide exactly how he should approach the part. He initially had few ideas of his own, and was happy to be guided by Barry Letts and the series' new script editor, Robert Holmes.

'We had a meeting in the Balzac restaurant in Shepherd's Bush,' says Letts. 'There was Tom, Philip Hinchcliffe, Bob Holmes and me. This was before Philip took over from me as producer. We discussed the way Tom was going to play the Doctor. The floppy hat and so on was Tom's idea stemming from me saying that the one thing he mustn't be was a dandy, as Jon had played him that way. And what came out of that conference was fed back to costume designer Jim Acheson.'

'The production team kept saying that they wanted a new image for the Doctor,' recalls Acheson. 'So what I did was to spend a lot of time with Tom Baker and have what we call stock fittings, where one takes the actor to a costume house and tries all sorts of different jackets and hats on him with the idea of building up an image.

'I seem to remember a fitting with Philip

The Doctor examines his new face on regaining conciousness after his regeneration. *Robot.*

Elisabeth Sladen, Alec Linstead (Jellicoe) and Patricia Maynard (Miss Winters) rehearse a scene with Michael Kilgarriff wearing a light-weight version of the Robot costume created especially for the rehearsals. *Robot.*

LOCATIONS

Robot
> BBC Training Centre,
> Wood Norton, Hereford
> and Worcester

The Ark in Space
> No location work

The Sontaran Experiment
> Hound Tor, Nr
> Manaton, Devon

Genesis of the Daleks
> Betchworth Quarry,
> Betchworth, Surrey

Revenge of the Cybermen
> Wookey Hole, Somerset

Hinchcliffe, and maybe the director Christopher Barry. I don't remember them having too much input really. I was left pretty much to my own devices to come up with something.

'The eventual costume was eccentric rather than flamboyant. Whereas Pertwee had been the sartorial, frilly, velvety, greying Doctor, Baker was this manic, scarecrow, slightly more dangerous Doctor. I don't know how the scarf happened really except that we decided we should have a scarf. There's a poster by Toulouse-Lautrec of a man with a big red scarf and a fedora, and I think one was probably unconsciously influenced by that.'

Acheson also recalled a distinctive multicoloured scarf which had been knitted for one his friends, the freelance prop maker Allister Bowtell, by a woman named Begonia Pope.

'I bought a pile of wool and gave it to this little lady in Putney, who I knew was a knitter, and said "Start knitting". When I went back to collect the scarf it was 20-feet long! This is a true story. When I got it round Tom Baker's neck, he liked the idea. I think we cut a few feet off it, but he used it as a prop; he tripped villains up with it. I seem to remember the first time Tom walked onto the set dressed in his outfit it was kind of well-liked. I always remember wanting him to wear a longer jacket to start with, which he did later on.'

Philip Hinchcliffe, although not involved in the casting of Tom Baker, had some quite firm ideas about the new Doctor's character:

'I discussed with Tom what we thought he could do with it. We discussed what he ought to look like. I also did a sort of crash course on *Doctor Who* — I hadn't really seen that much of it, although luckily I'd seen quite a lot of the Jon Pertwee stuff. That

was the first thing I did, in fact. Then I formulated a view of the character, which I suppose was partly from that tradition, and the Sydney Newman "cosmic hobo" phrase stuck in my mind. I'd read a fair bit of science fiction, not a lot, so I spent my preparation time reading further from writers and authors whom perhaps I knew about but had never really read. I read voraciously throughout the whole genre.

'I got really interested in all sorts of concepts. It was like suddenly discovering a really fascinating area which I had only vaguely known before. Bob Holmes already had a very good background and was very well-read. He also had the drop on me because he could remember a lot of old movies which I've never seen! So out of all that we formulated the character. I liked the idea of him being sort of bohemian.

'At the time, heroes were really going out of fashion. Your hero could be a little bit more vulnerable, a little bit more complex. So our Doctor wasn't quite the same moral authority. He was getting a little bit back to the first Doctor — he was irascible, unreliable, and humans were not quite sure whether they should trust him or not. But basically he was an heroic character. He was less powerfully heroic, though. He had to work a bit harder to get out of problems; and we gave him some pretty tough opposition, I think, so he couldn't just "with one bound" be free all the time!

'Tom kept going round saying "I'm not really human — how do I portray a 500-year-old Time Lord?" And I said "Olympian detachment, Tom. You're very good at Olympian detachment." So he used to quote this back at me. But basically, the Doctor is a human hero — we all identify with him so easily. He is the ultimate essence of human virtue. But at the same time, biographically as it were,

MUSIC

Dudley Simpson provided the incidental music for the first four stories of season twelve. For the fifth, Revenge of the Cybermen, director Michael E. Briant commissioned a score from composer Carey Blyton, but the end result proved disappointing to producer Philip Hinchcliffe, who decided to have it enhanced by Peter Howell at the BBC's Radiophonic Workshop.

The music heard by Sarah Jane as she is prepared for cryogenic freezing in The Ark in Space was an excerpt from 'Concerto Grosso Opus 3 Number 2' by Largo and played by the Academy of St. Martins in the Field.

RADIO TIMES

Season twelve marked a notable downturn in the amount of promotion that Doctor Who received in Radio Times. Its first episode failed to merit a front cover photograph – unlike each of the five Jon Pertwee seasons – and the small black-and-white illustrations which had previously accompanied the programme listings were phased out. The only major feature to appear – and then only in certain regional editions – was an interview with Terry Nation to publicize the start of Genesis of the Daleks. This reduced level of coverage would set a precedent for the remainder of the decade.

Sarah is held hostage ▲ by the Robot. Robot.

THE SIZZLAS

The small power boats featured in the Wookey Hole location filming for **Revenge of the Cybermen** *were experimental prototypes called Sizzla Boats, produced by a company called Dorhill Ltd. Contrary to what the production team had been told prior to filming, these proved very difficult to operate in a confined space and at low speeds. Elisabeth Sladen had to jump into the water at one point when the boat in which she was being filmed ran out of control, necessitating quick action by Terry Walsh to rescue her from the strong currents of the underground lake. Dorhill Ltd subsequently submitted a £250 charge for extra work carried out on the boats during filming, but the production team refused to pay. A lower sum was eventually agreed upon as a compromise.*

ALADDIN

Doctor Who *stuntman Terry Walsh, who often doubled for Jon Pertwee and later Tom Baker during potentially dangerous scenes, went one better by portraying the Doctor himself in a brief appearance during an hour-long production of the pantomime* **Aladdin** *transmitted on BBC1 at 4.14 pm on Christmas Eve 1974 – four days before season twelve began with the first episode of* **Robot.** *Also amongst the cast – which included numerous TV celebrities such as Peter Glaze, Don MacLean, Jan Hunt, Dana, Deryck Guyler, Richard Wattis, Derek Griffiths, Ed Stewart, Michael Aspel, the Goodies, Pan's People, Jack Warner and James Ellis – was Barrie Gosney playing a Dalek.*

he's got to be sort of non-human. So Tom was quite keen to get some of his "non-humanness" into it. Bob was as well, which is probably why, at times, we showed him being a bit detached.'

Another participant in the process of developing the new Doctor's character was Terrance Dicks, who had just handed over the script editor's job to Holmes and had been commissioned to write season twelve's opening story, *Robot.*

'There was very little to go on,' notes Dicks, 'except that I had actually met Tom Baker by then and talked to him, so I had some idea what he was like. I'd also been in on the casting of Tom before I wrote the script. Tom in the flesh does have a kind of loony scatter-brained quality, so I played on that very much. I also used the device, which can always be used in a new Doctor's first episode, that the regeneration is unstable. So he starts off being rather crazy and gradually quietens down and becomes more reasonable by the end of it. I thought, if they don't like that interpretation, or if Tom doesn't like it, they can always say "Well, he was a bit weird then but he's different now, he's stable." In fact I think they always kept quite a lot of that arbitrary erraticness with which I started him off.'

It was Holmes's idea to do a story about a robot, and Dicks then devised a plot which paid homage to the 1933 RKO film *King Kong.*

The newly-regenerated Doctor joins UNIT in an investigation into the theft of top secret plans and equipment from supposedly secure premises. He quickly realizes that the raids have been perpetrated by something distinctly non-human. It is Sarah Jane Smith who first meets the culprit: a massive robot invented by one Professor Kettlewell while he was working for Think Tank, an official body involved in developing emerging technologies. The robot has been reprogrammed on the orders of Miss Winters, director of Think Tank, and used to obtain the means for constructing a disintegrator gun with which the Scientific Reform Society — of which she is a leading member — can steal the computer codes controlling the nuclear weapons of the world's leading powers. In this way, the SRS hope to hold the world to ransom unless their demands for a purer way of life are met.

Kettlewell, although claiming no knowledge of the SRS's scheme, is actually a party to it, but is ultimately killed by his creation after he balks at Miss Winters's ruthlessness. The robot suffers an electronic mental breakdown upon killing its creator and tries to activate the nuclear weapons. Brigadier Lethbridge-Stewart then attempts to destroy it with the disintegrator gun, but this merely causes it to grow to gigantic proportions, following which it

goes on the rampage through the UNIT troops. The Doctor saves the day by destroying the behemoth with a virulent metal virus described in Kettlewell's notes.

Now fully recovered from the after-effects of his regeneration, the Doctor persuades Sarah and bemused UNIT medic Harry Sullivan to join him on a trip in the TARDIS.

Robot was the first Doctor Who story to be originated entirely on videotape, its location scenes being shot using portable outside broadcast equipment rather than the usual film cameras so as to facilitate the extensive CSO work required for the scenes where the robot grows to giant size. Its first studio session on 21 May 1974 was hit by industrial action, and the scenes attempted that day were later abandoned as being unsatisfactory. Studio recording was eventually carried out on 1–2 June and 6–7 June 1974, bringing to an end *Doctor Who's* eleventh production block. Editing and dubbing took place a little later, and the first episode was eventually transmitted on 28 December 1974.

The last element required to complete the story was another new title sequence, again designed by Bernard Lodge.

'The new producer, Philip Hinchcliffe, didn't want to spend a fortune on the titles,' says Lodge, 'and as the slit-scan version had been on for only a season he was happy for the same technique to be used again. He suggested including the police box as it had never been in the titles before, so we did that with a TARDIS-shaped slot. For the image behind the slot, I used a vacuum-formed plastic chrome material and bounced lights off it. We also reflected a pattern of black lines off it to add to the image.'

Save for this new sequence, and for the new Doctor himself, there was little in *Robot* to distinguish it from the *Doctor Who* to which viewers had become accustomed in recent years. It took place in near-contemporary England — the setting used for the majority of the Pertwee stories — and featured not only the Doctor's established companion, Sarah Jane Smith, but also the familiar characters of Brigadier Lethbridge-Stewart, Sergeant (now RSM) Benton and the UNIT organization. Barry Letts explains the thinking behind this:

'As the audience have not yet accepted the new Doctor, their sympathies are with the characters they know, and they are identifying with these characters as they react to the new and eccentric Doctor. The old characters — the Brigadier, Benton and Sarah — are there to reassure the viewing public that they are still watching *Doctor Who.*'

Sarah and the Doctor in the cryogenic chamber of Nerva Beacon – now better known as the Ark. On the right, a Wirrn lies dead, killed by a massive electric discharge. *The Ark in Space.*

▲ Vira (Wendy Williams) and Rogin (Richardson Morgan) in the Ark's shuttle craft. *The Ark in Space.*

▲ The model of the Ark under construction in the Visual Effects workshop.

This was a philosophy which was to underpin much of the rest of season twelve. Although it would follow the trend of the later Pertwee seasons by moving away from the tried-and-trusted UNIT set-up and into more unfamiliar territory, continued viewer reassurance would be provided by way of the inclusion of a succession of popular returning monsters.

Robot was the last story on which Letts received the producer's credit. By the time it went into studio, he was already well on the way to handing over the reigns to his successor Philip Hinchcliffe.

'*Planet of the Spiders* was far more my epitaph than *Robot*,' reflects Letts. 'I had far more input and directed it myself, and we said goodbye to Jon. With *Robot*, the main thing was to try to get a good exciting show for the first one of the new Doctor, so that I could hand the success over to Philip.'

The cross-over between the two producers was in fact a relatively lengthy one. Hinchcliffe had been trailing Letts for some weeks by the end of the eleventh production block, and Letts would remain on hand for the making of the first two stories of the twelfth, offering comment and advice. Moreover, all the scripts for season twelve had already been commissioned during Letts's time as producer, so his influence would continue to be felt.

A large part of the responsibility for shaping the new season, however, fell to new script editor Robert Holmes.

'Bob Holmes had quite a large influence,' confirms Hinchcliffe. 'He was very much anti-UNIT — he thought it was all rather silly, running around shooting at monsters. It had had its day.

'When I got there, they had already commissioned a Dalek story from Terry Nation and a Cyberman story from Gerry Davis. From Bob Baker and Dave Martin they had commissioned one about a Sontaran — which was a character that Bob himself had invented. Although none of those stories was completed — the Sontaran one had been written, and the Dalek one was half-written — they were on the go. Bob didn't like the idea of using the old monsters, but he was enough of a show-

◄ The Wirrn gain access to the shuttle craft. *The Ark in Space.*

Styre (Kevin Lindsay). ▲
The Sontaran Experiment.

Erak (Peter Walshe), Vural (Donald Douglas) and
Krans (Glynn Jones) are captured by Styre's robot.
The Sontaran Experiment.

Dr Who (Saturdays, BBC1) was once a fantasy adventure serial for children. Not any more though: in today's episode we saw the Doctor and his friends, lost in a corpse-strewn minefield, wrenching gas masks from the faces of dead soldiers in order to survive an attack by poison gas themselves, captured by Nazi-pattern storm-troopers and finally pursued through a foggy, nightmarish landscape by the the repulsive results of 'failed experiments in human genetics'.

It was brutal, violent and revolting – totally without point or plot – yet convincingly enough done to be really terrifying for many normal children, and to put some very nasty ideas into the heads of some of the growing number of disturbed ones.

Does the producer of this unpleasant effort really expect a not-too-bright child to know the difference between grim reality on the Falls Road or in Cambodia, and a jolly little Saturday romp with the Doctor? **Alison Duddington, London**

Philip Hinchcliffe, Producer, Dr Who, replies: Though I am sure that most of our audience realize they are watching fiction not fact, of course, ultimately, we have to rely upon parents in the home to decide whether a programme is suitable for their child. We do take great pains to ensure that we never depict any act of violence which could be dangerously copied by children. The episode to which Ms Duddington refers was the first of a six-part story, The Genesis of the Daleks, which, in fact, will be seen to adopt a clearly moral attitude towards senseless warfare.
From **Radio Times**

man to know that probably it was a safe bet to beef up the season.'

The next story in transmission sequence — although not the next to be recorded — was an exception to the rule, in that it featured no established monsters.

The story originally considered for this slot was one by Christopher Langley entitled *Space Station*, but this fell through and was formally written off on 17 June 1974. Its replacement, *The Ark in Space*, had started life as an outline commissioned by Terrance Dicks from the highly experienced writer John Lucarotti, who had previously contributed three historical stories — *Marco Polo*, *The Aztecs* and *The Massacre of St Bartholomew's Eve* — during William Hartnell's time as the Doctor.

Lucarotti's idea revolved around a space station, the Ark, on which the last remnants of humanity had been placed in cryogenic suspension in order to survive a burst of solar flare activity. The story would have seen the Doctor and his companions arriving to discover that a race of fungus creatures called the Delc had infiltrated the station and taken over in its huge hydroponic garden, treating the sleeping humans as nothing more than a convenient food source. The Delc would have taken two different forms, some of them appearing as giant, immobile puffballs communicating purely by telepathy and the others as multi-legged headless bodies serving as mindless drones. The Doctor's attempts to put matters to rights would have been constrained by the fact that the adult puffballs could not be simply blown up without causing their spores to be released, thereby spreading the menace. His eventual solution would have been to destroy most of the creatures with massive discharges of electricity and to dispose of the remaining puffballs by jettisoning them from the Ark with the use of a golf club.

Lucarotti was given the go-ahead to write a four-part story based on this idea. As his scripts arrived, however, the production team became increasingly concerned about the direction being taken.

'As far as I can recall,' says Barry Letts, 'what came in was too clever by half. What John had done was very involved — the scripts were incredibly complex. They were too hard, too difficult, too complicated and sophisticated for the slot.'

To compound the problem, liaison with Lucarotti proved somewhat difficult due both to his preference for writing scripts while sailing on his yacht in the Mediterranean and to unexpected delays in the post.

'There was a postal dispute,' recalled Robert Holmes, 'so the scripts came in a bit later than expected. When the second episode arrived, we could see it was veering off the course that we wanted, but it was too late to do anything about it. Then, when the last bit came in, Philip said "We can't use this thing — we've got 18 days to get it right". That was just before the director, Rodney Bennett, arrived.'

As an emergency measure, Hinchcliffe asked Holmes to take on the onerous task of rewriting the story from scratch. Although Lucarotti was paid in full for his scripts and retained copyright in them, the final version was therefore almost entirely Holmes's work and went out under his name.

The transmitted story sees the TARDIS arriving on space station Nerva — otherwise known as the Ark — orbiting Earth in the far future. On board, the Doctor, Sarah and Harry discover the last survivors of the human race held in suspended animation, the Earth having been evacuated thousands of years ago when solar flares threatened to destroy all life. The human sleepers begin to revive after the Doctor repairs some control systems damaged by a now-dead Wirrn Queen which earlier infiltrated the ship. The Wirrn, first encountered by humankind on Andromeda, are an insect species which lay their eggs close to a food source so that their larvae have access to nourishment — both physical and mental. The larvae secrete a slime which can physically invade other creatures, transforming them into Wirrn whilst retaining the knowledge of the host.

Before succumbing to the Ark's defence system, the Wirrn Queen laid her eggs close to its power source, the solar stacks. The humans' leader, nicknamed Noah, becomes infected by one of the emerging larvae and is slowly taken over. The Doctor and his friends meanwhile gain the trust of the other humans, now led by a medic named Vira. Together they manage to lure the hatched Wirrn

Styre tests the abilities of the Galsec crew members. *The Sontaran Experiment.*

insects into a shuttle craft and then eject it into space. In a final act of humanity, Noah — by this time fully transformed into a Wirrn — deliberately neglects to set the shuttle's stabilizers, causing it to explode. The Doctor decides to pop down to Earth using the Ark's transmat system to ensure that the receptor beacons are correctly tuned to receive the returning sleepers. Sarah and Harry tag along.

The situation encountered by the three travellers upon their arrival on Earth is revealed in the following story, a two-parter by Bob Baker and Dave Martin entitled *The Sontaran Experiment* (working title: *The Destructors*). Although transmitted immediately after *The Ark in Space*, *The Sontaran Experiment* was actually made immediately before it as the first story of *Doctor Who*'s twelfth production block. It was shot entirely on location around the Hound Tor area of Dartmoor in Devon — like *Robot*, using lightweight Outside Broadcast (OB) equipment rather than film cameras — over the period 26 September to 1 October 1974. The decision to make an all-location two-parter followed by an all-studio four-parter was taken mainly for budgetary reasons, as it meant that two separate stories could be made for the same amount of money as would normally have been spent on a single six-parter following the same production pattern.

All went smoothly on location apart from the fact that, during recording of a fight scene on Sunday 29 September 1974, Tom Baker slipped and broke his collar bone. After being briefly admitted to a local hospital, the actor returned to Dartmoor

and completed his remaining scenes with his scarf and coat concealing a neck-brace.

The story opens with the Doctor, Sarah and Harry arriving on the desolate surface of the supposedly deserted Earth. The Doctor starts realigning the transmat receptors while Sarah and Harry go off to explore. Harry falls into a pit, so Sarah runs back to get the Doctor's help. The Doctor, however, has been captured by a group of shipwrecked space travellers from a human colony world, Galsec, who have been lured to Earth by a fake distress call. Sarah meets another of their number, Roth, who tells her of an alien conducting gruesome experiments on him and his crewmates. Before long, they are both captured by a robot and dragged off to the alien's ship. Harry finds his own way out of the pit via a series of underground tunnels and emerges nearby. He watches as Sarah and Roth are presented to the alien, who turns out to be a Sontaran.

Field-Major Styre is compiling a report on human physical and mental capabilities as a prelude to a Sontaran invasion of Earth, which has now taken on a strategic importance in his race's perennial war with the Rutans. The Doctor interrupts Styre's experiments and challenges him to unarmed combat. The Sontaran readily agrees but is quickly weakened as he attempts to keep up with his more agile opponent in Earth's unfamiliar gravity. Harry meanwhile enters Styre's ship and, using the Doctor's sonic screwdriver, removes the terrulium diode bypass transformer. When the alien returns there to revitalize himself, he is consequently

PHILIP HINCHCLIFFE
PRODUCER

After leaving college with a degree in English Literature, Philip Hinchcliffe worked briefly for a travel company, and then took a teaching job for six months or so before landing a job in the script department of ATV where he worked on **The Kids from 47A** *(1974) amongst others. His work also involved sifting through the unsolicited submissions, and handling the contract negotiation for the writers. He was determined to make a name for himself in television and eventually became involved in a soap opera called* **General Hospital** *and several children's programmes in the capacity of an associate producer. Unusually for someone on the production side of television, Hinchcliffe had an agent and it was through this contact that he was offered the producership of* **Doctor Who** *in November 1973. Following the end of his tenure, he went on to produce shows like* **Private Schultz, Nancy Astor, Strangers and Brothers** *and* **Target.** *In addition, he has novelized three* **Doctor Who** *scripts for the Target imprint:* **The Keys of Marinus, The Seeds of Doom** *and* **The Masque of Mandragora.**

GERRY DAVIS
WRITER

Gerry Davis became a BBC story editor in 1965 at the invitation of Head of Serials Donald Wilson, who had been impressed by a course he had written on TV scriptwriting. He had previously been a newspaper reporter, a merchant seaman and a writer for the Canadian Broadcasting Corporation, and had studied opera and worked as a cinema translator in Italy. His first BBC assignments were on **199 Park Lane** *and* **United!** *and he was then given the chance to take over from Donald Tosh on* **Doctor Who.** *Although he never saw entirely eye to eye with producer Innes Lloyd, he remained in this post for over a year before moving on to edit another show,* **First Lady.** *He later returned to freelance writing, his greatest success coming in the early seventies with the BBC's ecological drama series* **Doomwatch,** *which he co-created with Kit Pedler. From the mid-seventies he spent most of his time in Hollywood, writing for American films and TV series and teaching screen-writing courses at the UCLA Film School. He died on 31 August 1991, aged 64.*

DAVROS

*'Davros served two roles,' says his creator Terry Nation. 'First, he was half-man, half-Dalek, a sort of mutated link between the two species – the Kaleds as they once were, and the Daleks as they were to become. Secondly, he was someone who could **think** like a Dalek, but talk in a much more human fashion. With the Daleks' slow speech pattern, to have had a Dalek as a spokesperson for their point of view all the way through would have been dull and – worse – would have slowed down the action of the story. I feel very strongly that the Daleks themselves should be left to speak in short, snappy sentences, not long speeches.'*

Visual effects designer Peter Day modelled Davros's chair on the familiar lines of a Dalek base, as specified in Nation's script: 'Davros is contained in a specially constructed self-powered wheelchair. It has similarities to the base of a Dalek.'

Nation goes on to describe Davros himself: 'A single lens wired to his forehead replaces his sightless eyes. Little of his face can be seen, tubes and electrodes attached to what does show.' To acheive this effect, a mask was designed by effects sculptor John Friedlander and the costume by Barbara Kidd. Chair, mask and costume were all specifically tailored to fit actor Michael Wisher, who had not been the first choice for the role but had eventually been cast largely on the strength of his previous experience in providing Dalek voices for the series.

STOCK FOOTAGE

*Footage was obtained from NHK in Japan for the shots of the Thal missile taking off en route for the Kaled Dome in part 3 of **Genesis of the Daleks**.*

*In episodes one and two of **Revenge of the Cybermen**, some silent film was used entitled 'Rocket Man' for the shots seen by Sarah on the educational video just before she is attacked by a Cybermat. This footage had previously been used in a programme called **Thanks for the Frying Pan**.*

drained of all his energy and destroyed. The Doctor then sends a message to the Sontaran fleet, warning them that without Styre's report they cannot know the strength of human resistance and so had better look elsewhere — brinkmanship at its most effective. The Doctor, Sarah and Harry then leave via the transmat with the intention of returning to the Ark.

Kevin Lindsay, who had played Linx in *The Time Warrior*, returned to portray both Styre and the Marshal of the Sontaran fleet in *The Sontaran Experiment*. As the actor suffered from a heart condition, which had resulted in him collapsing at one point during the recording of *The Time Warrior*, the Sontaran costume was redesigned on this occasion to be less bulky and to give better ventilation for breathing. Although Lindsay was still unable to act for more than short periods at a time, his acclaimed performance went a long way towards establishing the Sontarans as the most popular *Doctor Who* monsters created in the seventies. The series' fans were sad to learn of his death not long after *The Sontaran Experiment* was transmitted.

Like *The Ark in Space* and *The Sontaran Experiment*, the next two stories were made in reverse order. Last to be recorded but first to be seen by the viewing public was a Terry Nation six-parter entitled *Genesis of the Daleks* (working title: *Daleks — Genesis of Terror*).

'It was my idea to do a story about the origin of the Daleks,' recalls Barry Letts. 'What happened was that we decided it would be good if Terry Nation did another Dalek story. He said he'd love to, and put in a storyline. I looked at it, and he came in to talk about it. I said "It's quite a good story, Terry. The only snag is, you've sold it to us three times already!" And I detailed the likenesses to the first Dalek story, and to one or two of the others.

'Then I suddenly said, "You know, what you've never shown us is where the Daleks came from in the first place — the genesis of the Daleks." And Terry said "Oh great," and went away and wrote it.'

Genesis of the Daleks sees the Doctor, Sarah and Harry being diverted by the Time Lords to an early point in the history of the planet Skaro. There, a Time Lord emissary gives the Doctor a mission to prevent or alter the Daleks' development so that they become less of a threat to the future of the Universe. The travellers subsequently learn that the planet is in the grip of a 1000-year war of attrition between its two humanoid power blocs, the Kaleds and the Thals. The Kaleds' crippled chief scientist, Davros, has been carrying out experiments to discover the final form into which his race will mutate as a result of all the chemical and radiation weapons used in the war, and has devised a protective

casing in which they can continue to survive. This casing — the Mark 3 Travel Machine — is instantly recognized by the Doctor and Sarah as a Dalek.

Escaping from the bunker where Davros and his Elite are based, the Doctor and Harry persuade the Kaled leaders to put the Dalek experiments on hold. Davros, however, retaliates by conspiring with the Thals to destroy the Kaled city with a rocket. He then activates the Daleks and orders them to wipe out the Thals. When some members of the Elite revolt, protesting at the genetic alterations Davros has made to the Daleks to eliminate compassion and instill a ruthless instinct for survival, they too are exterminated. Now fully autonomous, the Daleks seize control, killing the remainder of the Elite and ultimately Davros himself.

A group of Thal survivors detonate explosives at the entrance to the bunker, sealing the Daleks inside. Having earlier passed up an opportunity to destroy the Dalek mutants at birth, balking at the prospect of committing genocide, the Doctor estimates that his intervention will have delayed their development by about 1,000 years. He tells Sarah and Harry to take hold of a time ring which the Time Lord gave him at the start of the adventure, and together the three friends are whisked away into time and space.

Genesis of the Daleks is one of Terry Nation's own personal favourites of all the *Doctor Who* stories he wrote.

'I tried very hard,' he says, 'to make it fit with what had been established about the Daleks — to adjust and change where I could, but not to step on too many traditions. I was starting with the "complete version" and working backwards to see how they might have begun.

'After the first Dalek story, I had begun to see some influences in it. By the time of *Genesis of the Daleks*, I had convinced myself that the Daleks were closer to the Nazis than to any other political group I could think of. It worked terribly well for them. I grew up during the war, and was aware of the Nazis and their totalitarian state. If you look at this story, the uniforms and the Elite — all those things — seem to have echoes of what the Nazi regime was like. I was tremendously influenced by that. I would have said that was in the script, but I won't swear to it; so many things change from the moment I put them on the typewriter to the moment they're on the screen. But the Elite was mine, and the general idea was — I believe — mine.

'*Genesis of the Daleks* was a highly moral tale. It was always intended to be a kind of anti-war piece — anti-politics, and certainly anti-totalitarianism. Trust

The Doctor attempts to reason with Davros (Michael Wisher). *Genesis of the Daleks.*

The Daleks are given their orders by Davros as Nyder (Peter Miles) looks on. *Genesis of the Daleks.*

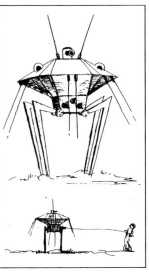

▲ **Visual effects designer Tony Oxley's design sketches for Styre's robot.** *The Sontaran Experiment.*

▲ **Visual effects sculptor John Friedlander puts finishing touches to his mask for Davros.** *Genesis of the Daleks.*

▼ **The new style Cyberman costume for *Revenge of the Cybermen* modelled by its maker Allister Bowtell, with his daughter.**

no one, especially governments! We had so many good elements going — we almost overloaded ourselves with elements. We had two different cities, we had two different races of people, we had highly complex political manoeuvring going on. And within all this we had the Daleks developing. It was a complex story, with a lot of story to tell. It could have gone on for another four episodes, in fact. It's always been one of my favourites as it stayed very true to the script. I had demanded tremendous things — like the rocket ship the Thals were building — and I think the producer gave me almost everything I asked for. I think the production was brilliant on that show — they did wonderful things.'

There was however at least one change made by director David Maloney about which Nation expressed reservations shortly after the story's transmission, commenting in a radio interview about the addition of 'elements of visual brutality' such as the slow motion opening sequence of a group of soldiers being shot down.

The final story to be transmitted in season twelve was *Revenge of the Cybermen*, which saw the return of the only monster race ever seriously to rival the Daleks in popularity. This was the first Cyberman adventure since *The Invasion* in 1968, although images of them had appeared fleetingly in *The War Games* (1969), *The Mind of Evil* (1971) and *Carnival of Monsters* (1973). Commissioned from Gerry Davis — a former *Doctor Who* script editor who, with Kit Pedler, had co-created the Cybermen — it started out in a rather different form from that in which it finally reached the screen.

Davis's original idea had been for a story involving a gambling casino in space, where — due partly to budgetary restrictions and partly to the writer's own preferences — most of the scenes would have been confined to one main set. The production team, however, suggested switching the action to the Nerva space station first seen in *The Ark in Space* so that some of the sets from that story could be reused and money thereby saved to be spent on

other aspects of the production. Davis consequently reworked the story for this setting and added in the concept of a gold-rich asteroid, populated by a forgotten colony of human prospectors, which the Cybermen would attempt to destroy as the metal was anathema to them. The scripts for this four-parter, which like *The Moonbase* and *The Invasion* had the working title *Return of the Cybermen*, subsequently underwent a further major rewrite at the hands of Robert Holmes, who retained Davis's basic concept and most of his characters for the Nerva crew but changed the details of the plot and replaced the gold prospectors with an alien race called the Vogans.

In the story as transmitted, the time ring takes the Doctor, Sarah and Harry back to Nerva, but to a period many thousands of years earlier than their previous visit. At this point in its history, the ship is acting as a beacon warning space traffic of the existence of a new asteroid orbiting Jupiter. This is Voga, nicknamed the planet of gold as that metal can be found in abundance there. Exploring, the three friends learn that a space plague has killed all but a handful of Nerva's crew. It transpires that a visiting civilian named Kellman, an exographer who has been surveying Voga, is a traitor working with a small group of Cybermen to destroy the asteroid and thus eliminate a major source of gold — a metal which in dust form can coat their breathing apparatus and suffocate them. The 'plague' is in fact the result of poison injected into its victims by rodent-like Cybermats smuggled aboard Nerva.

The Cybermen invade the beacon and force the Doctor and two of the remaining humans to carry down into the heart of Voga some cobalt bombs which will then be detonated to destroy the planet. What the Cybermen fail to realize is that Kellman is a double agent, secretly working with one faction of the Vogan race on the planet below. Their plan has been to lure the Cybermen onto the beacon and destroy it with a missile. The Doctor rids himself of the bomb he has been forced to carry

The Cyberleader ▶ (Christopher Robbie) orders a change of course in the control room of the Cybermen's space ship. *Revenge of the Cybermen.*

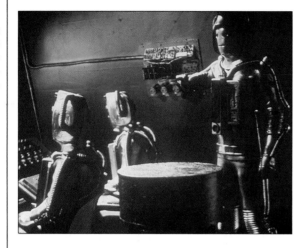

Vogan leader Tyrum's ▶ forces defend their position in the caverns of Voga, the planet of gold. *Revenge of the Cybermen.*

Vorus (David Collings), ▲ leader of a rival Vogan faction. *Revenge of the Cybermen.*

The Doctor ▼ contemplates destroying the embryo Daleks. *Genesis of the Daleks.*

and returns to the beacon, which the Cybermen subsequently evacuate on learning of the Vogans' intentions. The missile is launched, but the Doctor gives instructions for it to be redirected away from the beacon and onto a collision course with the Cybermen's ship, which is thus destroyed.

The TARDIS arrives on the beacon, having been gradually drifting back to this point in time, and the Doctor, Sarah and Harry leave for a rendezvous with the Brigadier, who has sent an urgent message requesting assistance with a problem on Earth.

Transmission of *Revenge of the Cybermen*, which concluded on 10 May 1975, brought *Doctor Who's* twelfth season to an end after only 20 episodes — by far the shortest of the series' history up to that point. The original intention had been that it would be followed by a further six-part story, but the programme planners had decided to cut short this run of transmissions and bring forward the next so that *Doctor Who's* seasons would in future span from autumn to spring, rather than from spring to summer. Season twelve had done very well in the ratings, reversing a slight dip registered during season eleven, and it was felt that the change to an autumn start would give the BBC an added edge against the rival ITV network in the fierce competi-

tion for viewers. In particular, it was hoped that *Doctor Who* would prove an effective counter to an expensive new science-fiction drama entitled *Space: 1999* which was due to begin transmission on ITV in autumn 1975.

This change of scheduling meant that production of the next batch of 26 episodes had to be advanced by some three months to ensure that they would be ready in time for transmission. The division between the twelfth and thirteenth production blocks was consequently more notional than real, as work continued effectively without a break after completion of the last studio session for *Genesis of the Daleks* on 25 February 1975.

Despite the presence of some reassuringly traditional elements, season twelve had contained strong hints that *Doctor Who* was undergoing an important change of style under Philip Hinchcliffe and Robert Holmes. *Robot*, for all its military hardware, gun battles and explosions, had been essentially larger-than-life, fantasy-based family drama, very much akin to most of the Pertwee-era UNIT tales, but productions like *The Ark in Space* and *Genesis of the Daleks* were infused with a harder, grittier quality. *The Ark in Space*, for instance, had a Gothic horror flavour in its portrayal of people being physically and mentally possessed by the Wirrn, while *The Sontaran Experiment* depicted what was, in effect, the brutal and systematic torture of a group of human spacemen. *Genesis of the Daleks*, with its themes of warfare, racial hatred and genetic experimentation, was even more graphic and disturbing, provoking complaints from some viewers and from TV watchdog Mary Whitehouse.

'Although we'd got all the old favourites in the first season,' recalls Hinchcliffe, 'both Bob and I felt that we'd like to move the show away from what had been the "Barry Letts formula". Not because we didn't rate that — I think Barry was a terrific producer of the show, and Jon Pertwee was a very good Doctor . . . But I felt that that was now slightly played out.

'I felt that we could move the show in a different direction — more into genuine science-fiction and fantasy. We didn't want to be so reliant on monsters in funny masks all the time, but in a way to take the audience on a genuine journey of fantasy by creating an atmosphere in the stories. And that tied in with Bob's idea of not relying totally on monsters that weren't very interesting and didn't have very interesting motives. I thought we could add a bit more power — I was quite interested in doing something in the science-fiction area which, okay, would be *Doctor Who*, but we could make it a bit more ballsy!'

CHAPTER TWELVE

Season Thirteen: Worlds of Horror

Season thirteen began transmission on 30 August 1975 — the new, earlier date decreed by the programme planners — with the first of a four-part story entitled *Terror of the Zygons*. This was the debut contribution to *Doctor Who* by Robert Banks Stewart, a highly experienced TV writer whose credits included episodes of *The Avengers, The Saint* and *Undermind*.

'I knew Robert Holmes quite well,' recalls Stewart. 'He said, "How about writing a *Doctor Who* story?" and we kicked a few ideas around.

'One of those ideas — the one I happened to be particularly fond of — was about the Loch Ness Monster. Being Scottish it was something I was familiar with. Not that I knew a lot about it, because nobody knows much about the Loch Ness Monster — therefore I suppose one could take a great deal of licence in fiction. It seemed to me it was an ideal theme for a *Doctor Who* story, because here was a kind of Earth monster: whether we know it exists or not, it's very much of this Earth, so rather than inventing a monster from space, or wherever, here was something I could use anyway. Also, it seemed to me that Scotland was a good location for a story — although subsequently it wasn't actually filmed in Scotland as the budget wouldn't run to it.'

Stewart's story was commissioned on 3 April 1974 as a six-parter under the working title *Loch Ness* and was originally intended to be transmitted immediately after *Revenge of the Cybermen* at the end of season twelve. When that six-part slot was lost, however, it was held over to the start of season thirteen and revamped as a four-parter, gaining the new working titles *The Secret of the Loch* and *The Secret of Loch Ness*.

'When the decision was taken to make it into a four-parter rather than a six-parter,' says Stewart, 'Bob Holmes and I sat down and agreed on what we would take out. Bob did quite a major amount of that editing work, to make it fit. I think there was quite a lot of action in the Scottish highlands that was cut. A lot of it was simply local colour because, as I say, it was originally meant to be filmed in a highland village and in the mountains.'

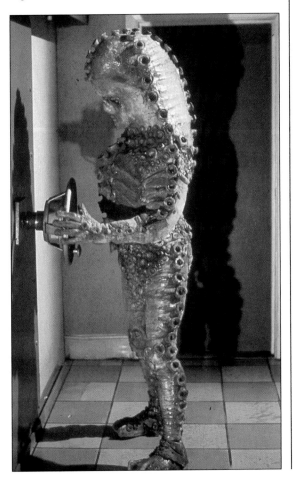

SEASON THIRTEEN

CODE	TITLE
4F	TERROR OF THE ZYGONS
4H	PLANET OF EVIL
4G	PYRAMIDS OF MARS
4J	THE ANDROID INVASION
4K	THE BRAIN OF MORBIUS
4L	THE SEEDS OF DOOM

RATINGS

Figures in millions

Story code: 4F 4H 4G 4J 4K 4L

◀ **A Zygon locks Sarah and the Doctor in a compression chamber.** *Terror of the Zygons.*

LOCATIONS

Terror of the Zygons
    Charlton, Sussex;
    The Mill, Climping, Nr
    Littlehampton, Sussex;
    Ambersham Common,
    Nr Midhurst;
    Furnace Pond,
    Crabtree, Nr Lower
    Beeding

Planet of Evil
    No location work

Pyramids of Mars
    Stargroves, East End,
    Nr Newbury, Hants

The Android Invasion
    Worsham Quarry, Nr
    Witney;
    East Hagbourne,
    Oxfordshire;
    National Radiological
    Protection Board,
    Harwell, Didcot

The Brain of Morbius
    No location work

The Seeds of Doom
    Dorking Quarry, Surrey;
    Athelhampton House,
    Athelhampton, Dorset

MUSIC

*The incidental music for **Terror of the Zygons** and **The Seeds of Doom** was provided by Geoffrey Burgon, but all the other season-thirteen stories were handled by the series' regular composer, Dudley Simpson.*

*For the music played on the bagpipes by Angus in **Terror of the Zygons**, the following tracks were used, both played by Bob Murphy: 'Strathspey Reel' and 'Flowers of the Forest'.*

*The distinctive pipe organ passages in **Pyramids of Mars** were recorded on 16 May 1975 (after an initial attempt on 14 May 1975 proved unsuccessful) at St Augustine's Church in Kilburn Park Road, London NW6.*

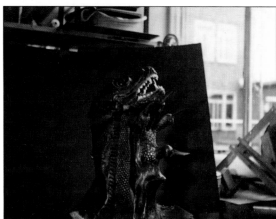

The scale models of the Skarasen used in *Terror of the Zygons*. Top: the complete creature. Bottom: A larger model of the head and claw.

The transmitted story opens with the Doctor, Sarah and Harry returning to Earth in response to the summons received from the Brigadier at the end of *Revenge of the Cybermen*. UNIT are investigating a series of unexplained attacks on North Sea oil rigs and have set up a temporary HQ in the remote Scottish village of Tulloch. The Doctor discovers that the attacks are being carried out by a huge cyborg, the Skarasen, under the control of a group of aliens called Zygons whose spaceship lies at the bottom of Loch Ness. The Zygons plan to take over the Earth as a

Harry (Ian Marter) is held prisoner by the Zygons in the space ship at the bottom of Loch Ness. *Terror of the Zygons*.

substitute for their own planet, which has been devastated by solar flares. To this end, they are using their shape-shifting abilities to take on the identities of a number of local inhabitants whose inert bodies are meanwhile held aboard their spaceship.

The Doctor releases the Zygons' prisoners and causes their ship, which has now emerged from the Loch, to self-destruct. Only their leader, Broton, survives. He has assumed the form of the Duke of Forgill and travelled to London in order to infiltrate a World Energy Conference. His plan is to give a show of strength by destroying the Conference with the Skarasen, which is swiftly approaching up the Thames. Broton is shot by UNIT troops, and the Doctor then throws the Skarasen its homing device, which it promptly devours. Now without a controlling influence, the creature makes its way back to Loch Ness — the only home it has ever known — there to be occasionally mistaken for the fabled Loch Ness Monster.

Having returned to Scotland in the aftermath of the adventure, the Doctor and Sarah decide to travel back to London by TARDIS. Harry, however, opts for the more reliable method of British Rail.

Veteran *Doctor Who* director Douglas Camfield was persuaded by Philip Hinchcliffe to return to the series to handle *Terror of the Zygons*. Two of the biggest challenges he faced were the realization of the story's monsters and the extensive location filming required.

Scotland having been ruled out as too expensive, the filming was carried out in and around the village of Charlton in Sussex. This proved ideal for the story's needs, and work progressed largely according to schedule. One problem encountered, however, was the very changeable weather, which made it difficult to achieve continuity of lighting between different shots. The script for episode one had included a scene in which the TARDIS materialized and then became invisible, but this had to be dropped as the completed footage was considered too poorly matched to be convincing.

Two different models were used to achieve the Skarasen effects. One was a complicated stop-motion version built by an outside contractor and the other a hand-operated puppet of the creature's head and neck. Although a great deal of money and time were set aside for these effects, Camfield and Hinchcliffe were both disappointed with the end results. Shots of the models were therefore kept to a bare minimum in the finished episodes, and some scenes were rewritten to avoid the Skarasen having to be seen at all.

The Zygons, on the other hand, were very impressively realized by costume designer James Acheson and visual effects sculptor John Friedlander.

'I remember I was looking at a lot of half-formed embryos in amniotic sacks,' says Acheson. 'I did a model along those lines and then John worked in a face for it. So that was a very close collaboration. We made the whole body; John made the rib cage, the cranium and the face, but working pretty much to my designs.

'I wanted to give the costume a translucent quality. I'm not sure we ever used this as it was too distracting, but in fact the rib cage and the head had lights inside which were meant to glow. It was always a question of not having enough voltage. Either one had to build a battery pack into the guy or one had to plug him in. I think we used it occasionally, when he got angry. I seem to remember his head throbbing a bit.'

Terror of the Zygons was also notable for being the last seventies story to feature the Brigadier.

'I think there was a genuine feeling that we had come to the end of an era,' remembers actor Nicholas Courtney. 'The production team had told us UNIT was going to be phased out and so, particularly in the case of John Levene and myself, we were under a terrible cloud of thinking we were playing our characters for the last time.'

The second story of the season to be transmitted, although the third to be made, was a four-parter entitled *Planet of Evil*. Written by Louis Marks, who had previously been responsible for season two's *Planet of Giants* and season nine's *Day of the Daleks*, it drew inspiration from Robert Louis Stevenson's *The Strange Case of Doctor Jekyll and Mister Hyde* (1886) and the classic MGM science-fiction film *Forbidden Planet* (1956).

'We'd decided that we wanted to do a Jekyll and Hyde story,' recalls Philip Hinchcliffe. 'In the end I came up with the notion that we could perhaps have a Jekyll and Hyde planet — one minute one thing, the next another. Out of that grew the idea of a planet of evil. Then we had to think about how to do it. I remember thinking about it very hard, as I didn't want it to look just like a studio! I spoke to Roger Murray Leach, who was to be the designer, and he said, "I can do you a good jungle. We can shoot that on film at Ealing and it'll look really good." This was how we worked: it was a combination of having a good idea, then working out how we thought we could do it; of talking to the production professionals very early on so that we knew we had something strong enough.

'The thing in *Planet of Evil* that was a straight lift

Sarah and the Doctor discover that anti matter is on board the Morestran space ship. *Planet of Evil.*

Sarah makes her way through the jungle on Zeta Minor. The jungle set, designed by Roger Murray-Leach, was later used in BBC publications about set design. *Planet of Evil.*

The Doctor and Sarah discover the desiccated body of one of the Morestrans after a visit by the force which inhabits the planet. *Planet of Evil.*

was the Id monster from *Forbidden Planet*. That was probably a bit too like the original. The idea was that one had somehow to discover the evil; it had to be represented in some way. So that's what we had a go at.'

In the story as transmitted, the TARDIS picks up a distress call from the edge of the known universe and the Doctor and Sarah hurry to respond. They arrive on the planet Zeta Minor to find that the members of a Morestran geological

▲ The Doctor in the anti-universe. *Planet of Evil.*

▲ A concept sketch of the anti-man by make-up designer Jenny Shircore.

▲ Professor Sorenson (Frederick Jaeger) becomes anti-man.

▲ The costume for the anti matter monster worn by Mike Lee Lane. The image was treated for use on the final episodes.

Effects designer Ian ▲ Scoones sets up the model TARDIS on the model future Earth set for a scene cut from the final story. *Pyramids of Mars.*

The Doctor and Sarah investgate a series of attacks against North Sea oil rigs. *Terror of the Zygons.*

The TARDIS arrives in a room full of Egyptian relics in Marcus Scarman's English home. *Pyramids of Mars.*

Ian Scoones hangs the ▲ model TARDIS on wires against a space background for the sequence of the ship spinning in space. *Pyramids of Mars.*

expedition have fallen prey to an unseen killer. Only the leader, Professor Sorenson, remains alive. A military mission from Morestra has also arrived to find out what has happened to the expedition. Sorenson is confused and unable to supply the answer but, as the deaths continue, the Doctor and Sarah are the obvious suspects.

The true culprit is a creature from a universe of antimatter. It has been attacking the Morestrans in retaliation for the removal by Sorenson of some antimatter samples from around the pit which acts as an interface between the two universes. The Morestrans take off in their ship, but it is slowly dragged back towards the planet due to the antimatter on board. Sorenson himself becomes infected by antimatter and gradually transforms into anti-man, a hideous monster capable of draining the life from others.

The Morestran commander, Salamar, goes berserk and attacks Sorenson with a radiation source. This causes him to multiply, and the ship is soon overrun by deadly creatures capable of walking straight through the walls and doors. The Doctor finds the original Sorenson anti-man, takes him back to the planet in the TARDIS and throws both him and his samples into the pit, thus fulfilling a bargain

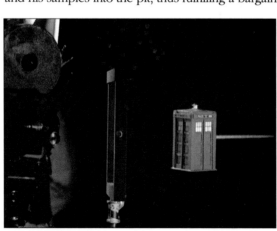

The TARDIS model is attached to a spinning rig. *Pyramids of Mars.*

he earlier made with the antimatter creature. Sorenson reappears unharmed and the Doctor returns him to the Morestran ship, which is now freed of the planet's influence. He and Sarah then leave in the TARDIS to try to keep their appointment with the Brigadier.

'*Planet of Evil* was a strange one,' says Louis Marks. 'It changed as it went through. The Jekyll and Hyde business was certainly in there right from the start, but the antimatter theme tended to take over more and more as I worked at the plot. I read a lot about antimatter beforehand from writers like Asimov, to get some thoughts and get the brain cells ticking over. But the more I read, the more I got into the subject. Consequently, I ran into a bit of trouble when it was suddenly realized we were half-way through the story and the Jekyll and Hyde monster hadn't even appeared yet!

'Ultimately the script went through several versions. The first version did rely a little too much on simple action to solve it. But we'd got ourselves into such a strange world with this planet on the border of matter and antimatter which we had to show changing mood and nature as it went from night to day and then back to night again.

'At one point things were getting very complicated, although that was when Bob Holmes was at his best, bringing the plot back on course while keeping within the scientific framework we'd set up for the story. It almost got out of hand, as we were getting near to crossing the line between what people will accept as credible and what they won't. That again is one of my penchants. I like trying to take my subject matter as far as one can go. I think they're better stories in the end when one enlivens people's imaginations.'

Planet of Evil was a prime example of a story which owed much of its on-screen impact to the combined efforts of its various designers. Roger Murray Leach's jungle set served as an eerie and convincing backdrop to the action — an important consideration as the story was afforded no location filming. Constructed in such a way that it could be shot from a number of different angles to increase its apparent size, it was considered sufficiently impressive to be featured for a number of years afterwards in BBC educational publications about set design. Many of the more alien-looking vacuum-formed trees and plants were supplied by visual effects designer Dave Havard, who also collaborated with costume designer Andrew Rose in the creation of the antimatter monster. The padded silver costume provided by Rose and worn by actor Mike Lee Lane was shot under harsh coloured lighting and its image then electronically enhanced with a red tint before being overlaid onto the final picture using CSO. Make-up designer Jenny Shircore was responsible for transforming actor Frederick Jaeger into the anti-man version of Sorenson. The scenes in which he was seen fully transformed were all recorded together at the beginning of one studio day, so that only a single application of this complex make-up was required.

Although Dave Havard also provided the models of the Morestran ship and of the planet Zeta Minor as seen from orbit, one model sequence for which he could take no credit was that of the TARDIS spinning through the time vortex. This had been created by his colleagues Ian Scoones and Mat Irvine as part of the effects work for *Pyramids of Mars* — the story which was made immediately before *Planet of Evil* and transmitted immediately after it.

The main action of *Pyramids of Mars* takes place on Earth in the year 1911. Egyptologist Marcus Scarman has uncovered a lost pyramid which is in reality the prison of Sutekh, last survivor of the Osiran race. Although held immobile by a signal transmitted from a pyramid on Mars, Sutekh uses his god-like powers to kill Scarman and take control of his corpse. The TARDIS then encounters Sutekh's influence in the time vortex and, thrown off course, materializes in the grounds of Scarman's family home, an old priory on the site which will one day be occupied by UNIT HQ.

The zombie Scarman returns to the priory via a space-time tunnel and, with the help of servicer robots in the form of Egyptian mummies, constructs a rocket with which to destroy the Martian pyramid and thereby free Sutekh to wreak havoc throughout the cosmos. The Doctor manages to foil this plan by using explosives to blow up the rocket. He then falls under Sutekh's control himself and is made to transport Scarman to Mars in the TARDIS. There the animated cadaver gains access to the heart of the pyramid and destroys the Eye of Horus — the device transmitting the signal which holds Sutekh captive.

The model of the pyramid rocket outside Scarman's house. *Pyramids of Mars.*

The Doctor, Dr Warlock (Peter Copley) and Laurence Scarman (Michael Sheard) hide from Sutekh's mummy-like robots. *Pyramids of Mars.*

The Doctor, now freed of Sutekh's influence, realizes that there will be a short delay before the signal ceases to have effect, owing to the time taken for it to reach Earth. He rushes back to the priory and, using equipment from the TARDIS, moves the end of the space-time tunnel far into the future. Sutekh, travelling down the tunnel, is unable to reach it in his lifetime, and dies. The energy from the tunnel sets fire to the priory which burns down as the Doctor and Sarah leave.

Pyramids of Mars grew out of a desire on Robert Holmes's part to do a story based around Egyptian mythology. It was commissioned in the autumn of 1974 from Lewis Griefer, an experienced writer who was known to be interested in the subject. When Griefer delivered his scripts, however, it became clear that he had taken an approach out of keeping with the style of the series, as Holmes later recounted:

'Lewis Griefer's story, as I recall, started with two museum keepers being chased through the British Museum by a mummy, for some reason. And the reason, it suddenly transpired, was something to

▲ **Sutekh (Gabriel Woolf).** *Pyramids of Mars.*

▲ **The servant of Sutekh (Bernard Archard) confronts Namin (Peter Mayock).** *Pyramids of Mars.*

▲ **Marcus Scarman (Bernard Archard).** *Pyramids of Mars.*

A sequence of ▲ photographs taken during location filming for *The Android Invasion*. In the bottom photograph, stuntman Terry Walsh, doubling for the Doctor, jumps from the roof of one of the buildings.

do with frightening them out of the place so that the sarcophagus could be opened. Because in it there was some wild rice left over from ten thousand years ago; some grains with which this particular group wanted to seed Mars — so that they could make a lot of money. But the story veered all over the place, and it wasn't anything to do with Egyptian mythology. I wanted Osiris and all those people in it.

'*Pyramids of Mars* was his original title. He was very into pyramids and all the alleged magical properties they have. If one leaves a razor blade under a pyramid, it's supposed to stay fresh for ever.'

Philip Hinchcliffe, in a memo dated 10 December 1975, described the background to these script problems and explained how they were overcome:

The scripts for Doctor Who *4G* Pyramids of Mars *were originally commissioned from Lewis Griefer. He is a professional writer of high standing and since he was commissioned in good time there should have been no undue problems with the scripts. However, he unfortunately fell ill during this time and was suspected of having cancer until a final operation in hospital to remove his prostate gland proved successful. The scripts that were due in October 1974 did not arrive until Christmastime. Understandably perhaps in the circumstances, the scripts were not usable but by this time Lewis had to fulfil a teaching engagement at the University of Tel Aviv. An attempt at rewriting the scripts was made in these difficult circumstances but there came a point when I had to ask the story editor to attempt a speedy and total rewrite in order to prepare the show in time for the studio. As it turned out this task became one of writing fresh scripts rather than doctoring the existing ones — a case of drastic steps for a drastic situation.*

We felt honour bound to pay for the original scripts in full and so copyright in the story resides with Lewis Griefer...

Incidentally this story was billed in the Radio Times as written by 'Stephen Harris' — a pseudonym at the request of Lewis Griefer.

Hinchcliffe subsequently gained agreement from Head of Serials Graeme McDonald that Holmes could if necessary be commissioned to write up to two complete stories per season for the remainder of his tenure as script editor.

The location filming for *Pyramids of Mars* was carried out over the period 29 April to 2 May 1975 in the grounds of Stargroves House in East End, Hampshire. This property belonged at the time to rock star Mick Jagger, but the production team discovered that by a curious coincidence it had once

been the home of Lord Caernarvon — the man who had funded the archaeological dig which uncovered the tomb of Tutankhamen.

The season's fourth story, both in production and on transmission, was a four-parter entitled *The Android Invasion*. The original storyline was commissioned from writer Terry Nation on 29 November 1974 under the title *The Enemy Within*, a detailed treatment on 13 February 1975 under the title *Return to Sukannan* and the full scripts on 27 February 1975 under the title *The Kraals*.

'*The Android Invasion* was a shot at doing something quite different,' says Nation. 'I don't know why particularly. I didn't want to do a Dalek story at that point, I think. So we talked about doing a different sort of story, keeping the Daleks out of it.'

Nation's central idea was of a race of aliens who had set up a training area for a forthcoming invasion of Earth. What most appealed to Philip Hinchcliffe, however, was the use of robots, as he explains:

'Robotics fascinated me. I'd read all the Asimov stuff. The idea behind *The Android Invasion* was to do a sort of double-double-double thing with androids, but to do it really well — really shock the viewer. We didn't want it to seem like people pretending to be robots. We actually showed their faces coming off. We wanted to do it so it actually worked!'

The Android Invasion sees the TARDIS materializing on the planet Oseidon, where the Doctor and Sarah discover that an alien race called the Kraals have created an exact replica of the English village of Devesham and its nearby Space Defence Station. This is being used as a training ground for a force of androids with which the creatures intend to infiltrate and take over the Earth. A human astronaut, Guy Crayford, is collaborating in this scheme as he has been duped into believing that he was abandoned by his own people after an accident in space.

The TARDIS travels on to Earth alone, and the Doctor and Sarah are forced to follow in Crayford's rocket, the XK5 space freighter, which is being used to carry the spearhead of the invasion force. The Kraals' leader, Styggron, intends to release a virulent virus on Earth in order to weaken resistance to the forthcoming invasion.

On reaching Earth, the Doctor and Sarah try to convince UNIT troops at the Space Defence Station of the imminent danger. The Brigadier is away in Geneva, however, and Crayford is being hailed by all as a hero. The Doctor uses the Station's transmitters to jam the control signals of the now active

Styggron (Martin Friend) and Chedaki (Roy Skelton) in the Kraal base on Oseidon. *The Android Invasion*.

The Doctor is subjected to the Kraal's disorientation chamber as Styggron looks on. *The Android Invasion*.

androids — including duplicates of himself, Harry Sullivan and RSM Benton — and prevents Styggron from releasing his virus. Styggron accidentally infects himself during a fight with the android Doctor and is killed. The Doctor and Sarah then slip back to the TARDIS, leaving UNIT to clear up in the aftermath of the incident.

The Android Invasion was the penultimate UNIT story of the seventies and the last to feature John Levene and Ian Marter in their regular roles as RSM Benton and Harry Sullivan — albeit in android form. Nicholas Courtney was unavailable, so the lines originally written for the Brigadier were given instead to a new character, Colonel Faraday, played by Patrick Newell.

Also making his final contribution to the series was sculptor John Friedlander, who created the masks for the Kraals. The script had described them as insectoid creatures covered with heavy carapaces which made them impervious to radiation. Friedlander, however, was unhappy with this idea and based them instead upon mammals such as rhinoceroses and wild boar.

Three former members of the *Doctor Who* production team had stories under consideration during the period when season thirteen was being planned. Sixties story editor Dennis Spooner was commissioned on 4 February 1975 to write a four-parter entitled *The Nightmare Planet*, the storyline for which had been accepted on 31 January 1975, but was ultimately unable to complete it to the production team's satisfaction. Philip Hinchcliffe's predecessor Barry Letts similarly finished just the first of the four scripts he had been commissioned to write for a story entitled *The Prisoner of Time*.

'I came up with a story based on the scene I had written for Elisabeth Sladen's audition,' says Letts. 'I wrote the storyline and then the script. But meanwhile Philip had had other thoughts and wanted it

changed radically — the whole *raison d'être* of the story was altered. I did my best, but there were so many changes. We never really got anywhere with it. So I just left them the work I'd done.'

The third idea came from Robert Holmes's predecessor Terrance Dicks, who towards the end of 1974 submitted a storyline entitled *The Haunting*. This too proved unsuccessful, but Dicks was shortly afterwards commissioned to write what would eventually become the season's fifth story, *The Brain of Morbius*.

'We'd been talking about various myths,' remembers Dicks, 'and one of them was the *Frankenstein* myth of a man making a monster. I came up with the idea of a galactic super-criminal who has a super robot assistant — a sort of devoted robot Jeeves. The criminal, Morbius, is fleeing from his enemies and his spaceship crashes. He is smashed up to the extent that the robot can save only his head. And having been saved like this, he demands a new body. The robot is well-intentioned, but limited as robots are. Now, for some reason, spaceships crash on this planet. So the robot goes out, scoops up the remaining bits of alien life forms and whacks them together into a roughly-functioning body, onto which he puts Morbius's head. But as Morbius has always been something of a handsome Greek god, he is far from pleased.

'That was the story — it was gruesome, macabre and funny. But it was also logical: the robot would do that. Bob and I worked out the story, and I wrote a set of scripts which he seemed happy with. The mistake I made was in delivering them on the day I went away on holiday! During subsequent discussions I was out of the country and could not be contacted. And Philip Hinchcliffe turned against the robot. He thought that it would be too expensive to realize. So Bob was instructed to remove the robot from the story. Now, the robot was the whole *core* of the story. Poor old

CASTING FOR PYRAMIDS

Often, directors would have several ideas as to who might play a given part. The following were director Paddy Russell's original casting ideas for the guest characters in **Pyramids of Mars:**

Marcus Scarman
Maurice Kaufmann; Christopher Benjamin; Leonard Kavanagh; Ronald Howard; Leonard Sachs; Peter Welch; Bernard Archard*.

Laurence Scarman
Maurice Kaufmann; Colin George; Reg Pritchard; Michael Sheard*.

Namin
Lee Crawford; Renu Setna; Al Garcia; Barry Martin; Mike Lewin.

Ernie Clements
Chubby Oates; Tommy Wright; Mostyn Evans; Walter Sparrow; Anthony Kenyon; Freddie Earlle; George Tovey*; Eric Francis.

Dr Warlock
Martin Dempsey; Andrew Lodge; John Baskcomb; Roger Booth; John Wentworth; Colin George.

Collins
Jeffrey Segal; Eric Francis; Arthur Hewlett; Michael Bilton*.

Sutekh
Gabor Vernon; John Quentin; Malcolm Rennie; Paul Bacon; Gabriel Woolf*.

Ahmed
David Rayner; Vik Tablian*.

Mummies
Jon Glover; Malcolm Mudie; Paul Lamont; Douglas Gorin; Dave Carter; Philip Ryan; David Jackson; Miles Hoyle.

* indicates that this actor played the role on screen. Namin was eventually played by Peter Mayock, Dr Warlock by Peter Copley and the Mummies by Nick Burnell, Melvyn Bedford and Kevin Selway.

STOCK FOOTAGE

Planet of Evil *part two featured footage from a programme called* **Orang-Utan** *in the BBC2 series* **The World About Us** *on one of the Morestran ship's monitors to represent the ship flying over the jungle.*

Footage from NASA was used for the launch of the rocket in part three of **The Android Invasion.**

The Seeds of Doom *part six featured some footage from World Backgrounds.*

MORBIUS OR THE DOCTOR?

*During the mind battle at the conclusion of **The Brain of Morbius**, several faces are seen to appear on the screen sited between Morbius and the Doctor, supposedly representing past incarnations of the duelling Time Lords. In fact these were specially taken photographs of production team members for both **The Brain of Morbius** and **The Seeds of Doom**, together with a treated photograph of the clay bust of Morbius featured in earlier episodes and photographs of the first three Doctors: William Hartnell, Patrick Troughton and Jon Pertwee. The production team members featured were: Philip Hinchcliffe (producer), Robert Holmes (script editor), Douglas Camfield (director), Graeme Harper (production assistant), Robert Banks Stewart (writer), Christopher Baker (production assistant), George Gallaccio (production unit manager) and Christopher Barry (director). It has long been a subject of debate as to which of the contestants – the Doctor or Morbius – these additional faces relate to, but as Morbius lost the contest it is generally assumed that they were past incarnations of him.*

LEWIS GRIEFER
WRITER

*Lewis Griefer used two names for his writing: his own, and that of Joshua Adam. In the following listing, those written as Adam are marked with an *. Griefer wrote **The Voodoo Factor** for ATV in 1959/1960, contributed scripts to **Crossroads** and worked as a story editor for HTV in the sixties. In 1963 he wrote three episodes for **Ghost Squad*** and in 1964 did one episode for the third season of **Ghost Squad** which had been renamed **GS5***. In 1967 he contributed the episode **The General*** to Patrick McGoohan's **The Prisoner** and in 1969 wrote one episode for a series called **Fraud Squad***, contributing two further scripts under his own name for the second series in 1970. 1971 saw him contribute to a series called **The Trial** for the BBC and in 1972 he wrote one episode for **New Scotland Yard**. In 1973/1974 he wrote two episodes for **Special Branch**. After completing the initial scripts for **Pyramids of Mars** he took up a teaching assignment in Tel Aviv.*

The Sisterhood of Karn. Maran (Cynthia Grenville) is seated in the centre while Ohica (Gilly Brown) is standing to the right. *The Brain of Morbius*.

Bob, in a state of some desperation, came up with a mad scientist instead. It wasn't the most original idea in the world, but it was the only one available. Of course Bob was a very good writer, and it worked out all right. I'm not saying that it wasn't a good show, but it just wasn't my show by the time I came back from holiday.

'Technically, a production team is not allowed to do that to a script without consulting the writer. But Bob was an old friend, and I did not want actually to block the show and put them in terrible trouble. However, I was furious when I got the scripts. I rang up Bob and shouted at him down the telephone. He was apologetic, but asked what else he could have done. Eventually I said, "All right, you can do it, but I'm going to take my name off it. Not because it's a bad show, but because it's now much more you than me." He asked, "Well, what name do you want to put on it?" I said, "I don't care. You can put it out under some bland pseudonym," and slammed the phone down. Weeks later, when I saw the *Radio Times*, I noticed it was "The Brain of Morbius by Robin Bland." By then I'd cooled down, and the joke disarmed me completely.'

The Brain of Morbius brings the TARDIS to the planet Karn. This is the home of a mystic order called the Sisterhood, the guardians of a sacred flame which produces an Elixir of Life used by the Time Lords to help them through difficult regenerations. Also resident on the planet is Mehendri Solon, a fanatical scientist who, with the aid of his man-servant Condo, is using the remnants of spaceship crash victims to put together a new body for the still-living brain of the executed Time Lord criminal Morbius. When the Doctor and Sarah seek shelter at his citadel, Solon decides that the Doctor's head is just what he needs to complete his work.

The telepathic Sisterhood are aware of the Doctor's arrival on Karn and fear that he has been sent by the Time Lords to steal the last precious drops of Elixir produced by the dying scared flame. They kidnap him and attempt to burn him at the stake but he

The Morbius monster (Stuart Fell) grapples with Solon (Philip Madoc). *The Brain of Morbius*.

is rescued by Sarah, who is temporarily blinded in the process. The Doctor is tricked by Solon into believing that his companion's condition is permanent. He subsequently seeks the Sisters' help and, to prove himself to them, restores their sacred flame to its former glory using a firework to clear its blocked chimney.

Returning to Solon's citadel, the Doctor and Sarah become trapped in the cellar. The Doctor releases cyanide fumes into the ventilation system and Solon is killed, but not before he has used an artificial brain-case to complete Morbius's new body. The now-mobile Morbius accepts the Doctor's challenge to a mind-bending contest, which takes a heavy toll on both of them. The Sisters force the crazed Morbius over a cliff and he falls to his death. They then use the precious Elixir to heal the Doctor, who bids them farewell and leaves with Sarah in the TARDIS.

The Brain of Morbius was a rare example of a fourth Doctor story recorded entirely at Television Centre, with no filming either on location or at the BBC's Ealing studios. This presented unusual challenges for set designer Barry Newbery, whose involvement with *Doctor Who* extended right back to the very first story:

'The usual time given in the mid-seventies to design the settings for a 30-minute recording was nine days, with extra allowed for any filming. *The Brain of Morbius* had no filming, so therefore I had just 36 days — four of which were the studio days — to complete my work on it. Thinking about all the things that had to be done before the first studio — that is, in the first four weeks — I find it incredible now that I managed to do it. But of course that goes for everyone else on the production as well.

'I decided that the formal structure of Solon's citadel would be unlike traditional Gothic structures in that it would have supporting columns on the inside instead of buttresses on the outside. It has been said that I based the designs on the work of Antonio Gaudi. That's not so — although I did look at his

The Doctor with the clay bust of the renegade Time Lord Morbius. *The Brain of Morbius.*

buildings in my research. The only place in which that influence did perhaps show through was in the shape of the window in Solon's laboratory. My starting point was to try to think of ways in which a civilization parallel to that on Earth — one which had the same genetic make-up and lived on a planet nearly identical in its circumstances — would develop at the same rate but solve its problems differently. So the architecture was inside out.

'The columns also enabled the director, Christopher Barry, to get some interesting camera angles and compositions, but in this instance that wasn't something I'd consciously thought of. I was simply trying to make the structure of the room echo the constructional principle of internal buttressing. However, Christopher looked at it visually, and two lines at an irregular angle are always going to make the picture more interesting than two parallel ones.'

'I enjoyed *The Brain of Morbius* a lot,' says Christopher Barry. 'I revelled in it. I thought, "Here is a Gothic story, so let's treat it that way." It was obviously based on the *Frankenstein* idea, so I thought we'd have fun with it — "We'll see how far we can go."'

'I think the thing people really complained about was the scene where Morbius's brain fell on the floor, but to me that was humorous rather than grisly. I think most people laugh at that sort of thing. But it's possible that if your attitude to life is that the brain is a sacred object, then it's like dropping the Holy Grail or dashing the communion wine to the floor.'

The production team had at one point considered dividing season thirteen into six four-part stories and one two-part story. To this end they had in the late summer of 1975 commissioned from writer Eric Pringle a two-parter entitled *The Angurth*. This

turned out to be unsuitable, however, and so the season ultimately consisted of five four-parters and one six-parter. This set a precedent which would be followed for the remainder of the seventies seasons.

The concluding six-parter of season thirteen was *The Seeds of Doom* by Robert Banks Stewart — the writer who had earlier been responsible for the season opener, *Terror of the Zygons*.

The story opens with a vegetable pod being found buried in the permafrost near an Antarctic research station. Photographs of the discovery are sent to England, where the Doctor identifies it as having come from a Krynoid — an alien life-form which feeds off a host planet's animal population and then expels its pods into space where they fall to other worlds to germinate. The Doctor and Sarah race to the research station but get there too late to prevent the pod from opening and infecting one of the scientists, Winlett, who slowly mutates into a vicious Krynoid hybrid. News of the pod has meanwhile reached millionaire botanist Harrison Chase (amended from Harrington Chase in the original draft scripts), who decides that he must add this unique specimen to his collection. Two of his agents, Scorby and Keeler, arrive at the research station and seize a second pod which has been found, then plant a bomb to cover their tracks. The first Krynoid is destroyed in the explosion, but the Doctor and Sarah escape.

On returning to England, the two friends trace

▲ Sarah and the Doctor realise that they have not arrived on Cassiopeiae after all. *The Seeds of Doom.*

▼ Designer Barry Newbery's design painting for Solon's clifftop citadel. *The Brain of Morbius.*

The Krynoid (Ronald ▲ Gough and Keith Ashley). *The Seeds of Doom.*

ROBERT BANKS STEWART
WRITER

Robert Banks Stewart is one of the most prolific writers working in television. He was script consultant and writer on **Undermind** *(1965) and wrote for* **The Avengers** *(1965),* **Adam Adamant Lives!** *(1966),* **Public Eye** *(1968),* **Special Branch** *(1969),* **Fraud Squad** *(1969),* **Callan** *(1967–1969),* **New Scotland Yard** *(1972),* **Jason King** *(1972),* **Arthur of the Britons** *(1972) and* **The Sweeney** *(1975). He had also contributed scripts for* **Dr. Finlay's Casebook** *and script edited as well as written for* **Van Der Valk** *before he was commissioned to write the season thirteen story* **Terror of the Zygons** *in 1974. This commission was shortly followed by another* **Doctor Who** *story,* **The Seeds of Doom**, *after which Stewart worked on* **Sutherland's Law** *and episodes of* **Robin Hood**, *the BBC's 1975 classic serial. In 1976 he contributed one further storyline to* **Doctor Who**, *called* **The Foe from the Future**, *which was eventually produced as* **The Talons of Weng-Chiang** *with scripts written by Robert Holmes. At this time he was also script editor at Thames TV and for the BBC he provided scripts for* **The Mackinnons** *and* **The Legend of Dick Turpin** *(another BBC classic serial). In 1979 he devised and wrote three episodes for* **Charles Endell Esquire** *and also co-created and produced* **Shoestring** *(1979–1980). In 1981 he devised* **Bergerac**, *a show which ran for over ten years and he also set up and produced* **Lovejoy** *(1986),* **Call Me Mister** *(1986) and* **The Darling Buds of May** *(1991). In 1992 he created* **Moon and Son** *which ran for one season.*

Charles Winlett (John Gleeson) is slowly converted into a Krynoid. *The Seeds of Doom.*

the second pod to Chase's mansion. They gain access to the grounds with the help of Amelia Ducat, an ageing painter of flora, but are caught by patrolling guards. Chase, intrigued by what Scorby and Keeler have told him about the infected man at the Antarctic, arranges for the pod to be opened under controlled conditions while a human host — Sarah — is forcibly held nearby. The Doctor rescues his companion in the nick of time, but Keeler is less lucky and is infected by the plant.

Keeler's transformation into a Krynoid is accelerated by Chase, who has him fed with raw meat. The creature then escapes and goes on the rampage through Chase's estate. Becoming ever stronger, it rapidly grows to giant proportions. Chase, now totally insane, decides to turn the Doctor into compost for his garden by feeding him into a pulverizing machine. The Time Lord escapes this grisly fate, but Chase falls into the grinder following a struggle and is killed. UNIT have meanwhile been called in, and they arrange for the Krynoid to be bombed before it can spread its pods across the Earth. The danger over, the Doctor and Sarah leave for a holiday on Cassiopeiae — but are taken back to the Antarctic by the ever-unpredictable TARDIS!

In plot terms, *The Seeds of Doom* was reminiscent of numerous hostile-plants-attack-mankind tales like John Wyndham's *The Day of the Triffids* (1951) and, on TV, *The Quatermass Experiment* (1953) and the *Out of the Unknown* episode *Come Buttercup, Come Daisy, Come . . . ?* (1965). The first two episodes, set in the Antarctic, also bore a number of similarities to the 1951 Christian Nyby film *The Thing from Another World.* This Antarctic segment was quite heavily rewritten by Robert Holmes and director Douglas Camfield but was not, as has sometimes been

reported, a late addition to the story to extend it from four episodes to six. The story was intended as a six-parter from the outset, and was commissioned as such on 30 September 1975.

'The first two episodes were always designed as part of the story,' asserts Robert Banks Stewart, 'as our idea — again, Robert Holmes and I discussed it at length — was that this strange pod should be found in the ice and that we should have, just for a change in *Doctor Who*, some immediate action in Antarctica. The intention was always to start in Antarctica and to play most of the first two episodes there, and then to develop the story in England.

'In any case, one couldn't have started that story with the pod simply arriving at this private, Kew Gardens-type laboratory; that just wouldn't have worked.'

Stewart's six scripts were delivered and accepted during the course of October 1975.

The phasing out of UNIT which had been begun in season twelve was finally completed in *The Seeds of Doom.* This was also the last story to be directed by Douglas Camfield, who had earlier overseen UNIT's introduction in the season-six story *The Invasion.*

'Douglas was marvellous for *Doctor Who*,' says Stewart. 'In fact, in retrospect — and with no disrespect to all the other directors who've worked on it — I think that Douglas Camfield was probably the finest *Doctor Who* director of all. He gave a terrific kind of lift to every story he did; he applied the same standards as he would to other forms of drama. In a way, one might almost say that Douglas was a bit of a schoolboy at heart, and he went into *Doctor Who* with a feeling of fun and inventiveness. He always had a tremendous enthusiasm for the series.'

The Seeds of Doom concluded not only season thirteen, its closing episode being transmitted on 6 March 1976, but also the thirteenth production block. Its outside broadcast recording took place at the end of October 1975 and its three studio sessions over 16—18 November, 1—2 December and 15—16 December 1975 respectively.

This had been a season in which Tom Baker had consolidated and built upon his popularity as the Doctor. It had also seen a new kind of *Doctor Who* emerging; one which relied more on Gothic horror and fantasy than on the Earth-bound action-adventure style of the third Doctor's era. These were trends which would continue in season fourteen, as Philip Hinchcliffe and Robert Holmes embarked upon their third year in charge of the series.

CHAPTER THIRTEEN

Season Fourteen: Gothic Quality

The stories of season fourteen were made and transmitted in exactly the same order — something which had been the norm during the series' first decade but which was now becoming very much the exception.

First in line was *The Masque of Mandragora* (working titles: *The Catacombs of Death, The Curse of Mandragora*), the opening episode of which was aired on 4 September 1976. Set largely in Renaissance Italy, this was a rare example of a seventies *Doctor Who* story with a historical flavour. It was Philip Hinchcliffe who had suggested this setting to writer Louis Marks after making a visit to Portmeirion, the mock-Italian village in North Wales which had become famous as the principal location for the cult Patrick McGoohan series *The Prisoner*.

'I'd been to Portmeirion,' recalls Hinchcliffe, 'and also seen Roger Corman's film *The Masque of the Red Death*, and I thought "Let's do something like that." Bob Holmes had always said "These historicals are boring," but I thought we could do quite an interesting one, and give it some bite. I said we should do one about the Machiavelli Italian era.'

This suggestion was seized upon by Marks, who

The Doctor and Sarah in the TARDIS's secondary control room as the ship heads into the Mandragora Helix. *The Masque of Mandragora.*

SEASON FOURTEEN	
CODE	TITLE
4M	THE MASQUE OF MANDRAGORA
4N	THE HAND OF FEAR
4P	THE DEADLY ASSASSIN
4Q	THE FACE OF EVIL
4R	THE ROBOTS OF DEATH
4S	THE TALONS OF WENG-CHIANG

RATINGS

Figures in millions

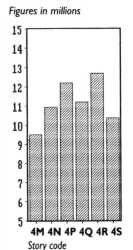

Story code

Barry Newbery's ▲ detailed set for Hieronymous's study. *The Masque of Mandragora.*

The Doctor stands ▲ outside the TARDIS on a green CSO set. *The Masque of Mandragora.*

DOCTOR WHO AND THE HELL PLANET

On Friday 31 December 1976 the Daily Mirror ran a full page Doctor Who adventure by Terrance Dicks in their Junior Mirror section. It told of a small group of space explorers who find themselves on a planet inhabited by monsters. They meet the Doctor who persuades them to leave the planet after he saves their spaceship from being destroyed by one of the monsters. The explorers won't be recommending the planet for colonization, which, the Doctor muses when they have left, is just as well, for in 70 million years the monsters will have died out and a new species called Man would have emerged.

Count Federico (John Laurimore) and Captain Rossini (Antony Carrick) stand in another of Barry Newbery's impressive sets. *The Masque of Mandragora.*

in 1954 had written a post-graduate thesis called *The Development of the Institutions of Public Finance in Florence during the Last Sixty Years of the Republic, c. 1470—1530* and was consequently something of an expert in the Renaissance era. The story he came up with was one which mixed themes of astrology and political in-fighting.

'It was the idea of astrology which intrigued me,' he says. 'Astrology is, after all, trying to find the forces in the stars which actually affect us — which decide our destinies and so forth. I applied what could be called "*Doctor Who* thinking" to this idea, to suggest "What if these aren't just chance forces but are being manipulated by somebody or something making them happen?" So the basic premise arrived at was not just mumbo-jumbo but a force within the Universe which could be controlled and directed. Against that force one has the power of science, which becomes the Doctor's weapon. He uses the new knowledge first to understand the nature of his enemy and then finally to fight back against it.'

The story opens with the Doctor and Sarah investigating some unfamiliar areas of the TARDIS and coming across a wood-panelled secondary control room. On activating the scanner, the Doctor sees that they are approaching the Mandragora Helix, a spiral of energy with a controlling influence. The ship is temporarily captured by the Helix and drawn to a still point at its centre, where — unbeknown to the Doctor — it is infiltrated by a sparkling ball of energy.

The travellers' next port of call is the Dukedom of San Martino in Renaissance Italy, where the Doctor quickly realizes that the Mandragora energy is loose and up to no good. The energy enters an underground temple and reveals itself to the outlawed Brotherhood of Demnos, whose leader, the court astrologer Hieronymous, receives instructions to make ready for Mandragora's full appearance.

Hieronymous (Norman Jones) and an acolyte of the Brotherhood of Demnos in the Brotherhood's crypt headquarters. *The Masque of Mandragoa.*

Hieronymous is one of the pawns in the evil Count Federico's schemes to usurp his young nephew Giuliano, whose accession to the Dukedom is being marked with a celebratory masque. At the height of the ball, the Brotherhood attack the court and kill many of the guests. Hieronymous, now completely absorbed by Mandragora, confronts the Doctor in the underground temple and attempts to blast him down. The Doctor, however, has earthed both himself and the altar so that the energy simply drains away, leaving the planet safe — at least until the constellations are again in the correct configuration for the Helix to make contact.

Two notable aspects of *The Masque of Mandragora* were the location filming carried out in Portmeirion during April 1976, which gave the story an authentic Italian ambience, and the impressive sets designed by Barry Newbery for the studio recording which got underway on 3 May 1976.

'I always researched the historical settings pretty thoroughly,' says Newbery. '*The Masque of Mandragora* took place in 15th-century Italy, so I decided to base my designs largely on paintings of the period, and particularly those of Vittore Carpaccio, a very fine Renaissance artist.'

Another important task which fell to Newbery was that of designing the TARDIS's secondary control room.

'It was Philip Hinchcliffe's idea to have a new TARDIS interior. There was always a problem with the old one: it took up such a lot of room in the studio. It was rarely needed for more than one or two scenes, but once it had been put up it was stuck there for the whole day. I think the feeling was that if they could only get rid of it they would have more room for other sets. So Philip asked me if I could come up with a smaller one to a different design.

'I decided to go for a Jules Verne look, with wood panelling, brass fittings, bits of stained glass and so on. I retained the familiar roundels — this was still part of the TARDIS, after all — but had them arranged in parallel rows, rather than staggered as they had been previously. This meant that I could incorporate doorways and so on without leaving lots of untidy semicircles around the edges. My brief for the scanner screen was to use CSO rather than a real monitor — there is a limit to the amount of information one can put on a monitor, and luminosity is also a problem in a TV studio — so I had a pair of mechanically-operated wooden shutters built into one of the walls with a CSO cloth behind them.

'The new control console I made something akin to a little davenport, only six-sided in keeping with the spirit of the original. The control panels were behind little flaps, although only one of them actually had controls fitted for this story as I knew that the others wouldn't be seen. The director, Rodney Bennett, was quite keen to have a central column which rose and fell, again like the original, but Philip and I thought it best to avoid this. For one thing it would have been very costly, and for another it would have created unnecessary problems — the central column on the original console was always breaking down!

'As Philip had requested, I made the new set much smaller than the original. I also put the console on a raised dais, allowing for a greater variety of shots.

'Incidentally, I also had a new police box built for this story. The original one had undergone quite a lot of repairs and modifications over the years, before it wore out altogether, so for this new one I tried to go back more to what it had looked like when the series first began. The new version was much lighter, too, and so easier to take out on location.'

The season's second story marked the final regular appearance of Elisabeth Sladen as Sarah Jane Smith — not only one of the longest-serving of the Doctor's companions, but also one of the most popular. This farewell adventure was originally to have been written by long-time *Doctor Who* director Douglas Camfield, who came up with a pseudo-historical sword-and-sorcery tale set in a Foreign Legion outpost and involving feuding factions of a powerful alien race. Sarah was to have been killed off at the end, and the closing scenes would have shown her receiving a full ceremonial burial at the military fortress. Ultimately, however, Camfield's scripts were rejected and *The Hand of Fear* by Bob Baker and Dave Martin was taken forward as a replacement.

'Eventually I'd had enough,' recalls Sladen. 'I had nothing to go to, nothing lined up, but I went to Philip Hinchcliffe and said, "I think I should go while my character is still popular. I can't stay forever, I don't want to be asked to leave, and I'd rather go on my own terms." I said, "Please don't marry me off to anyone else, and please don't kill me off."

'Philip said, "How do you want to go?" I said, "I don't want the entire story to be about me going. Let it be a *Doctor Who* story, and right at the end just let me go." Lennie Mayne, the director, said, "What do you want to do for the last shot?" and I replied, "Can we do it like the Americans, and freeze frame?"

'I adored Sarah, and I'd defend her to anyone. I know she was so stupid at times, but always with the best will in the world. So she went down the same hole every time, and she tripped over, and it got to be like *The Perils of Pauline*. I really found it a challenge. I asked Barry Letts at the start, "What do you want? What's she supposed to be like?" He said, "She jumps before she thinks — she's an instigator." They tagged the journalist thing on. So he left me alone, saying, "Just do what you think is right!" '

Sarah is rescued from the rubble by the Doctor and a quarry worker. *The Hand of Fear.*

Eldrad (Judith Paris) admires his new form which has been patterned on Sarah. *The Hand of Fear.*

▲ Setting up the visual effects shot of the Mandragora Helix spinning in space. The top photograph shows Ken Bomphray assisting with a mechanical 'galaxy' against a front axial projection (FAP) screen. *The Masque of Mandragora.*

▲ Sarah with the stone hand. *The Hand of Fear.*

▼ The model of the Kastrian Obliteration Module. *The Hand of Fear.*

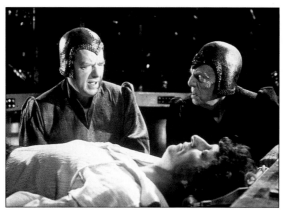

The emaciated Master ▲ (Peter Pratt). *The Deadly Assassin.*

CASTING LEELA

It was often the case that when casting a new companion, the production team would hold extensive auditions with artistes suggested by agents as being suitable for the role. The following auditions were held for the part of Leela:

10 August 1976: Carol Drinkwater; Katherine Fahy; Deborah Fairfax; Gail Grainger; Louise Jameson; Kay Korda; Pamela Salem; Lois Hantz.

17 August 1976: Colette Gleeson; Marilyn Galsworthy; Ann Pennington; Carol Leader; Celia Foxe.

18 August 1976: Belinda Sinclair; Belinda Low; Carol Leader (second audition).

20 August 1976: Gail Harrison; Irene Gorst; Sally Geeson; Janet Edis; Michelle Newell; Phillipa Vavzey; Heather Tobias; Elaine Donnelly; Sue Jones-Davies.

25 August 1976: Lydia Lisle; Susan Wooldridge; Louise Jameson (second audition); Janet Edis (second audition); Carol Drinkwater (second audition).

The five actresses seen on 25 August were those on the production team's short-list. Others who fell only just short of this were Irene Gorst, Sally Geeson, Michelle Newell, Heather Tobias, Elaine Donnelly, Belinda Sinclair and Carol Leader. The remainder were considered unsuitable for the role.

Coordinator Engin (Eric Chitty) and Castellan Spandrell (George Pravda) watch over the Doctor's body as he battles the Master in the Matrix. *The Deadly Assassin.*

The Master in his lair beneath the Time Lord's citadel. *The Deadly Assassin.*

The Hand of Fear (working titles: *The Hand of Time, The Hand of Death*) sees the TARDIS materializing in a quarry on present-day Earth. A mining explosion is triggered nearby and Sarah is buried under the resulting rubble. As the miners and the Doctor frantically search for her, she regains consciousness to find herself entombed. Seeing a hand reaching for her, she grasps it only to find that it is a fossil. A burst of energy moves from the hand into her mind, knocking her unconscious once more.

Sarah is found and taken to hospital. Recovering, she removes a blue-stoned ring from the fossil hand and places it on her own. She then leaves the hospital in a trance, taking the hand with her, and makes her way to a nearby nuclear power station. The hand soaks up the radiation from the reactor core and comes alive, growing into a creature named Eldrad. Eldrad is a criminal who plotted to destroy his home planet, Kastria, when he was denied power. Sentenced to death, he was placed in a syllenic obliteration module and launched into deep space, where the module was blown up. However, parts of Eldrad's silicone-based body drifted to Earth where they lay for centuries until the hand was uncovered.

Eldrad — who, having patterned his new body on Sarah's, appears to all intents and purposes female —

persuades the Doctor to take him back to Kastria where he might reclaim his heritage. There he discovers only a dead planet: the Kastrians are extinct and their race banks were destroyed by their last King, Rokon, in case Eldrad should ever return. Furious, Eldrad, whose body has now been reconfigured into its proper form, tries to get the Doctor to return him to Earth so that he might rule there instead. The two time travellers use the Doctor's scarf to trip him into a deep crevasse.

On returning to the TARDIS, the Doctor receives a summons from the Time Lords. He tells Sarah that she must leave him as outsiders are not permitted on his home world. Sarah is deposited supposedly in her home town of Croydon but does not recognize the street — it seems the Doctor has got it wrong again!

Writers Bob Baker and Dave Martin had suggested the story's power station setting to the production team after finding a suitable location at Oldbury on the Severn estuary. This was originally to have represented the Nuton complex first seen in season eight's *The Claws of Axos*, the story with which Baker and Martin had made their *Doctor Who* debut, but the name was changed to Nunton in the transmitted episodes. The management at Oldbury reacted enthusiastically to the idea of filming taking place there and gave the production team full co-operation. The concept of the fossil hand came from Robert Holmes, who had in mind the horror film *The Hands of Orloc*. Baker and Martin also drew inspiration from another film, *The Beast with Five Fingers*. Sarah's farewell scene at the end of the story was largely rewritten by Tom Baker and Elisabeth Sladen themselves, with some input from Holmes.

After Sarah's departure, the production team decided to do a story in which the Doctor would be companionless — something that Tom Baker had long been suggesting. 'We were between girls,' recalled Holmes, 'so it seemed like a good time to test out whether or not the Doctor needed an assistant at all. Could the Doctor carry the programme on his own? I think we proved he could, but the first episode, before he became involved with other people, was very difficult to structure.'

The story, commissioned on 27 May 1976 under the working title *The Dangerous Assassin* and later renamed *The Deadly Assassin*, was written by Holmes himself and, at Philip Hinchcliffe's suggestion, took place entirely on the Doctor's home planet, Gallifrey.

Experiencing premonitions of the assassination of the Time Lord President, the Doctor materializes the TARDIS on Gallifrey. After gaining access to the Capitol, he quickly learns that this is the day on

The Doctor, Tomas (Brendan Price) and Leela (Louise Jameson) during rehearsals for *The Face of Evil*.

▲ Leela (Louise Jameson). Note that she is wearing dark make-up in this shot.

▲ Visual effects designer Mat Irvine with the Horda props. *The Face of Evil*.

which the President is to resign and name his successor. Favourite for the post is Chancellor Goth, but only the President knows for sure. Donning the robes of one of the assembled Time Lords, the Doctor makes his way to the ceremonial meeting hall, the Panopticon, and from there to an overlooking balcony where he has noticed someone taking aim with a staser weapon. The balcony turns out to be deserted but, seeing a gun raised in the crowd below as the President appears, the Doctor picks up the staser and fires. The President falls down dead, apparently shot by the Doctor.

The Doctor is put on trial for murder but manages to gain a temporary immunity by nominating himself as a Presidential candidate. With the help of Co-ordinator Engin and Castellan Spandrell, he investigates the assassination and discovers that it is part of a plot hatched by his old adversary the Master. Having used up all twelve of his regenerations, the Master is now a wizened husk — the result of an accident on the planet Tersurus. He is seeking to control the Presidency in order to obtain the official regalia, the Sash and Rod of Rassilon, which are in truth the keys to the Eye of Harmony, the source of all Time Lord power.

The Doctor links his mind to the Amplified Panatropic Computer Net containing the accumulated wisdom of the Time Lords, which he believes to have been responsible for his earlier premonitions. In the virtual reality of the Matrix, he finds himself in a life-or-death struggle with a hooded opponent. The Doctor proves the stronger and his opponent is revealed as Goth, whom the Master has been using as a puppet. Following his defeat, Goth dies. The Master meanwhile seizes the Sash and Rod of Rassilon and starts to access the Eye of Harmony, located beneath the Panopticon floor, in the hope of drawing off enough energy to enable himself to regenerate. The Doctor manages to intervene before Gallifrey is destroyed, and the Master falls down one of the fissures which have opened up in the floor. The Doctor then departs in the TARDIS, unaware that the Master has survived his fall and escaped to fight another day.

The Deadly Assassin was the first story to feature the Master since the death of the original actor, Roger Delgado, in 1973. On this occasion he was played

A Tesh in the corridors of their space ship. *The Face of Evil*.

CHRIS BOUCHER
WRITER

After leaving school Christopher Boucher went to Australia for a year before returning to England and starting work at Calor Gas as a management trainee. The company sent him to Essex University to read Economics where he received a BA. It was while at university that he turned to writing as a means to supplement his income. His first work was for **Braden's Week** *and he went on to write gags for Dave Allen amongst others. It was his agent who suggested he submit some ideas to* **Doctor Who** *as a means of broadening his range and this led to several commissions for the series in the late seventies. When David Maloney was looking for a script editor for* **Blake's 7** *in 1977, it was Robert Holmes who suggested Boucher. Upon getting the job he immediately quit his other job at Calor Gas. Boucher worked on almost the entire run of* **Blake's 7**, *contributing eight scripts as well as working as script editor. Following the end of* **Blake's 7** *in 1981, Boucher worked on* **Juliet Bravo** *(1982) and* **Bergerac** *(1983–1986) as script editor and writer and then developed a new science fiction series,* **Star Cops**, *for the BBC in 1987, for which he also wrote five scripts.*

The model cliff carved ▲ into the likeness of 'the Evil One'. The Face of Evil.

Leela in Victorian ▲ costume. The Talons of Weng-Chiang.

Magnus Greel (Michael ▲ Spice), alias the Chinese god Weng-Chiang, in his Limehouse lair. Beside him is the Peking Homunculous (Deep Roy). The Talons of Weng-Chiang.

by Peter Pratt, a former member of the d'Oyly Carte opera company, who was cast by director David Maloney as he had not only a very rich voice but also the necessary stature to act in a major role opposite Tom Baker. He appeared throughout the story wearing a cadaverous mask which he later described as resembling 'a rather over-cooked set of fried eggs'.

'Philip Hinchcliffe felt it was time to reintroduce the Master in a physically transitional stage,' explained Robert Holmes. 'This was so that our successors, if they wished, would be free to appoint a new actor to this popular role.'

Another notable aspect of *The Deadly Assassin* was the fact that the third episode consisted almost entirely of location-filmed sequences of the mind battle in the Matrix, the surrealistic nature of which Holmes felt widened the series' vocabulary:

'*The Deadly Assassin* was, I think, the first *Doctor Who* in years that did not feature a monster. We decided instead to go for these surrealistic sequences of episode three. This meant putting all our film effort into one episode. And this meant writing the other three episodes totally for studio. David Maloney took all these difficulties in his stride, as he always does, and directed the show brilliantly.'

The season's fourth story marked the debut of writer Chris Boucher. Robert Holmes had suggested the concept of a world controlled by a powerful computer which began to malfunction, causing civilization to break down. The Doctor's problem would be to recognize what was happening and put things to rights. Boucher's initial inclination was to set the story on a multi-generational colonist ship, and on this basis he produced two successive storylines, *The Dreamers of Phados* and *The Mentor Conspiracy*, neither of which was quite what the production team were looking for. Philip Hinchcliffe then suggested changing the setting to a planet and incorporating a giant sculpture of the Doctor's head — a visual image he had always wanted to see used in the series. Boucher consequently proceeded to produce a third storyline, *The Tower of Imelo*, on the strength of which he was commissioned to write the full scripts for a four-part story.

It was only at this point that Boucher learned that Sarah was no longer to be the Doctor's companion. He was told that there were no immediate plans to replace her, and that this would probably be left until the break between the fourteenth and fifteenth production blocks. One idea under discussion was for a Cockney waif character, loosely based on Eliza Doolittle in *Pygmalion*, who might possibly be played by well-known actress and former model Twiggy — tying in with tentative casting plans for *Doctor Who meets Scratchman*, the cinema film script written by

Tom Baker, Ian Marter and James Hill for which finance was currently being sought. Philip Hinchcliffe also considered casting Emily Richard as the new regular, having greatly admired her performance in the title role of a recent BBC adaptation of *Lorna Doone*, but she turned out to be unavailable. Robert Holmes, drawing on his experience of writing *The Deadly Assassin*, advised Boucher to develop one of his own characters to serve as a companion figure for the duration of the story. Boucher at first considered using his male lead, Loke (later renamed Tomas), for this purpose. It was then suggested, however, that the companion should be female, so he decided instead to incorporate the character of Leela, who had first appeared in *The Mentor Conspiracy* storyline.

By the time Boucher had delivered the script for the second of his four episodes, which he had decided to call *The Day God Went Mad*, Philip Hinchcliffe was sufficiently impressed with Leela that he was considering using her as a continuing character — a kind of futuristic Eliza Doolittle. Boucher therefore wrote two different endings to his story — one in which Leela went with the Doctor in the TARDIS, and one in which she stayed behind on the planet. It was the former of these which was eventually used in the transmitted story, now renamed *The Face of Evil* by the production team in view of potential religious objections to Boucher's title.

After extensive auditions, the actress chosen for the role of Leela was 25-year-old Louise Jameson. Her skimpy leather costume, designed by John Bloomfield, ensured that her debut received extensive coverage in the tabloid press, earning her descriptions such as 'this sexy, space-age cave girl', 'sexy superwoman' and 'sexiest assistant so far'. Her contract covered the fourteen episodes remaining in the season and, in addition to a standard clause about fight sequences, required her to wear special contact lenses to change her eye colour from blue to brown. Philip Hinchcliffe also had her agent notified that she might be required to wear a wig or a special hairstyle. Another idea under consideration was that she might wear dark make-up for the part, but this was eventually dropped after some tests proved unsatisfactory.

The Face of Evil sees the TARDIS materializing on a planet where a tribe of savages, the Sevateem, worship a god called Xoanon. Xoanon speaks to the tribe through their holy man, Neeva, and exhorts them to find a way through a deadly energy barrier which separates them from a forbidden land controlled by the Tesh. The Doctor finds that his face is recognized by the Sevateem as that of the Evil One, and that there is a massive carving of it on a cliff near their village. Only one member of the

The Doctor and Professor Litefoot (Trevor Baxter) prepare to go hunting giant rats in London's sewers. *The Talons of Weng-Chiang.*

The Doctor and Leela in the London sewers. *The Talons of Weng-Chiang.*

THE TIME MACHINE

A one-off **Doctor Who** episode was transmitted at 2.00 pm on Monday 4 October 1976 on BBC Radio 4 VHF as part of the children's educational geography series **Exploration Earth**. Subtitled **The Time Machine**, the programme was 20-minutes long and starred Tom Baker as the Doctor, Elisabeth Sladen as Sarah Jane Smith and John Westbrook as the Megron.

Written by Bernard Venables, the story opens with the Doctor and Sarah in the TARDIS. A strange force brings the ship to a halt 4,500 million years in Earth's past. The Doctor and Sarah see the Earth being created from boiling gases. The Doctor programs the TARDIS to follow Earth's development.

The next time the ship stops, the Earth is a ball of molten rock and gases in the process of cooling. As the Doctor and Sarah watch, an echoing voice demands to know who they are. This is the Megron, High Lord of Chaos, Chief of the Karlions, who has taken over the formless ball. He proclaims that nothing now can alter its disorder. The Doctor points out that a rock crust is forming on the planet, and order is coming whether the Megron likes it or not. The Megron flies into a rage and the Doctor and Sarah slip back to the TARDIS.

At the travellers' next stopping off point, the Earth is steadily being shaped by massive eruptions and earthquakes. The Doctor compresses time, and he and his companion watch as seas, mountains and continents are formed. The Megron appears again and asserts that order will never come out of this chaos. The Doctor taunts him, saying that even now there is oxygen being generated and that before long there will be life. The Megron rages once more, and the Doctor and Sarah leave.

The TARDIS finally halts in an idyllic landscape of trees, flowers, birds and animals, fresh air and bright sunlight. Sarah is very impressed and the Doctor comments that it is incredible what oxygen can do – it has made all this life possible. The Megron is still about, though, and the Doctor challenges him to a duel of telepathic will deployment. The Doctor wins this contest easily and the Megron is banished forever from the Earth.

tribe is willing to trust him. This is Leela, an outcast who has dared to question the wisdom of Xoanon.

Leela helps the Doctor to investigate further, and he manages to get through the barrier by way of passages behind the carving of his face. He discovers that the situation which now exists on this planet is the indirect result of his own actions on an earlier visit, when he repaired the computer of a crashed spaceship and inadvertently drove it mad by giving it a multiple personality. The computer, Xoanon, subsequently arranged for the ship's crew to be split up, raising the technicians — or Tesh — as ascetic telepaths who would tend with religious fervour to its every need while allowing the survey team — the Sevateem — to descend into savagery.

The Doctor manages to wipe the additional personalities from the computer, leaving it sane and in proper control once more. Leela, deciding that she no longer wants to stay on her own planet, pushes her way on board the TARDIS. It seems that the Doctor has gained another companion.

Following transmission of *The Face of Evil*, a dispute arose between Chris Boucher and the BBC as to who owned the rights to Leela. This was finally resolved in 1978.

'Leela was actually named after a Palestinian woman called Leila Khaled,' says Boucher, 'who would now be regarded as a terrorist — she and her two companions were the first hijackers — but in those days was something of a celebrity. She was very glamorous and very bright.

'The character came out of the whole atmosphere of that time. The women's movement had begun to

get underway and people in general, and the media, were starting to see women in a different light. We had also had *The Avengers*, and I had fallen deeply in love with Emma Peel. She was just unbelievably gorgeous and depended on absolutely no one — she didn't scream, didn't play second banana to any man. So it seemed to me that it was time that *Doctor Who* followed that example.

'So I wrote this girl who was brave, bright, primitive, proud and curious and who, despite her basic naivete, didn't have the habit of deference. The production team liked this and said, "Yes, that's a good character, and as you've managed to write it we'll commission you to do another story, and you can use Leela again." By the time I had finished that next story, *The Robots of Death*, they had pretty much decided that she was going to be the regular companion.'

The Robots of Death (working titles: *The Storm-Mine Murders*, *Planet of the Robots*) was commissioned on 29 September 1976. After Boucher had completed a draft script for the first episode, Robert Holmes telephoned him to suggest that Leela's character should be further refined by giving her supernatural powers, possibly inherited from a witch-priestess grandmother. Boucher rejected this idea but proposed instead that her senses should be so well-developed, by reason of her being a warrior and a huntress, that she seemed to have such powers, and in particular a 'sixth sense' alerting her to danger.

LOCATIONS

The Masque of Mandragora
Portmeirion, Gwynedd, North Wales

The Hand of Fear
Oldbury Nuclear Power Station, Avon;
ARC Quarry, Crowhall, Avon

The Deadly Assassin
Gardens of Royal Alexandra and Albert School, Reigate, Surrey;
Betchworth Quarry, Dorking, Surrey

The Face of Evil
No location work

The Robots of Death
No location work

The Talons of Weng-Chiang
The Royal Theatre, Northampton;
St Crispin's Hospital, Northampton

NOTES
Uvanov

The part of Uvanov, captain of the sandminer in **The Robots of Death**, was first offered to Ronald Lacey but eventually went to Russell Hunter, well known for his role as Lonely in the **Callan** series.

Magic Tricks

To ensure that Li H'Sen Chang's magic act at the Palace Theatre in **The Talons of Weng-Chiang** was as authentic as possible, the production team hired two magicians, Larry Barnes and Ali Bongo, as advisers.

STOCK FOOTAGE

The Hand of Fear featured material from World Backgrounds in part one, and in part three, shots of Buccaneers from **Tomorrow's World** and footage of Harriers from World Backgrounds.

In part three of **The Deadly Assassin**, a shot of a lone condor flying above the Doctor was taken from **El Condor** and supplied by Dr J. McGahan.

The Robots of Death takes place on a massive sandminer vehicle, Storm-Mine 4, combing an alien world for precious minerals. The sandminer is run by a small human crew with the aid of numerous robots, which are split into three classes: Dums, Vocs and a single controlling Super Voc. The arrival of the Doctor and Leela in the TARDIS coincides with the start of a series of mysterious deaths, the crew being picked off one by one by an unseen killer. The time travellers immediately come under suspicion but are able to convince two undercover government agents — Poul and his robot associate D84, a Super Voc posing as a Dum — that they are innocent.

The culprit is eventually revealed to be one of the human crew, Dask, who is in truth the scientist Taren Capel. Raised by robots, Capel regards them as superior to humans and has been reprogramming those on board the miner with orders to kill the other members of the crew. He is tricked by the Doctor into outlining his plans for conquest while a helium canister discharges itself into the room, and is consequently killed by one of the robots as it can no longer recognize his voice.

As was often the case with stories at this point in Doctor Who's history, the basic premise of The Robots of Death was suggested to the writer by the series' production team.

'Bob Holmes wanted a traditional whodunnit,' explains Chris Boucher, 'but he wanted it set in the future and preferably somewhere that moved. That was how The Robots of Death came about. The basic approach was to do something like Agatha Christie's Ten Little Niggers — something that could be set in an isolated, claustrophobic environment. But it became for me a very fascinating conundrum, working with the whole concept of machine intelligence and asking, "At what point does machine behaviour become intelligent?" '

The Doctor and Leela are held prisoner on the Sandminer. The Robots of Death.

One particularly notable aspect of The Robots of Death was the distinctive Art Deco style which ran through all the story's design aspects, including sets, costumes and make-up. This was conceived by director Michael Briant and set designer Ken Sharp as an indication of the decadence of the future civilization from which the sandminer came, and also as a means of avoiding the usual science-fiction clichés of silver sets and hulking metallic robots.

A story by writer Basil Dawson had at one point been considered for inclusion in season fourteen but had ultimately proved unsuitable. Further scripting problems arose on the season's closing six-parter, which was originally to have been written by Robert Banks Stewart on the basis of a storyline entitled The Foe from the Future commissioned on 7 May 1976.

'I had asked Robert Banks Stewart to write the last story of that season,' recalled Robert Holmes, 'and suggested he work on the idea of somebody from Earth's future returning either to the present day or to the recent past. I had finished The Deadly Assassin and, thinking the season was sewn up, took off for only the second holiday I had had since joining the programme.

'My wife was then taken ill in Germany and had to go into hospital, so I got back to the office three weeks later than expected — only to find a note from Bob Stewart saying that other sudden commitments prevented him from writing the scripts. It was far too late to find and brief another writer, so it became a case of "Once more unto the breach . . ." '

Taking Stewart's outline as his starting point, Holmes developed a story which drew inspiration from The Phantom of the Opera and the Fu-Manchu canon and was set in the romanticized Victorian London of Sherlock Holmes.

'I am not a fan of Sherlock Holmes,' the writer later said, 'but I am a fan of that fictitious Victorian period, with fog, gas lamps, hansom cabs and music halls. We look back on it and say that's what it was like, although of course it wasn't — people were slaving in dark, satanic mills and starving in London gutters. But the popular concept of Victoriana is this, with colourful language.'

Written under the working title The Talons of Greel, the story was eventually transmitted as The Talons of Weng-Chiang.

The story begins with the Doctor taking Leela to Victorian London to show her how her ancestors lived — an idea arising from the production team's original Eliza Doolittle concept for the new companion. On their way to a music hall they witness the abduction of a man, Buller, by a group of

Chinese coolies. Leela incapacitates one of the thugs until the police arrive. The Doctor then learns of other disappearances and makes friends with the police pathologist, Professor Litefoot. He finds that hairs taken from the clothing of a victim found floating in the Thames seem to have originated from a very large rat.

The Doctor explores the sewers and discovers that there are indeed giant rats there. He also notes that the river Fleet, which empties into the Thames, runs directly underneath the Palace Theatre, which is central to the recent disappearances. His investigations lead him to Li H'sen Chang, a stage magician at the Theatre, and from Chang to an ancient Chinese god, Weng-Chiang, who has apparently been reincarnated on Earth. Weng-Chiang is in fact Magnus Greel, a war criminal from the 51st century, whose experiments in time brought him back to 19th-century China. The journey through time has disrupted his molecular structure and he now needs to feed on the life force of others — hence the disappearances.

Greel has come to London to retrieve his lost time cabinet, which is in the possession of Litefoot. Infiltrating Litefoot's home with Chang's ventriloquist doll Mr Sin — a computerized homunculus with the brain of a pig — he retrieves the cabinet and prepares to travel back to his own time, abandoning his loyal worshipper Chang to death in an opium den. The Doctor, aided by Leela, Litefoot and Henry Gordon Jago, the proprietor of the Palace Theatre, tracks him down to his lair and traps him before he can escape. Greel falls into his life force extraction machine and disintegrates. The Doctor is then attacked by Mr Sin but manages to disconnect its circuitry, rendering it inanimate. As the London fog closes in, the Doctor and Leela take their leave in the TARDIS. Jago and Litefoot look on in astonishment.

The Talons of Weng-Chiang was an unusual production in that its location work was split between film and OB video. The filming took place in mid-December 1976 on the streets of Wapping in East London, while the OB recording was carried out in mid-January 1977, mainly at the Northampton Repertory Theatre — where *Doctor Who*'s regular incidental music composer Dudley Simpson made a cameo appearance as the conductor of the music hall orchestra. Studio recording then took place in two sessions — 24—25 January and 8—10 February 1977— which, barring final editing and dubbing, brought to a close the series' fourteenth production block.

The transmission of the final episode of *The Talons of Weng-Chiang* on 2 April 1977 was followed the next evening by the screening on BBC2 of an hour-long documentary entitled *Whose Doctor Who*

Leela is threatened by SV7 (Miles Fothergill). *The Robots of Death*.

▲ A robot prepares to kill. *The Robots of Death*.

— the first factual programme ever to be devoted to the series. The idea of a *Doctor Who* documentary had originally been mooted by the BBC's Arts and Features Department in the spring of 1976, the intention being that it should be included in the youth-orientated *2nd House* series. Producer Tony Cash was assigned to devise a suitable format, and in the summer of 1976 invited former *Doctor Who* script editor Terrance Dicks to act as a consultant. Dicks suggested a number of possible approaches, including one in which Tom Baker as the fourth Doctor would call up a succession of clips on the TARDIS scanner, the opening line being 'When I was younger, I used to be an older man . . .'

Shortly after this, *2nd House* was cancelled, and it seemed for a time as if the *Doctor Who* documentary would die with it. In November 1976, however, Cash managed to get it commissioned by Bill Morton, the executive producer of another BBC2 arts series, *The Lively Arts*. The programme then gained two researchers — Ben Shephard, who had the task of tracking down suitable interviewees, and Bridget Cave, who was given the responsibility of choosing a selection of clips from the relatively meagre stock of old episodes then extant in the BBC's Film and Videotape Library. Dicks still favoured a programme based largely around a succession of clips, but Cash eventually decided on a more traditional documentary fronted by the regular presenter of *The Lively Arts*, Melvyn Bragg.

As transmitted, the documentary consisted of a mixture of clips, behind-the-scenes footage and interviews. Much of the specially shot material was obtained during the making of *The Talons of Weng-Chiang*, and amongst those appearing were Tom Baker, Philip Hinchcliffe, David Maloney and Dudley Simpson. Also interviewed were a number school-

MUSIC

All the specially composed incidental music was supplied for the season by Dudley Simpson.

The music for the masked ball at the conclusion of **The Masque of Mandragora** was from an LP called 'Tanzmusic Der Renaissance' by Ulsamer Collegium. The tracks used were 'Basse dans La Brosse' by P. Attaingnant, 'Branle de Champagne' by C. Gervaise and 'Istampita Cominciamento di Gioia', composer unknown.

Simpson elected to make use of organ music in his score for **The Deadly Assassin**. Musician Leslie Pearson was brought in to provide it using the organ of St Gabriel's Church in Cricklewood.

The background music for the relaxation of the human crew in episode one of **The Robots of Death** was all from an LP arranged by Simpson called 'In a Covent Garden Electrophon'. The tracks used were 'None but the Weary Heart' by Tchaikovsky and 'Girl with the Flaxen Hair' by Debussy.

To provide a suitable period feel for **The Talons of Weng-Chiang**, some cylinder piano music was used, played by Roy Mickleburgh, from an LP called 'Music of the Streets'.

Leslie Pearson was again brought in to provide organ music for **The Talons of Weng-Chiang**.

Now Mrs. Whitehouse

takes on Dr. Who

Dr. Who orbited into a new conflict yesterday – with Mrs. Mary Whitehouse.

She slapped her own X certificate on B.B.C. TV's popular Doctor (that's him above; actor Tom Baker) and his unearthly foes.

The Saturday serial is giving nightmares to under sevens and even making them wet the bed, she claimed.

Mrs. Whitehouse, secretary of the Viewers' and Listeners' Association, said the programme was screened too early in the evening.

She was answering a claim by a top B.B.C. official that Dr. Who taught children about courage, morality and humour.

Mr. Shaun Sutton, B.B.C. T.V.'s drama chief, told a Manchester University symposium on broadcasting: "Courage must be a basic ingredient of Dr. Who. It is expected that the hero will be brave and this is right."

But Mrs. Whitehouse said doctors told her that the programme could cause nightmares and bedwetting among under-sevens.

From an unknown newspaper, c.1976

children, fans and assorted experts — including an educationalist, a consultant physician and an educational psychologist — who it was hoped would give an indication of the series' impact on the viewing audience.

This question of the public's perception of *Doctor Who* was a very topical one at the time. The three seasons produced by Philip Hinchcliffe and edited by Robert Holmes had seen the series coming under heavy criticism from TV watchdog Mary Whitehouse over its increasingly horrific content. The most vociferous of her complaints had concerned a scene at the end of *The Deadly Assassin* part three in which the Doctor had appeared to be on the point of being drowned. This had even prompted a written apology from BBC Director General Charles Curran, who noted that the scene in question had been shortened prior to transmission but that, with hindsight, 'the head of department responsible would have liked to cut out just a few more frames of the action than he did'. Although expressed in relatively mild terms, this apology marked a significant change of policy by the BBC, where at one time Mary Whitehouse had been very much *persona non grata*.

In an interview with *Daily Express* journalist Jean Rook, published on 11 February 1977 under the title *Who do you think you are, scaring my innocent child?*, Holmes gave his response to some of the standard criticisms of the programme's new style:

'Of course it's no longer a children's programme. Parents would be terribly irresponsible to leave a six-year-old to watch it alone. It's geared to the intelligent fourteen-year-old, and I wouldn't let any child under ten see it.

'If a little one really enjoys peeping at it from behind the sofa, until Dad says "It's all right now — it's all over," that's fine. A certain amount of fear is healthy under strict parental supervision. Even then I'd advise half an hour to play with Dad and forget it before a child goes to bed.

'That's why we switched the time-slot from 5.15 to after 6.00, when most young kids are in the bath.

'When *Doctor Who* started, as a true children's programme, the monsters were rubber and specific and you saw them almost at once. What horrifies far more is the occasional flash of monster — bits and pieces of one. People are frightened by what might come round the corner or in at the window.'

When challenged about the portrayal of death in the series, Holmes told Rook:

'They're strictly fantasy deaths. No blood, no petrol bombs, nothing a child could copy. We're not in

business to harm children. We learned our lesson years ago, with some plastic daffodils which killed just by spitting at people. We didn't consider that people actually have plastic daffodils in their homes. They caused screaming nightmares, so we scrapped them. You must never attack the security of a child in its home. If you make something nasty, you don't stick it in a nursery.'

In fact, Holmes's memory was at fault here: seasons thirteen and fourteen did feature both blood and (in *The Seeds of Doom*) petrol bombs. However, the impact of *Doctor Who* under Hinchcliffe and Holmes relied not so much on the presentation of a succession of gory and shocking images as on the chilling concepts underlying the stories and the realistic and frequently Gothic style in which they were produced. These stories also benefited from the fact that they were made during a period now widely regarded as a golden age of BBC drama, with extremely high production values being achieved across the entire range of series, serials and plays. Having reached an almost unprecedented level of popularity, *Doctor Who* was at this time regarded as one of the BBC's flagship programmes, and the production team were able to call upon not only the highest real-terms budget the series had ever had but also some of the cream of the Corporation's considerable creative talent to help bring it to the screen.

Notwithstanding the undoubted success of the approach adopted by Hinchcliffe and Holmes, BBC executives determined in the wake of the recent furore to impose a tighter reign on the horror content of future seasons — a decision which would have a long-term and far-reaching impact on the series. This was a problem with which Hinchcliffe himself would not however be faced: having been asked to take over a new, hard-hitting police series called *Target*, he left *Doctor Who* at this point and handed over to the man who had earlier created *Target* — Graham Williams.

'Basically I had no choice but to leave,' he recalls. 'I was a producer within the BBC's Drama Department and in those days one was asked to move on and produce another show. I didn't know that I was being replaced until Graham Williams walked in the door. It was an on-off situation. I think I had said initially that I would like to move on, that three years was enough. They had then asked me to stay on, and I'd agreed a bit grudgingly — not because I disliked working on the show but because I wanted my career to move in new directions. Then their decision was reversed. Graham was made up to be a producer and *Doctor Who* was the first thing he was given. It meant musical chairs for the other producers in the Department, including me.'

CHAPTER FOURTEEN

Season Fifteen: Year of Transition

Newcomer Graham Williams was immediately faced with a minor crisis when the story which should have been his first *Doctor Who* production — a vampire tale by Terrance Dicks entitled *The Witch Lords* — had to be dropped at virtually the last minute on the insistence of BBC Head of Serials Graeme Mcdonald, who thought it might be construed as a send-up of the prestigious BBC serial *Count Dracula* which was then in the pipeline. Dicks had already completed a draft script of his first episode at the point when he heard of the story's cancellation, and the start of production was only weeks away.

The loss of *The Witch Lords* not only necessitated the hasty commissioning of a replacement, which Dicks himself provided under the initial working title *Rocks of Doom*, but also completely disrupted the schedule for the early part of the fifteenth production block. *The Invisible Enemy* by Bob Baker and Dave Martin, which should have been the second story into the studio, had to be moved forward and made first, with recording taking place in two sessions over 10—12 April and 24—26 April 1977 respectively. Dicks's story, renamed *Horror of Fang Rock*, then followed, but had to be recorded at the BBC's Pebble Mill studios in Birmingham — making this the first *Doctor Who* story to have had its studio work done outside London — as no space was available at the usual Television Centre facilities on the dates when needed. The two Birmingham sessions were held over 25—26 May and 7—9 June 1977 respectively.

Despite these late changes of plan, *Horror of Fang Rock* was still completed in time to launch the fifteenth season on transmission, its first episode going out at 6.18 pm on Saturday 3 September 1977.

The TARDIS's latest point of arrival is Fang Rock, a small island off the English coast, in the Victorian era. The island's only inhabitants are the lighthouse keepers — Ben, Vince and old Reuben — who operate the recently-installed electric light to warn ships off the treacherous rocks close by. The Doctor and Leela seek shelter at the lighthouse, where Vince has just seen a bright object fall from the sky into the sea. Ben then disappears and his body is later discovered hidden behind the generator — he has been electrocuted.

The Doctor in the pump room of the lighthouse.
Horror of Fang Rock.

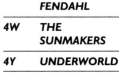

SEASON FIFTEEN

CODE	TITLE
4V	HORROR OF FANG ROCK
4T	THE INVISIBLE ENEMY
4X	IMAGE OF THE FENDAHL
4W	THE SUNMAKERS
4Y	UNDERWORLD
4Z	THE INVASION OF TIME

RATINGS

Figures in millions

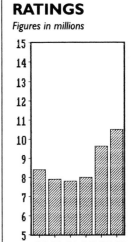

Story code

A series of pictures ▲ showing the impressive lightouse sets designed by Paul Allen. *Horror of Fang Rock.*

GRAHAM WILLIAMS
PRODUCER

*Graham Williams had been working in theatre for nearly five years when, in 1966, he decided to join the BBC in order to earn enough money to return to the theatre. He found that television was far more exciting and started working in the Script Unit. He then moved to become an assistant floor manager and it was whilst doing this job that he gained an attachment as a script editor – a job in which he was to stay for seven years. He worked on series like **Barlow at Large**, **Z Cars** and **Sutherland's Law**. He had devised the hard-hitting series **Target** in 1977 and was involved in producing an ultimately aborted twelve-part film series called **The Zodiac Factor** for the BBC when he was offered the producership of **Doctor Who**. After leaving **Doctor Who** in 1979 he later produced **Supergran** for ITV before becoming disillusioned with television and retiring to Devon in 1987, where he ran a hotel near Tiverton. In 1985 he wrote the scripts for a **Doctor Who** adventure called **The Nightmare Fair** which was to have formed a part of season twenty-three but which was ultimately dropped. The scripts were eventually novelized by Williams in 1989 for the Target range of novelizations. Williams died in a shooting accident on 17 August 1990.*

Reuben (Colin Douglas) and the Doctor at the top of the lighthouse. *Horror of Fang Rock.*

A passing ship crashes on the rocks as a freak fog bank descends, and the survivors stumble into the lighthouse. There they find themselves prey to an alien creature which is picking them off one by one. Ben was just the first to die. The Doctor realizes that the creature is in fact a Rutan — one of the race engaged in a perennial war with the Sontarans — whose spaceship has crashed in the sea. The Rutan can change its form at will and has been masquerading as Reuben, having killed the old keeper and hidden his body. These revelations come too late, however, as Vince and the wreck survivors are also killed.

The Doctor fights back by blasting the Rutan, now reverted to its natural form of an amorphous jelly,

Leela stands outside the TARDIS which has arrived on Fang Rock. *Horror of Fang Roak.*

with a makeshift mortar bomb. The creature dies, but further danger looms as it has been sending a homing signal to its mothership. The Doctor rigs up the lighthouse lamp with a diamond taken from a cache held by one of the now-dead survivors of the wreck, thereby creating a powerful laser beam. He focuses it on the approaching Rutan mothership, which is destroyed in a huge explosion. The Doctor and Leela then depart in the TARDIS, leaving only bodies and a mystery in their wake.

The lighthouse setting of *Horror of Fang Rock* was suggested by script editor Robert Holmes and accepted only reluctantly by Terrance Dicks. It also caused problems for director Paddy Russell, who asked for a number of scenes to be switched from the lamp room to other sets due to the difficulty of shooting in an area with transparent walls. Designer Paul Allen also found the setting a challenging one, as he recalls:

'Who knows how to design the inside of a lighthouse tower, and who knows what the engine room of a lighthouse looks like? Particularly in Victorian or Edwardian times. So we went off to the Needles lighthouse and established the fact that the rooms were round and that what little furniture there was was built-in. I also went to the lighthouse at Southwold and took loads and loads of photos of the light area. I based the lighting system of *Doctor Who's* lighthouse on a mixture of the one at the Needles and the one at Southwold, although it probably leant more towards the latter.'

Although the story's setting presented challenges, the move to Birmingham proved unproblematic.

'It was a delight to work at Pebble Mill,' says Allen. 'They had their own studio teams up there, and they were all so enthusiastic and polite. They were trying to outdo the Londoners at being keen and efficient — the Cockneys working at Television Centre had a terrific reputation and these guys were determined to prove their worth too.

'For example, we had a problem with the light housing in the lamp room. That had been designed by me and constructed out of flat sheets of perspex in London. The housing was all glued together and taken very carefully by special transport up to Birmingham. When the sets were struck at the end of the first studio session, the whole thing fell apart. I had no idea how to go about getting it repaired in Birmingham, but the studio manager simply told me to leave it all to him, and by the second session it had all been repaired. The point is that there was far less demarcation of jobs up there. Down in London, the unions would have been on my back if I had even suggested to the wrong person that they might be able to fix something. Everyone up there was so friendly and helpful, and that made my job a lot easier.'

Louise Jameson had originally intended to give up the role of Leela at the end of season fourteen but had been persuaded to renew her contract by the incoming Graham Williams during a visit he made to the Northampton location for *The Talons of Weng-Chiang*. She did however gain agreement to dispense with the brown contact lenses that she had been asked to wear during her first batch of episodes. The change of eye colour from brown to her natural blue was explained in plot terms as being a consequence of the intense light emitted from the explosion of the Rutan mothership.

The season's second story, *The Invisible Enemy* (working titles: *The Enemy Within*, *The Invisible Invader*), saw the Doctor and Leela returning to outer space.

While in flight, the TARDIS is infiltrated by the Virus — a space-borne intelligence which wishes to spread itself across the Universe — and the Doctor is infected by its Nucleus. The TARDIS subsequently materializes on Titan, one of the moons of Saturn, where the human occupants of a refuelling station have also been taken over by the Virus. The Doctor eventually collapses as a result of his infection, but first manages to relay to Leela the coordinates of a local hospital asteroid.

At the Bi-Al Foundation, based on the asteroid, Professor Marius clones the two time travellers, miniaturizes the clones and then injects them into the Doctor's body in the hope that they can find and destroy the Virus Nucleus. The plan backfires as the Nucleus escapes from the Doctor in place of the clones and is enlarged to human size. The creature arranges for itself to be taken back to Titan, where breeding tanks have been prepared prior to its invasion of the galaxy.

The Doctor, now cured of the Virus's influence, enlists the help of K-9, Professor Marius's dog-shaped robot computer, and sets a booby-trap which results in the breeding tanks being blown up, thus killing the Nucleus. Marius gives K-9 to the Doctor as a parting gift as he himself is returning to Earth.

Designer Barry Newbery, who had created the TARDIS's secondary control room introduced in season fourteen's *The Masque of Mandragora*, found himself having to come up with yet another TARDIS interior for *The Invisible Enemy*.

'The new producer, Graham Williams, wanted to go back to the traditional white-walled control room. The old console was dug out of stock and refurbished by Visual Effects, so I had only to provide

The Nucleus of the swarm (John Scott-Martin) is grown to giant size. *The Invisible Enemy.*

The infected Doctor is attended by Professor Marius (Frederick Jaeger) in his laboratory. *The Invisible Enemy.*

the main structure of the set itself. I aimed to make a modified set which was simple to assemble and as flexible as possible. I decided to use slatted columns constructed to go in the corners. The slats were vertical strips of wood, about two inches square, with spaces in between so that the ends of the wall flats just slotted in between them. Depending on which particular slots were used, the walls could be arranged with one another at virtually any angle. They could be moved round the column like the hands of a clock. That's where the flexibility came in. For the scanner screen, I retained the arrangement of a CSO cloth behind a pair of mechanically-operated shutters.'

Perhaps the most important development in *The Invisible Enemy* was the introduction of K-9. Bob

▲ The Doctor in Barry Newbery's 'brain' set. *The Invisible Enemy.*

▲ Leela inside the Doctor's brain. *The Invisible Enemy.*

▲ The model of the Bi-Al Foundation. Note the medical shuttle on the landing pad. *The Invisible Enemy.*

INVISIBLE EFFECTS

To achieve the complex model sequences for **The Invisible Enemy,** *effects designer Ian Scoones elected to use the facilities at Bray Film Studios rather than the BBC's own studios.*

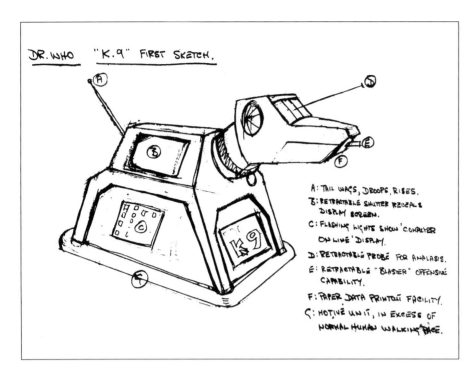

DR. WHO "K.9" FIRST SKETCH.

A: TAIL WAGS, DROOPS, RISES.
B: RETRACTABLE SHUTTER REVEALS DISPLAY SCREEN.
C: FLASHING LIGHTS SHOW 'COMPUTER ON LINE' DISPLAY.
D: RETRACTABLE PROBE FOR ANALASIS.
E: RETRACTABLE "BLASTER" OFFENSIVE CAPABILITY.
F: PAPER DATA PRINTOUT FACILITY.
G: MOTIVE UNIT, IN EXCESS OF NORMAL HUMAN WALKING PACE.

Tony Harding's initial ▲ design sketch for K-9 and the finished prop. *The Invisible Enemy.*

K-9 DESIGN

*Visual effects designer Tony Harding had only three weeks in which to design and build K-9 for the first studio session of **The Invisible Enemy**. The prop was modelled in plywood and plasta-board and then moulded in fibreglass. The proportions of the final version differed slightly from those in Harding's initial concept sketch owing to the need to leave sufficient room inside for all the mechanical parts, the power source – small, motorcycle-type wet-cell batteries – and the radio control apparatus, which had already been bought by Harding's colleague Ian Scoones and consisted of two Futuba sets, one four-channel and one six-channel, working on the AM frequency. The head was made somewhat larger than had originally been intended as Harding was asked at a late stage to incorporate a ticker-tape read-out into the dog's mouth.*

of course, and it was a right pain because it hardly ever worked properly. Its remote control interfered with the cameras and it would get stuck on bits of debris, causing further delays.'

Despite these problems, Williams decided that K-9's obvious appeal to viewers — particularly those in the younger age groups — made it too good an opportunity to pass up. Tom Baker, on the other hand, was less than enthusiastic about the dog's arrival, having considered for some time that the Doctor had no need of any regular companions — a fact which also contributed to his intense dislike of Leela, who he felt was too inclined to resolve situations through violence. However, while he had a generally strained working relationship with Louise Jameson, he remained on good terms with John Leeson, the actor cast by director Derrick Goodwin to provide the voice of K-9. Leeson was much admired by his fellow cast members for his habit of crawling around on his hands and knees during rehearsals to indicate the intended position of the radio-controlled prop in the studio. His dedication to the role was further illustrated by the fact that he quickly dispensed with the electronic modulation with which his voice was initially treated and thereafter created K-9's distinctive tones entirely through his own vocal artistry.

The Invisible Enemy was one of the most effects-intensive *Doctor Who* stories ever to be produced. For this reason, it was assigned two visual effects designers rather than the usual one. Tony Harding took charge of all the live-action effects,

Baker and Dave Martin had created the character purely for the purposes of their own story and were surprised to learn that the production team were considering keeping it on as a regular. The final decision was taken fairly late in the day, due largely to uncertainty on Graham Williams's part as to the practicability of the radio-controlled prop, designed by Tony Harding of the Visual Effects Department.

'Many retakes were necessitated by problems with K-9,' notes Barry Newbery. 'This was its first story,

Thea Ransome (Wanda Ventham) and Professor Fendelman (Denis Lill) discuss the recent happenings at Fetch Priory while Maximillian Stael (Scott Fredericks) stands in the background. *Image of the Fendahl.*

The entire cast and crew of *Image of the Fendahl.*

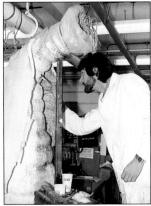

▲ A full-size Fendahleen creature is constructed by Colin Mapson.

▲ A full-size Fendahleen approaches. *Image of the Fendahl.*

▲ Thea Ransome begins her transformation into the Fendahl core. *Image of the Fendahl.*

while Ian Scoones — who before Harding's arrival had drawn up his own preliminary design sketches for K-9, depicting it as something akin to a rather fierce Doberman — was given responsibility for the story's extensive modelwork, which was generally acclaimed as some of the finest ever seen in the series.

As it had not been originally planned that K-9 would stay on after *The Invisible Enemy,* the character had not been included in the draft scripts for the next transmitted story, Chris Boucher's *Image of the Fendahl,* which had been commissioned on 2 May 1977. Two short scenes were therefore inserted in which the dog was seen to be confined to the TARDIS suffering from corroded circuitry.

The events of *Image of the Fendahl* are triggered off by an anachronistic 12 million-year-old human skull which has been discovered by archaeologists and is now being used by Professor Fendelman in his Time Scanner experiments at Fetch Priory in near-contemporary England. Drawn by the operation of the Scanner, the Doctor arrives as the experiments reach a peak. A strange force becomes active whenever the Scanner is in use, and two deaths have resulted. Thea Ransome, one of the scientists in Fendelman's team, has also been affected. The skull is exerting an influence over her mind, glowing with power each time the Scanner is activated and the connection is strengthened.

The Doctor realizes that the skull is a channel through which a powerful and ancient creature called the Fendahl is preparing to manifest itself on Earth. The Fendahl exists by sucking the life force from others. The Time Lords attempted to trap it in a time loop on what was then the fifth planet of Earth's solar system but, although the planet was effectively obliterated, the Fendahl's influence survived in the skull. Since then it has been subtly guiding the development of the human race in order to bring about the conditions whereby it can be recreated.

Thea is transformed into the Fendahl core, and a group of acolytes assembled by Maximillian Stael — another of Fendelman's team, who is trying to harness the creature's power for his own ends — are converted into snake-like Fendahleen. The Doctor fights back, showing the remaining scientist, Colby, and two locals, Granny Tyler and her son Jack, how to defend themselves against the Fendahleen using rock salt loaded into shotgun cartridges. By activating the Scanner once more, he triggers an implosion which destroys both the Priory and the Fendahl core. He then takes the skull to the TARDIS and prepares to dump it into a supernova, thus destroying the creature's bridgehead.

Image of the Fendahl took the fourth slot in *Doctor Who's* fifteenth production block, coming after *The Invisible Enemy, Horror of Fang Rock* and the story which would follow it on transmission, Robert Holmes's *The Sun Makers.* Its location work was carried out over 1—5 August 1977 and its two studio sessions took place over 20—21 August and 4—5 September 1977 respectively.

The Sun Makers and *Image of the Fendahl* were the last stories on which Robert Holmes worked as *Doctor Who's* script editor. He had in fact considered leaving some six months earlier, but had been

ROCKS OF DOOM

The following is the full text of the one-page outline which Terrance Dicks submitted to Robert Holmes for **Rocks of Doom,** *the story which eventually became* **Horror of Fang Rock:**

Tease: Subjective vp: the lighthouse; cascading foam, moving closer... Int. Lighthouse: Ben Travers having trouble with his telegraph: interference. Ext. Lighthouse: Old Ben goes out to check his wiring. Storm in full fury. Subjective: Old Ben mercilessly destroyed.

Int. Lighthouse: Two left to man carbon arc lamp. New-fangled device. Miss Old Ben's expertise. See steam yacht approaching as lamp fails. (JOSHUA and DAVY)

Ext. Rock. (T/C Model?) Tardis appears on stormlashed promontory. Doc and Leela emerge – this isn't Brighton. Screams of dying shipwrecked...

Int. Lighthouse. Joshua and Davy saying she's struck. Old Ben reappears dazed. Almost drowned. Doc and Leela arrive. Doc gets carbon arc lamp going again which attracts few survivors to rock.

Survivors: Lord Peach-Palmer; Adelaide, his secretary; Burkin, his valet; Rt. Hon John Skinsalde and wife, Veronica – MP, city financier, privy to Peach-Palmer's ploys.

Peach-Palmer incensed 'cos light wasn't working; lost his crew and his yacht and must, anyway, be in London by weekend for big political/financial coups he is about to pull.

Old Ben, resting meanwhile, in makeshift sick bay, rises and heads for generator room where Joshua is working; scream; Josh dead; Old Ben a pitiful gibbering wreck saying something came out of sea...

CAST:	SETS:
The Doctor	Generator Room
Leela	Lamp Room
Joshua Crockett	Crew Room
Davy Williams	Staircase & well
Ben Travers	Basement cellars
Lord Peach-Palmer	Sleeping Quarters
Adelaide Couchon	Ext. Rocks
Herbert Burkin	
John Skinsalde	
Veronica	

The Doctor, Leela and Cordo (Roy Macready) with the rebel leader Mandrel (William Simons). *The Sun Makers.*

persuaded to stay on until Graham Williams had settled in and managed to find a successor for him. The man eventually chosen for the job was Anthony Read, a writer with many television credits to his name but no previous experience on *Doctor Who* itself. Williams later recalled how Read's appointment had come about:

'Tony Read was, for me, a very obvious choice at the time to replace Bob Holmes, when Bob decided he had finally had enough as script editor. Tony had a very wide experience of script editing, both outside the BBC and inside. Originally, he had approached us to submit a storyline to *Doctor Who.* He and I knew each other from having worked on *The Troubleshooters,* and he and Bob for a lot longer than that. Bob thought very highly of him, so my response was very much to say, "Fine, we like the story. And while you're at it, would you like to become the show's script editor for a year?" '

Read worked alongside Holmes in the editing of his scripts for *The Sun Makers,* which had been commissioned on 30 April 1977. He also did much of the editing work on Chris Boucher's *Image of the Fendahl,* and was jointly credited with Holmes on the scripts, although it was Holmes's name which appeared at the end of the transmitted episodes.

The Sun Makers sees the TARDIS arriving on Pluto, where the Doctor is amazed to discover that there are six warm suns, a breathable atmosphere and a thriving industrial community. The people are not

so well off, however, as the Company which controls the planet works them to the bone, pays them a pittance and then taxes them on everything imaginable. The Doctor and Leela join forces with an underground band of rebels who are out to smash the system. They learn that the head of the Company's operations on Pluto, represented by the human tax official Gatherer Hade, is an Usurian known as the Collector. The Usurians are notorious for enslaving whole planets through economic means and then fleecing the inhabitants with exorbitant taxes.

The Company keeps the citizens in line by diffusing a repressant gas, PCM, through the air-conditioning system. The Doctor manages to stop the distribution of this gas, and the workers then rise up against the Company and hurl Gatherer Hade to his death from the roof of a tall building. The Doctor meanwhile gains access to the Company computer and programs it to apply a two per cent growth tax. The Collector, unable to cope with the loss of his profits, reverts to his natural form—a type of poisonous fungus — and is thus rendered harmless.

'*The Sun Makers* was a skit on the Inland Revenue system,' recalled Robert Holmes, 'with a Gatherer and a Collector and references to income tax forms, like a Corridor P-45, and to liquidation and things like that. And then there was the planet that the Collector originally came from, once it was revealed that he wasn't human and he himself went into liquidation and plopped down into this commode thing. I said he came from the planet Usurers.

The Doctor and the Collector (Henry Woolf). *The Sun Makers.*

Gatherer Hade (Richard Leech). *The Sun Makers.*

▲ **The Collector.** *The Sun Makers.*

Graham Williams was adamant that we couldn't have a planet with that name, but the director Pennant Roberts and I disagreed, so we changed it only slightly.'

'It would be true to say,' reflected Williams, 'that the archness with which Robert Holmes managed to send up the whole tax system was not entirely the way it had been explained in the story brief. He sold us a story very much along an anti-colonial, anti-empire line. These people were freedom fighters battling for independence — which was a good story to tell in 1977. Then he added the jokey parts about the Inland Revenue. Unfortunately, he was playing to a very sympathetic audience with Pennant Roberts. I think, with hindsight, that maybe it went a bit too far, although a lot of our audience probably did not get the joke anyway.

'Again with hindsight, I should have taken the edge off the humour, because we had not really prepared the ground for that type of story. In that respect it stuck out like a sore thumb. That element of sophisticated humour was certainly going to continue, though, for the rest of the time that I was doing the series, and that was not accidental. I wanted the humour to be there, available for those who wanted to grab it, and to add a little bonus without detracting from the story at all for those who did not want to catch hold. If people did not get the joke, then it should not impair their enjoyment of the show.'

Set designer Tony Snoaden and costume designer Christine Rawlins were keen to take a co-ordinated approach to the story's visual realization. Noting the allegorical nature of Holmes's scripts, Snoaden proposed that they draw their inspiration from propagandist art, and in particular the Aztec-influenced works of Mexican muralists Jose Clemente Orozco, Diego Rivera and David Alfaro Siqeiros. Had this plan gone ahead, all the story's sets, costumes and make-up would therefore have had an Aztec look to them. In the event, however, Pennant Roberts called for a rethink mid-way through pre-produc-

tion and only a few elements of this idea were carried through into the final designs.

'I remember Tony Snoaden and I started off very ambitiously,' says Rawlins, 'but it ended up simple again, at least as far as the costumes were concerned.

'There were a lot of walk-ons playing the workers in the city who weren't going to arrive until the day of filming, so we gave them "pyjama suits" with a badge of the Company symbol on them. They had different coloured costumes according to where they worked. The badge was the link.

'I remember the Collector very well. The idea of that costume was actually quite subtle — so subtle that everyone missed it! Or perhaps it wasn't particularly clever and no one had the courage to tell me. The theme of the story was money, so I put together the man in the City and the rich Arab and came up with a pin-striped kaftan!'

The season's fifth story, both in production and on transmission, was *Underworld*, commissioned from writers Bob Baker and Dave Martin under the

LOCATIONS

Horror of Fang Rock
No location work

The Invisible Enemy
No location work

Image of the Fendahl
Stargroves, East End, Nr Newbury, Hants

The Sun Makers
Hartcliffe Wills Tobacco Factory, Bristol, Avon; Camden Town Deep Tube Shelters, Camden

Underworld
No location work

The Invasion of Time
St Anne's Hospital, Redhill, Surrey; Laporte Industries Sandpit, Redhill, Surrey

▼ **A sketch of the Megropolis on Pluto.** *The Sun Makers.*

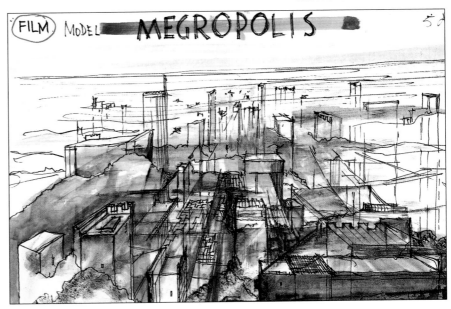

Tala (Imogen Bickford- ▲ Smith) in old-age make-up. *Underworld.*

The Doctor meets Herrick (Alan Lake) and Commander Jackson (James Maxwell). *Underworld.*

The crew of the R1C on their flight deck. Tala, Jackson and Herrick. *Underworld.*

The Doctor encounters ▲ the Oracle, watched by the Seers (Frank Jarvis and Richard Shaw). In this rehearsal shot the Seers are unmasked. *Underworld.*

early working title *Underground.*

The TARDIS's latest port of call is a Minyan space craft, the R1C, commanded by a man named Jackson. Jackson and his crew are on a long quest to recover the Minyan race banks from a ship called the P7E which left their planet centuries ago. They are immediately suspicious of the Doctor as they know his people of old: the Time Lords once shared some of their great knowledge with the Minyans, who then proceeded to destroy themselves through war as they were unable to cope with it.

The Doctor helps to free the R1C after it becomes buried in a meteor storm, but it then crashes into another newly formed planet at the heart of which is the P7E. Inside the new planet the time travellers and the Minyans discover a maze of tunnels and passages. The Doctor eventually makes his way to the centre, where the P7E's computer, the Oracle, holds court.

The Oracle was programmed to protect the race banks but subsequently went insane and — with the aid of its robotic servants, the Seers — imposed its

MUSIC

All the music for this season was provided by Dudley Simpson.

Tom Baker, as the Doctor, back on the Time Lords' own planet Gallifrey, for a new 6-part yarn. Last time there, he got in awful trouble but ended up elected president – now he's claiming the job, but it's all got twisted again and he's cast as the baddie once more. Louise Jameson in leggy support.
TV write-up from an unknown newspaper

The Doctor and Leela are threatened by Herrick and Commander Jackson. *Underworld.*

rule upon the Minyan survivors and their descendants. It allows Jackson to take what appear to be the race banks, but they are in truth imitations containing fission grenades. The Doctor realizes the deception and obtains the genuine race banks. He then tricks the Oracle's guards into taking the grenades back to their leader. The resulting explosion destroys the planet and the P7E and boosts the R1C off on a voyage to Minyos II, carrying with it all the Minyan survivors.

'*Underworld* was based on the voyage of Jason and the Argonauts,' recalls Bob Baker. 'The P7E was the Persephone and the characters had jumbled names from some of the Argonauts. It was a Golden Fleece they were after too, in the form of the race banks.'

Graham Williams faced a major difficulty during production of the story when he learned on returning from a two-week holiday that the sets of the Minyan spacecraft had proved much more expensive than anticipated, leaving no scenery budget remaining for the sequences set inside the new planet. After discussion with set designer Dick Coles, director Norman Stewart and electronic effects expert Mitch Mitchell, he decided that the only viable solution was to use CSO in conjunction with models to give the impression of caves and tunnels.

'We started talking and looking at the scripts,' he later recalled, 'with a view to saying "It's either going to be done that way, or all against black backdrops." Norman Stewart reckoned he could do it okay, although as it turned out I think he was a little over-confident. We really needed about four times as much studio time as we'd got, as we had to plan and line up every shot the way we wanted it. So the compromise was that we recorded CSO at a rate that was unheard of — cutting eight or nine minutes in an hour, when the normal rate would be about one minute per hour.

'In effect, we were trying things never done before — asking untutored crowd-scene actors to run into a blue studio and to stop on their blue marks on a blue cloth. An inch or two out of line and we'd have legs disappearing, and the shot wouldn't work. We'd retry it as often as we could, but there had to be a cut-off point where we would go into the next shot and take the best of what we had.

'So *Underworld* came in on time and within its budget, but I'm not that proud of its quality.'

The story did however benefit from one innovation which would gradually become standard practice on the series.

'The big change that happened on that story,' says

Costume designer Dee Robson's original design drawings for the aborted *The Killer Cats of Geng Singh* storyline. The designs show male and female Gallifreyan cat-creatures.

Mitch Mitchell, 'and that had to happen just to complete everything on time, was the introduction of post-production for the electronic effects.

'At the time, *Star Wars* had just come out. Graham Williams had seen the film, and wanted *Underworld* to look technically more sophisticated than earlier *Doctor Who*s. So he fought for, and got, a gallery-only day, when just the technicians and the director could come in and do post-production work — adding beams and ray-gun shots to tape and film that had already been shot.'

▲ **Christine Rawlins'
costume design for
Gatherer Hade.** *The
Sunmakers.*

I have just been watching episode 2 of *Dr Who – The Invisible Enemy* (8 October BBC1) and I am rather puzzled about one aspect of the episode.

I understand the theory of 'cloning', i.e. taking a single cell from an animal or person and developing an exact replica of that person from it, but I did not understand how their clothes came to be cloned too!

I saw the professor take a tiny sample of tissue from the arms of the Doctor and Leela and put the samples into the special machine, but when the door was opened, out stepped a replica couple who were even wearing the same outfits as the originals – long scarf, frayed mini-dress and all!

How did that happen? Surely the 'clones' should have been naked.
Amanda Jones (aged 12), Sheffield

Graham Williams, Producer, 'Dr Who', replies: You have hit exactly on the difficulty! A nude Doctor and Leela would be rather different from the usual *Dr Who*, and would have occasioned some comment. When Professor Marius took the skin sample, he said: 'You must realise, Doctor, that this isn't in any real sense a clone, but a short-lived carbon-based imprint, a sort of three-dimensional photograph.' He was of course referring to the Kilbracken technique, as mentioned in the programme. I am pleased that our efforts to cover the Doctor and Leela have not gone unnoticed.
*From **Radio Times***

The Vardan troops arrive ▲ on Gallifrey. *The Invasion of Time.*

Castellan Kelner (Milton ▲ Johns) talks with a Vardan. *The Invasion of Time.*

The Doctor and Leela arrive on Gallifrey to be greeted by Commander Andred (Christopher Tranchell) and the Chancellery Guard. *The Invasion of Time.*

Top: Designer Richard ▲ Conway stands by the model of the Vardan ship which was constructed by Bill Pearson. Bottom: The ship in flight. *The Invasion of Time.*

Further problems arose for Williams on the season's concluding six-part story. He had originally hoped that Robert Holmes would be willing to write this as a sequel to season fourteen's *The Deadly Assassin*, but Holmes turned down the invitation. The task was then passed on to David Weir, a very experienced writer with whom Anthony Read had previously worked on the *Troubleshooters* series in the sixties. In discussions with Read, Weir devised a story entitled *The Killer Cats of Geng Singh* (spelling uncertain) which involved both the Time Lords and a race of cat-like beings who were also native to Gallifrey. He was then commissioned to write the full scripts, while Williams set pre-production work in motion. The problems began when Weir's scripts were finally delivered, as Williams later explained:

'When the scripts eventually thudded onto the desk a week before the director was due to join, they were totally unusable. There were crowd scenes in Wembley Stadium stipulated which would have required something like 96,000 human-shaped cat costumes! In a way, that is text-book proof that some writers are more suited to *Doctor Who* than others, irrespective of their background and work on other shows. David Weir is a fine writer, and had obviously been brought in by Tony Read on the basis of work they had done together in the past. But I still remember Tony in my office, with his head in his

hands, saying "I don't understand it. How can he have done this to me?" And that didn't help matters much either.'

After seeking advice from Robert Holmes, Williams and Read decided that they would have to write a replacement story themselves. Williams suggested the storyline during a lengthy session in the BBC bar, then Read went away and wrote first drafts of the scripts over the following two weeks, during which time the production was put on hold. The story, entitled *The Invasion of Time*, retained the Gallifreyan setting but dispensed with the cat-like creatures that Weir had created. After Read had completed his drafts, Williams took them home and re-wrote them, effectively performing the script editor's function, over a four-day period in which he scarcely broke for sleep.

It was during this period of intense activity that Louise Jameson informed Williams that she would be leaving *Doctor Who* at the end of the season. He was by no means disappointed to learn this as he considered Leela to be a character of limited potential and was also concerned that the working relationship between Jameson and Tom Baker had deteriorated to such an extent that their animosity was starting to show on screen. Jameson's announcement did come at the worst possible time, however, and this affected the way in which Williams chose to write her out, as he later admitted:

'I shouldn't have written Louise's character out quite so blandly as I did. I'm afraid that was just me in a tiff for which I can only apologize. The horrors of getting *The Invasion of Time* underway with such horrendous production conditions prevailing on *Underworld* had just about got to me when Louise strolled up and announced she was definitely not going to do the next year after all. That was just about all I needed to hear then. So I figured that my two options were either to kill the character off — which I dismissed as it would have ended the season on a downer — or to have her stay behind on Gallifrey to the hum of Hollywood strings playing the wedding march.'

The Invasion of Time opens with the Doctor returning to Gallifrey after a meeting in space with a group of unseen aliens. On his arrival he immediately claims the Presidency, which is his by right following the events of *The Deadly Assassin*. Leela, meanwhile, tries to work out what has got into him as he is behaving completely out of character. At his Presidential inauguration, the Doctor is 'crowned' with a device giving him access to the Matrix, the repository of all Time Lord knowledge. He then arranges for the transduction barriers around Gallifrey to be put out of action by K-9. When this is done, his alien 'friends' materialize in the Panopticon. They are Vardans — telepathic invaders intent on usurping the Time Lords' power.

The Doctor links K-9 to the Matrix in order to determine the Vardans' point of origin. His plan is to place a time loop around their home planet, but he must avoid arousing their suspicions until he is ready — hence his erratic behaviour. He banishes Leela to the wastelands of outer Gallifrey for fear that she might unintentionally jeopardize his plans. There she meets up with a group of outlaw Time Lords, and together they organize an attack on the Capitol to fight off the invaders. The Doctor finally springs his trap and the Vardans are banished. Almost immediately, however, Gallifrey is invaded by Sontarans who, unknown to the Doctor, were using the Vardans as a bridgehead to enable them to conquer the Time Lords.

The Doctor and Leela, with the help of the outlaws and some of the Time Lords, lure the Sontarans into the TARDIS, where they can be picked off one by one. Realizing that the invaders are after the Matrix, the Doctor uses knowledge extracted from it by K-9 to construct a forbidden de-mat gun, activated by the Great Key of Rassilon. He uses this to kill the remaining Sontaran in the TARDIS and then confronts the Sontaran leader, Stor, in the Panopticon. Stor intends to destroy the Time Lords' power centre with a bomb, but the Doctor activates the gun as the charge detonates. The Doctor survives the release of energy, but his memory of recent events is wiped. He prepares to leave Gallifrey to resume his travels. Leela, however, announces that she wishes to stay behind with Andred, one of the Chancellery guards, with whom she has fallen in love. K-9 decides to remain with her. As the TARDIS dematerializes, the Doctor pulls out a large box marked 'K9 MII'.

Production of *The Invasion of Time* was disrupted by the latest recurrence of an industrial dispute, then of over ten years' standing, which stemmed from a demarcation wrangle between electricians and props staff as to who should be responsible for switching on an electric clock at the start of a popular children's programme.

'In 1977,' recalled Graham Williams, 'this dispute occurred half way through the pre-prep for *The Invasion of Time*. The planning people phoned up and said: "We can't let you have the studio dates you want as we've got too big a backlog of Christmas shows queuing up. Nor can we offer you an extra option on filming."

'What they could offer us, however, was one studio session, one on OB, and then our filming. But, as things turned out, we were able to get only about two days' filming as the film crew were needed else-

The Doctor gets K-9 to trace the location of the Vardan homeworld through the Matrix. *The Invasion of Time*.

Castellan Kelner assists the Sontarans with their enquiries. *The Invasion of Time*.

where. The rest had to be rejigged onto OB.

'They did offer me another alternative: "Just don't make *The Invasion of Time* and reuse the money elsewhere on the show." But I didn't want to do that. I really wanted to do the story, despite its problems.'

By drawing money from a special BBC 'strike fund', the production team were able to afford two weeks' use of an OB unit using new, lightweight cameras, and thus managed to compensate for the loss of two of the three studio sessions which would normally be required to complete a six-part story. In a complete reversal of the normal production routine, the studio work was carried out first, followed by the location filming and then finally the two weeks' OB work.

The transmission of the final episode of *The Invasion of Time* on 11 March 1978 brought to a close a season which had seen *Doctor Who* overcoming a number of behind-the-scenes crises and undergoing some important stylistic changes, foremost amongst which was the gradual toning down of the series' horror content.

ANTHONY READ
SCRIPT EDITOR/ WRITER

Anthony Read had always wanted to write, but moved instead into acting, appearing in school plays alongside Kenneth Ives and Frank Barlow amongst others. Upon leaving school he applied to RADA and the Central School of Speech and Drama and was accepted by both. He chose to join Central but had realized that acting was not for him before his studies were curtailed by National Service. Following his departure from the Forces, he worked in Fleet Street for a time before moving into public relations and publicity. He was also doing pieces of writing work and eventually found himself on the shortlist for script editing **The Avengers**. *He failed to get that job but shortly afterwards he became a script writer/adapter at the BBC on the strength of a play in the 1963* **Detective** *series called* **The Man Who Murdered in Public**. *He went on to work on shows like* **The Troubleshooters** *(1966–1971) (as producer and occasional writer and script editor),* **The Lotus Eaters** *(1972) (creator and producer),* **The Professionals** *(writer) and* **The Dragon's Opponent**. *It was following this latter production that Read went freelance and it was in this capacity that Graham Williams asked if he would script edit* **Doctor Who**. *Following his brief tenure on* **Doctor Who** *Read went on to work on several popular shows including* **Hammer House of Horror** *(he wrote the episode* **Witching Time** *and script edited the first thirteen episodes),* **One By One, Into the Labyrinth** *(writer) and* **Chocky** *and its sequels, which he adapted between 1984 and 1986 from John Wyndham's novels, as well as contributing* **The Horns of Nimon** *for Doctor Who's seventeenth season. He is currently a leading member of the Writer's Guild and has written several historical books with David Fisher.*

'To me,' explained Graham Williams, 'a lot of what Philip Hinchcliffe had done went too far. When I learned I was taking the show over, I made special efforts to watch it. One of the stories I saw — *Genesis of the Daleks* — had Lis Sladen climbing up a rocket gantry, being shot at by guards with rifles. She almost falls once, and then on reaching the top she gets caught and is deliberately tripped by her captors and left dangling in mid-air while they laugh.

'I had by then just become a father, and so was more aware that if children were going to be watching *Doctor Who* at 5.25 in the evening then a lot of this sadism and deliberate shock-horror, which Bob Holmes and Philip Hinchcliffe took a particular glee in producing, was not very defensible. I thought Philip was wrong to let the drowning sequence in *The Deadly Assassin* go through, because the violence was too realistic and therefore could be imitated. Even on *Z Cars* one did not show a fight using a broken bottle, for precisely that reason.'

This was in any case an aspect over which Williams had little room for manoeuvre, as senior BBC executives were keen for him to 'clean the series up' following the persistent criticisms which had been made during Hinchcliffe's tenure. As he would later reflect, this was the most difficult problem he had to face during his first year as producer:

'I was happy to tone down the realistic horror and gore. But then the BBC told me to go further and actually clean it up. It was over-reaction, of that I am sure, but it did not help that in my first year I was under a directive to take out anything graphic in the depiction of violence.'

While some of Williams's earliest productions, notably *Horror of Fang Rock* and *Image of the Fendahl*, retained the Gothic quality of the Hinchcliffe seasons, it was not long before his new policy took effect. This gradual removal of the series' more horrific elements left a void which was filled in part by an increased use of humour, particularly after Anthony Read succeeded Robert Holmes as script editor. The lighter tone at first manifested itself mainly in the way stories were directed and acted, Tom Baker taking the opportunity to inject a lot of his own ideas and dialogue into scenes during rehearsals to make them more off-the-wall and amusing. Robert Holmes's own *The Sun Makers* however was an exception to the rule, with its intrinsically humorous slant; and as time went by the series' writers increasingly picked up on the new, less serious approach and tailored their work accordingly, incorporating purely comedic scenes and dialogue.

At times there was a feeling within the BBC that the humour had gone too far. On 7 March 1978,

Williams had a meeting with Graeme McDonald in which they discussed *The Invasion of Time* — episode five of which had been transmitted the previous Saturday — and agreed that all directors who joined the series should in future receive a memo reminding them of the need to maintain the essentially serious nature of the stories. Williams later sent McDonald the following note to record the main conclusions of their meeting:

As an aide-memoire to our discussions of this afternoon:

1. Repetition of the location Interior Tardis was the joke — this was diluted by the further jokes from Tom Baker in particular; the 'trip' that happened on only one shot; the Colonel Bogey gag; the 'you're standing on my scarf'; 'I know this Tardis like the back of my hand'; 'that clock's slow' (tapping sundial).

2. More importantly — inability to take Stor, Derek Deadman, seriously.

3. Simply — the continual theme was carefully constructed to counterpoint the humour with the tension — the humorous approach by the Doctor against the tense threat of the Sontarans. The humour dominated. Surely any thriller situation needs comical relief, but if that comedy is overplayed, then tension must suffer and not gain as it should.

I enclose the memo which each director will receive on joining. Once again, I do not wish to cramp the flair and contribution made either by directors or actors to the programmes, and I do not wish to pre-empt contributions by attempting too draconian an attitude at the outset. In the light of our recent experiences, however, I believe I shall have to remind actors and directors of the continual purpose of the script, and ensure that the contributions they offer are additional to the basic material and are not misguided substitutions or actual detractions from that purpose.

'It was inevitable that the style of *Doctor Who* would change once Tony Read took on the burning torch,' Williams later reflected. 'But of course one can never predict how in advance. In all honesty, and with no detriment implied either to Tony Read or to his successor Douglas Adams, I have to say that I would have been a very much happier chap had I had Bob Holmes as my script editor throughout all my seasons, as Philip had done. I certainly felt I was on more of a wavelength from the word go with Bob than I was with either of the others. It took working towards with the other two, but Bob truly had found the natural slot for *Doctor Who* in the television universe.'

CHAPTER FIFTEEN

Season Sixteen:
The Key to Time -
A Universal Jigsaw

Season sixteen was unique in the history of *Doctor Who* in that its six individual stories were linked by a single over-arching plot. This idea had been conceived by Graham Williams when he was first appointed as producer and had originally been considered as the basis for season fifteen. In a three-page document dated 30 November 1976, Williams had set out his concept under the heading *Doctor Who (1977 Season)*. The full text of this was as follows:

Hypothesis:
To every action there is an equal and opposite reaction.

Thesis:
The universe, as we know it, is held in delicate balance by forces which we do not yet fully understand. We know, in the broadest terms, that the planets hold their course relative to the galaxy, that the galaxy holds its course relative to . . .? Discussion as to the force binding the galaxy in its equilibrium is a matter of constant speculation. Following investigation of elementary particles, gravity is the least likely force. Electromagnetic is the next most likely. Nuclear, or 'Strong Interaction' is the most significant force, though this is tempered by the fourth force 'Weak Interaction', (responsible for a number of phenomena of which the best known is Beta Radioactivity). This last force is that which is undergoing the most strenuous research. (REF: Plank, Einstein, Millikan on Photons, European Organisation for Nuclear Research, Geneva, on Elementary Particles.)

There exists the distinct possibility that the Fourth Force will discredit Einstein's Special Theory of Relativity and lend credence to Minkowski's extension of ordinary geometry — that of the fourth dimension, Space/Time.

Thus the state of all matter is held in balance by four forces, of which the weakest, most insignifi-

The Doctor and Romana (Mary Tamm) arrive on the planet Ribos. *The Ribos Operation.*

SEASON SIXTEEN	
CODE	TITLE
5A	**THE RIBOS OPERATION**
5B	**THE PIRATE PLANET**
5C	**THE STONES OF BLOOD**
5D	**THE ANDROIDS OF TARA**
5E	**THE POWER OF KROLL**
5F	**THE ARMAGEDDON FACTOR**

RATINGS
Figures in millions

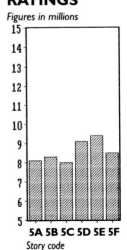

Story code

The White Guardian ▲
(Cyril Luckham). *The Ribos
Operation.*

Garron (Iain ▲
Cuthbertson). *The Ribos
Operation.*

A Shrivenzale (Stuart Fell) roams the catacombs
on Ribos. *The Ribos Operation.*

The Graff Vynda-K (Paul Seed) and Sholakh
(Robert Keegan) use the Seeker (Ann Tirard) to
locate Garron and Unstoffe. *The Ribos Operation.*

STOCK FOOTAGE

The Stones of Blood used
several pieces of stock footage.
Images of the moon and clouds at
night, waves crashing against rocks,
a sea horizon and light
disappearing into the sea were all
obtained from World Backgrounds.

cant, is the unexplained arbiter.

*Gravity can be controlled, to a certain extent.
Electromagnetism can be controlled, to a certain
extent. Nuclear Interaction can be controlled, to a
certain extent. But the Fourth Force . . . ?*

*The Time Lords have a degree of control over
this Fourth Force, by which they regulate the balance, in so far as they can, of their Cluster. (A collection of Galaxies.)*

*In the normal course of events, this control suf-
fices. But Time Lords, like human mortals, effect
control when and where they like, and to whatever ends they desire, either committed or ambiva-
lent.*

*Control cannot be allowed to rest in the hands
of so capricious a people. A further, and greater,
degree of control must vest in a higher, and more
responsible faculty.*

*Eternity and Infinity, as concepts, do not, by their
very nature, allow for an absolute Authority — the
Pyramidical Hierarchy stretches through Time and
Space and can have no apex. But the next step is
logical . . .*

*The balance must be kept by someone, or some-
thing, which enjoys a greater sense of responsibility, and a greater sense of objectivity. A sense of*

*right against a sense of wrong. A force for right
against a force for wrong. If a force for good were
to govern the balance there would be no balance.
Therefore the force of evil must have an equal control. Must responsibility and objectivity lie solely in
the hands of the good influence? Demonstrably not
so. Of our recent history there is no account nor
any evidence that Hitler believed in his principles
less sincerely than Churchill did in his. Where were
Nuremburg, had Hitler won?*

*Where would we stand if evil were the norm
and good . . . abominated? If the balance were to
shift, then this could, should, would become the
case.*

Hypothesis:
*All civilizations abhor the idea of authority with-
out responsibility. Therefore the Time Lords, with
their immense authority, must be responsible, as
civilized beings, to a yet higher authority. Even if
they are unaware of that authority's existence . . .
or have yet to admit to it . . .*

*The President of the High Council of Time Lords,
upon his ratification, is made aware of such a
Higher Authority. He is made aware that, awesome
as the Power of the Time Lords is to humans, or
indeed to other beings, it is only as awesome as the
power held over the Time Lords.*

*There exist in our section of the universe, our
section of the Cosmos, our section of the Cluster,
two Guardians. One is for 'Good' one is for 'Evil'.
One for 'Construction', one for 'Destruction'. One
for . . . the opposites are infinite, as they must be.*

*'Big fleas have little fleas upon their backs to
bite them. And little fleas have smaller fleas, and*

The Pirate Captain (Bruce Purchase) and his nurse (Rosalind Lloyd) on the bridge of Zanak. *The Pirate Planet.*

The Pirate Captain with Mr Fibuli (Andrew Robertson). *The Pirate Planet.*

▲ The Doctor and Romana are captured by the Pirate Captain. *The Pirate Planet.*

▲ The model of Zanak's Bridge. *The Pirate Planet.*

so ad infinitum . . .'

There is no evidence stronger to our earthly eyes than the difference between pure black and pure white. So, without any pre-judgement, let us call our two Guardians Black and White.

The source of power for both these Guardians resides in neutral territory — the Centre of Time. It is called the Key to Time and is in the form of six interlocking unequal segments, each of which, joined with the others, forms a perfect cube in the ratio of 6 x 6 x 6 units. This cube, this Key, is stolen by an agent of Black and scattered through space and time. Unless this Key can be recovered in a finite time, measured, naturally, not in minutes, hours, months or years, then the balance will be destroyed. It is easier to destroy than create; it is easier to kill than give birth; it is easier to demolish than to build. The Apocalypse will not be instantaneous — there would be no joy for Black in that. But for millennia worlds and their inhabitants would suffer ... famine, war, pestilence, despair, until finally they would be destroyed, or, better still, destroy themselves. And for all we know, that is what is happening now.

Prognosis:
The above is simply the background, or rather framework, in which we shall explore the Doctor's attempts to recover, as an agent of White, the Key to Time. Over 26 episodes, telling six individual stories, he will recover the Sections which form the Key to Time.

The time limit in which he has to work will be clearly defined by 'a candle' — a bright orb, so bright in its normal state that to look upon it by the uninitiated would be blinding, but now already diminished. As it fades, so do the hopes of all civilizations.

The Doctor will be seen to have six independent ventures, each linked by the common theme. He will, on occasion, have to decide whether to subordinate the individual problem to the overall plan. He will, on occasion lose a battle to win the war. But each venture in itself must be self explanatory. He may meet old adversaries or encounter new. They will remain, as they always have been, the agents of 'Black'. Those who wish to join him in episode one and follow him through to episode twenty-six will gain the momentum and bonus of following the story through. Those who choose to watch only one venture will enjoy it for its own sake — the scope in each venture is as wide and as free-ranging as ever — but should be encouraged as far as possible to see what happens next. But what does happen next?

Perhaps the Guardians are Time Lords advanced to a higher degree along their own paths. Perhaps this is a test as to whether the Doctor is to qualify for advancement. Perhaps this is a gigantic fraud. Does the good guy always wear the white hat? Whatever the outcome, either individually or overall, the Doctor will arrive at his own conclusions and decisions in his own fashion. As always.

This proposal was accepted by Head of Serials Graeme McDonald, but the enforced abandonment of Terrance Dicks's vampire tale *The Witch Lords* and the shortage of time remaining for advance planning meant that it could not in the end be taken forward for season fifteen. Williams therefore decided to hold it over and use it for season sixteen instead.

An important addition to the concept, necessitated by Louise Jameson's departure at the end of *The Invasion of Time*, was the idea that the White Guardian would give the Doctor a companion to assist him in his search for the six segments. Williams first asked Elisabeth Sladen if she would be willing to return as Sarah Jane Smith, but she

▲ The Mentiads and the Doctor use telekenesis to literally put a spanner in the works and prevent the Captain from destroying the Earth. *The Pirate Planet.*

K-9's operator (Nigel ▲ Brackley) and voice (John Leeson) during rehearsals for *The Stones of Blood*.

Tom Baker with other ▲ cast members during location filming for *The Androids of Tara*.

An unusual shot of the ▼ TARDIS control room taken during studio rehearsals for *The Stones of Blood*.

Beatrix Lehmann, Mary Tamm and Susan Engel on location for *The Stones of Blood*. Note the use of lightweight TV cameras.

The Doctor, aided by Professor Rumford (Beatrix Lehmann) constructs a 'beam machine'. *The Stones of Blood*.

declined the invitation. He then devised a new character called Romana, for whom he wrote the following outline dated 10 October 1977:

For the next season of Doctor Who, *the Doctor will have a new companion to assist in his quest for the Key to Time. She will be allocated to him by a Guardian of Time, initially against his own will and better judgement. She will, however, as the season progresses, prove her worth.*

Romanadvoratrelundar, to give her full name, will not enjoy the full use of that name whilst she is with the Doctor. She will initially be furious at his insistence on the diminutive 'Romana' and even more furious at his sometimes mischievous further foreshortening to 'Romy'.

This will however provide part of the key to the developing relationship which will form between Romana and the Doctor.

Romana is an acolyte Time Lord (Time Lords still refuse to admit to an official title, Time Lady) who has been brought up to believe entirely in the Time Lords' principles of non-intervention and academic observation. She has been firmly placed in the Gallifreyan Groves of Academe and knows nothing of other worldly matters. She will, at first, be horrified at the Doctor's dismissal of the Codes of Practice which have been instilled into her education. As the season progresses however, she will grow to appreciate the Doctor's sense of commitment and his breadth of vision. He, in turn, will be reminded of the youthful approach to problems and situations which, on occasion, will slip by his more sophisticated approach. He will be sometimes surprised, and even more annoyed at her knowledge of later techniques than were available to him during his *undergraduate years.*

Physically, Romana is a beautiful girl with an early appearance of about twenty years — she may, at the end of the season, be due for her first regen-

eration, which would make her in Gallifreyan terms, a mere hundred and forty year old slip of a girl. She possesses the virtues of youthful impetuousness, courage, agility — and an agility not only of body, but also of mind. She can therefore be expected to overcome the hidebound nature of her upbringing and slowly adapt to new patterns of thought and behaviour. Hence her selection by the Guardian. She will, for example, eventually see the sense in the Doctor's rather biting criticisms of her wearing the full length dress as being somewhat impractical and will, to his astonishment, hack it off above the knee to give herself more freedom of movement.

The Doctor will, as always, mistrust anyone's judgement but his own. He may, therefore, not give Romana the full facts of any situation, but try, even, to mislead her. As he grows to know and respect her through her own powers of logic and deduction he will combine his formidable powers with her latent talents.

Whilst her vulnerability will be born of inexperience, that same inexperience provides her with a freedom of temperament which, when unleashed, makes her actions as unpredictable and as mischievous as the Doctor's. She is, in short, the perfect foil to the Doctor in any situation throughout Time and Space.

'We decided to do the one remaining stereotype that had yet to be done,' remembered Williams. 'This was the exact opposite of the savage huntress, namely the ice goddess.

'We made an announcement in the trade press and, as I recall, got over 3,000 photographs and CVs back from interested hopefuls. From this we culled about 500 possibles and then whittled it down to a list of around 120 young ladies we wanted to interview. I did not have a face in my mind that I wanted to cast, but I think closer to Grace Kelly than to Ursula Andress was the image I was looking for. We were, after all, going through the whole female liberation business on television and so, as my step towards addressing that issue on *Doctor Who*, I thought to cast someone who could tackle the aggrievous Mr Baker on his own ground — at least in matters of background, education and awareness — whilst being still unworldly enough to take the side of the idealist.

'Anthony Read and I had rationalized that there is nothing idealistic in the Doctor's character. Like other Time Lords, all he really wants to do is observe and not get involved. But these wishes are constantly being tempered by a forced role of responsibility. And when you consider that he has got almost absolute authority over the savage, primitive cultures that he comes up against, he does handle it rather well.

'I therefore wanted Romana to be his idealistic conscience, having found it increasingly offensive that this renegade egocentric should be wandering around having a good time at everybody else's expense without even a hint of responsibility to a higher authority. The Guardians, I thought, could be that authority, and his companion could at least compete with him, even if she could never come off best. Romana could carry off an argument with the Doctor on moral or philosophical grounds that Leela never could.'

The actress eventually chosen from the extensive interviews carried out by Williams and Read was Mary Tamm, whom they considered to have just the right look for the part.

While Williams was still deeply embroiled in the problems surrounding the production of *The Invasion of Time*, Anthony Read set about commissioning the six stories which would make up the quest for the Key to Time. Robert Holmes, his predecessor as script editor, submitted a number of ideas, and one of these, under the working title *The Galactic Conman*, was commissioned on 9 December 1977 to form the season opener. The Key to Time elements were added by Read himself as the story progressed from storyline to script stage, acquiring in the process the new titles *Operation*, *The Ribos File* and, finally, *The Ribos Operation*.

The transmitted version of *The Ribos Operation* begins with the mysterious figure of the White Guardian sending the Doctor on his quest to find the six disguised segments of the Key to Time — which, when assembled, will be used to restore the balance of the cosmos. The Doctor is given little choice in the matter, and none at all in the selection of his new assistant, Romana.

With the aid of a tracer device, the two Time

An impressive miniature model of the stone circle designed by Mat Irvine for *The Stones of Blood*.

Lords track the first segment to the city of Shur on the planet Ribos. There, a con man named Garron and his assistant Unstoffe are engaged in a scam to sell the entire planet to the Graff Vynda-K, deposed ruler of Levithia, who wants to use it as a base from which to win back his throne. The Graff has been tricked into believing that Ribos is a rich source of jethryk, a rare mineral vital for achieving space warp drive. His interest is further piqued when he sees a large lump of the mineral on display in a reliquary. Unstoffe, disguised as a guard, tells the Graff an elaborate tale of hidden maps and caves full of jethryk, which he claims that the locals call scringe-stone.

The Doctor realizes that the jethryk is in fact the first segment. Before he can steal it, however, Unstoffe spirits it away again. The Graff, having discovered the trick that has been played on him, hunts the con men down and captures them, along with the time travellers, in the catacombs beneath the city. He is on the point of having them all executed when Riban guards blow up the entrance to the catacombs. The death of his officer and friend Sholakh in the ensuing rock fall unhinges the Graff's mind. He storms into the dust and is killed by a thermite bomb with which he had intended to destroy the catacombs entirely. The Doctor, Romana

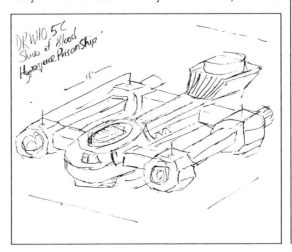

▲ Vivian Fay (Susan Engel) alias the Cailleach. Her necklace is the disguised third segment of the Key to Time. *The Stones of Blood*.

▲ Posing as the Cailleach, Vivian Fay encourages Druidic worship and blood sacrifice. *The Stones of Blood*.

▼ Left: Visual effects designer Mat Irvine's design sketch for the hyperspace prison ship and, below, the finished model resting against a CSO background. *The Stones of Blood*.

Romana searches for the ▲ next segment of the Key to Time on Tara. *The Androids of Tara.*

The Doctor on the steps ▲ of the Taran throne. The android prince is lying by his feet. *The Androids of Tara.*

A member of the ▲ production team on location with the Taran wood beast. *The Androids of Tara.*

and K-9 depart with the jethryk, which the tracer converts into its true form of the first segment, leaving Garron and Unstoffe to make off with the Graff's ship of plundered loot.

The Ribos Operation was the first story of Doctor Who's sixteenth production block. It was recorded entirely at Television Centre in two sessions over 9—11 April and 23—25 April 1978, with an extra gallery-only day on 3 May 1978 used primarily to complete the scenes with the White Guardian. Its opening episode launched the sixteenth season at 5.44 pm on Saturday 2 September 1978.

The decision to keep K-9 on for this season had been taken at a relatively late stage after Graham Williams had received assurances from the Visual Effects Department that the prop's internal workings could be redesigned to make it quieter and more controllable. This refit was carried out in collaboration with a specialist firm called Slough Radio Control, who allowed employee Nigel Brackley to be seconded to *Doctor Who* on a semi-permanent basis to look after the mechanical dog. A scene which had been recorded on a contingency basis was edited onto the end of *The Invasion of Time* to show the Doctor unveiling a Mark II K-9 after leaving the original with Leela on Gallifrey.

The Key to Time itself consisted of six solid pieces of clear perspex which could be assembled to form a complete cube. A cylindrical hole ran through the centre of the cube to accommodate the tracer device which the Doctor and Romana were given to track down the segments. A number of different versions of the prop were made, and a number of duplicates of each individual segment, to allow for the possibility of some going astray during the course of production.

The season's second story, *The Pirate Planet*, marked the TV debut of writer Douglas Adams, who had begun submitting ideas to the production office some time earlier while still a student at Cambridge University. He had recently completed his first scripts for a new BBC radio series called *The Hitch-Hiker's Guide to the Galaxy* — the creation for which he would eventually become famous.

'Douglas's enormous talent was immediately apparent to me,' says Anthony Read, 'as soon as I saw his first scripts for *The Hitch-Hiker's Guide to the Galaxy*, which is what led me to commission him. It was not always easy to see what would work on screen, but I knew there was enough there, if I could shape it correctly. He had that amazing imagination, firing off in all directions, some of which were right for *Doctor Who* and some of which were following quite different conventions — the jokiness of the series at the time was always a very fine line which

had to be walked with great care, and Douglas was naturally inclined to leap all over it, given half a chance.'

The transmitted version of *The Pirate Planet* differed greatly from Douglas Adams's original submission, as the writer later recalled:

'The original idea for *The Pirate Planet* was the basic concept of a hollow planet. Graham Williams was interested in space pirates, so we just married the two ideas together.

'The original storyline was of a planet being mined by the Time Lords. The inhabitants of this planet were a rowdy lot, and the Time Lords had erected a giant statue, the inside of which was in fact a giant machine for absorbing all the aggression from the people. When they had all the ore that they needed, they sent a Time Lord to disconnect the machine, but he got trapped in the works and absorbed all the aggression. None of the other Time Lords had bothered to find out where he had got to, so he decided to have revenge on them by letting the mining equipment completely hollow out the planet, then making it jump to surround Gallifrey . . .

'The plot was so complicated, even right from the beginning. I remember reading a synopsis of it to Graham, after which he sank into his chair mumbling that now he knew how Stanley Kubrick felt!'

'The big problem,' says Anthony Read, 'was that Douglas seemed to have absolutely no idea of shape and form for narrative drama; and, despite all the sci-fi effects, *Doctor Who* is essentially about telling stories within a proper, conventional dramatic structure. No matter how brilliant the imaginative ideas, the basic rules of drama still apply. When this is forgotten, the series fails. So it was down to me to perform the necessary surgery, with Douglas's willing co-operation.

'In fact, when this was all happening, I was on my own in the office. Graham had gone on a short holiday to Madeira, where he had tripped over a low wall and broken his leg. So he was out of action. When the first draft scripts came in, Graeme McDonald saw them and tried to pull the show, believing it would never work. It really did look that much of a mess.'

McDonald made his thoughts quite clear in a memo which he sent to Read and copied to Williams on 14 March 1978:

On the basis of the first two scripts this won't do. The situation is overfamiliar: the dominant Captain and the underground proles working in the mines. There's no plot development. The situation they are

A glowing Ogri forces its way through a gate in pursuit of blood. *The Stones of Blood.*

Prince Reynart (Neville Jason) sits on the Taran throne. *The Androids of Tara.*

LOCATIONS

The Ribos Operation
No location work

The Pirate Planet
Berkley Power Station, Gloucestershire;
Abercrave Caves, Dan-yr-Ogof, Powys, Wales

The Stones of Blood
Rollright Stones, Oxfordshire;
Reed Cottage, Little Compton, Oxfordshire;
Little Rollright Quarry, Oxfordshire

The Androids of Tara
Leeds Castle, Kent

The Power of Kroll
Boat landing at the Maltings, Snape, Suffolk;
The Wetlands, River Alde, Suffolk;
Iken Cliff, Suffolk

The Armageddon Factor
No location work

in is not stated until the end of Episode 2. Worse, there's no threat to the Doctor or the viewer. We're doing science fiction remember not comic cuts. The Captain with the parrot is a cod figure out of Treasure Island *with jokey lines which will inevitably lead Tom to stop taking himself seriously again. Indeed in Episode 1 p.38 the Doctor has lines like 'Take me to your leader' which will start the rot all over again. Again in Episode 2 p.6: the teacups routine is too jokey.*

Is Romana well enough set up in serial 5A? There's no development for her in this one. It's Leela all over again. And the 'Key to Time', which I had understood as being an important ingredient, is dismissed in a stage direction. I suggest we must substitute a stronger set of scripts before Pennant joins.

In any other season it might have been possible for Adams's story to be switched with one further down the production order to allow time for it to be reworked, but in this instance the strictures of the over-arching plot meant that there was no such room for manoeuvre. With less than two months to go before filming was due to commence, Read and director Pennant Roberts persuaded McDonald that there was no real choice but to proceed with the story as it stood.

The Pirate Planet sees the second segment being traced to the planet Calufrax — a location that the Doctor describes as 'paralysingly dull, boring and tedious!' The TARDIS makes a bumpy landing, and when the Doctor and Romana start to search for the segment they discover that they are not on Calufrax at all. They are in fact on Zanak, a planet which has been hollowed out and fitted with engines so that it can transmat through space and materialize around others — such as Calufrax — to plunder their mineral wealth, leaving them as shrunken husks held by gravitational forces in a 'trophy room'.

Zanak is governed from a complex known as the

Bridge. Ostensibly in charge is the Captain, a brilliant hyper-engineer whose body has been partially replaced with robotic parts following a near-fatal crash, but he is in fact merely a puppet controlled by his Nurse — a projection of Zanak's original ruler, the aged Queen Xanxia. Xanxia is using time dams, powered by the forces generated in the trophy room, to keep her feeble body alive until this new, younger form has stabilized.

The Captain prepares Zanak to 'jump' again — and this time the target planet is Earth. The Doctor realizes the truth about Xanxia — that there is no amount of energy that will give her a permanent new form — and attempts to thwart the Captain's plans. In this he is aided by the Mentiads, a gestalt of telepaths amongst Zanak's indigenous population who are sensitive to the life force of the destroyed planets. Under the Doctor's supervision, the Mentiads use their telekinetic powers to put Zanak's engines out of action. The Captain then rebels against the Nurse's control, but she retaliates by killing him. The Nurse herself is then destroyed by one of the Zanak natives whom the Doctor, Romana and K-9 have befriended. The Doctor realizes that the second segment comprises the whole of the planet Calufrax. He contrives to drop the compressed husks from the trophy room into a space-time vortex created by the TARDIS in the centre of Zanak, and is then able to pick up and convert the segment at his leisure.

The Pirate Planet, with its larger-than-life Captain and his robot parrot, the Polyphase Avitron, was season sixteen's most humorous story.

'The robot parrot idea, I must admit, was mine,' says Douglas Adams. 'I thought of it just before lunch actually. I had just finished a scene and thought that it seemed a bit dull — "We want something really silly in it, so how about a robot parrot?" I left that note for myself to discover after lunch. I came back and thought, "God, don't be stupid." But then I thought, "Why not?" It was partly because of the

MUSIC

All the music for this season was provided by Dudley Simpson.

Television Birthday

Congratulations and Happy Voyaging to the Tardis! On November 25, it's the 15th anniversary of the popular adventure series, *Dr. Who* – the gripping story of the eccentric Time Lord and his girl assistant, at present played by Tom Baker and Mary Tamm. Daleks rule OK, but the most appealing enemy was surely that concoction of spare parts housing Morbius' brain. Remember?
From **Woman's Realm**, *25 November 1978. In fact, 23 November was the date of the anniversary.*

The refinery crew: ▲
Dugeen (John Leeson),
Fenner (Philip Madoc) and
Thawn (Neil McCarthy).
The Power of Kroll.

Tony Harding's ▲
original design sketch for
Kroll appearing over the
horizon.

Long John Silver character, and partly for K-9 to have his own enemy for once; one specifically designed for him.'

The next two stories were both contributed by writer David Fisher, who was new to *Doctor Who* but had many other TV credits to his name, including on *The Lotus Eaters*, *Orlando* and — under its script editor and producer Anthony Read — *The Troubleshooters*. The storyline for the first was commissioned on 8 December 1977 under the title *The Nine Maidens* and the full scripts on 10 January 1978 under the revised title *The Stones of Time* (the production team having apparently decided at one point that each of the season's stories should have a title ending in . . . *of Time*). Later drafts became *The Stones of Blood*.

The Doctor, Romana and K-9 are led by the tracer to the Nine Travellers, a circle of standing stones on Boscowan Moor in present-day England, but the third segment is nowhere to be found. They meet up with elderly archaeologist Professor Amelia Rumford and her assistant Vivien Fay, who are surveying the site, and discover that the circle appears to have had a variable number of stones over the years. The Doctor visits Leonard de Vries of the British Institute for Druidic Studies (BIDS), whose members worship at the circle. He is knocked unconscious whilst at de Vries's home and is subsequently saved by Professor Rumford from becoming the Druids' latest sacrifice. He then revisits de Vries, only to find that the man has been killed by one of the stones from the circle — in truth an Ogri, a life form from the planet Ogros in Tau Ceti, which lives on blood.

Miss Fay turns out to be the latest guise of the Cailleach, a being worshipped by the Druids, who has been on Earth for four thousand years. She transports Romana to a spaceship suspended in hyperspace at the same coordinates as the stone circle. The Doctor follows and, whilst searching for his companion, accidentally releases two justice machines called Megara. The Megara put him on trial and sentence him to execution for breaking the seal on their compartment. When they attempt to carry out their sentence, however, he tricks them into knocking Miss Fay unconscious. Reading her mind to find out if she has been injured, they learn that she is in reality Cessair of Diplos — the alien criminal they were originally sent to try. Having established her guilt, they transform her into an additional stone in the circle, but not before the Doctor has grabbed her necklace — the third segment of the Key to Time.

The Stones of Blood had the honour of being *Doctor Who*'s one hundredth story, transmitted in its fifteenth anniversary year. In recognition of this fact, director Darrol Blake suggested amending the script

of episode one to include a scene where Romana sprang a surprise party for the Doctor's 751st birthday. This would have seen the Doctor entering the TARDIS's limbo room — an area, somewhere beyond the main control room, where they were assembling the collected segments of the Key to Time — to find streamers, balloons and a table laden with jellies and a huge birthday cake. Romana would then have given the Doctor a present which, when unwrapped, would have turned out to be a new scarf — identical to his old one. Although scripted and rehearsed, this scene was vetoed by Graham Williams just prior to recording, his reservations being that it was too self-congratulatory and raised the awkward question of where Time Lord babies come from.

David Fisher's second story was commissioned on 26 May 1978 under the title *The Androids of Zenda*. Based on Anthony Hope's novel *The Prisoner of Zenda* (1894), it was viewed by Graham Williams as a literary pastiche which would further the series' use of sophisticated humour as a replacement for the overt horror of the Philip Hinchcliffe seasons.

'Tony Read asked me what I thought about *The Prisoner of Zenda*,' recalls Fisher. 'I thought it was a brilliant story with a wonderful structure. Tony had the idea of reworking these old myths, which after all had stood the test of time and still had a lot of potency.

'Of course, once you're into androids, any comparison with *The Prisoner of Zenda* goes out the window.'

Later working titles were *The Prisoner of Zend* and *The Seeds of Time*, and the story was eventually transmitted as *The Androids of Tara*.

The search for the fourth segment brings the Doctor, Romana and K-9 to Tara, a seemingly peaceful planet where the technically skilled peasants are ruled by a ruritanian aristocracy. Expecting no trouble, the Doctor goes fishing whilst Romana explores alone. Romana quickly locates the segment, disguised as part of a statue, but is then attacked by a Taran wood beast. She is rescued by Count Grendel of Gracht, who sees off the beast but confiscates the segment.

Grendel is attempting to seize the Taran throne from the rightful heir, Prince Reynart. He initially believes that Romana is an android duplicate of the Prince's betrothed, Princess Strella, as they are identical in appearance. He is already holding Strella hostage and now imprisons Romana as well. The Doctor has meanwhile been taken to the camp of Prince Reynart and forced to repair an android

Kroll rises from the swamp beside the methane refinery. *The Power of Kroll.*

Ranquin (John Abineri), the leader of the Swampies. *The Power of Kroll.*

double of him to act as a decoy for potential assassins. Grendel then kidnaps the Prince, and the Doctor has to modify the android so that it can be crowned in his place.

Grendel's plan is first to force Reynart and Strella to marry and then to kill Reynart and marry Strella himself. Once Strella has in turn been killed, he will then become the legal heir to the throne. Strella is refusing to co-operate, however, and Grendel now wants Romana to stand in for her. Reynart's coronation goes ahead as planned, but Strella arrives towards the conclusion. The Doctor realizes that this is in fact an android sent to destroy the android Prince, and disables it. The ceremony is then put on hold until the following day. Grendel commissions another android duplicate of Romana — this time equipped with a lethal ray — and contrives for the Doctor to meet her at the Pavilion of the Summer Winds. K-9 recognizes the trap and saves his master. Meanwhile the real Romana escapes from Castle Gracht and rescues the Doctor and K-9, who have been attacked by Grendel's men.

Grendel turns the tables when he destroys the Reynart android and recaptures Romana. The Doctor gains access to the Castle by rowing across the moat and, having first found and pocketed the fourth segment, manages to halt the twin marriage ceremonies. Battle is then joined as the Prince's men attack the Castle in force. In the confusion, Romana saves Strella from being killed and the Doctor engages Grendel in a spectacular sword fight. Realizing that he has been defeated, Grendel dives into the moat and escapes to fight another day.

A number of unusual challenges arose during production of *The Androids of Tara*. One of the first came when the crew discovered that they were unable to complete the usual advance preparations for the story's location filming owing to the fact that the chosen venue, Leeds Castle in Kent, was being used

at that time for high-security Middle East peace talks. Other difficulties were posed by the inclusion in Fisher's scripts of a number of scenes in which actors playing dual roles had to be seen to meet their *alter egos*. Some of the required shots were achieved with the use of body doubles, but for the most part a time-consuming split-screen technique was adopted. So heavy were the story's electronic effects requirements that two gallery-only days were booked for their completion. In the event, however, half a day was lost to another programme owing to a spate of unofficial strikes. Electronic effects operator Mitch Mitchell consequently ran out of time and was unable to add all the proposed sparks, flashes and laser blasts to the scenes featuring electro-rapier duels.

Another writer new to *Doctor Who* who was commissioned for season sixteen was Ted Lewis, but his story proved unsuitable. The season's last two stories were ultimately provided by writers with very considerable experience on the series.

The fifth story, *The Power of Kroll* (working titles: *The Moon of Death*, *The Horror of the Swamp* and *The Shield of Time*), was the second to be written by Robert Holmes. The scripts were commissioned on 26 May 1978 and completed within a relatively short space of time, episodes one and two being delivered on 7 June and episodes three and four on 15 June. Holmes had however been unhappy with Anthony Read's stipulation that the story should be a predominantly serious one featuring the biggest monster ever seen in the series, and he remained dissatisfied with the end result.

The TARDIS's arrival point on this occasion is an

THE KRIKKITMEN

*The third of Douglas Adams's **Hitch-Hiker's** novels, **Life, the Universe and Everything**, actually started life as an unused **Doctor Who** storyline written for the fourth Doctor and Sarah Jane Smith. According to Neil Gaiman's book **Don't Panic**, the storyline was rejected by Graham Williams as being 'too silly', and Adams later revamped it as a film outline at the time Tom Baker was developing his **Doctor Who meets Scratchman** idea. The plot involved a race of xenophobic creatures from the planet Krikkit who built a force of anthropomorphic androids, the Krikkitmen, to wipe out all life in the universe. The Time Lords had trapped them on their own planet until the disparate elements of a key – the Wicket – combined together to release them onto the universe once more. This plot survives more or less intact in the novel, the role of the Doctor being split between Slartibartfast, Trillian and Arthur Dent.*

DAVID FISHER
WRITER

*David Fisher was approached by script editor Anthony Read to write for **Doctor Who** and the result was the 100th story, **The Stones of Blood** in 1978. Fisher had first met Anthony Read when the latter was setting up **The Troubleshooters** in 1965. Fisher also worked on **Orlando** (1967), **Dixon of Dock Green** (1969), **Sutherland's Law** (1973) and **General Hospital** (1977). Following **Doctor Who**, Fisher contributed some scripts to the **Hammer House of Horror** series. Fisher has, in more recent years, been collaborating with Read on a number of historical books dealing with subjects including World War Two espionage, the Nazi persecution of the Jews and the Nazi/Soviet pact of the early 1940s. He lives with his second wife in a 16th-century house in Suffolk.*

The Marshal's ship ▲ preparing for lift-off. *The Armageddon Factor.*

The Shadow's space ▲ station hanging in space between Atrios and Zeos. *The Armageddon Factor.*

area of marshland bordering a lake on the third moon of the planet Delta Magna. While trying to get an accurate reading on the tracer, the Doctor is shot at by Thawn and Fenner, two men from a nearby methane catalysing refinery. Romana is meanwhile taken prisoner by a group of green-skinned natives, the Swampies, who decide to sacrifice her to their god Kroll as a prelude to an imminent attack on the refinery. A man named Rohm-Dutt is running guns to the Swampies ostensibly on behalf of an anti-colonial organization called the Sons of Earth, who are sympathetic to their cause. In truth however this is all part of a plot by Thawn to discredit the Sons and have the Swampies wiped out. The Doctor, drawn by the sound of the sacrificial drums, arrives at the Swampies' temple just in time to rescue his companion.

The refinery crew notice that the bed of the lake is shifting, as if there is something massive moving beneath it. The Swampies, led by Ranquin, prepare their attack, but are stopped in their tracks when Kroll — an enormous squid-like creature — appears on the horizon. Kroll heads for the refinery and starts to assail it, while the Doctor, Romana and Rohm-Dutt are captured by the Swampies and sentenced to death. The Doctor and Romana manage to escape, but Rohm-Dutt is seized and killed by one of Kroll's tentacles.

The two Time Lords reach the refinery, where they learn that Thawn is planning to destroy Kroll by blasting it with one of the orbital plasma rockets normally used to seed the moon's atmosphere for methane. The Doctor disables the rocket, and Thawn is subsequently slain by the Swampies as they launch their attack. Kroll then returns its attention to the refinery, and the Doctor goes out to confront it armed only with the tracer — which transforms it into the fifth segment of the Key to Time.

Actor Philip Madoc — whose previous *Doctor Who* appearances had been as Eelek in *The Krotons*, the War Lord in *The War Games* and Solon in *The Brain of Morbius*—returned to the series to play refinery engineer Fenner in *The Power of Kroll*. This was after Alan Browning, director Norman Stewart's first choice, pulled out due to illness. Madoc had in fact been under the impression that he was being invited to play Thawn, and was disappointed to learn that his role was actually a much less substantial one. The part of Thawn was originally to have been played by George Baker, but when he proved unavailable it went instead to Neil McCarthy, who had previously been seen as Barnham in *The Mind of Evil*. Also recast was the part of Dugeen, another of the refinery crew. This had been offered to Martin Jarvis but was eventually played by John Leeson — a money-saving measure as Leeson was already under contract to provide the voice of K-9. The robot

dog was absent from this story owing to the unsuitability of the marshland location for the use of the radio-controlled prop.

Aside from these late casting changes, production of *The Power of Kroll* ran into further problems as filming got underway. The shots of Kroll were achieved primarily through the use of a split-screen effect — the top section of the picture consisting of model footage of the monster and the bottom of material filmed on location at Iken Marshes in Suffolk — but cameraman Martin Pathmore had been badly advised on this and made the mistake of physically masking off the top part of the camera lens for the location work. This meant that the horizontal join between the two sections of the picture was impossible to disguise in post-production and the shots were rendered largely unconvincing. Visual effects designer Tony Harding was disappointed also with the footage of the refinery model, which he considered to have been shot from the wrong angle due to inadequate tank facilities. Another difficulty which arose on location was that the bright green make-up used for the Swampies proved very difficult to remove, leading the cast to retire to a nearby air base to try to scrub it off — much to the amusement of the watching airmen.

The story's single studio session over 9—11 October 1978 was not without incident, either, as Graham Williams was absent due to illness and production unit manager John Nathan-Turner had to deputize as producer. David Maloney, a long-time *Doctor Who* director who was then working as producer of the BBC science-fiction series *Blake's 7*, was meanwhile brought in to cover for Williams in overseeing preparations for the following story, *The Armageddon Factor*.

This concluding six-parter was commissioned early in 1978 on the basis of a 15-page storyline entitled *Armageddon* which writers Bob Baker and Dave Martin had submitted on 19 December 1977. All six scripts were completed by 17 March and approved by Anthony Read and Graham Williams by the end of April. They were however far too long and ambitious as they stood, so Read later revised them quite extensively. This work, carried out during September, was his last major task as *Doctor Who*'s script editor. Having spent 18 months on the series, he felt in need of a rest and wanted to turn his attention to other projects. Faced with the task of finding a replacement for him, Williams tried in the first instance to persuade Robert Holmes to return to his old job. When Holmes declined, however, he decided at Read's suggestion to approach Douglas Adams instead. This time his offer was accepted, and Adams spent six weeks trailing Read before taking over fully at the end of November.

One of Adams's first acts as script editor was to

The Black Guardian, disguised as the White Guardian, tries to obtain control of the completed Key to Time at the conclusion of *The Armageddon Factor*.

The Doctor, Princess Astra (Lalla Ward) and Romana watch as Zeon forces invade Atrian air space. *The Armageddon Factor*.

rewrite the end of episode six of *Armageddon*, which he felt provided an insufficiently clear and dramatic resolution to the Key to Time plot. He was also responsible for renaming the story *The Armageddon Factor*.

The search for the sixth and final segment brings the Doctor, Romana and K-9 to the planet Atrios, which is engaged in a long and bloody war with the neighbouring Zeos. The Atrian people, desperate for victory, are unaware that the Marshal in command of their forces has fallen under the influence of a third party and is receiving orders from a skull-like communicator situated behind a two-way mirror. The Doctor eventually finds himself on an invisible third planet between Atrios and Zeos. This is ruled by the Shadow — the Marshal's controller — who, with his servants the Mutes, is working for the Black Guardian to try to prevent the Doctor from obtaining the segment. The Shadow has captured Princess Astra of Atrios and is holding her under threat of torture in the belief that she can tell him where the segment is hidden.

The Doctor learns that Zeos is being controlled by a computer called Mentalis, which is planning a final massive strike against Atrios to counter the Marshal's similar plan to obliterate Zeos. Mentalis was constructed for the Shadow by a Time Lord called Drax — an old college friend of the Doctor's. Drax helps the Doctor to disable the computer before both worlds are destroyed. The Doctor then creates a fake final segment from a substance called chronodyn and uses the Key to Time to place a time loop around the ship from which the Marshal is about to launch his strike against Zeos. The chronodyn is unstable, however, and the time loop begins slowly to decay.

It transpires that Princess Astra is herself the sixth segment. The Shadow converts her into the crystal, but the Doctor snatches it from under his nose and escapes to the TARDIS, where he finally completes the Key to Time. The White Guardian appears on

the TARDIS scanner screen and congratulates the Doctor on a job well done. He asks that the Key be handed over to him, but the Doctor decides that it is too powerful for any one being to control and orders it to re-disperse. Enraged, the Guardian reverts to his true colour — Black — and vows that the Doctor shall die for this defiance. In order to shake him off, the Doctor fits a randomizer to the TARDIS's controls. There is now no telling where or when his travels will take him.

The second of the three studio recording sessions for *The Armageddon Factor*, which took place over 20—22 November 1978, was disrupted by the latest bout of the long-running industrial dispute which had earlier caused problems on *The Invasion of Time*. Graham Williams explained the circumstances in a memo sent the following day to Graeme McDonald:

We were unable to start camera rehearsals on Monday at 11 am because of the union meeting which continued until 1 pm. The industrial dispute continued to affect recordings so that on Tuesday we lost three quarters of an hour of recording time and one quarter hour's recording time on Wednesday.

Thanks to the good will of the technical staff and the efficiency of the production team we were, however, able to complete all our scheduled recording with the exception of interior TARDIS scenes — the

NOTES
Pirated Planets

The eight planets in the Captain's trophy room in **The Pirate Planet** *were named Calufrax, Bandraginus V, Aterica, Temesis, Tridentio III, Lowiteliom, Granados and Bibicorpus. Amongst the minerals plundered from them were Oolian, Voolium and Madranite 1-5.*

Romana's Double

To achieve the effect of there being two Princess Strellas in **The Androids of Tara**, *a split screen process was used. Mary Tamm was doubled by actress Roberta Gibbs when the two characters were to be seen to interact. Gibbs also doubled for Tamm in part two of the previous story,* **The Stones of Blood**, *in the scene where Romana falls off a cliff edge.*

Breakdown

During part five of **The Armageddon Factor** *there was a 25-second break in transmission from 18:49:00 until 18:49:25. During the break a caption slide was displayed and a record called 'Gotcha' by Tom Scott was played. When the transmission of* **Doctor Who** *was restarted, the tape had been rewound slightly so there was a repeat of the action immediately prior to the break.*

smallest set in the studio. I have already discussed briefly with the production team the possibility of catching up with those scenes in our next recording (week 49) and we shall, of course, try to complete the programme by the end of that recording.

Whilst I am unable to offer any guarantees, of course, I am nevertheless as optimistic as the present circumstances allow.

Williams's optimism proved well-founded, as all the necessary scenes were completed during the third recording session on 3 and 5 December — which, barring final editing and dubbing, brought the series' fifteenth production block to a close.

The final episode of *The Armageddon Factor*, transmitted on 24 February 1979, saw Mary Tamm making her last appearance as Romana. As the actress later recalled, she had decided during production of *The Power of Kroll* to move on to other work when her year's contract expired:

'I would have done another year if the scripts — that is, my part — had improved. I thought Romana had started well, but towards the end had just degenerated into the traditional little girl figure, tagging along behind the Doctor. There was no sign of matters improving, so it seemed a good idea to go.

'Graham Williams really wanted me to stay on. He didn't believe I was actually going to leave, and wouldn't take no for an answer — which was quite extraordinary, I thought. I told the BBC a month before my contract was up that I wasn't going to renew.'

Although Tom Baker continued in the role of the Doctor, it had at one point looked as if he might also be departing at the end of season sixteen. This was due to disagreements which had arisen between him and Graham Williams over his increasing desire to influence all aspects of the series' production.

'We knew each other's strengths and weaknesses,' Williams later recalled, 'and it did get to a point when I had to say to him, "Look, we do know each other well. Now either you get on with your job and leave me to get on with mine, or I will have to find another leading man. And unfortunately you are not in the position of being able to find another producer." But that didn't work. I was called in and told that, unless I mended my ways and gave Tom story approval, casting approval and director approval next season, I would not be employed to produce it. Graeme McDonald actually called me in from sick leave to tell me that!

'This was all because Tom had pushed a postcard through my door a few days earlier to say that he wouldn't be doing *Doctor Who* any more. I had taken that card to Graeme McDonald with the argument that we were going to have to recast, as there was no way that I was prepared to give that amount of power to a leading actor. Graeme told me that he had had a meeting with Bill Cotton, the Controller of BBC1, and there was no question raised about my having failed in my job. It was simply a direct choice between Tom Baker and me. Bill Cotton and Graeme McDonald had agreed at that lunch that, if the choice had to be made, they would choose Tom Baker. The name of Graham Williams in *Radio Times* was not going to deliver 13 million viewers on Saturday night the way Tom Baker's did. My response was to say, "Fine, that's your decision. But still don't expect me to give the leading actor in a show script approval, casting approval and director approval."

'Shaun Sutton, the Head of Drama, was out of the country while all this went on, so I added that as it was Shaun who had appointed me as a producer, it was to Shaun that I should actually refer my reasons for not being able to continue. Graeme thought that was perfectly fair. We had a meeting with Shaun the day after he got back to the country. And that same afternoon Graeme McDonald came to me and asked me to fire Tom Baker! I told him that I didn't want to. I felt he should. And that didn't go down too well either. In the end, there was a meeting of the three of us in Graeme's office, with Tom airing his grievances and me airing mine. It went on for several hours, at the end of which the question was posed: could we two still work together? We both said yes, so Graeme said, "Fine. Get on with it."

'The crux of the whole matter had been Tom and I knowing each other too well, and Graeme not knowing Tom at all. Graeme had been approached by the extremely powerful personality of Mr Baker, which I had had time to get used to over two years, and he had come from a background of one-off plays where very potent and powerful actors and actresses are run-of-the-mill. He had taken Tom too much at his word.

'Tom, by and large, had been talking out of the back of his neck. By the time you've had your 95th drunken conversation with Tom, where he explains to you that the ideal companion for him in a *Doctor Who* story is a cabbage that could sit on his shoulder so he could turn to it from time to time to explain the plot, you're used to his eccentricities. Graeme McDonald, however, was hearing all this for the first time and, I think, was firmly convinced by the end of this business that Tom had been pulling his leg all along. Maybe he had.'

CHAPTER SIXTEEN

Season Seventeen: Crisis Point

Successful though season sixteen had been, Graham Williams considered that the use of a linking theme had imposed too many strictures to be repeated on a regular basis. For season seventeen he therefore decided to return to the more familiar format of a succession of unconnected stories, the transmission order of which could if necessary be changed during the course of production.

One of the first problems that Williams and his new script editor Douglas Adams had to face was Mary Tamm's decision not to renew her contract as Romana. They had hoped that she could be persuaded to change her mind, but this was not to be. The end result was that a new companion had to be chosen between seasons and a suitable plot explanation devised for Tamm's sudden disappearance. Williams and Adams concluded that, as Romana was a Time Lord, the simplest solution would be to have her regenerate. They briefly considered the idea of casting a different actress for every story, but decided that this would be impracticable. Tom Baker, meanwhile, reportedly suggested Miriam Margolyes to play Romana's second incarnation. In the end, the part went to Lalla Ward, who had impressed the production team with her performance as Princess Astra in *The Armageddon Factor* and had immediately hit it off with Baker. She signed her contract on 6 February 1979 and was presented to the press the same day.

Another pressing task was the selection of stories for inclusion in the new season. Anthony Read had already commissioned two from David Fisher, whose season sixteen scripts, *The Stones of Blood* and *The Androids of Tara*, had been generally well received. On the basis of a handful of submissions passed on to him by Read, Adams then commissioned one from Bob Baker, who had recently split from his long-time writing partner Dave Martin. He also decided to commission from Read himself a story based around the Minoan myths. Other ideas under consideration, which ultimately came to nothing, included *The Doomsday Project* by Alan Drury, John Lloyd and Allan Prior and *Erinella* by writer and director Pennant Roberts.

To launch the season, Adams and Williams agreed to go ahead with an adventure pitting the Doctor against his most popular adversaries, the Daleks. Their creator Terry Nation had been approached about this possibility back in November 1978, and had agreed on condition that he be allowed to write the story himself and to incorporate the character of Davros from his season-twelve success *Genesis of the Daleks*.

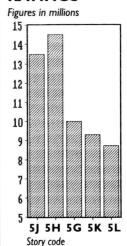

SEASON SEVENTEEN	
CODE	TITLE
5J	DESTINY OF THE DALEKS
5H	CITY OF DEATH
5G	THE CREATURE FROM THE PIT
5K	NIGHTMARE OF EDEN
5L	THE HORNS OF NIMON

RATINGS
Figures in millions

◀ **The newly-regenerated Romana (Lalla Ward) and the Doctor watch as the Movellan ship arrives on Skaro. *Destiny of the Daleks*.**

One of Romana's ▲ 'rejected bodies'. *Destiny of the Daleks.*

TERRY NATION
WRITER

Terry Nation was originally a comedy writer, and when David Whitaker first asked him to contribute to **Doctor Who** *– on the basis of his three previous science-fiction scripts for ABC TV's* **Out of this World** *– he initially declined. Following his work on* **Doctor Who,** *he went on to write for and script-edit a whole string of popular shows, including* **The Avengers, The Saint, The Baron** *and* **The Persuaders!** *– and, of course, he contributed many more stories to* **Doctor Who.** *In the seventies, he also created the successful BBC telefantasy series* **Survivors** *and* **Blake's 7.** *He has since emigrated to America, where he now lives in Hollywood.*

A unique monitor shot ▲ showing Tom Baker and David Gooderson as Davros, but without his mask. *Destiny of the Daleks.*

Back row: Agella ▶ (Suzanne Danielle), Commander Sharrell (Peter Straker) and Tysson (Tim Barlow). Front row: Romana and the Doctor. *Destiny of the Daleks.*

Davros (David Gooderson) is revived to aid the Daleks in their battle against the Movellans. *Destiny of the Daleks.*

The production team knew that other commitments would prevent Nation from delivering his scripts until the spring of 1979, but decided that the story — commissioned on 20 December 1978 under the title *Destiny of the Daleks* — could be slipped back to third in production sequence and still be

completed in time for transmission as the season opener. In the event, the scripts came in at the end of March 1979 — even later than anticipated — and Adams had to edit them quickly to ensure that they were ready for the start of filming in June.

Amongst the changes made by Adams were the addition of a regeneration scene to introduce the new Romana and the inclusion of an in-joke reference to his own *The Hitch-Hiker's Guide to the Galaxy* in the form of a book called *Origins of the Universe* by Oolon Coluphid. K-9 was confined to the TARDIS, supposedly suffering from a bout of laryngitis, as it was felt that the robot would not work well alongside the Daleks. In addition, although Williams had no desire to hark back to the Guardian theme of the previous season, a few lines of dialogue were incorporated to refer to the randomizer that the Doctor had fitted to the TARDIS's guidance systems at the end of *The Armageddon Factor.*

The TARDIS's first randomized journey sees it landing on the Daleks' home planet, Skaro, in the far distant future. Exploring, the Doctor and the newly-regenerated Romana discover that the Daleks are using explosive charges and a group of humanoid slave workers to mine the planet in search of their creator, Davros. A stalemate has arisen in an interplanetary war that the creatures are waging against the robotic Movellans, and their hope is that Davros will be able to give them the upper hand. A force of Movellans has also arrived on Skaro, determined to thwart the Daleks' plan.

Davros is found in the ruins of the old Kaled city and immediately revives, his life support systems having held him in suspended animation since his apparent death at the conclusion of *Genesis of the Daleks.* On assessing the situation, he realizes that the battle computers of the two warring races are locked in a logical stalemate and that he can break this by introducing an element of intuition. The Movellans, having reached the same conclusion, want the Doctor to do likewise for them.

Davros attempts to destroy the Movellan ship using a suicide squad of Daleks loaded with bombs, but the Doctor returns to the Kaled city and tricks him into inadvertently detonating the bombs before they reach their target. The Movellans are deactivated and Davros is cryogenically frozen on board their ship until the freed slave workers can take him to Earth and he can be put on trial for his crimes.

Michael Wisher, the actor who had played Davros in *Genesis of the Daleks,* was on tour in Australia when *Destiny of the Daleks* was made and so a replacement had to be found. David Gooderson was chosen, due both to his similarity in build to Wisher

Visual effects assistant Ken Bomphray sets up a shot of the Doctor's and Romana's feet against a vibrating table to simulate a minor earthquake. Steve Lucas and Barbara Horne double for the Doctor and Romana for this sequence. *Destiny of the Daleks.*

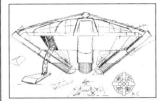

▲ Peter Logan's design drawing for the Movellan ship.

▲ The model of the Movellan ship under construction in the BBC's visual effects workshop.

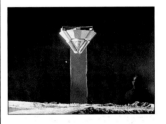

▲ A sequence of photographs showing the model of the Movellan ship arriving on Skaro and burying itself in the ground. The model and sequence were devised by visual effects designer Peter Logan. *Destiny of the Daleks.*

and to his talent for mimicry. The original Davros mask and chair were reused, although repair work had to be carried out on them as they had been damaged while on display in the *Doctor Who* exhibitions since their first appearance.

Much of the press coverage generated by the start of the new season, the first episode of which was transmitted on Saturday 1 September 1979, focused not on the return of the Doctor's most popular foes but on the casting of glamorous actress and former model Suzanne Danielle as one of the Movellans. Perhaps predictably, most of the tabloid newspapers carried publicity photographs of her clad in her skin-tight costume.

The season's second story on transmission was also the second to be made. It had started out as a David Fisher storyline entitled *The Gamble with Time* and was intended as a pastiche on the *Bulldog Drummond* tales of Herman McNeile. The basic idea concerned an alien, the last survivor of a race called the Sephiroth, trapped on Earth and rigging casino tables in order to finance time travel experiments. The main setting was originally to have been Las Vegas but was quickly switched to Monte Carlo, 1928. Graham Williams then learned from the series' production unit manager, John Nathan-Turner, that it would be feasible for a small amount of filming to be done in Paris — the series' first foray into overseas location work — so Fisher was briefed to include a few short scenes featuring well-known Parisian landmarks.

After Fisher had delivered his draft scripts it be-

came apparent that, by keeping the location crew to an absolute minimum, more overseas filming could be afforded than had previously been thought. Anxious to take advantage of this, Williams and Adams decided that the story should be rewritten

The suicide Daleks approach the Movellan space ship. Note that the Daleks are unfinished from this angle. *Destiny of the Daleks.*

Doctor Who **goes abroad ▲ for the first time. The Doctor and Romana stand outside Nôtre Dame Cathedral in Paris, France.** *City of Death.*

The set for Leonardo da Vinci's study designed by Richard McManan-Smith for *City of Death.*

SEASON TRAILER

A special trailer for season seventeen was made and transmitted. From an animated title sequence, the picture fades to a misty green planet – one of the sets from **Nightmare of Eden.** *An echoing disembodied voice repeatedly orders the Doctor to awaken but all the viewer hears is snoring coming from the TARDIS. Eventually the Doctor emerges, protests that he is awake and tells whoever has woken him up to go away as it is the middle of August. The voice tells the Doctor that it brings him a warning – he will be pitted against an evil force – a race known as the Daleks. The Doctor, suddenly alert, asks where and when but the voice says simply that forewarned is forearmed. The voice now tells the Doctor to forget the warning, to lose all conscious memory of it. The Doctor shakes his head and calls out asking who is there. There is no reply bar a low chuckle from the voice. The Doctor turns, complaining about the noise and that all he wants is a few months' rest. As he enters the TARDIS, the Doctor turns a notice pinned to the doors – 'Do Not Disturb Until September 1.' The TARDIS dematerializes.*

and set principally in Paris, 1979. They also decided that K-9 should be omitted, so that no members of the visual effects team would be required on location. Due partly to the tightness of the schedule and partly to reported family problems, Fisher was unable to perform the rewrites himself, so it was agreed — with no acrimony on either side — that in return for an additional fee he would allow the production team to take on the work and make whatever changes they saw fit. To get the rewrites done in time, Williams and Adams had to work literally around the clock, sitting at a typewriter from one Thursday night to the following Monday morning without breaking for sleep. The story was retitled first *Curse of Sephiroth* and then *City of Death* and— as agreed with Fisher, who retained copyright on his original characters — it went out under a BBC in-house pseudonym, David Agnew.

In the story as transmitted, the Doctor and Romana are enjoying a holiday in Paris when time starts to fracture around them. During a visit to the Louvre to see da Vinci's *Mona Lisa*, the Doctor purloins from a stranger, Countess Scarlioni, a bracelet which he recognizes as an alien scanner device. He then finds himself, along with Romana and a private detective named Duggan, 'invited' to the chateau home of Count Scarlioni to explain his actions. The three friends are subsequently locked up in the cellar, where the Doctor discovers that the Count has hidden away eight additional *Mona Lisas* – all of them originals!

The Count turns out to be an alien called Scaroth,

the last of the Jaggaroth race. He was splintered in time when his ship exploded above primeval Earth, and in his twelve different aspects has since been guiding mankind's development to a point where time travel is possible. His intention is to travel back in time and prevent the destruction of his ship. To finance the final stages of this project, he plans to steal the *Mona Lisa* from the Louvre and then secretly sell the multiple copies which one of his earlier splinters has forced da Vinci to paint.

The Doctor realizes that the Count must be prevented from carrying out his plan as the explosion of the Jaggaroth ship provided the infusion of energy which initiated life on Earth. Following Scaroth's trail in the TARDIS, he travels back 400 million years to primeval Earth. Duggan fells Scaroth with a punch and thereby ensures that history stays on its proper course.

City of Death received the highest ratings ever recorded for a *Doctor Who* story, the final episode reaching 16.1 million viewers. This was due in part to the fact that a strike had blacked out the ITV network during the period in question, which meant that the series' only competition came in the form of minority interest programmes on BBC2. Even taking this factor into account, however, the story was a highly popular one — an assessment which can be applied to the season as a whole, the figures for which showed a marked reversal of the gradual downward trend seen during seasons fifteen and sixteen.

A first for *Doctor Who* was the inclusion in *City of Death* of a humorous cameo appearance by John Cleese and Eleanor Bron, playing art-lovers at a Parisian gallery. They admire the TARDIS as a magnificent piece of art and are completely unfazed when the Doctor, Romana and Duggan rush inside and it dematerializes before their eyes.

'It was lovely to do,' says Cleese. 'It just took an hour and a half, so I enjoyed it. Douglas Adams suggested to the director that we should do it. It was very painless and quick — I live only six minutes from the BBC Television Centre.'

Also recorded were some jokey scenes involving Cleese and Tom Baker which were destined for inclusion in the BBC engineers' Christmas tape — a collection of bloopers, out-takes and other material exchanged with a similar collection from ITV on Christmas Day.

The Creature from the Pit, at one time planned as the season's second story, eventually went out third. It was however the first to be made, and thereby marked the start of the series' seventeenth production block. Filming took place on Stage 3B at the BBC's Television Film Studios in Ealing over the period 18—26 March 1979, and the main studio recording was completed in two sessions over 9—10 April and 22—24 April 1979, both in TC6.

This story — David Fisher's other contribution to the season — sees the Doctor and Romana arriving on the planet Chloris to investigate a distress call. Chloris is a lush and verdant world but has only small quantities of metals, all of which are controlled by its ruler, Lady Adrasta. Adrasta keeps order with the aid of her Huntsman and his wolfweeds — mobile balls of vegetation — while a band of scruffy thieves organize raids on her palace to steal whatever metal they can lay their hands on.

The Doctor identifies the distress signal's source as a large eggshell-like structure in the forest. Before he can investigate further, he is taken prisoner by Adrasta's guards. In order to escape, he then leaps into the Pit — the entrance to a cave system into which all those who incur Adrasta's wrath are consigned to be devoured by an immense green globular creature living within. The Doctor discovers that the creature is not an unthinking killer but an ambassador from the planet Tythonus, which has a lack of chlorophyll but an abundance of metal. The Tythonians had hoped to trade with Chloris, but the first person their ambassador Erato encountered on arriving in his eggshell-like ship was Adrasta, who took his communicator device and trapped him in the Pit so as to preserve her monopoly on metal.

Erato retrieves his communicator and kills Adrasta.

Scaroth of the Jaggaroth (Julian Glover). *City of Death.*

DUDLEY SIMPSON
COMPOSER

Born in Australia in 1922, Dudley Simpson was introduced to music at the age of four by his mother and went on to win an award as the top amateur musician in Australia in 1936. Following the war, he studied at Melbourne University and eventually came to England to conduct at the Royal Opera House in Covent Garden. He started composing music for television in 1963 on a series called **Moonstrike** *which led to his being asked by Mervyn Pinfield to compose for* **Doctor Who.** *Simpson continued to work on* **Doctor Who,** *as well as* **Thirty Minute Theatre,** *several* **Wednesday Plays** *and* **Blake's 7** *amongst others, up until 1980. In 1988 he returned to Australia where he worked as a freelance composer. He returned to England to work in 1994.*

▼ **Left: Ian Scoones's original concept painting for the Jaggaroth ship on primeval Earth. Below: the model ship designed by Scoones on a model stage constructed at the BBC's Ealing studios.**

ANIMAL MAGIC

During the filming at Ealing for **The Creature from the Pit***, the production team of* **Animal Magic***, a children's nature programme hosted by Johnny Morris, recorded Tom Baker as the Doctor (wearing the wooden stocks used in* **The Creature from the Pit***) talking about some of the creatures he has faced, with colour photographs of them included at appropriate points (indicated in the transcript below). The segment was transmitted on 1 May 1979.*

'Now a little while ago I happened to be on Earth and I was having a discussion with a friend of mine who said that on Earth you have some ferocious animals, and he started to get a little bit competitive about certain animals and creatures you've got here on Earth that are either deadly or large, and naturally he quoted the elephant which he said was the largest, and he quoted among the deadly ones the puff adder.

'Of course, well I mean I didn't want to put him down but, I just had to tell him about some of the things I've bumped into on my travels. I mean, I remember in **The Ribos Operation***, do you remember the Shrivenzale? [photo] The Shrivenzale wasn't all that big really and I think smaller than an elephant, but it was extremely voracious in its appetite. It was a carnivore, that means it eats meat, and I'll tell you how fierce it was; six buffaloes a day it used to eat, and two wheel-barrow-loads of coconuts – unbroken! When it wanted to break open the coconuts, if it did, it had very short arms and it used to put the coconut in its arms like that, and crack it, like that!

'And after the Shrivenzale there was the Krynoid. Do you remember the Krynoid? [photo] Tall as a douglas fir and three times its circumference. That creature, the Krynoid, had a plan to recruit all the plant life on Earth and turn it against humanity. It had this idea that it could turn all the daffodils and hyacinths and elderberry bushes and blackberry bushes and things like that, and rose trees into deadly enemies of Man. Now that was a creature. Quite difficult to beat, that one. Somehow I managed it, with a bit of luck.

'Then, of course, there was the Wirrn [photo]. Now, the Wirrn, in the story **The Ark in Space***, remember that one? The Wirrn was a giant insect with a sting so fierce it could have done-in an elephant in five seconds. And that's only three!

'Then there was the Fendahl. Do you remember the Fendahl? This Fendahl was so deadly that when it used to pass anybody, it would just walk past someone and go ... (sucks in breath) ... and suck the life right out of them. That was a difficult one too, but somehow we managed it. What did you say? You don't believe it? Well, you look out next time I'm on. (He laughs manically.) Bye-bye!'

The model of the Chloran jungle with the Tythonian space craft and the TARDIS at the back. Pictured are effects assistants Morag McLean and Roger Perkins. *The Creature from the Pit.*

Erato, the Tythonian ambassador, is kept prisoner in a pit. *The Creature from the Pit.*

Lady Adrasta (Myra Frances) prepares to throw the Doctor into the pit. *The Creature from the Pit.*

He then warns the Doctor that the Tythonians have set a neutron star on a collision course with Chloris in retaliation for his imprisonment. With the Doctor's help he is freed from the Pit and, out in space, spins an aluminium shell around the star, pulling it off course and saving Chloris.

The Creature from the Pit marked the debut of actor David Brierley as the new voice of K-9, John Leeson having decided to move on to other work. Brierley was selected by director Christopher Barry after two rounds of auditions, on 9 March and 16 March 1979 respectively.

One major problem encountered in the making of *The Creature from The Pit* concerned the realization of Erato.

'The creature was a concept in the writing that was just impossible to fulfil,' says Christopher Barry. 'There was a lot of hassle and aggro about it, and in the end it just didn't work. We had an inquest about it afterwards. I blamed Visual Effects, Visual Effects blamed me. I think all of us should have blamed the writer and the producer for allowing it to go through like that. I was accused of changing my mind over it time and time again and making them build the monster in three different sizes. All of which is probably true — it was a failure in communication, although I went to the workshop again and again to look at it because I was so worried about it. Yes . . . big problems. I think we went about it the wrong way, and there wasn't time to design it and try it out and get back to the drawing board.'

To make matters worse, Barry had already had one disagreement with visual effects designer Mat Irvine's team when he demanded that the spaceship model footage be reshot as the wires holding up the models were plainly visible. Even the relatively simple effect of the wolfweeds rolling across the ground caused headaches for Irvine as the gear boxes kept burning out on the radio-controlled creatures.

'Tom Baker too was much more domineering by this time,' adds Barry. 'He had always been creative and full of ideas, but had previously had a certain humility, saying, "Shoot me down if you don't like it but . . . why don't we do it like this?" But by the time we did *The Creature from the Pit* together . . . I remember once in rehearsal him sort of pooh-poohing what I was planning to do and then going on to give a full scenario to the rest of the cast as to how the scene should go. I stood waiting for him to finish and then said, "Right, now we'll go back and do it my way." That isn't to say I didn't admire him. I did, tremendously.'

Due to the relatively high cost of *City of Death*

Erato uses Romana's voice to communicate with the Doctor. *The Creature from the Pit.*

and of the six-parter with which the production team planned to close the season, money had to be saved on the next two stories to be made. Thus both *Nightmare of Eden* — Bob Baker's first solo project, which had been commissioned in the spring of 1979 on the basis of an outline entitled *Nightmare of Evil* — and *The Horns of Nimon* — Anthony Read's Minoan-inspired adventure — were afforded a lower-than-average budget. In the case of *The Horns of Nimon*, this meant dropping some expensive night filming which had originally been planned. These economies were indicative of the increasingly difficult financial position that *Doctor Who* faced during Graham Williams's time as producer.

'During those three years,' recalled Williams, 'inflation was running at breakneck speed. We were almost hourly being told that costs had just gone up by another ten per cent. The knock-on effect was like compound interest, with everything spiralling up into quite lunatic sums. I had several long and very severe conversations with the bosses upstairs, to the effect that they didn't care how I spent my money as long as it was money from that year. Once that was gone, there was no question of over-funding. I would just lose episodes — end of argument. Philip Hinchcliffe had left me without too much of a reputation, as many of his *Doctor Whos* had gone massively over-budget on scenery.'

The setting for *Nightmare of Eden* is a luxury space liner, the *Empress*, which becomes locked together with a private ship, the *Hecate*, after colliding with it on emerging from hyperspace. The Doctor and

Romana arrive and meet the scientist Tryst, who has with him a continuous event transmuter (CET) machine containing crystals on which are stored supposed recordings of the many planets that he and his team have visited.

The Doctor discovers that someone on board the liner is smuggling the dangerous addictive drug vraxoin. To complicate matters, the interface between the two ships allows some Mandrels from the mud-swamps of Eden to escape from the CET machine and start to run amok. The smugglers are revealed to be Tryst and the *Hecate*'s pilot, Dymond, who are planning to send vraxoin to Azure, the planet below, by beaming down the sample of Eden from the CET machine.

Vraxoin turns out to be the material into which the Mandrels decompose when they are killed. The Doctor and Romana also learn that the CET machine does not merely take recordings but actually

▲ Romana and the Doctor discover that the Eden recording on the CET machine is not a recording after all. *Nightmare of Eden.*

▲ Organon (Geoffrey Bayldon) and two Chloran guards. *The Creature from the Pit.*

◄ K-9 destroys one of the Huntsman's deadly wolfweeds. *The Creature from the Pit.*

STOCK FOOTAGE

Nightmare of Eden part one featured a 22-second clip purchased from World Backgrounds at Elstree for one of the planets seen on the CET machine.

NOTES
Romana's Regeneration

*At the start of **Destiny of the Daleks**, Romana regenerates through several bodies before she settles on the form of Princess Astra from **The Armageddon Factor**. In fact, she starts the episode in that form, but then, on the Doctor's suggestion, also 'tries' a short body in a blue catsuit, a busty brunette in metal bra and white fur stole and finally a tall Grecian form before appearing – again as Astra – wearing the Doctor's clothes: hat, scarf and coat.*

The Planets

*The planets listed on the front dial of Tryst's CET machine in **Nightmare of Eden** were: Eden, Zil, Vij, Darp, Lvan, Brus, Gidi and Ranx.*

LOCATIONS

Destiny of the Daleks
Winspit Quarry,
Swanage, Dorset;
Binnegar Heath,
Wareham, Dorset

City of Death
Paris, France

The Creature from the Pit
No location work

Nightmare of Eden
No location work

The Horns of Nimon
No location work

MUSIC

*Dudley Simpson composed all the music for this season. He was also scheduled to work on **Shada** and had completed all his scores for it before it was cancelled, but received no payment.*

A Mandrel menaces Romana and Della (Jennifer Lonsdale). *Nightmare of Eden*.

The model of the *Empress* under construction. *Nightmare of Eden*.

Tryst (Lewis Fiander). *Nightmare of Eden*.

displaces whole planetary areas into its crystals. The Doctor prevents Tryst and Dymond from carrying out their plan, separates the two ships and returns the Mandrels to Eden.

One important change made to Bob Baker's draft scripts for *Nightmare of Eden* was a toning down of the portrayal of the use and effects of the drug vraxoin (originally to have been called xylophilin or, colloquially, xyp). This was done on the instructions of Graham Williams, who realized that the drug theme was a potentially controversial one.

The director's credit on *Nightmare of Eden* went to Alan Bromly, a semi-retired veteran who had previously handled season eleven's *The Time Warrior*. Bromly did not however direct the whole story. His unfamiliarity with the complexities of *Doctor Who*'s production resulted in numerous hold-ups and changes of plan during recording, drawing scathing criticism from Tom Baker, and Graham Williams decided part-way through the second studio session to dispense with his services and direct the remainder of the story himself.

Prior to the story's transmission, the *Sun* newspaper ran a feature headed 'Is this Dr Who monster far too scary?' in which actress Jennifer Lonsdale, who played Tryst's assistant Della, described how some young children visiting the studio had been so terrified of the Mandrels that they had left in tears. The article went on to say that no photographs had been taken of the monsters, and even quoted a BBC spokesman as explaining that there had been no photographers available. This was in fact untrue: numerous photographs had been taken and, far from inspiring terror, the Mandrels were later ridiculed by a *Doctor Who* Appreciation Society reviewer as being 'cute rejects from *The Muppet Show*'.

Nightmare of Eden was however notable for being one of the earliest *Doctor Who* stories to make extensive use of the Quantel image processing system, the possibilities of which had previously been explored on programmes like *Top of the Pops*.

The Horns of Nimon was a story which required very little script editing input from Douglas Adams. Its writer, his predecessor Anthony Read, was naturally well-acquainted with the techniques and demands of working on *Doctor Who* and delivered a very polished set of scripts.

Read's story, a pastiche on the legend of Theseus and the Minotaur, centres around the planet Skonnos. The inhabitants have been promised by an alien Nimon that he will restore their empire to greatness if they in return provide young sacrifices and radioactive hymetusite crystals, both of which they are obtaining from the nearby planet Aneth. With the TARDIS immobilized for repairs, the Doctor and Romana encounter the Skonnon spaceship transporting the latest sacrificial consignment from Aneth. Romana is captured and taken to Skonnos on board the ship, while the Doctor follows in the now-repaired TARDIS. Once there, they are consigned by the Skonnons' leader, Soldeed, into the Nimon's labyrinthine power complex.

The two Time Lords discover that the Nimon are a race of parasites which move from planet to planet like a plague of locusts. The bull-headed creatures send a lone representative to an unsuspecting world, offering assistance in order to gain the trust of its inhabitants, then arrive in force to drain it of its resources. The power complex, fuelled by hymetusite, uses a black hole to create a space tunnel through which the Nimon cross from one planet to the next. The Doctor manages to destroy the complex on Skonnos, thereby trapping the Nimon on their last home, the now-dead planet Crinoth.

Like the Mandrels in *Nightmare of Eden*, the Nimon presented a difficult challenge for costume designer June Hudson. Anthony Read had envisaged the creatures as cyborgs — part creature, part machine — but Hudson preferred to get closer to the 'body of a man, head of a bull' look of the mythical Minotaur. The final costume consisted of a large bull head, complete with horns, mounted on top of a grey body suit with a simple gold sash around the waist.

'The whole torso from the hips upwards was built onto a padded frame,' recalls Roger Oldhamstead, the freelance artist who constructed the costumes to Hudson's designs. 'It wasn't the actor's body at all; it was much, much bigger. The shoulders were widened and it had a 50-inch chest. The head was deliberately put on in a slightly artificial manner so that it appeared to be a cage concealing something underneath. A sort of head within a head. We reasoned that the creature was so hideous that it had caged itself in a kind of cover or mask — it couldn't bear to look at itself, let alone have anyone else look at it, so it had made itself humanly presentable by this means. I had a totally abstract view of it. The head was originally to have had transparent glass eyes, but the director decided about two days before studio recording was due to start that he didn't like the look of this and wanted it changed.'

The Nimon also wore shoes with ten-inch platform soles, adapted to look like hooves, so that they could be seen to tower over their victims. Ballet dancers were hired to play the creatures as it was felt that they would possess the necessary grace to move convincingly in such a cumbersome costume.

Having decided to commission *The Horns of Nimon* from Anthony Read, Douglas Adams sent a memo to Head of Serials Graeme McDonald on 23 March 1979 to explain why the season was relying so heavily on tried-and-trusted writers:

Our recent commissions, including this one for Tony Read, are as you see not in line with our originally declared principle of bringing as many new writers onto the show as possible. This is because we spent so much time and energy in the first few months of this season meeting, encouraging and commis-

The Doctor is threatened by Soldeed (Graham Crowden) while Teka (Janet Ellis) and Seth (Simon Gipps-Kent) keep them covered. *The Horns of Nimon*.

The Doctor and Romana reach the reactor core at the centre of the Nimon power complex on Skonnos. *The Horns of Nimon*.

sioning new writers who then turned out to be unable to produce scripts which came anywhere near what we required, that we now have to turn back to the tried and tested professionals in order to make up for lost time. It is a source of surprise and disappointment to discover that though the programme has been marching across our screens for fifteen years now, hardly anybody we approach seems to have the remotest idea as to what it might conceivably be about.

Since joining the *Doctor Who* production team, Adams had found demands on his time steadily increasing due to the burgeoning popularity of his *The Hitch-Hiker's Guide to the Galaxy* radio series. In the light of this, he decided to relinquish his script editor post at the end of season seventeen. It was also agreed in the summer of 1979 that, in common with a number of his predecessors, he should write his final story himself.

Adams's first idea was for a story in which the Doctor attempted to go into retreat but found himself being constantly called upon to solve other people's problems. This was vetoed by Graham Williams as being too jokey, so the writer then developed *Shada* (working title: *Sunburst*) as a Time Lord story

▲ A Nimon. *The Horns of Nimon*.

REPEATS

In the sixties, only eight episodes of **Doctor Who** *were ever repeated: the first ever episode (except in Northern Ireland), and* **The Evil of the Daleks** *to act as a lead in to the start of* **The Dominators** *in season six. In the seventies, however, repeats became more or less a standard feature of the summer break between seasons and sometimes with a compilation at Christmas. The following is a list of all the stories repeated prior to the start of the eighteenth season in 1980:*

Spearhead From Space	1971
The Dæmons	1971
The Sea Devils	1972
Day of the Daleks	1973
The Green Death	1973
The Sea Devils	1974
Planet of the Spiders	1974
The Ark in Space	1975
Genesis of the Daleks	1975
Planet of Evil	1976
The Sontaran Experiment	1976
Pyramids of Mars	1976
The Brain of Morbius	1976
The Deadly Assassin	1977
The Robots of Death	1977
The Invisible Enemy	1978
The Sun Makers	1978
The Pirate Planet	1978
The Androids of Tara	1978
Destiny of the Daleks	1978
City of Death	1978

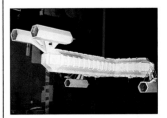

▲ The Skonnon ship under construction at the visual effects workshop. *The Horns of Nimon*.

The aged scientists ▲ aboard the think tank whose brains have been drained by Skagra. *Shada.*

K-9 is chased by a Krarg. ▲ *Shada.*

DAVID BRIERLEY
VOICE OF K-9

David Brierley was born in 1935 in Yorkshire. Among his many skills are being an expert sailor, a keen fell walker and a long-distance runner. He has worked in television on shows like **Storytime, Blind Justice, Howard's Way, Cover her Face, Tripods, Words and Pictures, Threads, Coronation Street, Juliet Bravo, The Law of the Land** *and* **Frankie Howerd Strikes Again,** *as well as playing the voice of K-9 for season seventeen of* **Doctor Who.** *On radio he has appeared as Doctor Watson in* **The Hound of the Baskervilles,** *Brutus in* **Julius Caesar,** *Mercutio in* **Romeo and Juliet** *and Puck in* **A Midsummer Night's Dream.** *He has also enjoyed a theatre career which includes seasons at Richmond On The Green, Aldershot, Wimbledon, Ventnor and Northampton, with specific productions including* **Sun of York** *and* **Sons of Oedipus.**

Professor Chronotis (Denis Carey), Claire Keightley (Victoria Burgoyne), the Doctor and Chris Parsons (Daniel Hill) during rehearsals for *Shada.*

without a Gallifreyan setting. It would explore how the Doctor's race handled their criminal element and would also draw on Adams's experiences as a student at Cambridge University. As in the case of *City of Death*, Williams helped out with the writing of the final scripts, acting in effect as Adams's editor.

The story begins with the Doctor bringing Romana to present-day Earth to visit his old friend Professor Chronotis, an elderly Time Lord who absconded from Gallifrey and now lives a quiet academic life at St Cedd's College in Cambridge. Also seeking Chronotis is a bizarrely-dressed scientist called Skagra who has in his possession a device, in the form of a floating sphere, with which he intends to steal the Professor's mind and thereby learn the location of a book entitled *The Ancient and Worshipful Law of Gallifrey.*

Despite opposition from the Doctor, Romana and K-9, Skagra eventually succeeds in obtaining the book, which had been inadvertently borrowed from the Professor's study by a student named Chris Parsons. He then kidnaps Romana and hijacks the TARDIS. It transpires that the book is the key to Shada, the ancient prison planet of the Time Lords. Skagra's ultimate objective is to use his sphere on one of the prison's inmates, Salyavin, whose unique mental powers he can then exploit to project his own mind into every other creature in the Universe. When the TARDIS reaches Shada, however, he discovers that Salyavin's cell is empty.

After a number of close encounters with the Krargs — Skagra's monstrous crystalline servants — the Doctor, Chronotis and K-9, along with Parsons and his friend Claire Keightley, arrive on Shada in Chronotis's TARDIS, which has been disguised as his study at St Cedd's. Chronotis admits that he is in fact Salyavin; he escaped from Shada centuries ago and has been living on Earth ever since. The Doctor eventually thwarts Skagra's plans for domination by winning a mind battle against him.

The Cambridge location shooting for Shada was completed as planned over 15—19 October 1979. By the time the first studio session took place over 3—5 November, though, a strike by BBC technicians was looming. This was a recurrence of the long-running demarcation dispute which had previously caused disruption to the production of season fifteen's *The Invasion of Time* and season sixteen's *The Armageddon Factor*. On this occasion, it put all the Television Centre studios out of action from 19 November and meant that the second of the three sessions for *Shada*, scheduled for 19—20 November, could not take place. Rehearsals for the third session, scheduled for 1—3 December, went ahead regardless as everyone hoped that the strike would be over by then. In the event, even though the strike did indeed end on 1 December, this session was also lost as BBC management decided that there were higher priority shows than *Doctor Who* to be completed for Christmas.

'The previous two Christmas times,' recalled Graham Williams, 'we had been able to skate around this dispute — this strike that happened every year over that bloody electric clock — either by rewriting or rescheduling. But we could not get out of it this time. The doors of the studio were locked. It was that simple. We just couldn't get in there.

'We turned up regularly in order for the actors to fulfil their contracts. Legally I had to say to them, "Look, I'll be there and I'll send you home," which was heartbreaking — one of the worst experiences I think I've ever come across.'

On 10 December 1979, *Shada* was formally dropped from season seventeen, which therefore ended with transmission of the final episode of *The Horns of Nimon* on 12 January 1980. A number of attempts were subsequently made to remount the story, but these ultimately came to nothing and in June 1980 it was officially cancelled, much to the regret of all those involved. The majority of the completed footage would eventually see the light of day many years later, in the form of a Tom Baker-narrated BBC Video compilation released in 1992.

The abandonment of *Shada* brought *Doctor Who*'s seventeenth production block to a rather unsatisfactory conclusion. This was especially galling for Graham Williams as he had decided during the making of *Nightmare of Eden* to give up the producer's post at this point. Having steered the series through three crisis-hit years without a proper holiday, he felt it was now time to let someone else take over the hot-seat. He and Douglas Adams therefore left together, marking their departure with a joint farewell party held on 14 December 1979 in one of the basement conference rooms at Television Centre.

CHAPTER SEVENTEEN

UNIT and the Companions

During the sixties seasons, the Doctor had been joined on his travels by a succession of friends who had come to be referred to in the media and by the series' production team as the 'companions'. With the adoption of a new Earthbound format at the start of the seventies, however, the role of the series' supporting characters changed significantly.

The Doctor was now seen to be working on a semi-permanent basis with the British branch of UNIT. Starting with commanding officer Brigadier Lethbridge-Stewart (Nicholas Courtney), a character established in the sixties stories *The Web of Fear* and *The Invasion*, the production team gradually built up a small ensemble of regulars. First was Sergeant Benton (John Levene), who had also appeared in *The Invasion* — then holding the rank of Corporal — and was reintroduced in season seven's *The Ambassadors of Death*. Then, at the start of season eight, Captain Mike Yates (Richard Franklin) was brought in as the Brigadier's second-in-command, a function previously fulfilled by a number of one-off characters — Captain Turner (Robert Sidaway) in *The Invasion*, Captain Munro (John Breslin) in *Spearhead from Space* and Captain Hawkins (Paul Darrow) in *Doctor Who and the Silurians* — and even by the relatively lowly Sergeant Benton in *The Ambassadors of Death* and *Inferno*.

CAROLINE JOHN
Doctor Elizabeth Shaw (Liz)

Caroline John trained at the Central School of Speech and Drama before working in repertory. For three-and-a-half years she was with the National Theatre, appearing in numerous productions like **The Dutch Courtesan, Rosencrantz and Guildenstern are Dead, Othello,** *and* **The Master Builder.** *In the late sixties at the LAMBDA Theatre she understudied the role of Minnie in D. H. Lawrence's* **Daughter-in-Law,** *and toured Yugoslavia, Romania and Italy with the play. She appeared in three films,* **Raising a Riot** *(1957),* **The King's Breakfast** *and* **Documentary of Romania** *and appeared on TV in three plays and in an episode of ITV's* **The Power Game.** *After leaving* **Doctor Who,** *she raised a family and resumed her career in the early eighties, winning numerous theatre roles and appearing in the BBC's* **The Hound of the Baskervilles,** *Channel 4's* **A Pattern of Roses** *and* **The Harry Enfield Television Show.** *She briefly returned to* **Doctor Who** *for* **The Five Doctors** *in 1983 and* **Dimensions in Time** *in 1993.*

Liz Shaw (Caroline John) and the Doctor appear to be having some engine trouble.

RICHARD FRANKLIN
Captain Mike Yates

Richard Franklin joined RADA in 1963 after working for a time in an advertising agency. His first professional acting job was with the Century Theatre which toured in a caravan. This was followed by several short-term jobs, including parts on TV in **Bed Sit Girl, The Saint** *and* **Dixon of Dock Green,** *and then a year and a half spent with the Birmingham Rep, which included a three-month run in* **As You Like It.** *He then appeared in the ATV soap opera* **Crossroads** *and played Charley on stage in* **Charley's Aunt.** *During 1969 he toured with a production of Shaw's* **Candida,** *had a small role in* **The Millicent Martin Show** *and appeared at the Bristol Old Vic. In January 1970 he appeared on the BBC's antiques series* **Going for a Song.** *After three months of radio and three TV commercials, he started work on* **Doctor Who.** *Since leaving the series, Franklin has continued acting and has also branched out into writing and directing. He appeared in* **Blake's 7** *for the BBC and as a regular in the YTV soap opera* **Emmerdale.** *He returned to* **Doctor Who** *for the* **The Five Doctors** *in 1983 and* **Dimensions in Time** *in 1993. He also wrote and appeared in the* **Doctor Who** *spin-off play* **Recall UNIT** *as part of the Edinburgh Festival Fringe in August 1984.*

NICHOLAS COURTNEY
Brigadier Alistair Gordon Lethbridge-Stewart

Nicholas Courtney was born in Egypt in 1931. He grew up in Kenya and France and at the age of eighteen was called up for National Service. Following the end of his eighteen-month duty, Courtney joined the Webber Douglas drama school. He left after two years and worked in repertory at Northampton before moving to London in 1961/62. He started in television with roles in **Sword of Honour, Spot the Birdies** *and other productions. His first appearance in* **Doctor Who** *was in* **The Daleks' Master Plan** *(1965). Then, in 1967, he was cast to play Captain Knight in* **The Web of Fear,** *but took the part of Colonel Lethbridge-Stewart when the original actor had to drop out. He reprised this role in* **The Invasion** *in 1968 and from 1970 played the character off and on for the next 23 years. In between appearances in* **Doctor Who,** *Courtney appeared in stage productions of* **The Dame of Sark, Donkey's Years, The Rocky Horror Show** *and* **The Mousetrap** *and television appearances included* **Then Churchill Said To Me, Minder, Juliet Bravo, All Creatures Great and Small** *and* **Sink or Swim.** *His film work includes* **To Catch A King** *(1984) and the TV film* **Jenny's War** *(1984).*

Captain Mike Yates (Richard Franklin). *The Dæmons.*

Katy Manning.

Lethbridge-Stewart, Benton and Yates would all go on to feature in many stories during the seventies. Another new regular, Corporal Bell (Fernanda Marlowe), was more short-lived, appearing in only *The Mind of Evil* and *The Claws of Axos*, and other UNIT personnel, such as Major Cosworth (Patrick Godfrey) in *The Mind of Evil* and Sergeant Osgood (Alec Linstead) in *The Dæmons*, continued to be brought in on a one-off basis.

The season seven regular who came closest to resembling an old-style companion, in that she was an attractive young woman who tended to work side-by-side with the Doctor, was Liz Shaw (Caroline John). There were, on the other hand, a number of significant differences. Whereas the sixties companions had tended to be — or to degenerate into — stereotypical screaming heroines, Liz was portrayed in a more realistic manner as a highly competent scientist with 'degrees in medicine, physics and a dozen other subjects'. Rather more mature than her predecessors, Liz conversed with the Doctor on a similar intellectual level and shared his general outlook, such as his distaste for military solutions to problems — as illustrated by her equally shocked reaction to the Brigadier's decision to blow up the Silurian base rather than talk peace at the conclusion of *Doctor Who and the Silurians*. It was in connection with Liz that the term 'assistant' started to be used more commonly than 'companion', reflecting this change in status of the series' principal female character.

Although Liz could be regarded as a step forward in the representation of women in *Doctor Who*, her intelligence and scientific expertise created a number of problems for the series' writers. One of the main functions of the companion in the past had been to act as a cipher allowing the Doctor to convey important plot information to the viewing audience. Liz, however, was felt to be poorly suited to this role as she had little need to rely on the Doctor for explanations. Another of the traditional functions of the companion had been to act as a point of audience identification, and again Liz was considered to fall short of achieving this as younger viewers found it difficult to relate to the mature scientist.

In an attempt to remedy this situation, the production team dropped Liz after the seventh season and introduced a new assistant, Jo Grant (Katy Manning). Jo was in some respects a throwback to earlier female companions. She was noticeably younger than Liz, rather naive, scatter-brained and definitely not an intellectual. One consequence of this was that the Doctor was able to take a much more paternal attitude towards her than he had towards Liz, spending a great deal of his time rescuing her from dangerous situations into which she had managed to stumble. Also in common with sixties companions such as Dodo, Polly and Zoe, she had a penchant for the latest fashions, including knee-boots and mini-skirts. This made her something of a sex symbol amongst fathers watching with their children, whilst the children themselves were drawn to her childlike qualities.

Jo was still a trained UNIT agent, however, and as such was able to show a measure of initiative which had been denied some of her predecessors. Examples included traversing a high, storm-swept ledge in order to escape from a locked room in *The Curse of Peladon* and rescuing the Doctor

The Brigadier (Nicholas Courtney) and the Doctor. *Terror of the Autons.*

JOHN LEVENE
Sergeant/RSM Benton

John Levene was born John Woods in 1941 in Salisbury. He left home at 21 and went to London where he ended up working in a men's clothing store. He eventually signed on at an agency which supplied walk-on actors and his first job was in **Adam Adamant Lives!**. Other appearances included **Z Cars** and **Doctor Who** where he played a Cyberman in **The Moonbase** (1967) and a Yeti in **The Web of Fear** (1968) and **The War Games** (1969). It was director Douglas Camfield who offered Levene the part of Benton in **The Invasion** (1968) and the character became one of the UNIT regulars from **The Ambassadors of Death** up until **The Android Invasion**. In 1977, Levene gave up acting and set up his own audio visuals company which specialized in conference presentations. More recently, he has worked as a compere and entertainer on cruise liners and emigrated to the USA where he has returned to acting and continued his work as an entertainer under the name John Anthony Blake.

from the Master's prison cell in *The Sea Devils*. She was also afforded a certain amount of character development, clearly growing in confidence and maturity during her time with the Doctor. She had romantic involvements with King Peladon in *The Curse of Peladon* and with the Thal Latep in *Planet of the Daleks*, and it was a logical extension of this when, in her farewell story *The Green Death*, she decided to marry Professor Clifford Jones and join him on an expedition up the Amazon.

There was in fact a relatively high degree of emphasis placed on the characterization of the regulars at this point in the series' history, as they came together to form what has often been described as the 'UNIT family' — a group of colleagues whose loyal friendship was mirrored by that which formed amongst the cast themselves.

The Brigadier was a soldier of the old school, a stickler for military correctness, and often showed a lack of imagination when dealing with alien menaces, choosing to shoot first and ask questions later. He had no doubt where his loyalties lay and was willing to do whatever was necessary to safeguard the world as he knew it. He did however mellow with age, his manner becoming less formal — as evidenced by the gradual lengthening of his hair — and his relationship with the Doctor less abrasive. He also became the focus for much of the humour which arose, such as in a scene in *Terror of the Autons* where the Doctor is led to speculate that 'military intelligence' might be a contradiction in terms. In short, in keeping with

the changes that the series itself underwent during this period, the Brigadier lost much of his original believability but gained an endearing larger-than-life quality.

While the only significant development in the

Sergeant Benton (John Levene). *Day of the Daleks.*

KATY MANNING
Josephine Grant (Jo)

Katy Manning was born in 1948 and trained at the Webber Douglas drama school for a year before joining a Wolverhampton repertory company. Her first job was in **Man at the Top** with Kenneth Haigh. Manning found that her height - only five foot - was a disadvantage in theatre and so moved to television. She made several commercials for ITV before appearing in an episode of **Softly, Softly: Task Force**. She landed the part of Jo Grant in **Doctor Who** in 1970, after nearly missing the auditions. Shortly after leaving **Doctor Who** she presented a television show called **Serendipity** before returning to the theatre, appearing with Derek Nimmo in **Why Not Stay for Breakfast** and Lionel Blair and Colin Baker in **Odd Man In**. Manning married **Rocky Horror Picture Show** star Raynor Burton in 1975, but the marriage only lasted five weeks. She had twins: a son, Jonathan, and a daughter, Georgina, by her boyfriend, actor Dean Harris, in 1978. Since 1982 she has been living and working in Australia.

ELISABETH SLADEN
Sarah Jane Smith

On leaving school Elisabeth Sladen attended drama school for two years before joining the local repertory theatre in Liverpool. She met actor Brian Miller during her first production with them and they were married after meeting again in Manchester three years later. Early television appearances included **Coronation Street** *(1970),* **Doomwatch** *(1972),* **Some Mothers Do 'Ave 'Em** *(1973),* **Public Eye** *and* **Z Cars**. *In 1974 she started work as Sarah Jane Smith in* **Doctor Who**. *After leaving the series in 1976, Sladen has returned four times:* **K-9 and Company** *(1981),* **The Five Doctors** *(1983), the 1993 radio production* **The Paradise of Death** *and* **Dimensions In Time** *the same year. Other work on television has included* **Stepping Stones** *(1977–1978),* **Send in the Girls** *(1978),* **Take My Wife** *(1979),* **Gulliver in Lilliput** *(1982),* **Alice in Wonderland** *(1985) and* **Dempsey & Makepeace** *(1985). In 1980 she appeared in the film* **Silver Dream Racer**. *Since the birth of her daughter, Sadie, in 1985, Sladen has spent most of her time being a mother and housewife, but has made occasional television appearances including* **The Bill** *in 1989.*

IAN MARTER
Surgeon-Lieutenant Harry Sullivan

Ian Marter left university in 1969 and joined the Bristol Old Vic as an acting stage manager. His first professional part was as a Russian soldier in **The Hostage**. *Around 1973 he started looking for television roles and one of his first roles was as John Andrews in the 1973* **Doctor Who** *story* **Carnival of Monsters**. *In 1974 Marter was offered the part of Harry Sullivan, companion to the fourth Doctor. In 1976 Marter, along with Tom Baker and James Hill, developed the idea for a* **Doctor Who** *feature film called* **Doctor Who meets Scratchman**. *Marter novelized several* **Doctor Who** *stories for the Target books range, and wrote a full length original novel,* **Harry Sullivan's War**. *Marter also novelized several films, including* **Baby** *and* **Splash**, *under the pen name Ian Don, and* **My Science Project** *under his own name. He was part-way through the novelization of the William Hartnell* **Doctor Who** *story* **The Rescue** *when he died suddenly in his London home on 30 October 1986.*

Journalist Sarah Jane Smith (Elisabeth Sladen). *The Time Warrior.*

Surgeon-Lieutenant Harry Sullivan (Ian Marter). *The Sontaran Experiment.*

life of the ever-dependable Sergeant Benton was his further promotion in *Robot* to Regimental Sergeant Major, Captain Yates was particularly well-served in terms of characterization. Although he seemed initially to be very much in the 'Boy's Own' mould of dashing army officers, debonair and athletic, it soon became apparent that there was a more sensitive, romantic side to his nature. This eventually led him in *Invasion of the Dinosaurs* to ally himself to the idealistic cause of Operation Golden Age, and in the process to betray his friends at UNIT. Allowed to resign quietly when his misguided actions were revealed, he was later seen in *Planet of the Spiders* to be developing the more spiritual side of his nature at a Buddhist meditation centre. This was perhaps more in keeping with his character than had been his previous military lifestyle, although he seemed to slip back quite comfortably into the role of a hero in the ensuing fight against the giant spiders of Metebelis 3.

The early decision to drop Liz Shaw in favour of Jo Grant was indicative of a dilemma which successive production teams would face throughout the seventies. On the one hand there was a desire to make the female companion strong, intelligent and independent, in keeping with changing attitudes towards the representation of women in the media, but on the other there was a need to ensure that she continued to fulfil the basic dramatic functions of aiding plot exposition and acting as a point of audience identification. A character devised specifically to circumvent this problem was Jo's successor, Sarah Jane Smith (Elisabeth Sladen).

Sarah was conceived as a strong-willed and independent young woman whose occupation as a journalist would allow her to be inquisitive without appearing unintelligent and to become involved in dangerous situations without seeming to be hanging on to the Doctor's coat-tails. This idea worked well during her first season, season eleven, in which there was a clear and logical reason for her involvement in each of the stories; and although seasons twelve and thirteen saw her slipping gradually into the more traditional role of a permanent travelling companion, her character really blossomed opposite the fourth Doctor and his new male assistant, UNIT's medical officer Surgeon-Lieutenant Harry Sullivan (Ian Marter).

Harry was seen initially as someone who could carry the more physical aspects of the stories if the fourth Doctor turned out to be played by an actor of advanced years. In the event, when Tom Baker was cast and it became apparent that he was more than capable of coping with action scenes himself, Harry became instead something of a bumbler who provided light relief during tense situations. His rather old-fashioned attitudes towards women gave Sarah something to play against, bringing her feminist outlook to the fore; and his propensity to stumble into danger afforded her a rare opportunity to take on the role of a rescuer.

Harry was the last new UNIT regular to be introduced. Shortly after his debut in *Robot*, UNIT was phased out of the series, being featured in only three further seventies stories — *Terror of the Zygons*, *The Android Invasion* and *The Seeds of Doom*. *Terror of the Zygons* ended with Harry remaining on Earth while the Doctor and Sarah continued their travels through time and space, and *The Android Invasion* then saw both Harry and Sergeant Benton making their final appearances in the series, while the Brigadier was replaced by a new character named Colonel Faraday (Patrick Newell). None of the UNIT regulars featured in *The Seeds of Doom*, which saw the troops being commanded instead by a Major Beresford (John Acheson).

The departure of Sarah at the end of season fourteen's *The Hand of Fear* broke the final link with the UNIT era. After *The Deadly Assassin*, which saw the Doctor operating without a regular supporting character for the only time in the series' history, *The Face of Evil* marked the introduction of another new companion in the person of Leela (Louise Jameson).

The popular image of Leela as a sexy leather-clad savage would seem to suggest that she represented a retrograde step in the depiction of women in *Doctor Who*. Her skimpy costume was however quite in keeping with her origins as a member of a primitive tribe on a temperate alien planet, and she was in truth one of the bravest and most independent women ever to have featured in the series. Although ignorant of high technology, she quickly became accustomed to the paraphernalia of time travel and proficient in the use of a variety of different blasters and laser guns. Effective though these weapons were, however, she always fell back in the last resort on the use of her trusty knife.

Leela was thus a character who mixed sex appeal with strength and intelligence, in a manner reminiscent of Cathy Gale or Emma Peel of *The Avengers* — or indeed of the more contemporary Purdey of *The New Avengers*. That said, she still had to fit within the constraints of a series aimed primarily at a family audience, and so lacked the sophistication and out-and-out sexiness of those other characters.

One thing that many of Leela's fans found disappointing was the way in which she was written out of the series, being hastily married off to Andred, a guard captain on the Doctor's home planet Gallifrey, at the end of the season fifteen story *The Invasion of Time*. It seemed quite out of

Leela (Louise Jameson).

Romana (Mary Tamm). *The Ribos Operation.*

LOUISE JAMESON
Leela

Louise Jameson was born in 1951 in Wanstead. On leaving school in 1966 she briefly trained as a secretary before joining RADA where she trained from 1969 to 1971. Since leaving RADA, Jameson has appeared extensively in the theatre, working for the Royal Shakespeare Company on several occasions and touring both England and America. On television she first appeared in Cider with Rosie and Tom Brown's Schooldays in 1971, followed by roles in Z Cars (1972), Emmerdale Farm (1973) and Play For Today: The Peddler (1976). She won the role of the savage Leela in Doctor Who in 1976. After leaving the programme in 1978, she went straight to the Bristol Old Vic to play Portia in The Merchant of Venice. Other stage work has included Romeo and Juliet (1973), several productions of King Lear and Blithe Spirit (1989). On television she starred in The Omega Factor (1979), Tenko (1981–1982), Bergerac (1985–1990), The Secret Diary of Adrian Mole (1985), The Growing Pains of Adrian Mole (1987) and Rides. Film work includes the Disney production Stick with me Kid. She has two children, born while working on Tenko, and in 1993 set up and administered an appeal bank account to help an orphanage in Northern Romania.

JOHN LEESON
Voice of K-9

After leaving school John Leeson worked in a bookshop, and then as a porter in the Leicester Royal Infirmary Hospital. He joined the Leicester Dramatic Society and was ultimately offered a place at RADA. On leaving RADA he worked in repertory and pantomimes including Toad of Toad Hall with Richard Goolden in which he met his future wife. His first work on television was as a walk-on in the BBC play The Wedding Feast. The Spanish Farm, Dad's Army and numerous situation comedies followed. He played the original Bungle the bear in the children's series Rainbow, set questions for Mastermind and did a lot of freelance voice work for the BBC. The part of K-9's voice came about because he bumped into the director, with whom he had worked previously, in a pub. Leeson stopped doing K-9's voice for a year as he felt he needed to get his face known as well as his voice, but in 1979, he returned for a final year. Since K-9 left Doctor Who, John Leeson has continued to provide voice-over services for the BBC and many other companies.

MARY TAMM
Romanadvoratrelundar (Romana)

*Mary Tamm was born in Dewsbury and raised in Bradford in the early fifties. She trained at RADA and began her career in 1971 working at Birmingham Repertory Company. She came to London in 1972 to appear in a rock musical called **Mother Earth** and the same year appeared in the film **Tales that Witness Madness**. Her first television work was in **The Donati Conspiracy** for the BBC and she also played Stan Ogden's daughter-in-law in **Coronation Street**. Other films included **The Odessa File** (1974) and **The Likely Lads** (1976). Other television work has included **Girls of Slender Means, The Assassination Run, The Return of the Saint, Casualty, Poirot, The Bill, Bergerac** and **Brookside**. After leaving **Doctor Who**, Tamm returned to the theatre to play Helen in **Action Replay** at Birmingham Rep, and has gone on to appear in numerous productions and the play **Why is Here, There, Everywhere Now** at the Riverside Studios. She was married to City businessman Marcus Ringrose in 1978.*

LALLA WARD
Romanadvoratrelundar (Romana)

*Lalla Ward, born Lady Sarah Ward, daughter of Lord Bangor - Edward Ward - and his writer wife Marjorie Banks, always wanted to act, paint and draw, and so joined the Central School of Speech and Drama in 1967. She left in 1970 and appeared in the film **Vampire Circus** (1971). Following this she worked extensively on stage, in films and on television including in a play about the poet Shelley and **The Duchess of Duke Street**. Her guest appearance in the **Doctor Who** story **The Armageddon Factor** in 1979 led to her being chosen to play Romana when the original actress, Mary Tamm, left after one season. Ward left **Doctor Who** in 1980, and in December of that year married Tom Baker. The marriage lasted only 16 months. Following **Doctor Who**, Ward won roles in **Schoolgirl Chums** and **Hamlet, Prince of Denmark** for the BBC and **The Jeweller's Shop** and **The Rehearsal** on stage. She has also developed her love of painting and has written and illustrated several books. In 1992 she was married to biologist Dr Richard Dawkins.*

K-9 and Lalla Ward.

character for her to choose to settle down to a quiet life in one of the Universe's oldest, stuffiest and most lethargic societies.

It was this society which was to provide the last of the seventies companions. Romanadvoratrelundar — Romana for short — was a young Time Lord graduate chosen by the White Guardian to assist the Doctor in his quest during season sixteen for the six segments of the Key to Time. In this incarnation (as played by Mary Tamm), she came across as being cool and aloof, clearly considering herself to be of superior intelligence to the Doctor — with some justification, as she had achieved better results than he at the Time Lord academy. She did however have an Achilles heel — a complete ignorance of life outside the cloistered confines of the Gallifreyan Capitol — which ensured that, like her predecessors, she would still spend much of her time asking the Doctor questions. Brought up in the knowledge of the awesome powers of her race, she had an air of self-importance which, when coupled with this lack of experience, often led her into trouble. She was then forced to suffer the added indignity of being rescued by the Doctor, with whom she had something of a clash of temperaments.

After her regeneration in *Destiny of the Daleks*, Romana (now played by Lalla Ward) mellowed quite considerably, losing much of her former haughtiness and acquiring a sense of fun. Her relationship with the Doctor also became closer and more harmonious than in the past — a development reflecting the off-screen romance then taking place between Lalla Ward and Tom Baker themselves.

No discussion of the seventies companions would be complete without referring to another character who travelled in the TARDIS alongside first Leela and then Romana. This was K-9 — the dog-shaped mobile computer that the Doctor acquired from the scientist Professor Marius in season fifteen's *The Invisible Enemy*. The late-seventies saw a proliferation of cute robots in science-fiction films and TV series, such as R2-D2 and C-3PO in *Star Wars* and Twikki in *Buck Rogers in the 25th Century*. K-9, however, was conceived prior to all these, providing another example of *Doctor Who* leading the way in its genre.

Much of K-9's success was due to the vocal skills of actor John Leeson, who supplied the distinctive electronic-sounding voice in all but four of its stories, with David Brierley taking his place for the others. The original K-9 chose to remain with Leela on Gallifrey at the conclusion of *The Invasion of Time*, but the Doctor had already produced a Mk II version which saw out the rest of the decade.

The seventies had seen significant developments taking place in the way *Doctor Who*'s regular supporting characters were portrayed, the UNIT team initially taking a central role and then being gradually phased out during the fourth Doctor's era. Further important changes lay ahead as the series moved towards its third decade.

CHAPTER EIGHTEEN

Doctor Who and the Daleks in Seven Keys to Doomsday

The first stage play spawned by *Doctor Who* had been the 1965 production *The Curse of the Daleks*, which had revolved entirely around the Daleks and had featured neither the Doctor nor the TARDIS. The second was a 1974 production, written by *Doctor Who*'s outgoing script editor Terrance Dicks, which saw the Doctor and the Daleks sharing equal billing.

Dicks had long harboured a desire to see *Doctor Who* on stage, and back in 1970 had tried to inter-est theatre companies in a musical starring Jon Pertwee as the Doctor along with the Daleks. This idea had not been well received, however, so he had let the matter rest until 1974, when the *Doctor Who* production office was contacted by two theatre producers, Robert de Wynter and Anthony Pye-Jeary, who wanted to mount a play based on the series.

'We decided a children's show had never really been done in the West End on the same level as, say, a children's film, a comic book adventure or a

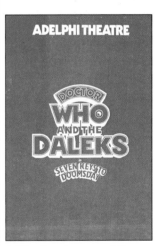

▲ The front cover of the programme booklet.

The Doctor (Trevor Martin), Jedak (Ian Ruskin), Tara (Patsy Dermott), Jimmy (James Mathews) and Jenny (Wendy Padbury) are menaced by the Clawrantulars (Peter Jolley, Mo Kiki and Peter Whitting) and the Daleks.

The Doctor takes one of ▲ the keys from the Master of Karn (Simon Jones).

James Mathews, Wendy Padbury and Trevor Martin meet a Dalek during publicity for the play.

Trevor Martin and a Dalek publicize the show.

television series,' explains Pye-Jeary.

Pye-Jeary and de Wynter met Terry Nation to discuss using the Daleks, and the BBC to obtain the rights to do the play. With these arrangements made, they set about raising the £35,000 budget they required.

'It was a very difficult show to do on stage,' admits Pye-Jeary. 'We had three huge screens and 2,000 slides that were run by computer. The computer was also programmed to work the music and the prerecorded voices. We went way over budget trying to get it right. The show we did was probably too good, as we were going to run only four weeks in the West End, twice nightly, and then go on tour.'

Dicks agrees with this assessment, noting that the scenery proved too big to fit on lorries for transportation and would have overshot most regional theatre stages.

Two key members of the production team were the director, Mick Hughes, and the designer, John Napier. Hughes was better known as a lighting designer and had worked on shows such as *Mrs Warren's Profession*, *Chez Nous* and *John Paul George Ringo ... and Bert*. *Doctor Who and the Daleks in Seven Keys to Doomsday* marked his West End debut as a director. Napier had previously received critical acclaim for his designs for the National Theatre production of *Equus*, and had worked extensively with the Royal Shakespeare Company. 'We asked and were thrilled when John Napier agreed to design it,' enthuses Pye-Jeary.

In what could be considered a strange move, the producers decided against offering the starring role in the play either to Jon Pertwee or to the new TV Doctor, Tom Baker. According to Pye-Jeary, they preferred to create their own Doctor; someone who

was a mixture of all the previous incarnations, including the Peter Cushing version from the cinema films of the sixties. They eventually chose Trevor Martin, citing his booming voice and his long white hair as being perfect for the part. Martin had in fact already played a Time Lord in the TV series. He was one of the three who sentenced the Doctor to exile at the end of the 1969 story *The War Games*.

'From a technical point of view I thought it was a very good production,' says Martin. 'I've worked on far less technical shows and seen how many times they go wrong, but I was full of admiration for the technical crew on the *Doctor Who* play. I really felt for the people inside the Daleks because they had to be very careful that they didn't lose control. There was a slight rake on the stage and if they'd gone slightly askew they'd have been sitting down in the front row of the stalls.'

To play the Doctor's two assistants, Jenny and Jimmy, Wendy Padbury and James Mathews were cast. Padbury had, like Martin, appeared in *Doctor Who* on television, playing the Doctor's companion Zoe in the late sixties.

'There wasn't a long time to rehearse,' recalls Padbury, 'which was a bit of a problem. There were loads of things that could have gone wrong. We used hundreds of back-projections and once started they couldn't stop. They were all operated on word cues, so you knew that if you forgot a line and you didn't give the poor guy who started the machine the cue, then forget it!'

Another member of the cast was Simon Jones, who normally played the 14-foot tall Master of Karn but was also called upon to appear as Jimmy for a few performances when James Mathews was ill.

The production's monsters were designed by

Jedak (Ian Ruskin) and the Doctor (Trevor Martin) at the controls of the TARDIS.

James Acheson, who had also worked on the TV series, creating such impressive visuals as the Robot in Tom Baker's debut story. He was responsible not only for the Master of Karn but also for a new race of evil crab-like creatures. These creatures had been called Crocs in Dicks's scripts but the producers, disliking this name, arranged to run a competition through the *Sun* newspaper to come up with another. Clawrantular was the winning entry and was therefore used in the production.

To construct the monsters, Acheson brought in freelance prop builder Allister Bowtell. For the Master of Karn, Bowtell first took an impression of Simon Jones's face with a plaster-soaked fabric. From this base he then built up the giant cranium in clay and copied the finished work in polyester resin. Lights were mounted inside the cranium, with wires leading to a battery. Finally the face was painted green and a long straggly beard added. Jones had to perform the part standing on a wheeled trolley to achieve the necessary height, his costume being draped over both him and the trolley in order to conceal it.

The plot of the play involves the Doctor being joined by Jenny and Jimmy — two teenagers who rush from the audience to help him — in a quest on the planet Karn for seven crystal keys. Together, these keys comprise the Crystal of All Power which will increase the power of an Ultimate Weapon built by the Daleks and enable them to conquer every planet in every galaxy in every universe. The Doctor manages to alter the molecular structure of one of the crystals so that when it is used in conjunction with the others, it destroys the Ultimate Weapon.

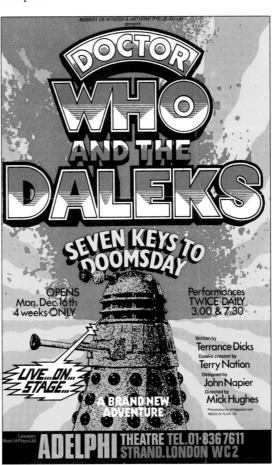

A handbill announcing the opening of the play at the Adelphi theatre.

From Shakespeare to Sam Shepherd, anything goes on the modern stage, but when it comes to Dr Who the theatre has to reckon with an expert public. The rules are inflexible and known to all; and the job of supplying an acceptable live equivalent for this electronic plaything is quite enough for any production team.

There is a moment in **Seven Keys to Doomsday** when Terrance Dicks allows authorship to go to his head, and permits the Doctor to open a Dalek like a hinged biscuit tin and scrape out its occupant while the rest of the cast avert their eyes in horror. For suggesting that Daleks contain anything more than standard printed circuits, Mr Dicks deserves a rehabilitation sentence down in the reactor room. But otherwise he knows his place and offers a blamelessly correct Tardis adventure, that makes up in self-containment what it lacks in time-slip complexities.

A bowed figure staggers out of the famous blue box; two plants in the audience (Wendy Padbury and James Mathews) rush to his assistance, while the past faces of the Doctor flash up on the back wall; finally he raises his head revealing his latest metamorphosis into Trevor Martin – a rather sardonic mask for so benevolent a character, but you get to accept it by the time he has ferried the party over to the planet Karn and stood his ground against its man-eating crabs and lobster-clawed, crocodile-muzzled guards.

Full electronic illusion is beyond the reach of any stage production; so Mick Hughes and John Napier, his brilliant designer, have settled for the only feasible alternative and magnified the scale of effects.

Besides the stage there is a bank of nine screens where interstellar skies mingle with fantastic vegetation, a bestiary of grotesque heads and enormous eyes. The screens are built around the equivalent of a Greek tragic portal: a black hole through which dreadful things happen and from which they stealthily emerge under cover of shadows and smoke.

When the ultimate horror is announced, a murmur of affection runs through the house, and on slide the Daleks to general applause. Nobody actually said 'Aah!', but they might just as well have been koala bears.

Review by Irving Wardle in The Times, date unknown

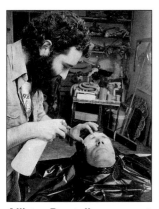

Allister Bowtell prepares ▲ to take a life mask from actor Simon Jones in order to construct the mask for the Master of Karn.

Dicks's script bore a number of similarities to the 1964 television story *The Keys of Marinus*, which had also seen the Doctor and his companions searching for a set of crystal keys which operated a powerful machine. In addition, it served as a foretaste of Dicks's own season-thirteen script *The Brain of Morbius*, which would likewise be set on the planet Karn and feature a monster with a giant crab claw in place of one of its hands.

One unusual aspect of the production was that the theatre curtains were not closed during scene changes. Instead, the lights were dimmed and the scene changed in the dark. The darkness was less complete than it could have been, however, and very often the scene-shifters could be seen moving the props about. The script's requirement for a large number of different settings was economically resolved by using a basic background throughout the play and just changing the trimmings. The background was a large backcloth with an arched entrance, while the trimmings consisted of rocks, machinery, the TARDIS console and other bits and pieces as required.

The aforementioned giant screens were placed either side of the stage and showed landscapes and other images as the story progressed. They were also used to achieve the regeneration of the Doctor from Jon Pertwee to Trevor Martin at the very start of the play.

'We had to start off with me coming on looking like Jon Pertwee,' explains Trevor Martin, 'and then going through one of those *Doctor Who* transformation scenes — turning myself into me!'

Another innovation was in the use of shadows to provide short linking scenes, generally involving the Daleks reporting to their Emperor. The shadows of the Daleks were cast onto the stage, giving the impression that there were a lot more of them than was actually the case.

The show opened at London's Adelphi Theatre on 16 December 1974 but audiences were low. Although the play had received a great number of very favourable reviews, the IRA were carrying out one of their sporadic bombing campaigns in the city. 'We had a lot of cancellations of bookings from frightened parents,' says Pye-Jeary ruefully. 'You couldn't blame them, so we gave them back their money.'

Ultimately, Pye-Jeary and de Wynter had to make a decision whether to go on tour as planned or to cut their losses and take the play off after the four week West End run. In the end they opted to pull the show after just the four week run, during which it took just under £27,500 at the box office.

Sir,
On a point of Dalek scholarship, may I take exception to one small part of your critic, Mr Irving Wardle's otherwise kind review of my play **Dr Who and the Daleks** at the Adelphi?

Mr Wardle chides me for assuming that the outer casing of a Dalek conceals a living creature. Yet such is, in fact, the case. The Daleks are not, and never have been, any kind of robot – a fact clearly established on television many times, since the Daleks were created by Terry Nation well over ten years ago.

The demonstration of this in every Dalek story is, in itself, one of the inflexible 'Dr Who' rules to which Mr Wardle himself refers at the beginning of his review.

In the hope that you will permit me to exterminate this minor inaccuracy, I am,
    Yours faithfully,
    Terrance Dicks.
**Letter to The Times,
date unknown**

A Clawrantular and Daleks patrol the stage at the Adelphi theatre.

CHAPTER NINETEEN

Exhibitions: On Display

The sixties had seen only two *bona fide Doctor Who* exhibitions being staged, both at the annual *Daily Mail Boys' and Girls' Exhibition* in London. The seventies, however, were to see a considerable growth occurring in this aspect of the series' presentation to the public.

The first example was not a static display but a one-off publicity venture which took place on 21 December 1971 at the London Planetarium. In the second half of a *Young Observer*-sponsored 'teach in' (the first half of which had consisted of a lecture on the workings of the Planetarium), Jon Pertwee took the stage with producer Barry Letts and actor Peter Purves, who had played the Doctor's companion Steven Taylor in the sixties. Purves, by this time better known as one of the presenters of the children's programme *Blue Peter*, acted as a master of ceremonies, inviting questions from the audience on all aspects of *Doctor Who*. Letts had brought with him a number of props to show the children, including masks of the Silurians, the Auton daffodil men from *Terror of the Autons* and the Axons. He also revealed that the Silurians' aquatic cousins, the Sea Devils, would be introduced in season nine, which was just about to begin its run on TV. The climax of the event came when two Daleks emerged and stormed the stage, and enthusiastic applause greeted the news that they too would be appearing in the forthcoming season.

The second seventies event was an exhibition staged over two weeks in March and April 1972 at the Ceylon Tea Centre in London's Lower Regent Street. The main purpose of this was to put on show some of the many entries that the *Radio Times* had received in the 'Win a Dalek' competition run to tie in with the transmission of *Day of the Daleks* earlier in the year. A number of original *Doctor Who* costumes were also displayed, including Aggedor and Alpha Centauri from *The Curse of Peladon*. Every competition entrant whose work was included in the exhibition received a certificate to commemorate the fact.

In December of the same year, a larger *Doctor Who* display was mounted as part of a BBC Visual Effects Exhibition in London's Science Museum. Several costumes and props from the series were grouped around a re-creation of the TARDIS control console, including a Draconian from the then-unseen *Frontier in Space*, along with some specially-designed exhibits demonstrating the creation

Displays at the 1972 exhibition at the Science Museum. Top left: The TARDIS entrance. Top Right: A Draconian. Bottom: The TARDIS console.

▲ **The Alpha Centauri costume on display at the Ceylon Tea Centre exhibition.**

▲ **The entrance to the *Doctor Who* exhibition at Longleat house.**

▲ **Part of the *Doctor Who* display at the 1979 Blackpool Illuminations.**

BLACKPOOL ILLUMINATIONS

In 1975, the Blackpool illuminations – a well-known annual tourist attraction – were switched on by an in-costume Tom Baker, who described the occasion as follows in his column for the weekly **Reveille** *newspaper:*

At last the day came to go to Blackpool for the great annual switch-on of the illuminations. They told me I was only the 43rd person to be invited to do the switch on, so I felt part of a very select group. Knees shaking, and with nervous jokes Ian Marter, Lis Sladen and I arrived in Talbot Square for the event!

There was a crowd – 20,000 strong! I've sometimes played to full houses, but 20,000!

The Mayor came out to address the people – and suddenly he was surrounded by Daleks. They told him to sit down or be exterminated. They went on about only Daleks being allowed to switch on illuminations and threatened to destroy the Blackpool Tower and blow up Woolworths.

Just then two Cybermen arrived. By a stroke of good fortune, I had my sonic screwdriver with me and we managed to put the Cybermen out of action. This caused great uproar among the children, screams of happy terror. Then the Daleks attacked. Luckily there were some very large 'Kiss Me Quick' hats on the dais and Lis and Ian popped them over the Daleks.

As you know, if there's one thing Daleks can't stand, it's being covered up. They spun around, and screamed and finally retired in sulky silence to the wings.

Then the switch-on. The crowd was hushed, I pressed the handle – and six miles of lights went on. We then toured the lights in Bessie. It was a wonderful evening.

Four years later, from 30 August to 28 October 1979, the illuminations featured a large tableau of Tom Baker's Doctor with K-9 beside the TARDIS control console. The display was previewed to the press on 4 July, when Baker himself was again on hand to pose alongside it for the photographers' cameras. He also presented the winner's sash in the Blackpool Queen of Lights beauty contest to 22-year old contestant Linda Lewis.

Tom Baker signs autographs for fans at an appearance to publicize the *Doctor Who* exhibition at Blackpool.

of visual effects such as the heat barrier in *The Dæmons*.

The Ceylon Tea Centre exhibition and the Science Museum display had both been overseen by Lorne Martin of BBC Licensing. Their success set the BBC thinking that there might be other ways in which they could exploit their treasure trove of props and costumes from all manner of programmes. Martin and others were therefore asked to set up a new department within BBC Licensing which would deal solely with exhibitions.

Almost the first task for the fledgling BBC Exhibitions team was to handle a request from Lord Bath, who had seen the exhibition at the Science Museum and who wondered if such a thing could be staged at his stately home of Longleat House in Wiltshire. Thus, in 1973, an exhibition, similar to that staged in 1972, was mounted in one of the old stable blocks at the back of the house. The following year, recognizing the popularity of the *Doctor Who* element, Lorne Martin and his team located, after much searching, suitable premises in Blackpool, Lancashire to stage a permanent exhibition of *Doctor Who* ephemera. At the same time, the Visual Effects Exhibition at Longleat was converted to a *Doctor Who* only exhibition.

The Blackpool exhibition was the larger of the two, situated in an empty basement under a cafe on the 'Golden Mile' — a long stretch of funfairs, amusement arcades and other tourist attractions in this popular family holiday resort. Within this space Martin, together with a team of specialists from other

Crowds pack the pavements and roads around the new *Doctor Who* exhbition in Blackpool, all waiting for Tom Baker, Elisabeth Sladen and Ian Marter to arrive for the official opening ceremony.

BBC departments, created a winding passage terminating in a representation of the TARDIS control room, complete with central console. All around the sides of the passage and the control room were placed open areas to house the exhibits, as well as wall-mounted display cases and numerous photographs. As an added attraction, two tracks were installed around which mechanically operated Daleks paraded. A third Dalek acted as sentry to the TARDIS control area, warning visitors by way of a prerecorded voice track that they would be exterminated if they smoked. The exhibition was entered through an oversized police box exterior constructed at the head of the flight of stairs leading down to the basement. The first visitors were admitted on 10 April 1974.

The exhibition at Longleat House was slightly smaller than its counterpart in Blackpool but followed the same format, with a winding passageway leading the visitor past several display areas and into a mock-up of the TARDIS control room. The refurbished *Doctor Who* exhibition opened on 12 April 1974.

Both exhibitions were closed from around November to April each year to be re-fitted and decked out with new props and costumes from the latest televised season, ready for the next influx of visitors the following summer. Any exhibits no longer needed were either returned to the BBC's warehouses in Ealing or else held in the exhibitions' own store rooms. Occasionally, specific costumes would be recalled for use in the series itself, as was the case with Davros's chair and mask for *Destiny of the Daleks*.

Throughout the remainder of the seventies, these permanent exhibitions of *Doctor Who's* costumes and props attracted many hundreds of thousands of visitors and were amongst the most popular of all spin offs from the series.

CHAPTER TWENTY

Welcome to the Toyshop

I n the early sixties the BBC had pre-ferred to let external agents like Walter Tuckwell Associates handle the merchandising arrangements for their television programmes. Soon however the BBC's embryonic licensing depart-ment, BBC Exploitation, realized that they could handle this task without outside assistance and thus retain for themselves the percentage previously taken by the agent.

The department was being run then by Roy Williams, who handled the administration and the financial aspects and had the title of Exploitation Manager. In the late sixties the department was merged with BBC Radio Enterprises and renamed BBC Licensing, also taking on responsibility for a series of increasingly popular BBC-orientated ex-hibitions. The mandate of the department was, as its original title suggested, to exploit BBC proper-ties through the licensing of merchandise rights. The department would actively go out and sug-gest products to manufacturers as well as acting as a reference point for anyone who wanted to produce something connected with a BBC pro-gramme. In the seventies it became subsumed within BBC Enterprises, a company set up specifi-cally to handle all aspects of the marketing of BBC programmes.

Although there were a large number of *Doctor Who*-related products produced during the seven-ties, it was rare for any of them to do really well. The days of the mid-sixties Dalek boom were over and most licensees had no more than one royalty payment to make to the BBC. In many cases, only the initial license fee was paid, the product selling insufficiently well to cover even that advance. The one major exception to this rule was the range of novelizations based on the series, which formed the single most profitable area of *Doctor Who* merchandising in the seventies.

ACTIVITY BOOKS

World Distributors, continuing their long asso-ciation with *Doctor Who*, published **The Doctor Who Colouring Book** in 1973. The line draw-ings within this soft-cover book told a very loose story in which the third Doctor, his assistant (a sort of cross between Liz Shaw and Jo Grant) and UNIT battled aliens, historical figures, a giant oc-topus and so on. Several of the drawings were lifted from publicity stills from *Day of the Daleks*, *Terror of the Autons* and *Frontier in Space*, and the cover photograph was from *The Time Mon-ster*.

World Distributors had arranged a license for the **Doctor Who Press-Out Book** in August 1977, with an initial print run of 50,000. The book was eventually released late in 1978 after certain pic-tures of Mary Tamm's Romana were re-drawn at the BBC's request. It was however something of a disappointment for the publishers with under half the print run selling and the rest being remaindered in 1980.

The food manufacturer Crosse & Blackwell brought out in 1977 a three-dimensional **TARDIS**

◄ **A selection of activity books released during the seventies.**

HALLOWEEN BOOK

*One book about which no information can be found, and which may not even exist, is the **Doctor Who Halloween Book**. It was advertised as a 'want' in a book collector's magazine in the eighties and was described as having been published around 1976 with a glossy dust jacket.*

BOOKS

In August 1975, Allan Wingate (Publishers) Ltd came up with the idea of producing a series of books tentatively themed as 'The Doctor Who book of …', which would make no reference to Doctor Who other than the title. On 3 August 1976 W.H. Allen, who had by then taken over the company, requested the BBC's permission to publish the **Doctor Who Dinosaur Book**. *Written by Terrance Dicks and illustrated by George Underwood, this large format paperback saw the Doctor meeting all manner of dinosaurs while the sparse text told the reader a little about them. Published late in 1976, this was followed, starting in November 1977, by a range of similar publications under the generic title* **Doctor Who Discovers**.

Edited by Fred Newman and designed by Frank Ainscough, these books took the idea of the Doctor visiting various times and places as a way of conveying a brief history of the subjects covered. Photographs from the TV series were included to add authenticity to the brief text. **Space Travel** *(published November 1977),* **Prehistoric Animals** *(November 1977),* **Strange and Mysterious Creatures** *(December 1977),* **Early Man** *(February 1978) and* **The Conquerors** *(February 1978) were not the success that the publishers had hoped - Strange and Mysterious Creatures, for example, sold only 10,140 units worldwide - and further titles,* **The Inventors, The Pirates** *and* **The Miners** *planned for publication in 1978, were cancelled.*

The unused cover ▲ artwork for Doctor Who Discovers Miners.

colouring book together with some 'pop-a-point' colouring pencils. The set could be obtained by sending the company 95 pence, together with four labels from their tins of baked beans. Other items available (for more money!) in the promotion were a Thomas Salter chemistry set and a Radionic Electronic kit. Artwork posters were also produced which were given away in exchange for labels from the tins during a promotional tour by Tom Baker.

In March 1977, Alan Fennell of Children's Leisure Products Ltd approached the BBC for permission to release a painting book, an activity book and a poster magazine. The poster magazine was not progressed as, at that time, the BBC's photographic department was preparing what was described as a 'Picture Encyclopedia' on *Doctor Who* (an idea which was subsequently dropped), but the go-ahead was given for the other products. When the final artwork for the books was submitted to the BBC for approval, though, the Head of Serials, Graeme McDonald, commented that it seemed to be of a significantly lower standard than products he had seen before. He was particularly

The third Doctor Annuals.

The fourth Doctor Annuals.

concerned about poor quality likenesses of Tom Baker and Louise Jameson and was appalled at the prospect of the BBC's name being associated with what he described as 'trash'.

Fennell was dismayed at this rejection but agreed to terminate the license if the BBC would refund his initial payment. This they did and the license was officially terminated on 1 June 1978. Nevertheless, that same year, Children's Leisure Products released **The Daleks Colouring Book** and **The Daleks Activity Book**. The pictures in these were in many cases very basic copies of photographs. Recognizable images were from *Planet of the Daleks* and *Genesis of the Daleks*. There were no obvious likenesses of Leela, but images of the Doctor and Davros were both used.

The final colouring book appeared in 1979, when World Distributors published another **Doctor Who Colouring Book**. This followed the same pattern as their previous titles and in evidence here were drawings of photographs from *The Ribos Operation, The Androids of Tara* and *Pyramids of Mars*.

The same year, W.H. Allen & Co, building on the increasing popularity of their Target range of novelizations, released two 'B' format paperbacks, one in September entitled **The Adventures of K9 and Other Mechanical Creatures** and the other in October called **Terry Nation's Dalek Special**. The former contained a selection of photographs, games and puzzles featuring various mechanical creatures to have crossed the Doctor's path over the years, with text by Terrance Dicks. The latter followed a similar format, being compiled and edited by Terrance Dicks, but also featured a reprint of a story written by Terry Nation originally for a London newspaper, the *Evening News*, in 1974. Both books had cover paintings and internal illustrations by Andrew Skilleter.

ANNUALS

World Distributors continued their policy of publishing a *Doctor Who* Annual each year, except one for 1972 (which, if it had followed the usual schedule, would have been published in September 1971). The 1980 annual (September 1979) was published under their new World & Whitman logo and imprint. All the annuals during this period followed the same basic pattern. The contents consisted of a mixture of comic strip stories, text stories and puzzles, along with factual features on space travel and astronomy. The front covers of those for 1973, 1974, 1975, 1976 and 1980 featured photographs while the rest were graced with artwork.

World Distributors rarely credited any of their writers or artists, but some are known. *The House that Jack Built*, the first story in the 1975 annual (published September 1974), was written by Keith Miller, the then organizer of the *Doctor Who* Fan Club. This was one of two stories for which Miller had submitted ideas, and he was paid £9 for it. The cover of the 1970 annual was painted by World Distributors' Production Manager Ron Smethurst. Steve Livesy was responsible for the comic strip stories in the 1974 annual (September 1973) and Edgar Hodges for those in the 1975 one. The 1976 annual (September 1975) contained artwork by P.J. Crompton, as did the 1977 annual (September 1976), which had a different page size from all the others (it was 22cm by 29cm as opposed to 20cm by 27½cm), the 1978 annual (September 1977) and the 1979 annual (September 1978), in the latter of which he actually received a credit.

To accompany their regular *Doctor Who* publication, World Distributors reached agreement with Terry Nation's agents, Roger Hancock Ltd, to publish a Dalek equivalent. **Terry Nation's Dalek Annual** appeared four years running, the first being for 1976 (published September 1975) and the last for 1979 (September 1978). The format was similar to that of the *Doctor Who* annual. The stories were all reminiscent of the Dalek material of the sixties, and a number featured Mark Seven, a humanoid android who had first appeared in *The Dalek Outer Space Book* in 1966. The lead characters, who featured in all four annuals, were Joel Shaw and Reb Shavron. The 1977 and 1978 annuals featured material reprinted from *TV Century 21*, while the majority of the artwork for the 1979 one was provided by Paul Mark Tams, a member of the *Doctor Who* Appreciation Society, as a nod to which he incorporated the initials 'DWAS' on the side of a spacecraft pictured on page four.

The Dalek Annuals.

The final annual-format book of the seventies was **Doctor Who and the Daleks Omnibus**, published in 1976 by Artus Publishing (a division of Weidenfeld and Nicholson) for the Marks and Spencer chain of shops. It featured abridged reprints of two novelizations, *Genesis of the Daleks* and *Planet of the Daleks*, interspersed with articles and photographs. Script extracts from *Genesis of the Daleks* were included, and there was also a wildly inaccurate listing of TV, film and stage appearances by the Daleks.

CONFECTIONERY

In 1971, the Nestlé Company added *Doctor Who* to their range of **chocolate bars** featuring several TV programmes. The chocolate itself had an image of the third Doctor's face moulded into it and there were fifteen different wrappers to collect. In artwork form they told the story of *Masterplan Q*, and how the Doctor foils it. The Master also made an appearance, coinciding with his debut in the TV series. The bars were available singly or in packs of four.

It was also while Jon Pertwee was the Doctor that a **TARDIS toffee** was produced. This took the form of a long flat toffee stick, but no further details are available.

The next item was the **Dalek's Death Ray** ice lolly from T. Wall & Sons, which was produced from 1975 until 1977. This green and brown, mint and chocolate flavoured lolly came with several variations of wrapper during its lifetime. There was a plain wrapper with a simple Dalek design on both sides; one giving details of a competition to win a real life-size Dalek in 1975; one explaining how to 'Make a Dalek' out of a yoghurt pot and a toilet roll tube, also in 1975; a set of eight entitled *From the World of the Daleks ...* in 1976;

A selection of confectionery.

CLOTHING

The seventies saw only a few items of Doctor Who clothing available to buy. Only three examples of T-Shirt are known to have been commercially produced. The first was a silk screen printed **Doctor Who logo T-Shirt** from a company called Rumpelstiltskin. The second, available in June 1975 from a firm known variously as Kaleidoscope Services, Silly Things and Arthur Howe's Associates Ltd (Aha Ltd), was a **Doctor Who and the Daleks T-Shirt**. White with a red, yellow and black transfer on the front, this came in two different sizes: Junior (26-32") and Adult (34-40"). The third example was a black **T-Shirt** with a glittery logo, produced in Portugal in 1976 for BBC Enterprises.

There was also a **Doctor Who Scarf** produced by Today Promotions in 1976. This came in two lengths, 8 and 10 foot. It had a fourth Doctor patch sewn into it to officially identify it, and the colours and design were taken from the authentic BBC version.

WHERE'S THE DOCTOR?

Producer Graham Williams sent BBC Enterprises a memo when approving the proofs of **Terry Nation's Dalek Special** on 12 July 1979. He asked if there was a precedent for a Dalek story, set in contemporary London, which was completely divorced from **Doctor Who**. He ended by pondering whether younger viewers would be confused as to how the Daleks' most familiar adversary and the Earth's most familiar defender did not meet in the most familiar surroundings! He wondered whether the **Doctor Who** element had been avoided deliberately and it is unknown what answer he received. Nation had actually written the story in 1974 for serialization in the London newspaper, the **Evening News**, and it was being reprinted in the Dalek Special.

The wrappers for the ▲ Dalek's Death Ray Ice Lolly featured useful Dalek information on the back.

FILMS

*Writer Don Houghton contacted the BBC in 1971 to see if there was any interest in an approach which an unknown company had made to him about producing a **Doctor Who** film, but nothing came of this. Later, in 1977, Tom Baker, Ian Marter and James Hill began their ultimately unsuccessful attempt to obtain finance for a film script they had written under the title **Doctor Who meets Scratchman**. With the increase in popularity of film formats – particularly **super-8 films** – for home viewing, it was only a matter of time before the two Dalek films of the sixties were made available to the public. They were finally released in 1977 by Walton Sound and Film Services Ltd, one of the major super-8 dealers. **Daleks' Invasion Earth 2150 A.D.** was also available in a widescreen format.*

and a set of eight entitled *The Incredible Daleks …* in 1977.

1975 also saw Nestlé releasing a second set of **chocolate bars**, this time with wrappers featuring illustrations and profiles of, respectively, the Doctor, the TARDIS, Harry, Sarah, Sergeant Benton and the Brigadier. This time the chocolate itself did not feature the Doctor's face. As with the first set, the bars were available singly or in packs of four.

Another 1975 product was the first *Doctor Who* **rock**, made by Regent confectionery. The *Doctor Who* exhibition had recently opened in Blackpool, and the rock was an obvious product to be placed on sale in its shop.

Doctor Who **candy favourites** arrived on the scene in 1979 from Goodies. These were white chocolate pieces in four different shapes: the TARDIS, K-9, a Dalek and a Cyberman.

FACTUAL BOOKS

At no time during the sixties had a wholly factual book or publication about *Doctor Who* been made available. Home video was still a thing of the future, so fans had to rely on their own memories, personal notes and audio tape recordings to

The factual books released during the seventies.

keep the programme's history alive. By the early seventies, the time was ripe for a proper retrospective to be published.

Pan Books took the initiative in April 1972 with **The Making of Doctor Who**, published under their Piccolo imprint and written by two of the series' most prominent contributors, Malcolm Hulke and Terrance Dicks. The project had been suggested to Pan by Hulke, who had then asked Dicks to become involved. The book contained features on the series' origins, history and major characters, along with brief biographies of the then current regular cast members and of William Hartnell and Patrick Troughton. The largest section consisted of a summary of the Doctor's adventures up to and including *The Sea Devils*, presented in the form of supposed extracts from his trial by the Time Lords and, for the seventies stories, a batch of UNIT memos and other reports. The authors then took *The Sea Devils* by way of example and looked at how *Doctor Who* was actually made, using extracts from filming schedules and scripts. The book also included a section of black and white photographs and was finished off with a 'could it all be possible' look at the real-life science involved, and even a religious viewpoint. As the first of its kind, *The Making of Doctor Who* was a landmark publication which served to make viewers more aware of the series' rich heritage and to leave the inquisitive wanting further information.

The next factual book was **The Doctor Who Monster Book**, published in November 1975 by Tandem Publishing Ltd and written by Terrance Dicks. It celebrated *Doctor Who*'s monsters by presenting photographs and artwork (taken from the covers of the Target novelizations) of selected creatures, along with a brief text. Included were perennial favourites such as Daleks, Cybermen and Ice Warriors, along with one-off monsters including Zarbi, Axons, Dæmons, Spiders and Zygons. Perhaps the most appealing aspect of the book was its generous photographic content, as few such stills had been published in the past. The print run of the first edition was 100,000 and Tandem negotiated a special one per cent royalty deal with the BBC — the normal royalty payable to the BBC on a book being two-and-a-half per cent — to compensate for the fact that they had to pay copyright clearance on all the photographs on top of their normal publishing costs.

Tandem came up trumps again on 16 December 1976 when they reissued Pan's **The Making of Doctor Who**. Whereas the bulk of the first edition had been written by Malcolm Hulke, this revised version was almost solely the work of Terrance Dicks. Dicks reused material from *The*

Doctor Who Monster Book and substituted a section on his own story *Robot* in favour of that on *The Sea Devils*. The photographic section was retained, but featured different stills. The extracts from the Doctor's trial and the UNIT memos were removed completely, and in their place was included a set of brief story synopses in transmission order, up to and including *The Hand of Fear*.

Following the success of *The Doctor Who Monster Book*, 20 October 1977 saw W.H. Allen — a successor to Tandem — release **The Second Doctor Who Monster Book**. This was a physically smaller book and featured the era of the fourth Doctor, with monsters from *Robot* to *The Talons of Weng-Chiang* presented through photographs and Terrance Dicks's text. A third *Monster Book* was suggested by Dicks in 1979, the intention being to cover the stories from *Horror of Fang Rock* to *The Armageddon Factor*, but the publishers did not follow this up.

JIGSAWS

Doctor Who jigsaws were to prove very popular in the seventies. The first, produced by Michael Stanfield Holdings in 1971, were a set of two 100-piece 11" x 9" puzzles: *Dr Who and Bessie* (showing the third Doctor in his car — a publicity photo) and *Dr Who at Work* (a photo from *Terror of the Autons*). On the back of each box was a large artwork picture of the Doctor together with information about the other jigsaw in the set. These puzzles were also available together in a two-in-one box the same year.

Michael Stanfield Holdings reissued the two separate jigsaws in 1972, and added another two to the series: *Dr Who and the Daleks* and *Odds Against Dr Who* (each featuring a publicity photo from *Day of the Daleks*). The reissues can be differentiated from the 1971 releases as in this case the back of each box displayed columns of information about other TV-related products in Michael Stanfield Holdings's Pleasure Products range.

In total, these jigsaws sold in excess of 215,000 units. Although Michael Stanfield Holdings suggested other items of *Doctor Who*-related merchandise to the BBC, most notably a Magic Pen in 1971 and a 'Slotty' Press-Out Book — which apparently would not have used the image of the Doctor — a range of Nightwear and a Magic Picture Book, all in 1972, nothing came of them.

In 1973, Whitman produced a set of four 15" x 11¼" 125-piece photographic jigsaws featuring the third Doctor. Two of the photos were from *The Green Death*, one was from *The Three Doctors* (and

A selection of *Doctor Who* jigsaws.

showed the second Doctor as well as the third) and one was from *Day of the Daleks* (from the same photo session as that on the third Michael Stanfield Holdings jigsaw, but a slightly different pose).

Another set was produced by Whitman in 1974 and released early in 1975, following the transmission of *Robot*. It featured four photos from that story: two publicity shots of the fourth Doctor, one of the Doctor, Harry and the Brigadier in a jeep and one showing the Robot being attacked by UNIT soldiers. This time the puzzles contained 224 pieces each and measured 18½" x 13". This set sold in excess of 60,000 units.

In 1977, Whitman issued a further set of four jigsaws featuring artwork representations of the Doctor in a variety of locations. One, inspired by *The Deadly Assassin*, showed him in the Panopticon wearing his Time Lord robes. The number of pieces and the size of each puzzle were the same as for the previous set.

Whitman's final set was issued in 1978 with the overall title **Enemies of Doctor Who**. The four artwork jigsaws were individually titled: *The enormously powerful Giant Robots*, *Sontarans the war-obsessed space travellers*, *The evil Kraals planning to conquer Earth* and *The Zygons emerging from their crippled spaceship beneath Loch Ness*. The number of pieces and the size remained the same as for the 1977 set.

While these jigsaws were the last to be issued under the Whitman name, Whitman was itself owned by the Pentos group who also owned World Distributors, and it was the latter company which released the next set of artwork jigsaws in 1979. This set of four had the title **The Amazing World of Doctor Who**. Two featured K-9, the other two featured the Daleks (*TV Century 21* versions). Again, the number of pieces and the puzzle size were unchanged.

▲ **The reverse of the first edition Michael Stanfield Holdings jigsaws.**

The promotional poster ▲ produced to publicize Crosse & Blackwell baked beans.

POSTERS

In 1972 a firm called Personality Posters released a large photographic poster of the Doctor being threatened by a giant claw in Colony in Space. This item was subsequently withdrawn, however, as Jon Pertwee felt that the Doctor's fearful expression was out of character. A poster of the Doctor and a Sea Devil was issued in its place.

Although promotional posters were produced to publicize the release of the Doctor Who and the Pescatons record in 1976, for the Crosse & Blackwell baked beans promotion in 1977 and also the range of Target books, the next commercially available examples came from Denis Alan Print in 1979. There were four in all - one of the Doctor (portrait), one of the Doctor with a Dalek (medium shot) and two of the Doctor with K-9 (medium long shot and close-up respectively) - using stills specially taken by the company.

A Doctor Who cover ▲ from TV Action + Countdown, 22 April 1972.

MAGAZINES

The final issue of *TV Comic* to feature the second incarnation of the Doctor in its long-established *Doctor Who* comic strip was number 936. There was then a break of eight weeks before readers encountered the third Doctor in issue number 944. The strip appeared in black and white on two pages of each issue, was drawn by John Canning and written initially by Roger Cook and then later by Alan Fennell. UNIT, Liz and Bessie all featured in the stories as well as the Doctor himself. The strip continued in *TV Comic* until issue 999, when publishers Polystyle switched it to a new magazine called *Countdown*.

Now written by Dennis Hooper and illustrated by Harry Lindfield, the strip was back in colour and firmly in an action-adventure vein. For issue 23 only, it was extended to three pages and moved right to the front of the magazine, where the cover was in colour but the other two pages in black and white. From issue 33, Frank Langford took over the artwork for one seven-part story. After a short relegation to black and white for issues 35 to 39, the strip was back in colour again from issue 40. Harry Lindfield at this point returned as the artist for two issues before handing over to Gerry Haylock, who would continue to provide the artwork until the end of the third Doctor's era.

From issue 59 in April 1972, when *Countdown* was relaunched as *TV Action + Countdown*, the strip went back to the format it had held in issue 23. Then, from issue 101 in January 1973, the magazine was given a second relaunch and the name changed again to *TV Action*, at which point the strip reverted once more to the interior of the magazine with two colour pages per issue. Every so often during this period, each of the magazine's action-orientated strips would be featured as a 'big picture story', in which case it would appear on seven black and white pages and also on the colour cover, following which it would generally be dropped altogether for a few weeks. The issues in which *Doctor Who* was featured as the 'big story' were numbers 104, 112, 120, 123 and 131, and those in which it failed to appear at all were numbers 105, 106, 113—115, 121—122, 124, 130 and 132.

Issue 132 of *TV Action*, in August 1973, was in fact the last to be produced, the magazine having been cancelled due to falling sales. The *Doctor Who* strip subsequently returned to its original home in *TV Comic*. From this issue — number 1133 — the title was temporarily changed to *TV Comic Plus TV Action*, reverting to *TV Comic* from issue 1150 at the end of the year. The strip still consisted of two Gerry Haylock-illustrated pages per issue, but was now in black and white rather than

in colour. The title changed again to *TV Comic Plus Tom and Jerry Weekly* from issue 1182 before reverting once more to *TV Comic* from issue 1202.

In issue 1204, Tom Baker's Doctor made his debut in the strip. The first story for the fourth Doctor was also the last to be illustrated by Gerry Haylock. He was succeeded by Martin Asbury, who provided the artwork for two stories, and then by John Canning.

From issue 1292, in September 1976, *TV Comic* was retitled *Mighty TV Comic* and its format changed to a folded broadsheet printed on pulp paper. The strip continued to be drawn by John Canning, and the stories were written by, amongst others, Geoff Cowan (who had also been the writer of a number of the later *TV Action* strips, as had Dick O'Neill). The last new *Doctor Who* strip appeared in issue 1385. From the following issue, a new policy was introduced of reprinting second and third Doctor stories with the faces and costumes of the Doctor and his companions overdrawn by Canning to convert them into fourth Doctor adventures. The magazine dropped the 'Mighty' from its title from issue 1353, and from issue 1393 was renamed *TV Comic with Target*. It went back to *TV Comic* once more from issue 1401.

The *Doctor Who* strip continued in *TV Comic* until issue 1430 in May 1979, after which it was dropped. *TV Comic* itself continued to run for a further five years before it folded in June 1984 with issue 1697.

Readers had only a short time to wait before *Doctor Who* reappeared in comic form, though, as in October 1979 a new magazine was launched which featured *Doctor Who* in a big way. This was Marvel Comics's **Doctor Who Weekly**, the brainchild of editor and publisher Dez Skinn. Given away free with the first four issues were sets of transfers which could be used on a scene printed on the inside of the debut issue's front cover.

The weekly's contents consisted of a mixture of strip stories and text features. The former were initially handled by artist Dave Gibbons and writer Pat Mills, while the latter were commissioned from *Doctor Who* Appreciation Society historian Jeremy Bentham, who also acted as a consultant to the title. The end of the seventies saw the magazine steadily increasing in popularity.

In addition to its regular weekly appearances, *Doctor Who* also featured in a number of one-off publications during the seventies.

From Polystyle came regular *TV Comic*

Holiday Specials and *TV Comic* Annuals and also, during the period of its run, *Countdown/TV Action* Holiday Specials and Annuals. In addition, they produced several specials devoted entirely to *Doctor Who*. The first, a **Doctor Who Holiday Special**, was published in June 1973 and featured a cover photograph of Jon Pertwee, Katy Manning and Roger Delgado from *Frontier in Space*. It contained several articles and numerous photographs, including a two-page spread of behind-the-scenes shots from *Frontier in Space*, and also some Dalek strip reprints from *TV Century 21*. In June of the following year a second *Doctor Who Holiday Special* appeared, this time with a cover photo of the Doctor standing in the TARDIS doorway from *Invasion of the Dinosaurs*. The format was the same as for the first, but there were slightly fewer photographs. Next came the **Doctor Who Mighty Midget Comic**, given away free with the debut issue of the relaunched *Mighty TV Comic* on 18 September 1976. This contained two strips — *Doomcloud* and a reprint of a *TV Century 21* Dalek story — both of which were modified reprints from the 1974 *Holiday Special*. The final special from Polystyle was a November 1977 **Doctor Who Winter Special** which had a cover shot from *The Talons of Weng-Chiang* and again mixed photographs and stories. Of note here was a text story, *The House of Wax*, which appeared to have been written around the photographs available to illustrate it. These were from *The Masque of Mandragora* and *The Talons of Weng-Chiang*. The strip stories were modified reprints from *TV Action*.

To celebrate the tenth anniversary of *Doctor Who* in 1973, *Radio Times* brought out a special covering the entire history of the series. It featured interviews with, and specially taken photographs of, some of the main cast and brief synopses of all the stories in transmission order, with titles (some inaccurate), brief credits and representative stills. It also included an all-new 'origins of the Daleks' story by Terry Nation and some 'build your own Dalek' instructions. This publication increased the awareness of *Doctor Who* amongst the general public and was, like *The Making of Doctor Who* the year before, a milestone in *Doctor Who* merchandise.

Also produced in the seventies were two fold-out **Poster magazines** devoted to *Doctor Who*. The first, published on 29 May 1975 by Legend Publishing, consisted of a collection of photographs and illustrations and was aimed at the younger end of the *Doctor Who* market. Its print run was around 65,000 and it was to be found on sale for many years after publication. The second, called **Doctor Who — A Special Monster Packed Issue**, was published in April 1976 by Harpdown Publishing Ltd and contained factual articles, photo-

The cover of the *Radio Times* special released to celebrate *Doctor Who*'s tenth anniversary.

graphs and posters. This too remained available for many years.

Doctor Who featured in many general interest magazines throughout the seventies, the popularity of the third and fourth Doctors ensuring a steady stream of interviews and features. Of particular note were the following: **Mad** number 161 carried a *Doctor Who* cover and a spoof, written by Geoff Rowley and illustrated by Steve Parkhouse, of *The Ark in Space*. Issues 124, 126 and 155 of the US magazine **Famous Monsters of Filmland**, published in April 1976, July 1976 and May 1979 respectively, all contained *Doctor Who* articles, the first concerning the film *Dr Who and the Daleks* and the other two looking at the TV series itself. 1976 also saw the launch of a monthly magazine called **TV Sci-Fi Monthly** which contained mainly *Star Trek* material but which touched on *Doctor Who* several times during its eight-issue run. **Screenscene** number 2, published around 1977, featured a photo of K-9 on the cover and more photos from the series inside. **Outer Space** was another title from the same publishers which contained several full-page full-colour photos from *Doctor Who*. **Starforce** was a 1977 magazine which used several photos from *Doctor Who* as a part of an A—Z of British TV sci-fi. Issue one of **Screen On**, a 1979 magazine, printed numerous photographs from *Doctor Who* alongside others from TV series and films such as *Star Trek* and *Battlestar: Galactica*. Other magazines to feature *Doctor Who* on a fairly regular basis were **World of Horror**, which ran for nine issues in 1976/77, and **Starburst**, which was

POSTER POSER

Prior to arranging a special location photographic session with Tom Baker, the TARDIS, a Dalek and K-9 for their posters and greetings cards, Denis Allen Print arranged a studio session with Tom Baker and a Dalek. The Dalek had been built by fan Richard Berelson based on the plans in the Radio Times tenth anniversary Doctor Who special. Richard attended the studio session and was subsequently told that the photographs could not be used due to difficulties with the BBC.

▲ The cover of the first issue of *Doctor Who Weekly*. 17 October 1979.

TARGET COVER ART

The first choice of cover artist for the Target range was Frank Bellamy. He was too busy to take on the job, however, so it went instead to Christos Achilleos, a new talent just out of art school. Achilleos was instructed to produce the covers in Bellamy's style and was happy to do so as he had long admired the artist's work on the **Dan Dare** *strip in* **Eagle** *magazine.*

By the end of 1974, Achilleos was feeling the strain of producing effectively a painting a month. **Radio Times** *artist Peter Brooks was therefore contracted to provide covers for four of the 1975 titles. His style was less realistic than Achilleos's and was reportedly unpopular with readers. Achilleos was therefore enticed back to provide the covers for more than a year's worth of books. When he finally threw in the towel, the commissions were shared out between Jeff Cummins and Mike Little. Later, a number of covers were painted by Roy Knipe and by John Geary. The end of 1979 then saw the Target debut of Andrew Skilleter, an artist whose work was to dominate in the early and mid-eighties.*

The BBC were normally sent proofs of the artwork prior to publication. For the most part these were accepted without comment, but occasionally changes were requested. The only problem on the first batch concerned the depiction of the Zarbi. Achilleos had painted them to look like real ants, but the BBC asked that they be changed to represent those seen on TV. Another example arose in 1975 when Brooks was asked to improve his likeness of Tom Baker on the cover of **Planet of the Spiders**. *In August of that year, producer Philip Hinchcliffe commented that he felt the cover artwork was generally very poor but accepted that there was little he could do about it. He suggested that the publishers contact Frank Bellamy, whom he described as 'the best graphic illustrator in the country'. On doing so, however, Target found that the artist was still too busy to work for them.*

When the proof for **The Web of Fear** *was submitted in January 1976, the BBC questioned its depiction of a Doctor other than the one currently being seen on TV. In response, Target dropped plans to feature the third Doctor on the cover of* **The Space War** *(the*

LISTING OF DOCTOR WHO NOVELIZATIONS 1970-1979

KEY	PUBLISHER
A	Allan Wingate (Publishers) Ltd
B	Universal-Tandem Publishing Co. Ltd
C	Tandem Publishing Ltd
D	Wyndham Publications Ltd
E	W.H. Allen & Co. Ltd

TITLE: Doctor Who and the ...	PUB DATE	PRICE FORMAT (PUB.)
Daleks	05/73	h/b(A)25p p/b(B)
Crusaders	05/73	h/b(A)25p p/b(B)
Zarbi	05/73	h/b(A)25p p/b(B)
Auton Invasion	01/74	£1.75 h/b(A)25p p/b(B)
Cave-Monsters	01/74	£1.75 h/b(A)25p p/b(B)
Day of the Daleks	03/74	h/b(A)30p p/b(B)
Doomsday Weapon	03/74	h/b(A)30p p/b(B)
Dæmons	08/74	h/b(A)30p p/b(B)
Sea-Devils	08/74	h/b(A)30p p/b(B)
Abominable Snowmen	11/74	h/b(A)30p p/b(B)
Curse of Peladon	11/74	h/b(A)30p p/b(B)
Crusaders	../75	£2.25 h/b(White Lion)
Daleks	../75	£1.95 h/b(White Lion)
Zarbi	../75	£2.25 h/b(White Lion)
Cybermen	02/75	h/b(A)35p p/b(B)
Giant Robot	03/75	h/b(A)35p p/b(B)
Terror of the Autons	04/75	h/b(A)35p p/b(B)
Green Death	08/75	h/b(A)35p p/b(C)
Planet of the Spiders	10/75	£2.25 h/b(A)35p p/b(C)
- The Three Doctors	11/75	£2.25 h/b(A)35p p/b(C)
Loch Ness Nonster	01/76	£2.25 h/b(A)40p p/b(C)
Dinosaur Invasion	02/76	£2.25 h/b(A)40p p/b(C)
Tenth Planet	02/76	£2.25 h/b(A)40p p/b(C)
Ice Warriors	03/76	£2.25 h/b(A)40p p/b(C)
Revenge of the Cybermen	05/76	£2.25 h/b(A)40p p/b(C)
Genesis of the Daleks	07/76	£2.25 h/b(A)45p p/b(C)
Web of Fear	08/76	£2.25 h/b(A)45p p/b(D)
Space War	09/76	£2.50 h/b(A)45p p/b(D)
Planet of the Daleks	10/76	£2.50 h/b(A)45p p/b(D)
Pyramids of Mars	12/76	£2.50 h/b(A)45p p/b(D)
Doctor Who Omnibus, The	../77	£4.95 h/b(Book Club Associates)
Carnival of Monsters	01/77	£2.50 h/b(A)50p p/b(C)
Seeds of Doom	02/77	£2.50 h/b(A)50p p/b(C)
Dalek Invasion of Earth	03/77	£2.50 h/b(A)50p p/b(E)
Claws of Axos	04/77	£2.50 h/b(A)50p p/b(D)
Ark In Space	05/77	£2.50 h/b(A)60p p/b(E)
Brain of Morbius	06/77	£2.95 h/b(A)60p p/b(E)
Planet of Evil	08/77	£2.95 h/b(A)60p p/b(E)
Mutants	09/77	£2.95 h/b(A)60p p/b(D)
Deadly Assassin	10/77	£2.95 h/b(A)60p p/b(D)
Talons of Weng-Chiang	11/77	£2.95 h/b(E)60p p/b(E)
Masque of Mandragora	12/77	£2.95 h/b(E)60p p/b(E)
Face of Evil	01/78	£2.95 h/b(E)60p p/b(E)
Horror of Fang Rock	03/78	£2.95 h/b(E)60p p/b(E)
Tomb of the Cybermen	05/78	£2.95 h/b(E)60p p/b(E)
Time Warrior	06/78	£2.95 h/b(E)60p p/b(E)
- Death to the Daleks	07/78	£3.25 h/b(E)60p p/b(E)
Android Invasion	11/78	£3.25 h/b(E)60p p/b(E)
Sontaran Experiment	12/78	£3.25 h/b(E)60p p/b(E)
Hand of Fear	01/79	£3.25 h/b(E)60p p/b(E)
Invisible Enemy	03/79	£3.25 h/b(E)60p p/b(E)
Robots of Death	05/79	£3.50 h/b(E)70p p/b(E)
Image of the Fendahl	07/79	£3.50 h/b(E)70p p/b(E)
War Games	09/79	£3.75 h/b(E)75p p/b(E)
Destiny of the Daleks	11/79	£3.50 h/b(E)75p p/b(E)
Ribos Operation	12/79	£3.75 h/b(E)75p p/b(E)
Junior Doctor Who and the Giant Robot	12/79	£2.50 h/b(E)

NB: *All the hardback editions of the Doctor Who novelizations prior to Planet of the Spiders, with the exception of The Auton Invasion and The Cave-Monsters, were library editions. This means that the books were produced in limited quantities for library sale only, and were not available for the general public to buy.*
The Three Doctors and Death to the Daleks did not have the 'and the' words in the book title.

started in 1978 by Dez Skinn (who later launched Marvel Comics's *Doctor Who Weekly*) and has enjoyed publication on a monthly basis ever since.

NOVELIZATIONS

In 1972, the Universal-Tandem Publishing Company was starting up a new children's imprint called Target and the editor of the range, Richard Henwood, was looking for suitable titles to publish. At a trade fair he came across the three *Doctor Who* novelizations put out by Frederick Muller in the sixties. Enquiries revealed that these titles — *Doctor Who in an exciting adventure with the Daleks* and *Doctor Who and the Crusaders* by David Whitaker and *Doctor Who and the Zarbi* by Bill Strutton — were available for sale, so he negotiated the rights. The books were eventually published under the Target imprint both as hardbacks and as paperbacks in May 1973.

By the time these books appeared, Henwood had already contacted the BBC to discuss publishing further titles. In a letter dated 3 November 1972 he had set out his intentions, requesting: first option to novelize all *Doctor Who* scripts; access to photographs from the stories in question; and permission to re-illustrate the first three William Hartnell titles with likenesses of Jon Pertwee's Doctor. This final idea seems later to have been dropped by Henwood, as by the time the BBC received the cover roughs from the publishers on 10 January 1973, Hartnell's face was shown.

Henwood wanted to publish a further three or six paperbacks, depending in part upon the success of the re-issues. He was put in touch with the *Doctor Who* production office and spoke to script editor Terrance Dicks. Dicks was enthusiastic about the idea — he had previously written to Frederick Muller and suggested the same thing, but had received no reply to his letter — and he offered to write some of the novelizations himself. The intention was to concentrate on stories featuring the then current third Doctor, and the initial schedule of titles was to be *Spearhead from Space* and *Doctor Who and the Silurians* in December 1973, *The Ambassadors of Death* and *Terror of the Autons* in March 1974 and *The Claws of Axos* and *Colony in Space* in May 1974. Dicks had recommended excluding *Inferno* and *The Mind of Evil*. It was thought that once the novelizations were up and running, then previous Doctors' stories could also be covered.

A contract was drawn up between the Universal-Tandem Book Publishing Company and the BBC allowing them to publish paperbacks with separate provision for hardbacks. After much negotiation, a royalty of two-and-a-half per cent of the cover price was agreed to be paid to the BBC for each copy sold.

In the event, the enormous success of the first three titles took everyone by surprise, the crowning glory being the appearance of *Doctor Who and the Daleks* at sixth place in W.H. Smith's top ten books in July 1973.

The final, revised, choice of stories for the initial tranche of new novelizations was *Spearhead From Space* (novelized as *The Auton Invasion*), *Doctor Who and the Silurians* (*The Cave Monsters*), *Day of the Daleks*, *Colony in Space* (*The Doomsday Weapon*), *The Dæmons* and *The Sea Devils*. These had all been commissioned by July 1973 for publication at the rate of one every two months starting in January 1974. Henwood contracted Terrance Dicks to handle Robert Holmes's *Spearhead from Space* and Louis Marks's *Day of the Daleks*, and Malcolm Hulke and Barry Letts to novelize their own stories.

A newsprint shortage at the end of 1973 caused a slight revision of the schedule, and *The Auton Invasion* and *The Cave Monsters* were eventually published together in February 1974. Richard Henwood left Target in May of that year, by which time he had already commissioned a second batch of *Doctor Who* books. His successor as editor was Michael Glover who, recognizing the strength of the range, made plans to release even more. The newsprint shortage meanwhile continued to throw the schedule into disarray. *Day of the Daleks* and *The Doomsday Weapon* eventually appeared in June 1974, and *The Dæmons* and *The Sea Devils* followed later in the summer. Things finally got back on course with the publication in November 1974 of *The Curse of Peladon* and *The Abominable Snowmen*, the first two titles in the second batch of commissions.

These eight new titles had, by spring 1975, collectively sold 154,917 copies worldwide, and the Target range was seen to be well established. It had indeed made such an impact that a publisher called White Lion, which had taken over Frederick Muller, re-issued the original sixties novelizations in hardback, using likenesses of the fourth Doctor on the jackets.

When the Target range first started, a Target Book Club was set up and run by the publishers to deal with enquiries. It was administered by Sandy Lessiter, who handled questions from readers and also mailed out advance schedules of books. The Club was eventually closed down during 1977.

Universal-Tandem had during this period been

A selection of Target books published in the seventies.

novelization of **Frontier in Space**). When Jon Pertwee's likeness was subsequently used on the cover of **The Claws of Axos**, the BBC again raised questions. This may have led to the dropping, around late 1976 or early 1977, of proposed covers for **The Tomb of the Cybermen**, which depicted

the second Doctor, and **The Mutants**, which depicted the third, and their late replacement with new paintings which featured no image of the Doctor. In the case of **The Mutants**, another factor may have been that the photographic reference used for the original painting had already been used once before, for the cover of **The Sea Devils**.

▲ Peter Brooks's original rough for the cover of **The Green Death**. Note the inclusion of the Doctor's face in the 'o' of 'Who', an idea which was ultimately only used for the release of **The Giant Robot**. Below: The final cover for **The Green Death**.

OVERSEAS EDITIONS

During the seventies, a number of the Target books were picked up by publishers outside the UK and issued in foreign language editions.

The first of these appeared in 1974 in Holland. Translated into Dutch by JJ vd Hulst-Brander and published by Unieboek B.V. Bussum, the titles available were: **Doctor Who en de Holen-Monsters** *(The Cave Monsters);* **Doctor Who en de Daleks** *(The Daleks);* **Doctor Who en de Kruisvaarders** *(The Crusaders);* **Doctor Who en de Zarbis** *(The Zarbi);* **Doctor Who en de Demonen** *(The Dæmons);* **Doctor Who en de dag van de Daleks** *(Day of the Daleks);* **Doctor Who en de invasie van de Autonen** *(The Auton Invasion); and* **Doctor Who en het dodelijke wapen** *(The Doomsday Weapon).*

In 1975, publishers Global Editora released in Brazil a Spanish translation by Márcio Pugliesi and Norberto de Paula Lima of Day of the Daleks entitled **Doutor Who e a Mudança da História**. *Unlike the Dutch books, which had reused the Target artwork in adapted form, this boasted a new cover painting by an artist named Darlon, albeit based very much on Chris Achilleos's work.*

Also in 1975, a number of the books were issued in Turkey by publishers Remzi Kitabevi, with translations by Reha Pinar. In these, **Doktor Kim** *found himself up against:* **ve Daleker** *(The Daleks);* **ve Korkunç Karadamlari** *(The Abominable Snowmen);* **ve Sibermenler** *(The Cybermen);* **ve Otonlar** *(The Auton Invasion);* **ve Dalek Baskini** *(Day of the Daleks);* **ve Peledon Gezegeni** *(The Curse of Peladon); and* **ve Gizli Silah** *(The Doomsday Weapon).*

Finally, in 1979, several titles were bought by Pinnacle Books in America. These were given impressive new covers by David Mann and contained an introduction by science fiction author Harlan Ellison. The text was in English, but had been slightly revised to replace English terms with equivalent or similar American ones. The titles released to the end of 1979 were: **Day of the Daleks** *(April 1979);* **The Doomsday Weapon** *(April);* **The Dinosaur Invasion** *(May);* **Genesis of the Daleks** *(May);* **The Revenge of the Cybermen** *(June);* **The Loch Ness Monster** *(June);* **The Talons of Weng-Chiang** *(September) and* **The Masque of Mandragora** *(November).*

renamed Tandem Publishing Ltd and been taken over first, in mid-1975, by Allan Wingate (Publishers) Ltd and then, in November 1976, by W.H. Allen & Co Ltd, who had been distributing the Target range since February 1976. Michael Glover had meanwhile been succeeded as editor by Elizabeth Godfrey, who had started out as Richard Henwood's secretary. Godfrey oversaw the books from January 1975 until she left Target in January 1977. No replacement was then appointed until May 1978, when Brenda Gardner took over, but as an interim measure Fanny Torrance, Managing Editor of W.H. Allen, looked after the range.

1977 saw publication of the first known Book Club Associates edition of a *Doctor Who* title. This special hardback was called **The Doctor Who Omnibus** and had a print run of 10,000 copies. The novelizations featured were Terrance Dicks's *The Web of Fear* and *Revenge of the Cybermen* and Malcolm Hulke's *The Space War*.

During 1978, Time Life Films of America approached W.H. Allen with an offer to handle distribution of the *Doctor Who* novelizations in that country. This was agreed, and a suitable package of books was arranged. As part of the deal, Time Life were given Chris Achilleos's original artwork for *The Doctor Who Monster Book* to use for promotional purposes, and it ended up appearing on posters, TV guides and all manner of other brochures and literature. Achilleos was less than pleased about this as his permission had not been sought and he had received no payment for the use of his artwork in this way. When he asked for it to be returned, Time Life replied that it had been mislaid.

The novelizations continued to be published on a regular basis, a total of eight new titles appearing in 1974, six in 1975, ten in 1976, eleven in 1977, seven in 1978 and seven in 1979. There were a few more glitches in the schedule during this period: July 1977 was the original publication date for Gerry Davis's *The Tomb of the Cybermen*, but the manuscript was delayed and the book was eventually published in May 1978; and March 1978 was the date planned for publication of Terrance Dicks's novelization of his forthcoming TV story *The Witch Lords*, which ultimately fell through and was replaced — both on TV and in the Target book schedule — by *Horror of Fang Rock*.

During 1978, with the *Doctor Who* range continuing to do well, W.H. Allen decided to release some versions of the novelizations adapted for younger readers. The first title to be chosen for this new 'Junior *Doctor Who*' range was *The Brain of Morbius*, written by Terrance Dicks. The tentative publication date of July 1978 was swiftly changed to April 1979 and a second title, *The Gi-*

ant Robot, was announced. This latter book ran into problems when producer Graham Williams commented that the likeness of Tom Baker in the internal illustrations was very poor. At the start of 1979, the publication date for both titles was moved again, this time to December of that year. By July, the publication of *The Brain of Morbius* had been put back yet again, to 1980. *The Giant Robot* was finally released in hardback in December 1979, although readers had to wait until the following year before the paperback edition came out.

As the Target range progressed, so pressure increased to link the publication dates of selected titles to the television transmission of the stories themselves. The first story for which this was attempted was *Destiny of the Daleks*, the book's publication being planned for November 1979, just two months after the story would finish on television. When sent a proof of the cover artwork, Graham Williams commented that it wasn't very 'individual' and that as the story hadn't actually been made at that time, it was tricky to provide any photographic reference for it.

As a final note for the seventies, Brenda Gardner was informed by the BBC in August 1979, following publication of the Dalek and K-9 specials, that although the television programme was called *Doctor Who*, this was not the name of the lead character, and that he should always be referred to as 'the Doctor'.

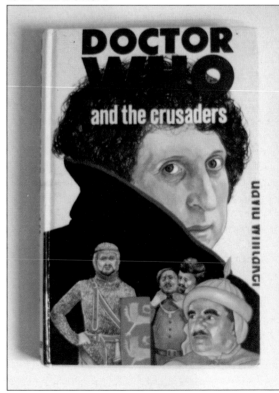

The cover of the White Lion hardback release of *The Crusaders*. Note the use of the fourth Doctor on the cover rather than the first.

PROMOTIONS

October 1971 saw *Doctor Who* arrive on the breakfast table in a promotion for Kellogg's **Sugar Smacks** cereal. An artwork likeness of Jon Pertwee was used on the packaging for a limited period, and a small metal badge was given away free inside each box (except the smaller 'variety' boxes which had the picture of Jon Pertwee but no badge). There were six different badges to collect, featuring artwork depictions of: the Doctor, Bessie, Jo Grant, the Brigadier, the Master and a UNIT symbol. The boxes featured information panels about the characters depicted, but gave no clue as to which of the six badges was actually inside. Kellogg's continued to use Pertwee's likeness on the packaging for a short time after the badge promotion had finished.

April 1975 then saw *Doctor Who* used in a promotion by **Weetabix**. Until the end of May, each special **Doctor Who And His Enemies** promotional pack contained four stand-up figures from a set of 24. The figures were very accurate artwork representations of characters from the series, and the set consisted of: Dalek (six different), the Doctor (two different), Sarah, Slaar (called Saarl on the box and card), Sea Devil, Silurian, Quark, Alpha Centauri, Cyberman, Ice Warrior, Ogron, Linx (described as Lynx the Time Warrior), Axon Monster, Giant Robot, Yeti, Draconian, White Robot and Aggedor of Peladon. To complement the figures, there was usually one of a set of six cut-out 'action settings' (including a TARDIS interior) on the back of the box. Some boxes had, instead, a cut-out TARDIS model.

In July 1976 **Ty-Phoo Tea** gave away octagonal photographic cards with every box of their tea bags. There was one card in a 36-pack, two in a 72-pack and four in a 144-pack. The company also offered, by mail order, a poster on which the cards could be stuck and an accompanying book, **The Amazing World of Doctor Who**. 15,000 copies of the latter were produced for the Sales Promotion Triangle by World Distributors. It cost £1 and featured reprinted comic strips primarily from the 1976 *Doctor Who* annual and *TV Century 21*, together with black and white and colour photofeatures on the series and its more popular monsters. The poster featured the same Chris Achilleos artwork as the book cover. It was sent free with the book or cost 20 pence if ordered separately. There were 12 cards in the set: the Doctor (publicity shot with Daleks in BBC car park on 24 February 1975), Sarah (*Pyramids of Mars*), the TARDIS (*The Seeds of Doom*), Alpha Centauri (*The Monster of Peladon*), Davros, Sea Devil, Dalek (*Death to the Daleks*), Giant Robot, Zygon, Krynoid, Ice Warrior (exhibition shot) and Cyberman (*Revenge of*

Chris Achilleos's original artwork for the Ty-Phoo tea promotional poster and book.

the Cybermen).

Weetabix ran another *Doctor Who* promotion in 1977. This time each pack of the serial contained a set of three artwork cards which could be used as playing pieces for a board game printed on the back of the box. There were six different sets of cards to collect, depicting: Bellal, Daleks, Davros (Set 1); Vega Nexos, Aggedor, Blor (Set 2); Daleks, Gellguards, Omega (Set 3); Zygons, Krynoid, Wirrn (Set 4); Vogans, Cybermen, Styggron (Set 5); and TARDIS, Field Major Styre, Hieronymous (Set 6). The cards also featured

▲ A small 'variety' type Sugar Smacks box.

The components of the ▲ Ty-Phoo *Doctor Who* promotion. Top to bottom: book, packaging and cards.

A newspaper ▼ advertisement promoting Jon Pertwee's record.

WHO IS THE DOCTOR
Jon Pertwee
PUR III

Jon Pertwee and the theme music of "Dr. Who" known to millions of viewers. Arrangement, production and special lyrics

messages in code, the cipher for which was printed on the inside of every box. The sets could be paired up to form continuous pictures as follows: Sets 3 and 2; Sets 6 and 1; and Sets 5 and 4. There were four different board-games: 'Travel through Time', 'Race through Space', 'Escape from the Underworld' and 'Discover the Lost Planet'. All four could be found on the 24-piece 'family size' boxes, but only the first two were available on the smaller 'standard size' 12-piece boxes.

RECORDS

The first *Doctor Who*-related record of the seventies was by the Doctor himself. Jon Pertwee released a single called '**Who Is The Doctor?**', released on 10 November 1972 to try to catch the Christmas market. Produced and arranged by Rupert Hines and written by David MacIver, it was a re-working of Ron Grainer's *Doctor Who* theme, but with lyrics sung by Pertwee. The song included lines like: 'I cross the void beyond the mind/The empty space that circles time/I see where others stumble blind/To seek a truth they'll never find/Eternal wisdom is my guide/I am the Doctor'. The 'B'-side, a song called 'Pure Mystery', was unrelated to *Doctor Who*.

1973 saw two further versions of the **Doctor Who theme** being released. One was a single by Homo Electronicus, a group led by jazz musician Don Harper who had composed the incidental music for the 1968 TV story *The Invasion*. The other was a BBC Records single release of the original Delia Derbyshire arrangement of the series' title music. There appear to have been five versions of this latter record: the first, dated 1973, had a picture sleeve showing the TARDIS against a 'spirograph'-type line design background and a record label bearing BBC Records's standard half-blue, half-white design; the second, also dated 1973, had a silver record label; the third, undated and apparently without a picture sleeve, was distributed by Pye for BBC Records and Tapes; the fourth was a 1976 re-issue; and the fifth was a 1978 re-issue which featured, in limited numbers, a picture sleeve with the same image of the TARDIS in the vortex as appeared on the cover of the '*Doctor Who* Sound Effects' LP (see below), but printed in blue and white rather than in full colour. The third and fourth of these versions may actually be the same item. In all cases, the 'B'-side was an instrumental track called 'Reg', which had nothing to do with *Doctor Who*.

Also in 1973, the BBC released a single of Dudley Simpson's theme for the series *Moonbase 3*, on the 'B'-side of which could be found some of the composer's incidental music from *Doctor Who*

under the title '**The World of Doctor Who**'. The 2' 40" track started with some music and effects from *Planet of the Daleks*, segued neatly into the Master's theme and ended with the Keller Machine attack music from *The Mind of Evil*.

The *Doctor Who* theme turned up again on a compilation album called '**Dr. Who and Space Adventures**' released by Damont records in 1975.

The next release of note came in 1976, when Argo Records commissioned writer Victor Pemberton (who had briefly story edited *Doctor Who* in 1967 and written the TV story *Fury from the Deep* that same year) to script a new adventure for the Doctor. With Tom Baker and Elisabeth Sladen contracted to star, the '**Doctor Who and the Pescatons**' album was born.

In 1977, a punk band called the Art Attacks released a single called '**I am a Dalek**', about which no further details are known.

1978 saw the release of an album of **Doctor Who sound effects**. It was Number 19 in the BBC's series of sound effects records and was produced and prepared by Dick Mills and Brian Hodgson at the BBC Radiophonic Workshop. The selection covered several stories between *Death to the Daleks* (1974) and *The Invasion of Time* (1978) and many tracks were listed under their working titles rather than their transmission titles.

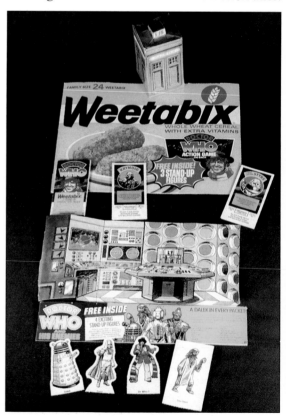

Weetabix featured *Doctor Who* twice in the seventies.

A selection of seventies *Doctor Who* singles.

An adaptation of a TV story followed in 1979 with the release of '**Genesis of the Daleks**'. This was a part-narrated (by Tom Baker), part-soundtrack album telling the general story that was seen on TV.

Doctor Who went disco in 1978 with a version of the theme by Mankind which reached number 25 in the pop charts before dropping rapidly out of sight. Released in both 12" and 7" formats, '**Doctor Who (Disco)**' was arranged by Mark Stevens and Don Gallacher and produced by Don Gallacher, and the **sheet music** was available from Chappell & Co. The 12" single was first released on the Motor label in blue vinyl, but Pinnacle records then bought out Motor and a sticker was placed over the label on some shipments until proper Pinnacle labels could be applied. Shortly after the blue vinyl copies had been released, the record was issued in several other colours as well. Of the 7" single there were only Pinnacle copies in evidence, but with two different labels; both showed four alpine peaks with the sun behind them, but the first was printed black-on-silver and the second in full colour.

There were several other record releases during the seventies which contained *Doctor Who*-related material. The following are perhaps of most interest.

The album 'BBC Radiophonic Music' (1971 BBC REC 25M) included Delia Derbyshire's 'The Delian Mode', which was used as incidental music in *Inferno*.

'Sounds from ... EMS' (1972 Electronic Music Studios (London) Ltd) was a very rare release issued to publicize EMS music equipment and included two tracks of Dudley Simpson's incidental music from *Doctor Who*, as realized by Brian Hodgson of the BBC's Radiophonic Workshop. 'The Axons Approach' was from *The Claws of Axos* and 'Dover Castle' was from *The Mind of Evil*. These two tracks appeared both on a tape and on a

Four 12" *Doctor Who* records were released.

shorter promotional flexidisc version of the release.

Finally, 'BBC Radiophonic Workshop 21' (1979 BBC REC 354) was an album including the original *Doctor Who* theme, the TARDIS dematerialization sound effect and some of Dudley Simpson's original music from *The Mind of Evil*.

STATIONERY

The ***Doctor Who* Space Mission Pad** was initially brought out in 1973 with the third Doctor's face on the cover and internal sheets and then reissued in 1974 with the fourth Doctor's image substituted. This was the first piece of merchandise to feature Tom Baker's Doctor, being produced several months in advance of his TV debut in *Robot*. The paper in the pads was specially treated so that a pen pressed on the top sheet would leave a copy on the lower one. The pad also included a code sheet, the idea being that the user could send coded messages to friends whilst retaining a copy. The pads were issued by John Morriss to support the Save the Children Fund. The third Doctor version was published by Naocroft Ltd and the fourth Doctor version by Morriss under his own name. Only 5,000 units were produced.

From about 1976, there were numerous BBC pens and pencils produced for sale in the newly opened BBC *Doctor Who* exhibitions at Blackpool and Longleat.

In 1978, Thomas Salter released a **Poster Art Kit**. This contained two 22-inch by 14½-inch posters and five felt-tip pens (yellow, brown, red, green and blue) with which to colour them in. The posters consisted of simple line artwork of the fourth

I wandered lonely as The Central Control Room in Exillon City that floats on The Mandragora Helix o'er fields and Metebelis III Atmosphere.

When all at once I saw a Kraal Disorientation Chamber A host of Dalek Hatching Tanks on Skaros.

Featuring the delights of a selection of aural locations from the Time Lord's travels, this album proves a must for Zygons, Daleks and Sisterhood of Karn. Boasts of such recordings as 'Tardis Interior (in flight)' and 'Tardis Interior (stationery)' as well as the much sought-after effects of 'Tardis Door Opens', this must surely be the most diverse album of the century.

Labels such as 'power-pop' and 'punk' fail miserably in attempting to describe the emotions and feelings behind the Doctor's journeys. The dreaded reverberations of 'The Cloning and Miniaturisation Process' bring to light the profundity and sensitivity behind the objet d'art. The intense weirdness of this album subjectifies what we must all know to be the future of music as-we-know it.

Doctor Who rools OK.
Review of Doctor Who Sound Effects album by Bev Briggs in Record Mirror.

MOVEMENTS

Mankind entered the UK record charts in 1978. Their first week in the top 40 was at no. 34 (moving in from no. 45). The next week they moved up to no. 27. On the third and fourth weeks they were at no. 25 and on the fifth week they dropped back to no. 35 before vanishing out of the 40.

This was the only Doctor Who-related record to enter the top 40 during the sixties and seventies.

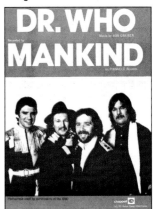

The third Doctor ▲ version of the Space Mission Pad.

The HCF *Doctor Who* ▲ pencil sharpeners were packaged in an attractive box.

Daleks still featured on ▲ some *Doctor Who* merchandise in the seventies like this transfer from Dodo Iron-Ons.

Doctor and the Daleks.

Also available, from Tangent Systems Ltd, was a *Doctor Who* **Data Printer**. This was a basic hand-operated Dymo labelling machine with a diamond *Doctor Who* logo mounted on the alphabet wheel. The machine came packaged on a card together with several strips of Dymo tape and a free *Doctor Who* badge. The production run of these label makers was 40,000 units.

The following year, Denis Alan Print, a company which was to specialize in mail-order *Doctor Who* merchandise, released a set of *Doctor Who* **Greetings Cards**. These cost 36 pence each or £5 for a set. There were two 'get well soon' cards, four cards without a message, three 'happy birthday' cards and a set of nine numbered birthday cards (ages two to ten). All featured photographs of Tom Baker's Doctor taken specially for the purpose.

Also in 1979, H.C. Ford (who traded as HCF) released four **Pencil Sharpeners**. These were of the same design as the Mini-Puzzles previously issued by the company in 1974 (see below), the only difference being that in this case the puzzles were mounted onto pencil-sharpener bases.

TOYS

The earliest *Doctor Who* toy to be released in the seventies was an **iron-on transfer** featuring the image of a Dalek. This was produced by Dodo Iron-Ons in 1971 and cost a mere 50 pence.

In 1974, Louis Marx, who had produced many Dalek toys in the sixties, released an upgraded version of their **battery-operated Dalek** in two colours (yellow and red).

Also in 1974, H.C. Ford brought out four **Doctor Who Mini-Puzzles**. These were circular in shape and the puzzle involved rolling a number of ball-bearings into indented holes on an artwork background.

The same year, Airfix released six **Doctor Who Painting By Numbers** sets, which were amongst the earliest items to depict Tom Baker as the Doctor. Each contained two pictures to colour and the titles were as follows: *Dalek Invasion, Dr Who and his Car, Dr Who and the Snake-Birds, Dr Who and the Sea Monsters, Dr Who and the Robots, The Daleks and the Octomen*. Airfix also got their knuckles rapped by the BBC over the unlicensed use of a Dalek in one of their 'Luminart' sets, but further details of this product are unknown.

A board-game called simply **Doctor Who** was

***Doctor Who* stationery.**

produced in 1975 by Denys Fisher in their Strawberry Fayre range. The box front bore a silhouette of the Doctor and the TARDIS against a blue vortex, and inside were a board, 56 cards, four coloured 'Doctor' counters and a TARDIS die shaker. The object of the game was to get around the board, avoiding monsters along the way. Presumably the game did not sell too well as the manufacturers later added a full colour photographic sticker of Tom Baker to the box front to make it more eye-catching.

The next game also came from Denys Fisher in 1975 but this time returned to the more familiar territory of the Daleks. **War of the Daleks** contained eight plastic Daleks (four gold, four silver), a

Denys Fisher's *Doctor Who* game and one of Airfix's Painting by Numbers kits.

Some pocket-money toys released in the seventies.

dynamic board and four player counters. This time the object was to get to the centre of the board (Dalek Control) and destroy the Emperor Dalek, avoiding the patrolling plastic Daleks along the way.

Denys Fisher's Doctor, Leela and K-9 figures.

Berwicks Toys' *Doctor Who* dressing up costume.

The same year, Palitoy Bradgate released a **talking Dalek** in two colours: red and silver. By pushing a button located at the top of the dome, the Dalek could be made to utter one of a number of pre-recorded messages such as 'I will obey' and 'Exterminate! Exterminate!'

Another **Dalek transfer** was issued in 1975, this time by Imagine Transfers Ltd.

Also in 1975, Louis Marx brought out a '*Doctor Who* and the Daleks' version of their popular **Yo-Yo**.

In 1976, after initially considering producing a range of plastic snap-together figures, Denys Fisher released a set of '**action dolls**' based on *Doctor Who*. The dolls available were the Doctor, Leela, a Dalek, a Cyberman, and the Giant Robot. The same company also released a TARDIS model scaled to match the figures. Although the figures were popular, the one of the Doctor was criticized as bearing more similarity to Gareth Hunt from *The New Avengers* than to Tom Baker. The explanation for this was that the head *was* of Gareth Hunt from *The New Avengers!* Between the prototypes being produced and the company being given the go-ahead by the BBC, the die for the Tom Baker head had been lost or damaged.

▲ **Imagine Products' iron-on transfer also featured a Dalek.**

▲ **Playtime's *Doctor Who* bagatelle.**

◀ **Denys Fisher's Giant Robot, TARDIS, Dalek and Cyberman figures.**

The War of the Daleks ▲
game.

Palitoy's talking K-9. ▲

Rather than go to the expense of creating a new one, the company made do with what they had, namely Gareth Hunt. The models were all made in Italy, and versions exist with Italian text on the packaging.

Also in 1976, the Letraset company issued a **Dalek Invasion of Earth** set in their Action Transfers range. Having nothing to do with the TV story of the same name, the transfers showed the fourth Doctor and Sarah battling numerous Daleks with the assistance of army troops. This item was still doing well by 1978, with over 8,000 units sold in January and February of that year alone.

Another toy produced in 1976 was the **Doctor Who Dressing Up Costume** from Berwicks Toys Ltd. This strange creation consisted of a small plastic tunic, on which was printed a jacket and a scarf, and a plastic Tom Baker mask. It was discontinued in September 1977, at which point only 309 had been sold.

1978 saw another increase in the number of *Doctor Who* toys produced. There were two different bagatelles: **Doctor Who Aim 'n' Shoot Bagatelle Game** from Jotastar and the **Doctor Who Bagatelle** from Playtime. Jotastar also brought out the **Doctor Who Trump Card Game**, which was notable for featuring many old monsters from the TV series, as well as for mixing up the captions for the Sea Devils and the Ogrons. The **TARDIS Tuner**, from Shortman Trading, was little more than a radio. It cost £19.95 and was on sale for many years after its initial release. Also in 1978, two different K-9 toys were released. There was a battery operated **talking K-9** from Palitoy Bradgate and a smaller **friction-action K-9** from Denys

Palitoy's talking Dalek in silver and red, and Louis Marx's friction action model in yellow and red.

Fisher.

The final toy of the seventies was a **Doctor Who 3-D Clay Picture Kit** released by Remus Playkits Ltd in their series of cheap children's products. The idea of the kit was to fill a plastic mould with different coloured plasticine to create a '3-D' scene which could then be mounted against a coloured back-board to make a picture. This product did extremely well, with over 18,000 units sold.

SUNDRIES

This section describes all those items which cannot be easily placed in any other category.

The BBC had for many years been producing small black and white photographic cards of the stars of their most popular programmes, to be used for autograph purposes or sent out free to fans who wrote in. *Doctor Who* was no exception, and cards were issued for all the Doctors and companions up to and including the first incarnation of Romana (Mary Tamm). After that, colour **postcards** were issued. These were also available for sale from the increasing number of BBC shops.

'All Stars' was the name of a brand of crisps released during the mid to late seventies, and each packet contained a small photo-card featuring a different television personality. Number 20 in the series of 24 was 'Tom Baker' and the card featured a photograph taken during a publicity session for *The Hand of Fear*.

Badges started to gain in popularity during the seventies, and the earliest *Doctor Who* examples were those offered by Sugar Smacks as a part of their 1971 promotion. There was also a BBC TV

A selection of sundry *Doctor Who* items. Shown are promotional postcards, badges, necklaces and rings.

'TARDIS Commander' badge, depicting the TARDIS against concentric blue circles on a white background. The style of the artwork and BBC TV logo on this suggest that it may actually have been produced in the late sixties, but the date is unknown. In 1972, a different 'TARDIS Commander' badge was put out to commemorate the BBC Visual Effects Exhibition mounted at London's Science Museum. In 1973, the BBC released a badge of the new diamond-shaped *Doctor Who* logo, which was printed in orange against a blue background. In 1975, they then produced two further *Doctor Who* logo badges — one red against white, the other blue against white — which each came in two different diameters, 1¼ inch and 1¾ inch. In 1976, the bookshop John Menzies ran a *Doctor Who* Monster painting competition and all entrants received a special badge, sent in an envelope printed with a graphic of the Doctor.

There were two sets of *Doctor Who* jewellery produced during the seventies. In 1974, A.P. Services & Co brought out **medallions** and **30 inch chains** in gold, silver, copper and satin finishes. Then, five years later, S. Weiner Ltd marketed a set consisting of Dalek and K-9 versions of a **brooch**, a **pendant** and a **ring**.

The two BBC Exhibitions, which stocked almost all the available *Doctor Who* merchandise, also sold some specially-produced items of their own. No complete list is available, but it is known that in 1976 a **car sticker** was available, as was a **leather key-fob**.

A **pottery TARDIS** was issued by Melwood in 1978, and several similar products were manufactured by unknown companies without a BBC licence.

Various items of printed ephemera were produced during the seventies. The 1974 stage play *Doctor Who and the Daleks in Seven Keys to Doomsday* spawned a programme and fliers (and presumably also a poster, although no examples are known to exist). Lastly, the popular BBC children's programme *Blue Peter* gave away a free **Doctor Who Theatre Leaflet** in April 1977.

In 1976, a company called The Water Margin released a **Dalek Bubble Bath**. This came in a box, and the soap was contained within a black moulded Dalek with a bright yellow dome and removable arm section. Following the success of this item — which sold over 26,000 units — The Water Margin, also known as Pewter Toiletries, put forward in 1978 the idea of a Dalek Soap, but this did not get the go-ahead from the BBC. The company also suggested a K-9 Bubble Bath, a K-9 Soap and even a Dalek Fly Exterminator (which was

▲ The Dalek bubble bath from The Water Margin and Melwood's pottery TARDIS.

vetoed by producer Graham Williams), but it went bankrupt in 1981 and ceased trading in 1982.

MISCELLANEOUS

During the seventies, far more so than during the sixties, there were numerous *Doctor Who*-related products which were proposed to the BBC but — often for reasons unknown — failed to reach fruition.

The earliest example arose when, in 1969, Louis Marx sought permission to release in 1970 a version of the Doctor's car, Bessie. The Meccano Triang company also requested the rights to produce a die-cast model of the car in 1970.

A Dalek poster was suggested in 1971.

In 1972, Transflair suggested iron-on transfers, DM Industries wanted to market a Dalek play-suit and both Jonbi and Withers proposed T-shirts. Withers were also interested in producing tank-tops.

An internal BBC list from 1976 giving details of potential licenses includes such things as mugs, plastic moulds, a bubble blow tray, a plastic Dalek money box, egg cups and PVC carrier bags, none of which ever seems to have seen the light of day.

The products suggested by The Water Margin in the late seventies are detailed in the Sundries

▲ The six badges given away free with packs of Sugar Smacks.

The TARDIS Tuner from Shortman Trading.

A piece of artwork based on *Pyramids of Mars* completed by Jeff Cummins for the aborted *Doctor Who* calendar in 1977.

AUSTRALIAN MERCHANDISE

*Although the bulk of seventies merchandise was originated in the UK, there were a couple of items of note released in Australia only. The first was the **Doctor Who** showbag which was released for the Australian Royal Melbourne Show in 1978. For $1 the buyer received a plastic printed bag which contained a make-it-yourself cardboard TARDIS, **Doctor Who** invisible ink, a **Doctor Who** badge, a **Doctor Who** game (based on the 'Escape From the Underworld' board game on the back of the 1977 Weetabix promotional boxes) and a **Doctor Who** jigsaw puzzle. The other item was a **Doctor Who** writing set which was printed in Australia by Ian Nicoll Enterprise and contained ten envelopes and twenty letter heads with colour pictures of the Doctor printed on them. It is believed that this item was released in 1979.*

section above.

A firm called Osman wanted to market a *Doctor Who* towel. This was agreed by the BBC, but the item appears not to have been produced.

The publishers of the *Doctor Who* novelizations suggested a *Doctor Who* calendar in 1977, with artwork by Jeff Cummins, Chris Achilleos and possibly others. They proposed a print run of 75,000 and a price of less than £1 per unit. The idea was subsequently dropped, even though the BBC were in favour of it.

Another item which would no doubt have been very popular was described as a Videomaster K-9. This would have been a remote-control version of the dog, operated by voice command rather than by a hand-held box. A change of management at the company suggesting the item prevented it from going ahead.

A similar fate befell some proposed *Doctor Who* watches in 1978, as the company concerned pulled out at the last moment.

Other items which got no further than the drawing board included: from Printstyle Ltd, a range of stationery consisting of note paper, pads, envelopes, calendars, greetings cards and posters; an *Enemies of Doctor Who* annual; and even a Tom Baker ice-pop.

Some products which did see the light of day but without BBC authorization were: the unlicensed pottery police boxes mentioned in the Sundries section above; a **Doctor Who-Style Slipover and Scarf Knitting Pattern** released by Mayfield Knitting Wools in 1976; a number of items, including badges and pens, made available by the *Doctor Who* Fan Club, the *Doctor Who* International Fan Club and the *Doctor Who* Appreciation Society; and numerous fanzines.

Lastly, **Jon Pertwee's Book of Monsters** was an anthology of children's fiction published in hardback in 1978 and in paperback in 1979. Although not a *Doctor Who* item as such, the book was promoted partly on the basis of Pertwee's popularity as the Doctor.

Denys Fisher's Giant Robot figure.

CHAPTER TWENTY ONE

Fandom Grows Up

By 1970, the *Doctor Who* Fan Club had been in existence for some five years. Its latest Secretary, Graham Tattersall, ran it single-handedly, producing a regular newsletter and occasional issues of a more substantial duplicated magazine entitled simply *Doctor Who*.

'The magazine was printed on an old Roneo duplicator at the office where I worked at the time, although I had to pay a considerable sum for the ink and paper. It was the cost of producing the magazine which caused me to abandon it after two or three issues.

'In the end I found the whole project of running the Club not only expensive but also very time-consuming. My job was taking up much of my spare time and I had no option but to give up the Club.'

In late 1971, a fourteen-year-old Edinburgh-based fan called Keith Miller wrote to the BBC to ask if there was a club devoted to *Doctor Who*. The production office sent him Tattersall's address. After two fruitless attempts to contact Tattersall, he wrote again to the BBC. They then contacted Tattersall themselves and he finally replied to Miller, explaining that he was no longer interested in running the Club. On learning this, Miller asked Barry Letts's production secretary, Sarah Newman, if he could take over. Not realizing how young he was, Newman agreed and arranged for a box of miscellaneous items, including the addresses of approximately forty of Tattersall's members, to be sent to him.

The new Club under Miller's leadership was officially founded on 30 December 1971 — the date when Newman wrote to Miller giving him the go-ahead to take over from Tattersall. Initially the only service it provided was a monthly A5 newsletter. This was a cheap affair printed by the silk-screen method — Miller himself later recalled that it was 'grotty' and looked as if it had been printed 'with tomato ketchup' — but in its favour was the fact that

it was sent out entirely free of charge to the Club's members. These early issues of the *Doctor Who Fan Club Monthly* were printed by Miller himself on equipment at the school he attended. As the Club's membership grew, however, he quickly realized that this was becoming impracticable. He discussed this with Sarah Newman, with whom he was now in regular contact by phone, and they agreed upon a new procedure for producing the newsletter. In future, Miller would type each issue on Roneo stencils and take these to the BBC's offices in Edinburgh, from where they would be sent down to the production office through the internal mail system. Newman would then run off all the required copies on a duplicator and send them out to the Club's members at the BBC's own expense.

From Issue 15 in April 1973, the newsletter — now bearing the title *DWFC Mag* — went bi-monthly, although with an increased page-count. As time went by, its contents became more and more interesting. Apart from the usual reviews, quizzes and so on, it featured short interviews with the stars of the series, news of commercial *Doctor Who* products and teasers for up-coming stories. There were also articles describing the early sixties stories, based on synopses supplied to Miller by the BBC. Miller even persuaded the production office to allow him to visit the Television Centre studios to see the series in the making. On his first such visit, he was accompanied by his mother:

'My mum recognized Barry Letts from his days as an actor. She told him all the old programmes she remembered seeing him in. He was very flattered, as few people remembered him as an actor. So my mum and Barry Letts left me on my own in the producer's gallery whilst they discussed the good old days.'

Jon Pertwee, although delighted that there was a *Doctor Who* fan club in existence, disliked the fact that Miller placed so much emphasis on the sixties stories. He therefore encouraged a young fan named

▲ The first issue of the *Doctor Who* Appreciation Society's newsletter, *Celestial Toyroom* published in June/July 1976.

▲ A sample membership card for the *Doctor Who* fan club run by Keith Miller.

▲ A selection of *Doctor Who* fanzines produced in the seventies.

ERASING THE PAST

During the sixties and early seventies the BBC had a policy of only keeping copies of television programmes which could be sold abroad. Up until the end of the Pertwee era, the BBC made 16mm black and white film recordings of all the **Doctor Who** *episodes for this purpose although the twelve part season three story* **The Daleks' Master Plan** *was the only one never sold abroad. For the stories made in colour (***Spearhead from Space** *onwards), colour copies were also available in both the PAL and NTSC standards.*

The episodes were transmitted from videotape which was subsequently reused or destroyed, often leaving the black and white film prints as the only record. After seven years, when the BBC's rights to sell a programme expired, the film negatives and prints were generally destroyed. In the case of **Doctor Who***, the destruction of old material started around 1972 and continued until 1978 during which time many stories were lost including many of the Jon Pertwee adventures.*

Among the last items to be destroyed in early 1978 was the William Hartnell story **Galaxy 4***. This fact was discovered by the* **Doctor Who** *Appreciation Society who had been negotiating to buy a print for their convention that year. In 1978, there was a greater awareness of the importance of retaining archive material and the BBC halted the destruction process. In the same year they established the post of Archive Selector and started to search for new copies of the material they had destroyed.*

The BBC's own film library turned up several **Doctor Who** *stories and episodes which had been feared lost, and other copies were retrieved from the British Film Institute, BBC Enterprises, several overseas television stations and private collectors.*

By the end of the seventies, only one Jon Pertwee episode did not exist in any form – **Invasion of the Dinosaurs** *part 1 (although a black and white copy was later recovered) – but some only existed in black and white, and 136 episodes of the 253 transmitted in the sixties remained missing.*

Stuart Money to set up a rival organization devoted solely to his own era as the Doctor. Miller promptly queried this with the production office, who informed Money that he was not to go ahead with his venture as the DWFC was the officially recognized club. They also told Miller that he should continue to print whatever was popular with his members.

The following 18 months saw only five more issues of the DWFC's newsletter produced, taking the total to 25. The Club's members now numbered in the thousands, including many in overseas countries such as Australia and Rhodesia (now Zimbabwe), and Miller was finding it increasingly difficult to cope as a one-man operation. Around the same time, the BBC told him that they could no longer afford to meet his printing and postage costs. New producer Philip Hinchcliffe was less accommodating to Miller than Barry Letts had been and was apparently keen to see the Club run on a self-supporting basis. At his suggestion, Miller subsequently contacted some of the more active members to form a network of distribution helpers, but still it seemed unlikely that he would be able to keep the organization going.

'I spoke to Tom Baker during the making of *Genesis of the Daleks*,' recalls Miller, 'and mentioned the problems I was having. He said, "Well look, if it's getting that bad, why don't you go to one of those places that do automatic printing of addresses and get them to make up a little metal address stamp for every member of the Club. Then they can do all your envelopes for you and you can send them through the BBC in the usual way. The BBC won't okay it, but just charge it to me." Tom Baker actually paid for this himself! He really cared about the fans, more so I think than anybody else at that time.'

In July 1976, after the eventual demise of the *DWFC Mag*, Miller published the debut issue of a new fanzine called *Doctor Who Digest*. This nominally monthly publication, priced 35p per copy, was similar in style to a one-off special he had produced some time earlier under the title *The Dimensions of Doctor Who*. It took advantage of recent advances in dry-paper photocopying and looked quite slick for its day. Its contents were varied and interesting and it had a highly distinctive visual style.

Nine issues of *Doctor Who Digest* were produced over a period of about 18 months, but it was then discontinued as Miller had finally decided to throw in the towel.

By this time, the DWFC had in any case been overtaken by other developments within fandom. The most significant of these had been set in train in June 1975 when a science-fiction and comics fan named Andrew Johnson from Ongar in Essex started up a fanzine called *TARDIS* under his Eyeball Productions banner. Although Johnson lost interest after only two issues, he then handed over to reader Gordon Blows, who continued the fanzine under his own editorship. Blows subsequently received a letter from another reader, Jan Vincent-Rudzki, and it transpired that they were both among the network of helpers which Keith Miller had set up for the *DWFC Mag*. Neither had ever been given any copies of the newsletter to distribute, however, and both had found Miller increasingly difficult to contact.

Blows soon began to have regular get-togethers with Vincent-Rudzki and his friend Stephen Payne, who were amongst a group of *Doctor Who* fans at the University of London's Westfield College. Around this time, Vincent-Rudzki also met Tom Baker and asked him what he thought of the idea of the Westfield group becoming a *bona fide* society. Baker approved of the idea and so, as the DWFC appeared at that time to be effectively defunct, Vincent-Rudzki and Payne founded the *Doctor Who* Appreciation Society, which came into existence on 5 October 1975.

Early in 1976, Vincent-Rudzki, Payne and Blows decided to expand the college-based Society to cover the whole country. The national DWAS was officially launched in May 1976 with an announcement in the seventh issue of *TARDIS*.

Membership of the DWAS grew slowly but surely from around 70 initially to over 400 by the end of 1977. The range of services on offer was also expanded, and a major landmark was passed when Keith Barnfather organized the world's first *Doctor Who* convention, Convention '77, on the Society's behalf. This event, which took place on 6 August 1977 at Broomwood Church Hall in Battersea, London SW11, proved highly successful and gave the Society the confidence it needed to organize much bigger events for the following two years. PanoptiCon '78 took place over the weekend of 12—13 August 1978 on the premises of Imperial College, London, and PanoptiCon III over 18—19 August 1979 on those of City University, London.

The strain of organizing such a large-scale operation whilst holding down full-time jobs took its toll on the original executive who began, one by one, to drop out. Other fans volunteered to replace the original executive, and reorganized the way the Society was run. David Saunders became the co-ordinator of the Society and the role of president disappeared in the shake-up. With its new executive team, the revived Society marched boldly on into the eighties.

CHAPTER TWENTY TWO

End of an Era

Such had been the difficulties involved in making *Doctor Who* in the late seventies that Graham Williams had repeatedly requested the appointment of an associate producer who could take over some of his workload. It had seemed to him that this would be an ideal promotion for production unit manager John Nathan-Turner, who had shown considerable skill in handling the series' budget and had been involved in many important production decisions. Although these requests had been turned down, Head of Serials Graeme McDonald had instead given former producer Barry Letts a 'watching brief' over most of season sixteen, when Williams had been incapacitated for a time with a broken leg, and over the whole of season seventeen.

On leaving the series, Williams suggested to McDonald that Nathan-Turner would be an obvious choice as his successor. McDonald agreed with the principle of appointing a PUM, but decided in the first instance to offer the job to Nathan-Turner's predecessor, George Gallaccio, who had already gained a year's experience as a producer on the BBC Scotland series *The Omega Factor*. When he was approached, however, Gallaccio declined, explaining that he wanted to concentrate more on the artistic side of television than on the technical, which he felt to be a major aspect of *Doctor Who*. Nathan-Turner was therefore finally invited to become producer, and gratefully accepted.

McDonald himself was in the process of changing jobs at this time as the Serials Department was being merged with the Series Department in a major reorganization of the BBC's Drama Group — the first to have taken place since Sydney Newman's establishment of the Serials, Series and Plays Departments in 1963. In view of this, and also of Nathan-Turner's inexperience, he decided to give Barry Letts an official post as executive producer of *Doctor Who* for season eighteen. This would entail commenting on scripts, giving advice and approving major production decisions — in short, the role usually played by the Head of Department.

An early priority for Nathan-Turner and Letts was to find a new script editor to replace Douglas Adams.

Nathan-Turner sought the advice of a number of colleagues at the BBC, and former *Doctor Who* writer Robert Banks Stewart, who was by this time working as producer of the detective series *Shoestring*, suggested Christopher H. Bidmead as a likely candidate.

'I had to confess to both John and Barry that I didn't actually want to do *Doctor Who*,' recalls Bidmead, 'as it had got very silly and I hated the show. They agreed with me — Barry wanted to go back to earlier principles and to find a way of familiarizing children with the ways of science. You can understand how deeply that idea had been subverted.

'Two things were going wrong, as we saw it. One was the pantomime element and the other was the element of magic which had come in. Magic is entirely contrary to science and to my mind the Doctor's view of the world is that he looks at a problem objectively and then tries to apply laws derived from experience to reach a scientific solution.

'So often in the past, it had been a case of the Doctor effectively waving a magic wand which amounted to teaching children that the scientific way of looking at things was nonsense. It was a sort of infusion of late sixties hippie ideas that derived from Third World cultures which had filtered its way down into *Doctor Who*. Now, John liked the idea that it was going to be as different from the previous era as possible. In other words I got the job on the premise that we would go back to basics.'

A completely new production team would consequently be in place to take *Doctor Who* into the eighties; and, although it was not immediately apparent to the viewing public, the series was about to undergo its most radical change since the switch from black-and-white to colour and the regeneration of the Doctor from Patrick Troughton to Jon Pertwee. The next year alone would bring developments such as: a new title sequence; revamped theme music; an increased allocation of episodes; the return of the Master; the departure of Romana and K-9; the arrival of three new companions; and, ultimately, the regeneration of the Doctor himself. One era of *Doctor Who* had come to an end, but another was about to begin.

OVERSEAS

The BBC had always sold **Doctor Who** for overseas transmission, and in 1972 a package of 72 Jon Pertwee episodes was made available via Time-Life Films to America. This was the first time that **Doctor Who** had been sold to that country. Following this, a package of 98 episodes was distributed there in 1978. In 1979, America's **Starlog** magazine noted that the surprise hit of the Los Angeles Science Fiction, Horror and Fantasy Convention was **Doctor Who**, and that screenings of episodes regularly packed the viewing hall. American viewers had the opportunity to watch episodes of **Doctor Who** as often as ten times a week, depending on which PBS station they watched, and the 98 episodes were repeated in syndication over and over again. Afforded an unexpected break in the schedules due to the cancellation of **Shada**, Graham Williams and Tom Baker travelled to America to guest at a **Doctor Who** convention late in 1979. Baker was an instant hit with the attendees but it wasn't until the eighties that the American fans embraced the programme with a vengeance.

The following list of countries to have bought **Doctor Who** for transmission was produced internally by the BBC as at 28 February 1977.

COUNTRY (NO. OF STORIES BOUGHT)

Algeria (4)	Lebanon (3)
Arabia (4)	Mauritius (15)
Australia (70)	Mexico (9)
Barbados (2)	Morocco (3)
Bermuda (2)	New Zealand (40)
Brunei (10)	Nigeria (24)
Canada (6)	Philippines (2)
Caribbean (13)	Rhodesia (11)
Cyprus (9)	Saudi Arabia (4)
Dubai (21)	Sierra Leone (13)
Ethiopia (14)	Singapore (58)
Ghana (5)	Thailand (9)
Gibraltar (26)	Trinidad and Tobago (6)
Holland (9)	Tunisia (4)
Hong Kong (53)	Uganda (15)
Iran (7)	USA (13)
Jamaica (16)	Venezuela (12)
Kenya (7)	Zambia (36)

LISTING OF *DOCTOR WHO* MERCHANDISE RELEASED 1970–1979

NAME	PUB/MAN	YEAR	PRICE	CATEGORY
Action Doll: Cyberman	Denys Fisher Toys	1976	£2.50	Toys
Action Doll: Dalek	Denys Fisher Toys	1976	£2.50	Toys
Action Doll: Doctor Who	Denys Fisher Toys	1976	£2.95	Toys
Action Doll: Giant Robot	Denys Fisher Toys	1976	£2.95	Toys
Action Doll: Leela	Denys Fisher Toys	1976	£2.95	Toys
Action Doll: TARDIS	Denys Fisher Toys	1976	£8.82	Toys
Adventures Of K9 And Other Mechanical Creatures, The (p/b)	W.H. Allen & Co. Ltd	1979	85p	Activity Books
Amazing World Of Doctor Who Jigsaws, The (set of four – series 8015)	World International Publishing Ltd	1979	99p each	Jigsaws
Amazing World Of Doctor Who, The (including poster) (h/b)	P.B.S. Limited	1976	£1.00	Promotions
Blue Peter Doctor Who Theatre Leaflet	BBC	1977	free	Sundries
Dalek (6.5", battery, talking)	Palitoy Bradgate	1975	£3.75	Toys
Dalek (6.5", battery)	Louis Marx & Co Ltd	1974		Toys
Dalek Bubble Bath	The Water Margin	1976	£1.59	Sundries
Dalek Enamel Brooch	S. Weiner Ltd	1979	75p	Sundries
Dalek Enamel Pendant	S. Weiner Ltd	1979	75p	Sundries
Dalek Enamel Ring	S. Weiner Ltd	1979	50p	Sundries
Dalek's Death Ray Ice Lolly (nineteen different wrappers)	T. Wall & Sons (Ice Cream) Ltd	1975-7	5p each	Confectionery
Daleks Activity Book, The (lfp/b)	Children's Leisure Products Ltd	1978	25p	Activity Books
Daleks Colouring Book, The (lfp/b)	Children's Leisure Products Ltd	1978	25p	Activity Books
Daleks Postcard (14.8cm x 10.5cm)	Larkfield Printing Co. Ltd	1974		Sundries
Daleks' Invasion Earth 2150 AD Super 8mm Home Movie (widescreen)	Walton Sound and Film Services	1977	£133.04 (eight reels colour/sound)	Films
Daleks' Invasion Earth 2150 AD Super 8mm Home Movie (Part 1)	Walton Sound and Film Services	1977	£16.33 (one reel colour/sound)	Films
Daleks' Invasion Earth 2150 AD Super 8mm Home Movie (Part 2)	Walton Sound and Film Services	1977	£16.33 (one reel colour/sound)	Films
Daleks' Invasion Earth 2150 AD Super 8mm Home Movie (Part 1)	Walton Sound and Film Services	1977	£5.49 (one reel b&w/silent)	Films
Daleks' Invasion Earth 2150 AD Super 8mm Home Movie (Part 2)	Walton Sound and Film Services	1977	£5.49 (one reel b&w/silent)	Films
Daleks' Invasion Earth 2150 AD Super 8mm Home Movie	Walton Sound and Film Services	1977	£133.04 (eight reels colour/sound)	Films
Doctor Who	Radio Times	1973	30p	Magazines
Doctor Who (Disco) by Mankind (12" & 7") (MTR 001/12, PIN 71)	Motor Records/Pinnacle records	1978		Records
Doctor Who (Poster Magazine)	Legend Publishing	1975	25p	Magazines
Doctor Who 3-D Clay Picture Kit	Remus Playkits Ltd	1979	£1.15	Toys
Doctor Who – A Special Monster Packed Issue (Poster Magazine)	Harpdown Publishing Ltd	1976	30p	Magazines
Doctor Who Aim 'n' Shoot Bagatelle Game	Jotastar	1978	£1.49	Toys
Doctor Who and the Daleks In Seven Keys to Doomsday Programme		1974		Sundries
Doctor Who and the Daleks Omnibus (h/b)	Artus Publishing Ltd (for Marks and Spencer Ltd)	1976	£1.99	Annuals
Doctor Who and the Daleks T-Shirt (red, black & yellow on white)	Silly Things (Aha Ltd)	1975	£1.55 (adult) £1.10 (junior)	Clothing
Doctor Who and the Daleks Transfer (Dalek)	Imagine Transfers Ltd	1975	50p	Toys
Doctor Who and the Daleks Yo-Yo	Louis Marx & Co. Ltd	1975	50p	Toys
Doctor Who and the Pescatons LP (ZSW 564)/cassette	Argo/Decca Record Company	1976		Records
Doctor Who and the Pescatons Poster		1976	free	Posters
Doctor Who Annual 1980 (h/b)	World Distributors (Manchester) Ltd	1979	£1.75	Annuals
Doctor Who Badge (orange logo on blue background)	BBC Enterprises	1973		Sundries
Doctor Who Badges (blue/red on white, 1¼" and 1 3/4" diameter)	BBC Enterprises	1975		Promotions
Doctor Who Badges, Sugar Smacks (set of six)	Kelloggs	1971	free	Promotions
Doctor Who Bagatelle	Playtime	1978	75p	Toys
Doctor Who Board-Game	Strawberry Fayre by Denys Fisher	1975	£3.60	Toys
Doctor Who Candy Favourites	Goodies	1979	3p each	Confectionery
Doctor Who Card Figures	Weetabix Ltd	1975	free	Promotions
Doctor Who Card Figures	Weetabix Ltd	1977	free	Promotions
Doctor Who Cards	Cadbury Ty-Phoo	1976	free	Promotions
Doctor Who Colouring Book (lfp/b)	World Distributors (Manchester) Ltd	1979	25p	Activity Books
Doctor Who Dalek Invasion of Earth Transfers	Letraset Action Transfers	1976	55p	Toys
Doctor Who Data Printer	Tangent Systems Ltd	1978	91p	Stationery
Doctor Who Dinosaur Book, The (lfp/b)	W.H. Allen & Co. Ltd	1976	75p	Books
Doctor Who Discovers Early Man (lfp/b)	W.H. Allen & Co. Ltd	1977	75p	Books
Doctor Who Discovers Prehistoric Animals (lfp/b)	W.H. Allen & Co. Ltd	1977	75p	Books
Doctor Who Discovers Space Travel (lfp/b)	W.H. Allen & Co. Ltd	1977	75p	Books
Doctor Who Discovers Strange And Mysterious Creatures (lfp/b)	W.H. Allen & Co. Ltd	1978	75p	Books
Doctor Who Discovers the Conquerors (lfp/b)	W.H. Allen & Co. Ltd	1978	75p	Books
Doctor Who Dressing Up Costume	Berwicks Toys Ltd	1976		Toys
Doctor Who Exhibition Sticker	BBC Enterprises	1976	25p	Sundries
Doctor Who Greetings Cards (set of 18)	Denis Alan Print	1979	36p each £5.00 set	Stationery
Doctor Who Holiday Special	Polystyle Publications Ltd	1973	10p	Magazines
Doctor Who Holiday Special	Polystyle Publications Ltd	1974	13p	Magazines
Doctor Who Jigsaws (set of four – series 7836)	Whitman Publishing (UK) Ltd	1977	99p each	Jigsaws
Doctor Who Keyring (leather)		1976	35p	Sundries
Doctor Who Logo T-shirt (black diamond logo on mustard)	Rumpelstiltskin	1975	£1.75 (l) £1.35 (s)	Clothing
Doctor Who Medallion and Chain (copper finish)	A.P. Services & Co.	1974	36p	Sundries
Doctor Who Medallion and Chain (gold plated finish)	A.P. Services & Co.	1974	39p	Sundries
Doctor Who Medallion and Chain (satin finish)	A.P. Services & Co.	1974	35p	Sundries
Doctor Who Medallion and Chain (silver finish)	A.P. Services & Co.	1974	37p	Sundries
Doctor Who Mighty Midget Comic (free with Mighty TV Comic #1)	Polystyle Publications Ltd	1976	free	Magazines
Doctor Who Milk Chocolate (15 different wrappers)	The Nestlé Company Ltd	1971	3p each	Confectionery
Doctor Who Milk Chocolate (six different wrappers)	The Nestlé Company ltd	1975	6p each	Confectionery
Doctor Who Mini-Puzzles	H.C. Ford	1974		Toys
Doctor Who Monster Book, The (lfp/b)	Tandem Publishing Ltd	1975	50p	Factual Books
Doctor Who Painting by Numbers sets (six different)	Airfix	1974		Toys
Doctor Who Poster Art Kit	Thomas Salter Ltd	1978	99p	Stationery
Doctor Who Poster, Ty-Phoo	Cadbury Ty-Phoo	1976	20p	Promotions
Doctor Who Posters (set of four)	Denis Alan Print	1979	95p each £3.45 set	Posters
Doctor Who Press-Out Book (lfp/b)	World Distributors (Manchester) Ltd	1978	30p	Activity Books
Doctor Who Rock	Regent Confectionery	1975		Confectionery
Doctor Who Scarf	Today Promotions Ltd	1976	£5.50 (8') £6.50 (10')	Clothing
Doctor Who Sound Effects LP (REC 316/cassette (ZCM 316))	BBC Records	1978	£2.99	Records
Doctor Who Space Mission Pad (fourth Doctor)	John Morriss	1974	35p	Stationery
Doctor Who Space Mission Pad (third Doctor)	Naocraft Ltd	1973	35p	Stationery

Item	Manufacturer	Year	Price	Category
Doctor Who T-shirt (glitter logo on black)	BBC Enterprises (Portugal)	1976	£2.00	Clothing
Doctor Who Theme by Don Harper's Homo Electronicus	EMI	1973		Records
Doctor Who Theme by Ron Grainer (RESL 11) (blue & white TARDIS sleeve)	BBC Records	1976		Records
Doctor Who Theme by Ron Grainer (RESL 11) (plain sleeve)	Pye/BBC Records	1973	48p	Records
Doctor Who Theme by Ron Grainer (RESL 11) (silver label)	BBC Records	1973		Records
Doctor Who Theme by Ron Grainer (RESL 11) (TARDIS sleeve)	BBC Records	1973		Records
Doctor Who Theme by Ron Grainer (RESL 11) (TARDIS in vortex sleeve)	BBC Records	1978		Records
Doctor Who Theme Sheet Music (Mankind version)	Chappell & Co	1978		Recordings
Doctor Who Trump Card Game	Jotastar	1978	70p	Toys
Doctor Who Weekly	Marvel Comics	1979	12p	Magazines
Doctor Who Winter Special	Polystyle Publications Ltd	1977	35p	Magazines
Doctor Who-Style Slipover and Scarf Knitting Pattern (No 1237 D/C)	Mayfield Knitting Wools	1976	12p	Miscellaneous
Dr Who and Space Adventures LP (Happy Time HT12)	Damont Records Ltd	1975		Records
Dr Who and the Daleks Super 8mm Home Movie (Part 1)	Walton Sound and Film Services	1977	£16.33 (one reel colour/sound)	Films
Dr Who and the Daleks Super 8mm Home Movie (Part 2)	Walton Sound and Film Services	1977	£16.33 (one reel colour/sound)	Films
Dr Who and the Daleks Super 8mm Home Movie	Walton Sound and Film Services	1977	£133.04 (eight reels colour/sound)	Films
Dr Who and the Daleks Super 8mm Home Movie (Part 1)	Walton Sound and Film Services	1977	£5.49 (one reel b&w/silent)	Films
Dr Who and the Daleks Super 8mm Home Movie (Part 2)	Walton Sound and Film Services	1977	£5.49 (one reel b&w/silent)	Films
Dr Who Annual 1973, The (h/b)	World Distributors (Manchester) Ltd	1972	70p	Annuals
Dr Who Annual 1974, The (h/b)	World Distributors (Manchester) Ltd	1973	75p	Annuals
Dr Who Annual 1975, The (h/b)	World Distributors (Manchester) Ltd	1974	90p	Annuals
Dr Who Annual 1976, The (h/b)	World Distributors (Manchester) Ltd	1975	£1.00	Annuals
Dr Who Annual 1977, The (h/b)	World Distributors (Manchester) Ltd	1976	£1.25	Annuals
Dr Who Annual 1978, The (h/b)	World Distributors (Manchester) Ltd	1977	£1.35	Annuals
Dr Who Annual 1979, The (h/b)	World Distributors (Manchester) Ltd	1978	£1.50b	Annuals
Dr Who Annual, The (h/b 1971)	World Distributors (Manchester) Ltd	1970	12s 6d (62.5p)	Annuals
Dr Who Colouring Book, The (lfp/b)	World Distributors (Manchester) Ltd	1973	10p	Activity Books
Dr Who Jigsaws (set of two)	Michael Stanfield Holdings	1971	20p each	Jigsaws
Dr Who Jigsaws (two-in-one set)	Michael Stanfield Holdings	1971		Jigsaws
Dr Who Jigsaws (two re-issues, two new)	Michael Stanfield Holdings	1972	25p each	Jigsaws
Dr Who Jigsaws (set of four – series 7408)	Whitman Publishing (UK) Ltd	1973	35p each	Jigsaws
Dr Who Jigsaws (set of four – series 7511)	Whitman Publishing (UK) Ltd	1975	50p each	Jigsaws
Dr Who Pencil Sharpeners (set of four)	H.C. Ford	1979	22p each	Stationery
Enemies of Doctor Who Jigsaws (set of four – series 7915)	Whitman Publishing (UK) Ltd	1978	99p each	Jigsaws
Genesis of the Daleks LP (REH 364/cassette (ZCR 364))	BBC Records	1979	£3.75	Records
I am a Dalek by the Art Attacks		1977		Records
Iron-on Transfer	Dodo Iron-Ons	1971	50p	Toys
John Menzies Monster Painting Competition Badge	John Menzies	1976	free	Sundries
Jon Pertwee's Book of Monsters (h/b)	Methuen	1978		Miscellaneous
Jon Pertwee's Book of Monsters (p/b)	Magnet	1979		Miscellaneous
K-9 (battery, talking)	Palitoy Bradgate	1978	£7.90	Toys
K-9 (friction-action)	Denys Fisher Toys	1978	£2.99	Toys
K-9 Enamel Brooch	S. Weiner Ltd	1979	75p	Sundries
K-9 Enamel Pendant	S. Weiner Ltd	1979	75p	Sundries
K-9 Enamel Ring	S. Weiner Ltd	1979	50p	Sundries
K-9 Postcard (from The Horns of Nimon)	Larkfield Printing Co. Ltd	1979		Sundries
K-9 Postcard (from The Invisible Enemy)	Larkfield Printing Co. Ltd	1978		Sundries
Leela (Louise Jameson) Postcard	Larkfield Printing Co. Ltd	1977		Sundries
Making of Doctor Who, The (p/b)	Pan Books Ltd	1972	25p	Factual Books
Making of Doctor Who, The (p/b)	Tandem Publishing Ltd	1976	60p	Factual Books
Moonbase 3/The World of Dr Who by Dudley Simpson (RESL 13)	BBC Records	1973		Records
Poster (third Doctor and IMC Robot Claw)	Personality Posters	1972	50p	Posters
Poster (third Doctor and Sea Devil)	Personality Posters	1972	50p	Posters
Poster (fourth Doctor – artwork)	for Crosse & Blackwell	1977	free	Posters
Pottery TARDIS	Melwood	1978	£2.99	Sundries
Publicity Cards	BBC Television	1970-79	free	Sundries
Romana (Lalla Ward) Postcard (from City of Death – publicity)	Larkfield Printing Co. Ltd	1979		Sundries
Second Doctor Who Monster Book, The (p/b)	W.H. Allen & Co. Ltd	1977	70p	Factual Books
TARDIS Colouring Book (p/b)	Crosse & Blackwell	1977	95p	Activity Books
TARDIS Commander BBC TV Special Effects Badge (two types)	BBC Enterprises	1972		Sundries
TARDIS Toffee				Confectionery
TARDIS Tuner	Shortman Trading	1978	£19.95	Toys
Terry Nation's Dalek Annual 1976 (h/b)	World Distributors (Manchester) Ltd	1975	£1.00	Annuals
Terry Nation's Dalek Annual 1977 (h/b)	World Distributors (Manchester) Ltd	1976	£1.10	Annuals
Terry Nation's Dalek Annual 1978 (h/b)	World Distributors (Manchester) Ltd	1977	£1.35	Annuals
Terry Nation's Dalek Annual 1979 (h/b)	World Distributors (Manchester) Ltd	1978	£1.50	Annuals
Terry Nation's Dalek Special (p/b)	W.H. Allen & Co. Ltd	1979	95p	Activity Books
Tom Baker full length 'Happy Days' Postcard		1976		Sundries
Tom Baker full length 'Welcome to Blackpool' Postcard		1976		Sundries
Tom Baker full length 'Welcome to Longleat' Postcard		1976		Sundries
Tom Baker full length 'Wish "Who" Were Here' Postcard		1976		Sundries
Tom Baker Greetings Card		1976		Sundries
Tom Baker head and shoulders Postcard		1976		Sundries
Tom Baker Postcard (pointing at lapel)	Larkfield Printing Co. Ltd	1978		Sundries
Tom Baker Poster	W.H. Allen & Co. Ltd	1976	free	Posters
TV Comic/Countdown/TV Action (assorted titles)	Polystyle Publications Ltd	1970-79	5p-10p each	Magazines
War of the Daleks Board-Game	Strawberry Fayre by Denys Fisher	1975	£5.25	Toys
Who Is The Doctor? by Jon Pertwee (PUR 111)	Purple Records Ltd	1972		Records

Authors' Note: We have made every effort to ensure that this merchandise listing is as complete as possible, but if you have any further information about any of the items mentioned, or know of any items which are not listed, please contact the authors at the publisher's address at the front of this book.

lfp/b = large format paperback

Number in italics denotes photographs.
Number in bold denotes entry in side column.
*=Working title.
+=story not made.

Acheson, James 49, **64**, 80, 91, 151
Acheson, John 147
Achilleos, Christos **162**, 164, 165, 172
Adam, Joshua (see also 'Griefer, Lewis') **96**
Adams, Douglas 126, 127, **129**, 130, **131**, 133, 134, 135, 136, 137, 140, 141, 142
Aggedor 153, 165
Agnew, David 136
Ainscough, Frank **156**
Allen, Paul 110
Alpha Centauri 153, *153*, 165
Ambassadors of Death, The 21, 25-28, **25**, **26**, **27**, *27*, *27*, *28*, *28*, 30, 143, **145**, 162
Andrews, Eamon **38**
Android Invasion, The 6, **89**, **90**, 94-95, *94*, *95*, **95**, **145**, 147
Androids of Tara, The 77, **121**, *124*, **126**, **127**, *127*, 128-129, **132**, 133, 156,
Angurth, The + 97
Animal Magic **138**
Anthony Read 120
Ark in Space, The 76, **79**, **81**, *83*, **83**, 84-85, 88, **138**, 161
Armageddon *130
Armageddon Factor, The **121**, **127**, 130-132, *130*, **131**, *131*, **132**, **148**, 159
Asbury, Martin 160
Automata, The + 63
Autons **24**, 153
Axons 153, 158, 165
Axons , The *37
Baker, Bob 36, **37**, 48, 49, 50, 53, 54, 83, 85, 101, 102, 109, 112, 115-116, 117, 130, **131**, 133, 139, 140
Baker, Christopher **96**
Baker, Colin **145**
Baker, George 130
Baker, John **51**
Baker, Jules **40**
Baker, Tom 68, 69-74, **69-74**, **75**, 80, 81, 82, 85, **90**, 98, 102, 104, *104*, **105**, 107, 112, **116**, 118, 120, **129**, 132, 133, 138, **138**, 140, 142, 146, **146**, 148, **148**, 150, **154**, 156, **158**, **161**, **162**, 166, 167, 170, 174, **175**
Baksh, Shakira 33
Banks Stewart, Robert 89, **96**, 97, 98, **98**, 106, 175
Barnes, Larry **106**
Barnfather, Keith 174
Barry, Christopher 50, 81, **96**, 97, 138
BBC Enterprises 1, **3**, 56, 155, **157**, **174**
BBC Radiophonic Workshop 10, **59**, **81**
Bellamy, Frank 38, 43, **162**
Bennett, Rodney 84, 101
Bennion, Alan 67
Bentham, Jeremy 160
Bentine, Michael 79
Berelson, Richard **161**
Bernard, Paul **50**, **57**, 58
Bessie **3**, 18, **54**, **154**, 159, 160, 165, 171
Bidmead, Christopher H. 175
Black Hole, The *54
Black, Ian Stuart 45
Blake, Darrol 128
Bland, Robin 96
Bloomfield, John 104
Blows, Gordon 174
Blyton, Carey 27, **67**, **81**
Bongo, Ali **106**
Boucher, Chris **103**, 104, 105, 106, 113, 114
Bowtell, Allister 81, **87**, 151
Boyle, Marc **50**
Brackley, Nigel 126

Bragg, Melvyn 107
Brain Drain, The + **11**
Brain of Morbius, The **89**, **90**, 95-97, *96*, **96**, *97*, 130, 152
Brain—Dead, The + 45, **52**
Breslin, John 143
Briant, Michael E. 39, 40, 48, 60, 66, **67**, **81**, 106
Brierley, David 138, **142**, 148
Briggs, Bev **167**
Bromly, Alan **64**, 140
Bron, Eleanor 137
Brooks, Peter **162**, *163*
Browning, Alan 130
Bryant, Peter **3**, 4, 6, 8, 9, **10**, 21, 22, 24, 28, 30, **30**, 31
Burgon, Geoffrey **90**
Caldinez, Sonny 67
Camfield, Douglas 22, 30, 90, **96**, 98, 101
Canning, John 160
Carnival of Monsters 18, **53**, *55*, **55**, 56, *56*, **56**, 63, 87, **146**
Carriers of Death, The * 25
Cary, Tristram **51**
Cash, Tony 107
casting 8, 9, 10, 32-34, 35, 39-40, 62-63, 79-80, **95**, **102**, 104, 124-125, 134, 135, 141
Catacombs of Death *99
Caunter, Tony 40
Cave, Bridget 107
Cerebroids, The + 34
Chase, The 60
City of Death 78, **133**, 135-137, *136*, **136**, 136, *137*, 138, **140**
Clarke, Malcolm **51**
Clawrantular 151
Claws of Axos, The 18, **31**, **33**, **35**, 36-38, *36*, **37**, **40**, 102, 144, 162, **163**, 167
Clayton, Gloria 67
Cleese, John 137
Coady, Matthew **24**, **33**
Coles, Dick 117
Collier, Ian **50**
Colony *38
Colony in Space **31**, **33**, *37*, 38-40, **38**, *38*, *39*, **39**, **39**, **40**, 42, **160**, 162, 163
Colour Separation Overlay **22**, 117
Conway, Richard *118*
Cook, Roger 160
Coombe, Timothy 35, 36
Cotton, Bill 132
Courtney, Nicholas 7, 10, 42, 91, 95, 143, **144**
Cowan, Geoff 160
Creature from the Pit, The **78**, **133**, 137-138, *138*, **138**, *139*, *139*, **140**
Crompton, P and J 157
Crowden, Graham 79
CSO (see 'Colour Separation Overlay')
Cully, Clifford 64
Cummins, Jeff **162**, 172
Curren, Charles 108
Curse of Mandragora, The *99
Curse of Peladon, The 18, 20, **43**, *44*, 45-47, *46*, **47**, **48**, **51**, 52, 66, 67, 144, **145**
Curse of Sephiroth *136
Curse of the Daleks, The 1, 149
Curse, The *45
Cushing, Peter 1
Cybermen 83, 87, **87**, **154**, 158, 165, 169
D'Oyly John, Christopher 68
Dale, Jim 79
Dalek Invasion of Earth, The 49
Daleks 43-44, **45**, 49, 56, 59, 66, **82**, 83, 133
Daleks 149, 150, **150**, **151**, 153, 154, **154**, 156, 157, 158, 159, **160**, 161, **161**, 165, 168, 169, 171
Daleks' Invasion Earth 2150 A.D. **158**
Daleks' Master Plan, The **144**, **174**
Daleks — Genesis of Terror *86

Daleks in London, The + 44
Dæmons 158
Dæmons, The 16, 17, **31**, *32*, **33**, **39**, 40-42, *40*, **40**, **40**, *41*, **41**, **42**, *42*, **42**, 47, 144, *144*, 163
Dangerous Assassin, The *102
Danielle, Suzanne 135
Darrow, Paul 143
Davey, Arthur 9
Davis, Gerry **10**, 49, 56, 83, **85**, 87, 164,
Davros **86**, *87*, 134-135, 154, 165
Dawson, Basil 106
Day God Went Mad, The *104
Day of the Daleks 18, **43**, *43*, **44**, *44*, 44, *45*, **45**, 49, **50**, **51**, *145*, 153, 155, 159, 163
Day, Peter 48, **86**
de Rouen, Reed **11**
de Wynter, Robert 149, 150
Deadly Assassin, The 77, **99**, 102-104, *102*, **102**, 104, **106**, **107**, 108, 120, 147, 159
Death to the Daleks 18, 18, **20**, 61, 65-66, *65*, **65**, **66**, **67**, 166
Delgado, Roger 34, **36**, 42, 58, 60, 65, 103, 161
Demons, The *40
Derbyshire, Delia 27, **59**, 166, 167
design 5, 9, 10, 24, 25, **28**, **40**, 50, **50**, **57**, 58, 59, 61-62, **64**, **65**, 66, 68, **80**, 80-81, 82, **86**, 90-91, 92-93, 95, 96-97, 100-101, 104, 106, 108, 110-111, 111, 112, 115, 117, *125*, 126, 129, 130, 135, *137*, 138, 141, 151
Destination: Daleks *57
Destiny of the Daleks 133-135, **133**, *133*, *134*, **134**, *135*, **135**, **140**, 148, 154, 164
Destructors, The *85
Dicks, Terrance 3, **6**, 7, **7**, 22, 23, **23**, 26, 27, 28, 30, 31, 32, **32**, 33, 36, 37, 40, 42, 44, 47, 49-50, 52, 53, 54, 55, 56, 58, 59, 60, 63, 64, 65, 67, 68, 82, 84, 95-96, **100**, 107, 109, 110, **114**, 123, 149, 150, **151**, 152, **152**, 156, **156**, 158, 159, **159**, 162, 163, 164
Dimensions in Time 16, **70**, 74, *143*, **144**, **146**
Doctor Who - The Ultimate Adventure 7, 16
Doctor Who and the Big Game + 73
Doctor Who and the Daleks in Seven Keys to Doomsday 7, 149-152, **149-152**, *149-152*, *149-152*, **149-152**, 171
Doctor Who and the Hell Planet 100
Doctor Who and the Pescatons 73, **160**
Doctor Who and the Silurians 17, **18**, 21, *22*, 22, 23-25, *25*, **25**, **26**, **27**, *25*, *26*, **30**, 35-36, 47, **50**,143, 144, 162, 163
Doctor Who Appreciation Society, The 160, **173**,174, **174**
Doctor Who Fan Club, The 58, 173, **173**, 174
Doctor Who meets Scratchman 73, 104, **129**, 146, **158**
Doomsday Project, The + 133
Dr Who and the Daleks **158**, 161
Draconians 58, 153, *153*, 165
Dreamers of Phados, The + 104
Drury, Alan 133
Ellis, David 23
Ellison, Harlan **164**
Emergents, The *48
Enemy of the World, The 6, 22, **49**
Enemy Within, The *(*The Android Invasion*) 94
Enemy Within, The *(*The Invisible Enemy*) 111
Erato 138
Erinella + 133
Evans, Tenniel 8
Evil of the Daleks, The **49**, 74
Exelby, Sandra **64**
Exploration Earth: The Time Machine **105**
Exxilons 165
Exxilons, The *65
Face of Evil, The **99**, *103*, **103**, 104, **104**, **106**, 147
Faceless Ones, The 23
Facsimile *23

Farries, Peter **65**
Farson, Daniel **72**
Fendahl **138**
Fennell, Alan 156, 160
Ferguson, Michael 27, 28, 38
Fisher, David **120**, 128, 129, **129**, 133, 135, 136, 137
Five Doctors, The 16, 73, **143**, **144**, 146
Foe from the Future, The * 98, 106
Franklin, Richard 33, 42, 143, **144**
Friedlander, John **57**, 58, **64**, 86, **87**, 91, 95
Friendly Invasion, The * 37
Frontier in Space 20, **53**, **55**, 56-58, *57*, **57**, *58*, 155, 161, *163*
Fury from the Deep 74
Galactic Conman, The * 125
Galaxy 4 **174**
Gallaccio, George **68**, **96**, 175
Gallacher, Don 167
Gamble with Time, The * 135
Gardner, Brenda 164
Geary, John **162**
Gell Guards 165
Genesis of the Daleks **76**, 77, *77*, **78**, **79**, 81, **84**, 86-87, **86**, *87*, 88, *88*, 120, 133, 156, 167, 174
Ghost Hunters, The * 44
Giant Robot 159, 165, 169
Gibbons, Dave 160
Gift, The * 36
Gleeson, Tim 50
Glover, Michael 163, 164
Godfrey, Elizabeth 164
Godfrey, Patrick 144
Gooderson, David 134
Goodwin, Derrick 112
Grainer, Ron **59**
Green Death, The **19**, *42*, **53**, **55**, **54**, **56**, **57**, 59-60, *59*, **60**, *60*, **63**, 64, 68, 145, 159
Green, Colin 66
Griefer, Lewis (See also 'Adam, Joshua') 93, 94
Gunfighters, The **25**
Hand of Death, The * 102
Hand of Fear, The **99**, 101-102, *101*, **101**, **106**, 147, 159, 170
Hand of Time, The * 102
Harding, Tony 112, **112**, *112*, 130
Harper, Don 166
Harper, Graeme **96**
Harris, Stephen 94
Harrison, Godfrey 56
Harry Sullivan's War **146**
Hartnell, William 1, 5, 14, **24**, 53, 54, **57**, **83**, **96**, 158
Haunting, The + 95
Havard, Dave 93
Hayles, Brian 45, **47**, **52**, 67
Haylock, Gerry 160
Hearne, Richard 79
Hemple, Anouska 33
Henwood, Richard 162
Hill, James 73, 104, **146**, **158**
Hinchcliffe, Philip 80, 81, **81**, 82, 83, **84**, **85**, 88, 90, 91, 94, 95, **96**, 99, 100, 101, 102, 104, 107, 108, 120, 139, **162**, 174
Hines, Frazer 10
Hines, Rupert 166
Hodges, Edgar 157
Hodgson, Brian **39**, **54**, 56, **56**, **59**, 166, 167
Holmes, Robert 23, **30**, **32**, 34, 56, 63, 65, 80, 81, 82, 83, 84, 87, 88, 89, 92, 93, 94, 95, 96, **96**, 98, **98**, 99, 102, **103**, 104, 105, 106, 108, 110, 113-114, 115, 118, 120, 125, 129, 130, 163
Hooper, Dennis 160
Horns of Nimon, The **120**, **133**, 139, 140-141, **140**, *141*, *141*, 142
Horror of Fang Rock **5**, 109-111, *109*, **109**, **110**, *110*, **114**, **115**, 120, 159

Horror of the Swamp, The * 129
Houghton, Don 28, 29, **29**, 34, **158**
Howell, Peter **81**
Hudson, June 141
Hughes, Mick 150, **151**
Hulke, Malcolm 7, 23, **23**, 25, 26, 38, 47, **50**, 56, 58, 64, 158, **159**, 163
Hunter, Russell **106**
Ice Warriors 45-46, 67, 158, 165
Image of the Fendahl 1, *78*, **109**, *112*, **115**, 113,*113*, *113*, 114, 120
Independence * 48
Inferno 18, 19, **21**, **25**, **26**, **27**, 28-30, **28**, *29*, *29*, 30, 32, **49**, 143, 162, 167
Invaders from Mars, The + 23
Invasion of the Dinosaurs 18, 19, 20, **23**, 61, *63*, 64-65, *64*, **66**, 146, 161, **174**
Invasion of Time, The 78, **109**, **115**, 118-119, *118*, **118**, *119*, **119**, 120, 126, 147, 148, 166
Invasion, The 7, 36, 87, 143, **144**, **145**
Invisible Enemy, The 109, **109**, 111-113, *111*, **111**, **111**, 112, *112*, **115**, 117, 148
Invisible Invader, The * 111
Jaeger, Frederick 93
Jameson, Louise 102, 104, 111, 112, **116**, 118, 123, 147, **147**, *147*
Jameson, Susan 40
Jarvis, Martin 130
Jerrard, Sue 74
John, Caroline 10, 32, **143**, 144
Johnson, Andrew 174
Jones, Matthew **63**
Jones, Simon 150, 151
K-9 37, 111-113, *112*, **112**, 126, 128, 134, 136, 138, **142**, **147**, 148, **154**, 156, 158, 159, **160**, 161, 170, 171, 172, 175
K-9 & Company **146**
Key to Time, The 121-123
Keys of Marinus, The **85**, 152
Kidd, Barbara **86**
Killer Cats of Gen Singh + *117*, 118
Kine, Jack **4**
Kingsland, Paddy 55-56
Knipe, Roy **162**
Kraals 95, 159
Kraals, The * 94
Krikkitmen, The + 129
Krotons, The 23, **30**, 130
Krynoid **138**, 165
Labyrinth, The * 56
Labyrinth, The + 11
Lacey, Ronald **106**
Lane, Mike Lee 93
Langford, Frank 160
Langley, Christopher 84
Leeson, John 112, 130, 138, **147**, 148
Leopold, Guy 40
Lessiter, Sandy 163
Lester, Rick 50
Letts, Barry 6, 22, 24, 25, 27, 28, **28**, 30, 31, 32, 33, 34, 35, 37, 38, 40, **40**, **42**, 42, 43, 44, 47, 48, 49, 51, 52, **54**, 55, 56, 58, 59, 60, 61, 62, **62**, 64, 65, **65**, 67, 68, 79, 80, 82, 83, 84, 86, 95, 101, 153, 163, 173, 174, 175
Levene, John 42, 91, 95, 143, **145**
Lewis, Ted 129
Lim, Pik Sen **29**, 35
Lindfield, Harry 160
Lindsay, Kevin **64**, 86
Linstead, Alec 144
Little, Mike **162**
Livesy, Steve 157
Lloyd, Innes **85**
Lloyd, John 133
locations 2, 21, 22, **26**, 30, **33**, 38, 42, 46, 48, **51**, 54, **55**, 56, **57**, 60, 66, **66**, **81**, 82, **82**, 85, 89, 90,

90, 94, 99, 100, 102, 104, **106**, 107, 113, **115**, **127**, 129, 130, 135, **140**, 142
Loch Ness * 89
Lodge, Bernard 10, **57**, 61-62, **80**, 82
Lord Bath 154
Lucarotti, John 84
MacIver, David 166
Mackay, Fulton 79
Madoc, Philip 130
Maggots, Giant **57**
Maloney, David 58, 87, **103**, 104, 107, 130
Man Hours * 35
Mann, David **164**
Manning, Katy 33, **38**, 42, 60, 144, **144**, **145**, 161
Mapson, Colin *113*
Marco Polo 1
Margolyes, Miriam 133
Marks, Louis 44, **48**, 91, 92, 99, 100, 163
Marlowe, Fernanda 144
Marsh, Jean 14, 15, *16*
Marsh, Ronnie 6, 31, **32**, 39, 40
Marter, Ian 33, 73, 80, 95, 104, 146, **146**, **154**, **158**
Martin, Dave 36, **37**, 48, 49, 53, 54, 83, 85, 101, 102, 109, 112, 115-116, 130, **131**
Martin, Lorne 154
Martin, Trevor 150, **150**, **151**, 152
Martinus, Derek 22
Masque of Mandragora, The 77, **85**, 99-101, *99*, *99*, *100*, **100**, **101**, **106**, **107**, 161
Master, The 33-34, 43, 58, 103-104, 165, 175
Mathews, James 150, **151**
Mayne, Lennie 67, 101
McCarthy, Neil 130
McCrae, John 6
McDonald, Graeme 94, 109, 120, 123, 126-127, 131, 132, 141, 156, 175
Mega, The + 45
Mentor Conspiracy, The + 104
Miller, Brian **146**
Miller, Keith 157, 173, 174
Miller, Russell 38
Mills, Dick 56, **59**, 166
Mind of Evil, The **29**, **31**, **33**, 34-36, *35*, **35**, *36*, 87, 130, 144, 162, 166, 167
Mists of Madness, The + 28
Mitchell, A. J. (Mitch) 117, 129
Mo—Hole Project, The * 28
Money, Stuart 174
Monster of Peladon, The 17, **61**, 66—67, *66*, **66**, **66**, **67**, 68
Monsters, The * 23
Moody, Ron 8
Moon of Death, The * 129
Moonbase, The **145**
Morton, Bill 107
Multiface + 56
Murray Leach, Roger 91, 92
music 27, **39**, **51**, **54**, 55-56, **56**, **67**, **81**, **90**, **107**, **116**, **127**, **140**, 166, 167
Mutant, The + 49
Mutants, The **43**, 48-50, *48*, **48**, **49**, **50**, **51**, 163
Myerscough-Jones, David **28**
Napier, John 150, **151**
Nathan—Turner, John **68**, 130, 135, 175
Nation, Terry 43-44, **45**, 57, 59, 65, **81**, 86, **86**, 87, 133, **134**, 156, 157, **157**, 161
Newbery, Barry 24, 96-97, 100-101, 111, 112
Newell, Patrick 95, 147
Newman, Fred **156**
Newman, Sarah 173
Newman, Sydney 3
Nicolotti, Aldo **62**
Nightmare Fair, The + 110
Nightmare of Eden **133**, **136**, 139-140, *139*, *140*, **140**, 142
Nightmare of Evil * 139

Nightmare Planet, The + 95
Nimon 141
Nine Maidens, The * 128
O'Neill, Dick 160
Ogrons 165
Oldhamstead, Roger 141
Omega 165
Operation * 125
Operation: Mole-Bore * 28
overseas **175**
Oxley, Tony **87**
Padbury, Wendy 10, 150, **151**
Palmer, Ben 10
Pandora Box, The * 35
Pandora Machine, The * 35
Paradise of Death, The **6**, 16, **146**
Parkhouse, Steve 161
Pathmore, Martin 130
Payne, Stephen 174
Pearson, Bill *118*
Pedler, Kit **85**, 87
Peepshow * 56
Pemberton, Victor 166
Pertwee, Ingeborg (see also 'Rhosea, Ingeborg') 38
Pertwee, Jon 8-9, 10, 11-16, **11-16**, *11-16*, **17**, *18*, 22, **24**, **28**, 32, **38**, 42, 43, 53, 58, 62, **62**, 65, **65**, 67, 74, **75**, 79, 81, **96**, 149, 150, 152, 153, **160**, 161, **163**, 165, 166, 172, 173
Pinfield, Mervyn **137**
Pirate Planet, The **121**, *123*, *123*, 126-128, **127**, **131**, **132**
Planet of Evil **89**, **90**, 91-93, *91*, **91**, **95**
Planet of the Daleks 17, **53**, **55**, 58-59, *58*, **59**, 60, 145, 156, 166
Planet of the Robots * 105
Planet of the Spiders 18, 19, **20**, 20, **42**, **61**, **63**, **65**, **66**, 67-68, *67*, **67**, 67, *68*, **68**, **75**, 83, 146, **162**
Plimmer, Charlotte and Dennis 28
Polyphase Avitron 127
Pope, Begonia 81
Power of Kroll, The **1**, **121**, **127**, *128*, 129-130, *129*
Power of the Daleks, The 74
Pratt, Peter 104
Primords **28**
Pringle, Eric 97
Prior, Allan 133
Prisoner of Time, The + 95
Prisoner of Zend, The * 128
production **2**, **4**, 5-7, **5**, 10, 22, 23, 24, 25, **25**, 27, 30, 31, **34**, 34, 35-36, 37, 38, 42, 43, 48, **49**, 50-51, 52, 56, 58, 60, 64, 68, **68**, **75**, 82, 85, 88, 98, 107, 108, 109, 110, 113, 119, 120, 126, 131-132, 137, 139, 142
Project Inferno * 28
Purves, Peter 153
Pye-Jeary, Anthony 149, 150
Pyramids of Mars **89**, **90**, 92, **92**, 93-94, *93*, **93**, **95**, **96**, 156
Quarks 165
Radio Times 1, 10, *21*, *33*, 34, 38, 43, **45**, *45*, **49**, *54*, 55, 61, **63**, *63*, **78**, **81**, **84**, **117**, 153, 161, **161**
Rathborne, Ray 10
ratings **21**, 26, 30, **31**, 42, **43**, 52, **53**, 60, **61**, **79**, 88, **89**, **99**, **109**, **121**, **133**, 136
Rawlins, Christine 9, 115
Ray, Trevor 22, 25, 26, **30**
Read, Anthony 114, 118, **120**, 125, 126, 127, 128, 129, **129**, 130, 133, 139, 140, 141
Recall UNIT **144**
Repeats **141**
Rescue, The **146**
Return of the Cybermen * 87
Return to Sukannan * 94
Revenge of the Cybermen **79**, **81**, **82**, **86**, 87-88, **88**, *88*, 90
Rhosea, Ingeborg (see also 'Pertwee, Ingeborg') 14, *14*, 15

Ribos File, The * 125
Ribos Operation, The **121**, *121*, **122**, *122*, **127**, 125-126, **138**, *147*, 156
Richard, Emily 104
Richards, Marion **28**
Roberts, Pennant 115, 127, 133
Robot 75, *76*, **79**, *79*, *80*, *81*, **81**, 82-83, **82**, 88, 146, 147, 159
Robots of Death, The **99**, 105-106, *106*, **106**, *107*, **107**, **107**
Robson, Dee *117*
Rocks of Doom * 109, **114**
Rook, Jean 108
Rose, Andrew 93
Rowley, Geoff 161
Russell, Paddy **95**, 110
Saunders, David 174
Scoones, Ian **47**, **58**, **92**, 93, **111**, **112**, 113, *137*
Sea Devils 153, **160**, 165
Sea Devils, The 18, **19**, 20, **43**, **46**, **47**, 47-48, **48**, **49**, **50**, **51**, 145, 158, 163, **163**
Sea Silurians, The * 48
Secret of Loch Ness, The * 89
Secret of the Loch, The * 89
Seeds of Death, The 1
Seeds of Doom, The **68**, 77, **85**, **89**, **90**, **95**, **96**, **97**, 97-98, **98**, **98**, **98**, 108, 147
Seeds of Time, The * 128
Shada 73, 74, **131**, **140**, 141, 142, *142*, **142**
Shadow People, The + 28
Shape of Terror, The + 45
Sharp, Ken 106
Shephard, Ben 107
Shepherd, Sandra 58
Sherwin, Derrick 4-5, 6, 7, 8, **8**, 21—22, 23, 24, 25, 30, **30**, 31
Shield of Time, The * 129
Shircore, Jenny **91**, 93
Shrivenzale **138**
Sidaway, Robert 143
Silurians 153, 165
Simpson, Dudley 27, **39**, **51**, **56**, **67**, **81**, **90**, 107, **107**, **116**, **127**, **137**, **140**, 166, 167
Skarasen 90
Skilleter, Andrew 156, **162**
Skinn, Dez 160, 162
Sladen, Elisabeth 62, 73, **82**, 101, 102, **105**, 120, 123, 146, **146**, **154**, 166
Slater, Bill 62, 80
Sloman, Robert 40, **42**, 42, 44, 51, 52, 59, 60, 67, 68
Smethhurst, Ron 157
Snoaden, Tony 115
Sontaran Experiment, The **79**, **81**, *84*, **84**, 85-86, **85**, **87**, 88, *146*
Sontarans 64, 83, 159, 165
Space Pirates, The 23
Space Station + 84
Space Trap The * 30
Space War, The (novelization) **162**
Space War, The + 45
Spare Part People, The + 11
Spearhead from Space 10, 17, *18*, 21-22, **21**, **22**, 23, *23*, **24**, **25**, **26**, **27**, 30, 34, 143, 162, 163, **174**
Spiders, Giant 68, 158
SPLINK **16**
Spooner, Dennis 95
Spray of Death, The * 34
Squires, Robin 22
Star Trek 2
Stevens, Mark 167
Stewart, Norman 117, 130
Stones of Blood, The 77, **78**, **121**, **122**, *124*, **124**, 125, **125**, **127**, *127*, 128, **129**, **132**, 133
Stones of Time, The * 128
Storm—Mine Murders, The * 105
Strutton, Bill 45, 162
Sun Makers, The **109**, **115**, 113-115, *114*, *115*, **115**,

117, 120
Sunburst * 141
Sutton, Shaun **8**, 9, **10**, 65, **108**, 132
Talons of Greel, The * 106
Talons of Weng-Chiang, The 77, 77, **78**, **98**, **99**, *104*, *105*, 106-107, **106**, **107**, 159, 161
Tamm, Mary 125, 132, **132**, 133, 148, **148**
Tams, Paul Mark 157
TARDIS, The 50, **56**, 100-101, 111, 153, *153*, 154, **154**, 157, 158, 165, 167, 169, 170, 171
Tattersall, Graham 173
Terror of the Autons 18, 19, **19**, **31**, *31*, **32**, 32, 32, **33**, **33**, **34**, *34*, 34, 38, **39**, **40**, 42, 145, **145**, 155, 159, 162
Terror of the Zygons 76, 77, 89-91, *89*, **89**, **90**, **90**, 92, **98**, 147
Thirkell, Arthur **150**
This Is Your Life **38**
Three Doctors, The 17, 18, 20, 53-55, **53**, *53*, **54**, *54*, **55**, 55, 57, 58, 159
Time Fugitive, The * 63
Time Monster, The **42**, **43**, **49**, 50-52, *50*, **51**, **51**, **50**, **51**, *52*, 56, 155
Time Survivor, The * 64
Time Warrior, The 61, *61*, **61**, 62-64, *62*, **62**, **63**, 66, 86, *146*
Timescoop * 64
Tomb of the Cybermen, The 16, **163**
Torrance, Fanny 164
Tosh, Donald **85**
Tower of Imelo, The * 104
Troughton, Patrick 1, 3, 4, 5, **6**, 10, **24**, 53, 54, **63**, **96**, 158
Tucker, Rex **6**
Twiggy 104
Underground * 116
Underwood, George **156**
Underworld **109**, **115**, 115-117, *116*, **116**
UNIT 6-7, 42, 95
Vampire from Space, The * 37
Venables, Bernard **105**
Vincent—Rudzki, Jan 174
Vogans 165
Walsh, Terry 15, 48, **82**, 83, **94**
War Games, The **6**, 7, **7**, 8, 17, 23, **23**, 87, 130, **145**, 150
Ward, Lalla 74, 133, 148, **148**
Wardle, Irving **151**, **152**
Ware, Derek 27, 48
Web of Fear, The 143, **144**, **145**, **162**
Weir, David **118**
Westbrook, John **105**
Wheatcroft, Anna 74
Whitaker, David 23, **23**, 25, 26, **134**, 162
White Robots 165
Whitehouse, Mary 108, **108**
Whomobile **15**, 64, **65**, 68
Whose Doctor Who 107—**108**
Wilkie, Bernard **63**
Williams, Graham 108, 109, **110**, 111, 112, 114, 115, 117, **117**, 118, **119**, **120**, 120, 121, 124, 125, 126, 128, **129**, 130, 131, 132, 133, 135, 136, 139, 140, 141, 142, **157**, 164, 171, 175, **175**
Williams, Roy 155
Wilson, Donald 23, **85**
wiping episodes 174
Wirrn **138**, 165
Wisher, Michael **86**, 134
Witch Lords, The * 109, 123, 164
Wright, Brian 28, 34
Years of Doom * 44
Yeti 165
Zarbi 158
Zygons 90-91, 158, 159, 165